The Word of the Guru

Other books from Narayana Gurukula !

Aitareya Upaniṣad: With the Original Text in Sanskrit and Roman Transliteration; by Muni Narayana Prasad.

The Bhagavad Gītā: A Sublime Hymn of Yoga. Translated from Sanskrit by Nataraja Guru, with explanatory Dialogue by Nitya Chaitanya Yati.

The Bṛhadāraṇyaka Upaniṣad: With Original Text in Roman Transliteration; by Nitya Chaitanya Yati (3 Vols.).

Experiencing One-World; by Nataraja Guru.

An Integrated Science of the Absolute: based on the Darśana Mālā (Garland of Visions) of Narayana Guru; translated by Nataraja Guru (2 Vols.).

Karma and Reincarnation: The Vedāntic Perspective; by Muni Narayana Prasad.

Kaṭha Upaniṣad: With the Original Text in Sanskrit and Roman Transliteration; by Muni Narayana Prasad.

The Kena Upaniṣad: With the Original Text in Sanskrit and Roman Translation; by Muni Narayana Prasad.

Love and Devotion; by Nitya Chaitanya Yati.

Muṇḍaka Upaniṣad: With the Original Text in Sanskrit and Roman Transliteration; by Muni Narayana Prasad.

Neither This Nor That But Aum; by Nitya Chaitanya Yati.

The Philosophy of Narayana Guru; by Muni Narayana Prasad.

Praśna Upaniṣad: With the Original Text in Sanskrit and Roman Transliteration; by Swami Muni Narayana Prasad.

The Taittirīya Upaniṣad: With the Original Text in Sanskrit and Roman Transliteration; by Muni Narayana Prasad.

That Alone, the Core of Wisdom: A Commentary on Ātmopadeśa Śatakam the One Hundred Verses of Self-Instruction of Narayana Guru; by Nitya Chaitanya Yati.

Vedānta Sūtras of Narayana Guru: with an English translation and Commentary; by Muni Narayana Prasad.

Wisdom — The Absolute is Adorable; by Nataraja Guru.

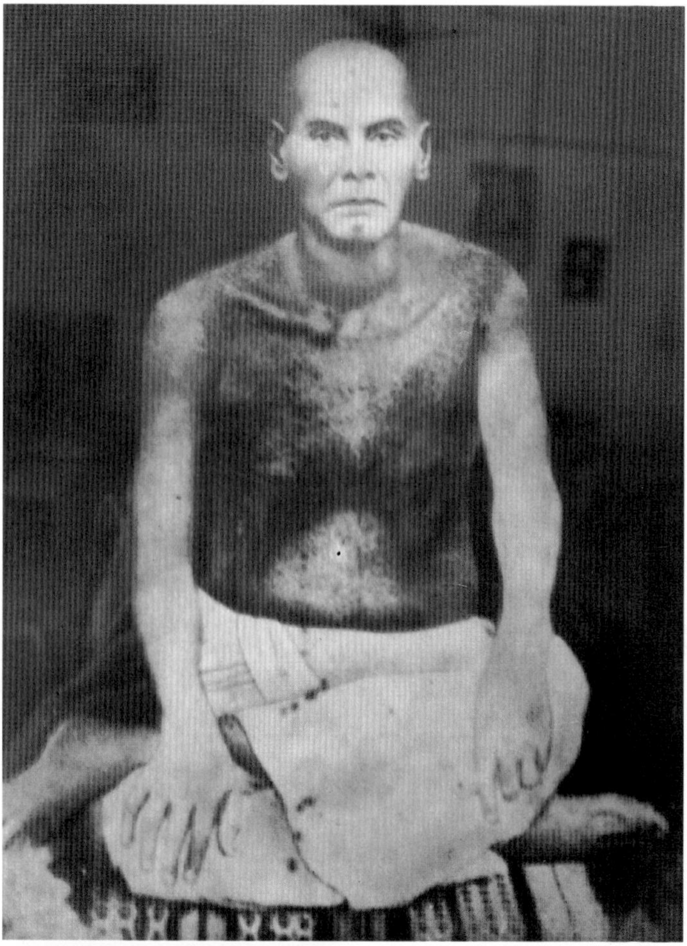

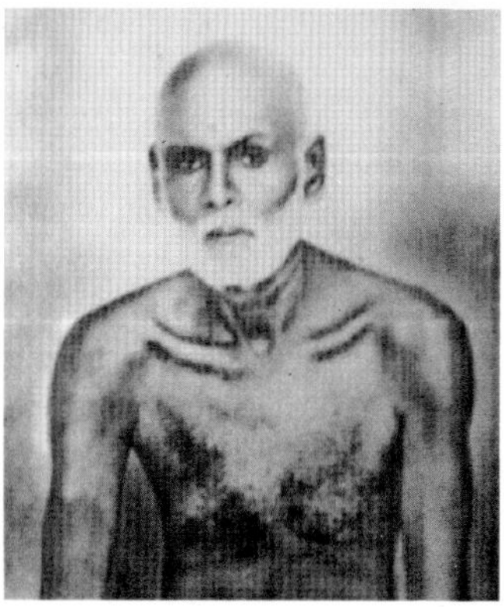

Nārāyaṇa Guru (1854-1928)

The Word of the Guru

The Life and Teachings of Guru Nārāyaṇa

by
Nataraja Guru

DK
PRINTWORLD
Publishers of Indian Traditions

Cataloging in Publication Data — DK
[Courtesy: D.K. Agencies (P) Ltd. <docinfo@dkagencies.com>]

Nataraja Guru, 1895-1973, **author.**

The word of the Guru : the life and teachings of Guru Nārāyaṇa / by Nataraja Guru. – Reprint.

pages cm

Includes bibliographical references and index.

ISBN 9788124602416

1. Narayana Guru, 1856-1928. 2. Hindus – India – Kerala – Biography. 3. Hindu philosophy. I. Title.

BL1175.N37N38 2022 DDC 294.5092 23

ISBN 13: 978-81-246-0241-6

First published in 1952
The third edition appeared as a part of
Life and Teachings of Narayana Guru in 1990

Reissued in this format in 2003
Reprinted in 2008, 2017, 2022

Printed and published by
D.K. Printworld (P) Ltd.
Regd. Office : "*Vedaśrī*", F-395, Sudarshan Park
(ESI Metro Station), New Delhi - 110 015
Phones : (011) 2545 3975; 2546 6019
e-mail : indology@dkprintworld.com
Web : www.dkprintworld.com

Foreword

THE author has asked me, 'as a Westerner', to write this foreword. But personally I do not think it is necessary. However, I respect the wishes of Dr. Natarajan, who is my Guru. I have known him for sixteen years and have been intimately associated with him for the last six years.

I am quite well aware that the mention of the word *guru* will probably cause some eyebrow raising, but not enough, I trust, to stop you from getting on with this book. Here you will find nothing escapist. Such religion as it presents is philosophically and psychologically interpreted rather than urging any creed or belief, least of all what is commonly called Hinduism. But when all that is said, I am aware of an archaic taste remaining. That cannot be helped. It belongs to the subject-matter. Indeed the pre-historic element evoked is a healthy reaction, fundamental, quite materialist or at least rebellious enough to satisfy the modern mind in revolt against the conventions of history. The majority of people have always been materialist. Here materialism is not rejected as a proper view in its proper place, but it is balanced by other aspects of human life.

This book represents the voice of the Guru. It is a solitary voice, recorded more or less against the stream of pressurised thought, both Indian and elsewhere. Its tone is as much foreign to India as to other lands. Certain old values lost to the world, had to be restated. The temper of modern India is flamboyant, nationalist, and in a hurry to exceed the dynamic Western world's successes in the material sphere.

Hence most of what is written here is very little known in India itself. Yet I have no hesitation in affirming, after many years active association with Indian thought and current literature, that you will find in these pages the authentic spirit of the contemplative East. It is not due to any bias for south India on the part of the author that he indicates certain reasons why the contemplative spirit should persist in this far too little known corner of the world.

South India has seldom been in the news. Nothing sensational happens here. Ever since the days of the Moguls north India has held the stage. The inner life of India, that strange factor of contemplation, on the other hand, has naturally withdrawn to its safe preserves. Even an author such as W. Somerset Maugham, on his quest for a background for a novel about a Guru, chose Malabar. Nobody visiting south India can be insensitive to its heritage of leisure. The northern Indian should not feel any offence. He too has to wander into the Himālayan regions to find a parallel refuge for contemplation. No antagonism is implied. The far South disarms all opposition by its poverty, mildness, simple ways and its deep roots, both primordially instinctive and intellectually strong, penetrating further into the past than perhaps anywhere in the world, with the possible exception of China.

Everywhere, in India no less than in other parts of the world, there exists a psychological unrest and tension, which nobody seems to be able to cure. There is besides a natural scepticism against all panaceas, certainly when proffered by the headline experts in politics, economics, science, religion and philosophy. It would be too much to expect repeatedly misled readers to come to this book with any new hope. All the same, there is hope here. You will not get that sense of a 'let-down' after reading it. This work is about an Indian, its background is Indian, the philosophical language is mainly a survival of what has matured in India, and it is written by an Indian. All that notwithstanding, I cannot sufficiently emphasise the fact that its vision is global, beyond locality and circumstance. Its theme is not so much the biography of a great man, as the biography of a central value which might be called unitive understanding, happiness, and in India, *ānanda*.

As a help to the reader, something may be said here about the structure of the book.

In the first place the whole volume is intended to clarify a subject, which is the genuine spiritual tradition of India. Around this noble subject, so many spurious, uninformed and sensational ideas have gathered — from the lowest level of cheap novels even up to the highly rarefied platforms of professional punditry — that it is a feat in itself to have cleared away all this mass of accumulated inane, misleading, vulgar litter. At the same time this subject is obscure enough in its own surroundings to need the pointed attention of a peculiarly qualified intelligence to unravel and expound.

The Word of the Guru therefore is quite the reverse of occult journalism. I am breaking no confidences when I say that it was rejected outright by a well-known firm of publishers in London, because it was not sensational enough by such standards. The author scorns to play up to the debased taste of those who relish books about the mysterious East, miracles, *fakīrs*, and the whole gamut of *yogī* tricks and stooge figures. Hollywood and colourful *swāmīs* can be left to cater for the lovers of mysteries. Commercial interest is not in the author's taste. 'Secrets' can be sold by the esoteric organisations and the various *yogīs* who trade upon the gullible.

Dr. Natarajan is one of the rare living authorities on Advaita Vedānta, which is the science and heart of the wisdom tradition of India. He has devoted his life to this subject. He is a philosopher who lives his philosophy, but he is not a 'Professor' of philosophy. He is too sincere to make good on a platform or to cut a charming figure in society. He himself is a *guru*. That is the long and the short of it. That qualification alone makes him and his book unique. In writing this volume he has done so in the only way possible, by centering his subject-matter around a real living being, his own *guru*, in relation to whom he himself was a disciple.

The first section of this volume stands by itself, and readers will be found to observe a vast difference in style and method, as if it were written by a different personality. This is almost the case, since not only is there a time-gap of over twenty years between its original publication and the remainder of the writing in this volume, but the mood of elation and youthful veneration has subsided to the self-assured certainty of philosophic maturity. In this first part, the Guru Nārāyaṇa as a man is described with some emotion.

But in the second and larger portion of this book the Guru-figure assumes a greater status, perhaps less impressionistically, but all the more important on the immense canvas of history, and he may seem, at times, almost to dissolve into symbolic rank, as a principle of *guru*-hood. This is partly intentional. It is only by taking the particular Guru Nārāyaṇa as a representative of a permanent, timeless *guru* model, as a typical example close to our own times, of the pure philosopher who stands, not for special view or argument, but for the principle of pure reason and wisdom of India, that the author can display with justice the meaning of *guru*-hood and *guru*-wisdom. In its full content this is only incidentally Indian, just as the *guru* is only incidentally the man who was the boy Nāṇu with certain parents and a certain environment on the West Coast of India. The universal value, the global vision, thus gets a chance to be represented.

In the third section, some examples are given of the literary works of the Guru Nārāyaṇa — the 'Word' as it was given on different occasions to fit the needs of popular and special exigencies. Much of this will appear abstruse and peculiar for non-Indian readers because of the intricate and unfamiliar Indian background material and terminology. But at the same time this third section will be appreciated for this very reason as it has a flavour of its own, a sampling of an exotic south Indian dish, so to say. It conveys the real mental and spiritual conditions of south India.

From the list of the literary works of the Guru Nārāyaṇa given at the end of the book, some idea of the vast material yet to be explored and annotated and commented upon will be noticed. It is Dr. Natarajan's intention to do this. This is his service to his *guru*. Christ had St. Paul and a whole sequence of mystics in Europe to continue this labour. Lao Tzu in China had Chuang Tzu and other

Tao writers fitted for the same expositionary task. Mohammed's commentators existed too in the form of the *sūfīs*. Plato and Aristotle were elaborated and understandable through the efforts of their linear successors such as Hypatia, Plotinus and Dionysius the Areopagite. The Zen masters in China and Japan had their aphoristic works interpreted by their disciples. Dr. Natarajan's book is but the breaking of the ice in regard to his *guru*'s works. More will follow. The present is largely introductory and by no means a final statement. There are far more serious treatments ahead, relating to contemplation as a science of tremendous value to modern thought.

This is not to say that Dr. Natarajan is merely an elaborator of the Guru Nārāyaṇa. He has not only his own original contribution to the subject, but — without departing an iota from the Guru's text — he has himself revalued and restated, with what can only be called his own contemplative insight or yogic intelligence, many of the puzzling enigmas of applied philosophy.

Indeed, if I may be bold enough to say so, he has made what amounts to revolutionary discoveries in philosophic thought and practice. He has taken up that much-abused term dialectics and given it a synoptic meaning. He has shown how polarised ambivalences can be resolved at any level, from the personal to the collective, psychologically. He has brought contemplation out of the closed system of private individual life and shown it to be the sanest human solution for every possible contingent problem, social, historical, religious and philosophical. In all this he has not deviated from or abused the teaching of his own spiritual Teacher. On the contrary, he has continued the method which had such success with the Guru Nārāyaṇa and former *gurus*. This method is logically clear and yet elusive enough to have puzzled the intelligence of all philosophers hitherto to bring down to understandable terms.

In preparing this book for publication, I have worried the author for six months over his terminology and his language, trying to put myself in the position of a lay reader to whom it is all new. This accounts for what may seem to the specialist in philosophical jargon, the banality of some of the footnotes. But the lay reader, for whom this book is meant as much as for the serious student, is not like Macauley's schoolboy. The glossary too is meant mainly for non-Indian readers, but even Indian readers will find many a novel and rational rendering of some of the puzzling terms which are too often given a slipshod English equivalent.

Thus my part in this publication is that of a critic and literary finisher. Any unorthodoxy in style or language is mainly due to the subject-matter and the appalling paucity of English or almost any other modern European language, with the possible exception of German, when it comes to finding exact terminological equivalents for the highly perfected words in Sanskrit, Malayālam and Tamil. Contemplative psychologists have developed in these languages an exactitude of precise technical terms to a degree bewildering and amazing for the newcomer, more than in any other language — not excluding scholastic or theological Latin and Greek. This process of accuracy of definition has a growth at least two or three thousand years old. From the philosophical point of view, or the psychological, Western languages in this respect are lisping a baby language. This is not said in disparagement of the enormous elasticity, fecundity and vigorous ability of Western languages to coin terms suitable for mechanistic description. But if new life is to flow into the world, not only must ancient peoples in Asian lands assimilate the language of modern science, the reciprocal or dialectical assimilation of the specialised psychological vocabularies of the East must be attempted by the West. That is a side-issue of some relevance which this volume may help to stimulate.

But I must leave the reader to discover other things of interest and value for himself. My role is that of an announcer, anxious now to step aside, to let the curtain rise, having, I hope, prepared you for a patient reading of an unusual and epochal book dealing with human understanding, and the welfare and happiness of us all.

Narayaṇa Gurukula, Kaggalipura P.O **John Spiers**
Bangalore South

Preface

THE first part this book was written when the Guru Nārāyaṇa was still living. I was then on a tour of Europe and, under the general title of *The Way of the Guru,* these first nine chapters appeared originally as contributions to *The Sufi Quarterly* of Geneva in 1928. The articles aroused much interest, and were later reprinted in book form, first in Geneva in 1931 and later in India in 1942, Sir Francis Younghusband was one of the first to welcome their publication and in a letter to the Editor of the Geneva journal he said:

> What an excellent number your January number is ! I look forward to further instalments of Śrī Nārāyaṇa's life. There are wonderful people in this wicked world still. . . .

The celebrated French writer M. Romain Rolland also noticed the articles in his now famous work on the life of Rāmakṛṣṇa, in which he admirably summed up the import and significance of the Guru's life as follows:

> Glasenapp does not say anything regarding the new religious manifestations in south India which are not negligible: such for example is the great Guru Śrī Nārāyaṇa, whose beneficient spiritual activity has been exercising its influence during the past forty years in the State of Travancore on nearly two millions of his followers (he passed away in 1928). His teaching, permeated with the philosophy of Śankara, shows evidence of a striking difference of temperament compared with the mysticism of Bengal, of which the effusions of love (*bhakti*) inspire in him a certain mistrust. He was, one might say, a *Jnānin* of

> action, a grand religious intellectual, who had a keen living sense of the people and of social necessities. He has contributed greatly to the elevation of the oppressed classes in south India, and his work has been associated at certain times with that of Gandhi.
>
> — *Cf.* the articles of his disciple P. Natarajan in *The Sufi Quarterly*, Geneva, December 1928 and in the following months.[1]

No doubt the reader will be aware of a difference in style and method between these chapters written more than twenty years before those that follow in the remainder of this volume. These early chapters were written unpremeditatedly, with very little intellectual planning, with the sole purpose of presenting something of the personality of the Guru, fresh from the anvil while he was still living, and before the intensity of the actualities of the Guru's presence evaporated by lapse of time and the mellowing of memory. The attempt was then made to delineate in broad outline a first distance view of the whole of the Guru's personality, stressing perhaps certain emotional and intellectual highlights, including some of his personal traits in a rather sketchy, general way, and without too much emphasis on any deeper philosophical aspects.

The Guru passed away at Varkala after the first two chapters had appeared in print, while I continued to live and teach in Switzerland. My studies in individual psychology on the one hand, and on Vedānta and philosophy in general on the other hand, taken together with preoccupation with brick and mortar in connection with establishing two idealistic institutions called 'Gurukulas' in India, one at Fernhill, Nīlgiris and the other at Varkala, Travancore, kept me occupied for nearly fifteen years thereafter.

Now that these years of necessary action have come to a natural close, I have been moved again to attempt the completion of my long cherished ambition of presenting the teachings and theoretical

1. Translated from the French from: *La Vie de Ramakrishna* par Romain Rolland, p. 160, Librarie Stock, Paris, 1930.

aspects of the Guru Nārāyaṇa's life in a form which I hope will be acceptable and understandable to seekers of truth in the West, as well as to those in the East, who are trying to comprehend, in terms of Western values, their own rare heritage of wisdom in revalued and restated language. The hospitality of the Gurukula founded by my friend, Harry S. Jacobsen, at the Schooley's Mountains in New Jersey, U.S.A., in 1949, gave me just that needed quiet retreat and access to libraries and books which has made it possible to write with some seriousness.

In dealing with the present work and with future projects, I must take the reader into my confidence, so that the general aim intended here will be understood.

The personality of the Guru is of such a rare kind that it does not fit itself into the usual scheme of biography. As a personality he is elusive and enigmatic, and therefore hardly capable of being appreciated with the hasty publicity which even ephemeral figures get. But, on the other hand, as has always been the case with the teachers of the perennial wisdom, his deeper message with all its real values will persist, like a glowing subterranean fire, which will influence thought through time.

In writing the life of a Guru it is essential for all readers, particularly those outside India, to know not only the background of the personality, but the background which is the setting for the teaching, in which the wisdom has its first meaning. To that extent background details are relevant, enabling the reader to surmount the merely personal and rise into the region which might be described as the biography of the Word-wisdom.

I have three volumes altogether in mind, of which this is the first, and perhaps in some ways the most difficult to write. I have here retained the earlier impressions and pen-pictures which constituted my first presentation of 1928, and this, being a section by itself, can be regarded as a preliminary introduction to the second part of this volume.

In the second part, as far as possible, I have attempted a rambling treatment of the whole subject-matter, lapsing where-ever possible into personal anecdote, and intentionally and consciously refusing to confine myself to any conventions of style, or what might be called an academic form. Such liberties as I have taken in these matters may be excused in the present work which is only meant to introduce the person of the Guru together with his teachings *grosso modo* rather than by way of a 'close-up.' For the ordinary reader some of the terms, phrases and ideas may at first sight appear unduly heavy. The wisdom-philosophy was so much part and parcel of the life of the Guru that such initial terminology is unavoidable if a true picture is to be presented. The loading of heavy or unfamiliar expressions has not been done on purpose. The wisdom-teaching has been lost or has been confused with much vestigial or irrelevant matter, all of which needs reasoned clearing and a fresh restatement of relevant values made before the Guru and his Word can be understood in its authentic grandeur.

In the third part of this volume translations of some of the writings of the Guru Nārāyaṇa will be found. These are only samples from the large body of writings left by the Guru. They have been selected and graded to illustrate some of the mystical yet always human values presented by the Guru.

The last of the selections on *The Science of the Absolute* or *Brahma-Vidyā,* sets the limit, as it were, to this volume. This science requires deep and critical study, of which only a foretaste is provided here. The major literary works of the Guru were concerned with this science, and the two further volumes which I hope to publish later will deal with this *in extenso.*

In connection with this present work, my indebtedness to friends is great, both directly and indirectly, and I shall not attempt to enumerate them all here. Above all, it is to the Guru that I am mainly indebted, and in acknowledging his personality conceived in general terms I include all others who love wisdom. In this sense, I incline inclusively before all, in the One.

During the summer of 1949 I was in Paris still working at my manuscripts, translating and taking notes. I availed myself of the use of the library at the Musèe Guimet and also at the Institut de

Civilisation Indienne at the Sorbonne. I frequented the lecture-rooms of the College de France and contacted thinkers such as Prof. O. Lacombe whose recent work, *L'Absolu Selon le Vedânta* (The Absolute according to the Vedānta), has been of considerable help to me. I have also had the benefit again of sitting in the study groups round Prof. Masson-Oursel. My indebtedness to these academic foundations of Paris has to be recorded here with gratitude. Such subjects as physiology, Assyriology, Egyptology, atomic physics and general philosophy interested me at Paris and to the various professors who have enlightened me I acknowledge my gratitude. The kindness, encouragement and hospitality of Madame L. Morin of Paris, who introduced me to the various intellectuals of that city is not to be forgotten.

In April 1951 I arrived back in India and reached the Gurukula at Fernhill, Nilgiri Hills in May. My friend and colleague John Spiers, with whom I had already established intellectual and, if I may say so, spiritual contact, for nearly five years, and who even substituted and deputised for me at the Gurukula there in my absence, was sufficiently interested and strangely well qualified to look through the manuscripts I had brought back. Much editorial revision, additions, including many footnotes, and ordering to make the meanings more explicit are to be attributed to the labours of this friend who comes from that same part of the world from which originated John the Scot in the ninth century and whom I consider as much as a Godsend in the context of the Word of the Guru. I have largely relied on him for all work requiring editorial sagacity and a sense of the public mind, from the stage of typing out the manuscripts in their final form to that of seeing them safely through the press.

To him and to all others I here express my thanks.

P. Natarajan

Contents

List of Illustrations

Part-I
The Way of the Guru

1

Introductory

WHERE is happiness ? Where is rest from the fever of life ? Where is the image of perfection? Where is the fountain-source of wisdom from which a thirsty traveller can drink? Where is that luminous something, in which we can live apart and be free — free from a sense of want and suffering ?

These seem to be some of the eternal questions echoing and re-echoing through the ages within the heart of humanity. Some think the answer can be found in material comforts. Some search for the answer in books. Some sit in meditation trying to tune their life-breath in unison with the Great Knowledge. Some others 'scorn delights and live laborious days.' All these attain degrees of success.

Once in a hundred years, solitary among a hundred thousand, there arrives at the caravanserai of life one, at the sight of whose features the seekers instinctively arise from their varied occupations and greet him, and see in him and his ways a clear commentary, a silent interpretation, a radiant centre of all that they were seeking. He is able to dispel age-long doubt and darkness by his words: and the hearers smile and for a moment feel a strange happiness. Literature and art and science grow round his person. Historical events find a centre round which to turn.

Nārāyaṇa Guru was one of such. He was one of those who followed in his life the ancient and immemorial programme of oriental saints and prophets. He left his home in search of Truth. He lived in lonely hill, cave or forest for years, unknown to men, performing *tapas*.[1] He emerged from seclusion, having solved some great riddle in life and he wanted to give his solution to the world

1. *Tapas*: meditation and self-discipline performed in retirement with a vew to illumination.

at large. Therefore, without any sort of hesitation whatever, he called himself a *guru* or Teacher. Penniless himself, he began to command an influence over rich and poor, educated and uneducated. People flocked to take the dust of his feet.

Today his words are recognised as a most modern echo of the ancient wisdom of the Orient. In him we had, combined once again, a bard who sang about the aspirations of the soul of man, a philanthropist whose one aim in life, night and day, was to devise ways to minimise human suffering, and a seer whose daily food and drink was the highest form of Truth.

Although out of reach of newspapermen and propagandists, this silent sage was the recognised spiritual leader of more than two million people in south India, to whom his word was more imperative than law. Within a period of less than a decade he had established more than one hundred places of worship on the west coast of India alone, which are day by day growing into centres of educational, philanthropic, and economic activity. Crowded meetings are held in which his name is the unifying element. His message to the people is the subject of weekly comment on many platforms, and scores of associations have been organised in various parts of south India to spread his ideals. By the spell of his name, young and old are seen to join hands in a common undertaking: rich and poor are seen to rub shoulders. It can be asserted that he has set in motion a force which is bound to spread into a new impetus for the regeneration of India and the world.

2

The Guru at Home

THE traveller who was animated by a desire to see this leader of one of the modern religious movements in India, would most probably have had to alight, as the present writer once did, at the small railway station called Alwaye, two stations to the north of the terminus of the Cochin State Railway. Alwaye is a small municipal town belonging then to the State of Travancore.[1] It is associated with the name of the great Indian philosopher, Śaṅkarācārya, who is said to have taken *saṁnyāsa,* the vow of renunciation in search of wisdom, while bathing in the broad river of crystal water winding its way through the town. If the traveller had directed his footsteps along one of the roads leading to the river-side, he would have come across a stile leading into a compound, which he must cross, keeping his way along the narrow avenue till he reached the bright river-side beyond the trees. He would have found, on turning to the right, a neat little white building strewn round with pure river-sand — the silence of the place broken only by birds or by the voices of occasional bathers in the river. On one side he would see below him, the river boiling over with a thousand whirlpools on its broad breast, the banks overgrown with luxuriant vegetation. If the Guru was in the *āśrama* (hermitage) he could invariably be found on a little raised seat overlooking the river. As he turned to look at the visitor, the latter would, if he had a keen eye, discover from the expression of his face that the Guru had just been disturbed from some all-absorbing subject while he sat gazing at the river scene. There could be discovered a peculiar composure in his features revealing a peaceful other-worldly contemplation. He would ask the newcomer who he was, in the

1. Under the Indian Union the two states of Travancore and Cochin now form part of Kerala State.

most gentle of voices; and treat him, probably to a meal of fruits and milk. After that, if he conversed, the topic in all probability turned on how human nature must improve; how there is no necessity for man to quarrel with man, as he does at present, on supposed religious, national, or racial distinctions; how, while a cow or a dog may be considered to belong to a different *'caste'*, it is absurd to think that one man differs from another except in trivial things like dress or language; and how it is immaterial, in everyday life, what school of philosophy or what creed a man professed so long as he does not transgress the bounds of common human goodness. Before the newcomer retired from the abode of the Guru leaving him to gaze on the river scene in absorbing meditation, let him walk round the humble hermitage, and he would not have failed to observe the neat little kitchen where a *brahmacārin* (dedicated student) prepared light food for the Guru, or noted how sparing the Guru's diet was. In the grounds of the hermitage he would have found trees, each one of them receiving its share of the Guru's care. Before leaving the precincts, had the visitor cast his glance on the inscription in golden letters on one of the walls of the *āśrama*, he would have read as follows:

> *One in kind, one in faith, one in God is man*
> *Of one same womb, one same form, difference none there is at all.*

3

Two Random Impressions

A JUNIOR officer of the Indian Civil Service once gave the following account of how he met the Guru for the first time in his life:

> My leave was about to expire and I was travelling back to Salem in a mail train. I was seated in a second-class compartment. At about ten o'clock in the morning the train steamed up to the crowded platform of Calicut. A number of people, dressed in spotless white, were seen on the platform. In the centre of the group was seated, on a chair, an old gentlemen dressed also in white, who was well-nigh sixty years. He was tall, slender, and erect. The arrival of the train and the consequent bustle did not seem to produce any effect on the composed features of this person.
>
> When the first bustle had subsided, the person slowly got up from his seat and walked into the very compartment in which I was seated. My curiosity to know who this revered man was, became aroused; and I began to watch him minutely. I soon guessed that he did not belong to the class of rich people, for he wore neither gold nor silver on him. His dress was of the simplest description, consisting merely of two pieces of white cloth. He wore no sort of headdress but, after the manner of the *saṁnyāsin,* had a clean-shaven head, which showed a spare crown of white hair. There was a sedate grandeur in his countenance, which was not suggestive on the one hand of the cold, calculating nature of a man of wealth nor, on the other, of the sternness of a fighter. Relaxed and restful, like the countenance of a child, it still revealed an undercurrent of seriousness which led

the critical observer into the unfathomable depths of something inexplicable.

The supreme restfulness and leisureliness of his manner, unaffected by anything that was passing round him, the spotless purity of his personal attire, the delicately artistic perfection of every one of his movements, even the manner in which the flowing dress clung round his person — half negligently, yet in a way that the artist would have the rumples adjusted — the silence and the gentleness of his ordinary behaviour made him carry with him, even in the busy atmosphere of a modern railway station, a still halo of reverence. When he talked, which was only now and then, his voice which, though not loud had still a rich mellow in it, exercised a peculiar lulling effect which could be compared to the far-off chiming of temple bells or the noonday murmur of bumble-bees. As I was watching him, I could observe that tears filled to the point of overflowing the eyes of this great man, as one by one the devotees, that had gathered on the platform, measured their lengths in prostration before him. Each one of them touched the foot of the strange leader and placed an offering of fruits and flowers before retiring from his presence. Age had not robbed his features of that soft freshness, richfulness, and restful relaxation so characteristic of the Indian *yogī*. A pair of not at all large eyes, which seemed to be constantly gazing at some object in the far-off fringe of the horizon, lips with the corners slightly turned down as if in open-eyed meditation, all these and many more little traits, revealed to me that the stranger was one of the *mahātmā*s or Holy Men of India.

The train soon left the station, and, as we stopped at the next station, I could observe that the Nārāyaṇa Guru — for the stranger was none other than this revered leader of whom I had heard so much — was engaged in giving away one by one, to some poor children who appeared at the

> carriage, all the fine oranges that he had received at the previous station, till not one was left of the pile beside him. A householder, I thought, would have reserved some, at least, to be taken home. When I had observed him thus far in silence, I was overcome by desire to talk to him, but having adopted the customs of the Western nations I felt some difficulty in introducing myself. I struck upon a plan. I was then carrying with me some oranges of the finest quality plucked from the orange groves of the Wynāḍ. I took out one of these and determined at last to break the silence. 'Swāmī', I said at last: 'Would you mind my offering you an orange ?' Those were the 'fitting words' with which I chose to break the silence; to which the saint replied rather pertinently, as I only realised later, 'Have you failed to find that out in spite of having watched me all this time?' Surely I had seen him receive a hundred oranges without any sort of protest, and felt for a moment how ridiculous a figure I cut in the presence of one whose manners belonged to the unalloyed past. This was how I met the Nārāyaṇa Guru the first time in my life.

To this effect, mainly, were the words of the officer. Coming from a perfect stranger to the Guru, this picture of him has its value inasmuch as it serves to show what the Guru appeared in the eyes of a casual stranger.

There is another impression of the Guru which the writer of this narrative had occasion to hear — this time from one of the representatives of the poor. Towards the small hours of the night it was — we were travelling together on the deck of a steam launch in the backwaters of Mālābār. The first blush of day was just appearing at the corner of the horizon. The boat at this time passed a big church, surrounded by palm trees, which moved in front of us, as we sat up in our beds, like a silhouette picture against the brightening sky. The rough hands of the fellow passenger and his dress, which were just beginning to be visible, revealed that he was a simple labourer. After some preliminary questions about my destination and antecedents, this new friend began to narrate the following anecdote, after he had crossed himself most reverently as we passed the church.

> Sir, I have seen the Guru, he said: It was the year before last, that one day I heard that he had arrived at the house of a landlord in the village where I live. I had heard of him long ago and wished very much to meet him and lost no time in going to see him in that house. When I saw him I could not resist the thought that he was like our Saviour Jesus Christ. He was surrounded by people who either wanted to be healed of sickness or came to seek his advice regarding some calamity that had befallen them. Some there were who were eager to take the dust of his feet and others were waiting for the water that had cleansed them. Surely this was the way in which, as we read in the Bible, Lord Jesus himself moved among the multitude. I am a poor man, without learning or wealth. I had a secret desire to invite this great man to my humble dwelling place, in spite of its being very poor and dirty. I mustered strength to express my wish to him. What was my joy when he consented to come forthwith. Within a short while, he had already started. As we were on the way the Guru asked me about all my affairs and my children and all the rest in a voice which was full of tender regard. When we were not far from my house, I excused myself and went ahead by a short-cut, in order to set things in order before the honoured guest arrived. I dressed my children up in their cleanest and spread a white cloth on an easy chair, had some incense sticks lighted, and with a brass vessel full of pure water, awaited his arrival at the outer entrance. Like the morning beam of light carrying the message of peace, the holy man entered. Although at first he resisted my approach to wash his feet with my own hands, I had my own way, on which, while I was bending, he gently placed his hand on my head. That solacing touch at once carried its message of blessing to the innermost recesses of my being.

When this honest man came to that part of the narrative, the day had almost dawned and the sun made the backwaters full of orange crested waves, and in the daylight could be seen the features of my fellow passenger showing visible signs of emotion. His voice cracked and his honest eyes grew dim. There was a pause for a few minutes, after which he continued as follows:

> When the Guru had finally taken his seat, I called my son and asked him to take the dust of his feet, which he did. The Guru asked him which class he was studying in and advised him to be a good and diligent boy. Turning to one of his men who was standing by, he then ordered a rupee to be given to the boy and told him that he was expected to re' turn that rupee, when he became a grown-up man, back into the public funds. Turning to me, he told me in so many words that I was not to consider myself as one who belonged to a different creed or religion: 'We are all one and the same'. His words are still echoing in my memory.

4

Brotherhood

It was a red-letter day in the history of the little *āśrama* (hermitage) at Alwaye, on which was to be celebrated, by some of the enthusiastic young men of the surrounding districts, the anniversary of their association for Universal Brotherhood. The celebration was to be held in the afternoon at the Sanskrit *pāṭhaśālā* (School) founded by the Guru. An extensive palm-leaf roof had already been put up to accommodate the delegates. It was known — almost instinctively, for no newspaper announcements were made — that the Guru would grace the occassion with his presence.

Batches of young men began to arrive at Alwaye early in the day, both by the north-bound and the south-bound trains. Before going to the Guru at the riverside hermitage, they had to plunge in the river and then put on their purest raiment. The Guru himself, who rose during the small hours of the morning, was usually ready, after his morning silence, to receive the visitors and talk to them on whatever subject they raised, and to clear away individual doubts that were brought before him, in the considerate, witty, and convincing manner usual to him. On this particular morning it was one of the new young men who had arrived at the hermitage and who had decided to be a worker among the people, who was standing reverently, talking to him about the meeting that was to take place. The Guru turned his face, with half-wakeful eyelids, towards the optimistic young man and asked him, his voice softened by the peaceful rest of the morning meditation. 'Do you think there is any use in holding big meetings ?' 'Yes', was the decided reply of the young man, 'meetings are the best means of spreading ideas'. 'But', said the Guru, 'they do not appear to produce as much action as noise. People come in crowds very seriously to take part in meetings. They speak at the tops of their voices and seem to rouse passions.

The speakers propose to reform the whole world, and the audience applauds and enthusiastically raises hands in unanimous votes of support — and, while someone is lecturing, if there is heard the whistle of a train, he excuses himself to the audience quite abruptly, takes up his bag and baggage, and goes back home. Meetings frequently end in this manner. But they may not be completely useless. It is good, all the same, to have some meetings now and then to rouse the public conscience. . . . Can you speak to the crowd?' 'I shall try to,' replied the young man humbly. 'It would be a good thing,' continued the Guru, 'to tell them about the excessive greed of human beings. Don't you think that the animal called man is worse than the rest of the animals in this respect ? The desires of animals in the forest are safely controlled, by natural instinct, from all abnormal excesses. The elephant is simple and fat, and does not need tonics or treatment to keep it so. The jackal hides in the woods all day and comes out only at night when all is quiet. It does not take much food — just a few fresh crabs, and the clear stream water, reflecting the moonlight, to drink — and it is content. It enjoys its life with its nightly music, and you can see that it is none the worse for this sort of life — its neck is as plump and glossy as a pillow. The animals have no exaggerated needs like man. Man trots about the earth as a veritable demon of destruction. As he marches, he carries behind him a trail of devastation. He cuts down the trees, and blasts and bleeds into paleness the green beauty of Nature for the sake of the plantations and smoky towns and factories which his unbridled desires necessitate. Not content with destruction on the surface, he tampers with the crust of the earth, making it weaker and weaker day-by-day; and he covers the surface with miles and miles of iron and coal. Man is terribly inconsistent. The state, which calls itself interested in humanity, would, for example, vehemently forbid even a man suffering from the worst form of skin disease to quit his miserable body. On the other hand, it will madly engage itself in wholesale man-slaughter, after due deliberation and in the holy name of altruism or religion. Man does not know what he does, although he prides himself on being more intelligent than the animals. It is all a mad deluded rush.' 'Oh, this man!' he said, lapsing into wistfulness. . . .'He must lay waste; his greed can be satisfied only by the taking away of life.' As the Guru repeated the word *Man,* the youthful orator watched his composed features and could not but discover a distant tinge of sadness in his voice and in his venerable features. 'Man knows not what he does,' the Guru repeated, and became silent for a moment. 'It would not have mattered so much', he continued, 'if the effect of man's misdeeds struck its blow only at mankind. But the innocent monkeys and birds in the forest have to forfeit their peaceful life because of man. The rest of Nature would be thankful if, in the process of self-destruction, man would have the good sense to destroy himself if he must, alone, leaving the rest of creation at least to the peace which is its birthright. . . .'

These words had their proper effect upon the young man, and by this time more young men had gathered round the Guru and he rose and walked 'gently as a summer's cloud' to the place where the preparations were going on for the afternoon celebrations. The public were to be the guests of the *āśrama* for the day and the *brahmacārins* were busy preparing a dinner of rice, vegetables, and buttermilk for the numerous persons who were expected. The palm-leaf lecture-hall was being decorated with festoons of young green coconut leaves.

The Guru walked round, interesting himself in the arrangements, and afterwards sat down on the floor of the verandah talking to young and old who surrounded him, anxious to imbibe his words. 'It is precipitate thought,' he went on, 'that makes a man try to proclaim his own opinion as the best. No one opinion, however loudly proclaimed, can justly represent the Whole. It is like the story of the blind men who went to examine the elephant. It is only waste of breath to argue vociferously to establish any one religion. It is impossible in the nature of things that only one opinion should prevail. Without realising this simple fact, men divide themselves into rival camps and fight for the mere words that seem to divide them, forgetting the most primary of human interests. Speeches should not be made with a spirit of rivalry or hate. All speech is for knowing and letting others know. A man's religion is a matter of his personal conviction, which is bound to be at varying stages of natural evolution in different people. Each man, therefore, may be supposed to belong to a different religion, and no two poeple belong to the same religion. On the other hand, all the religions of the world agree in *spirit,* the most essential part of religion. All religions represent values of Truth or Duty. The Goal is common. Why should man fight for his faith? It is an unwise act — one should not be swayed by the conflict of opinions, but should remain tranquil, knowing the Unity in all human effort, which is Happiness. Men differ in dress. Some poeple like to wear a beard; others are clean-shaven. Serious people do not quarrel over these things! Again, languages differ, but it requires no proof to see that humanity is one in spite of such differences. Why then should man differ and cultivate hatred? It is in vain — men have still to learn that fighting only destroys. If man only understood the simple truth, he would not fight. . . .' Thus continued the Guru, talking gently, and wafting home to simple folk that stood round him the eternal principles of human conduct which burned in his heart though his talk lacked oratorical perfection, for it was broken now and then by lapses into silence.

Another of the Guru's favourite topics on such occasions was *caste* or racial distinctions. He disapproved of all imaginary distinctions between man and man — in which he saw the cause of much unhappiness and unrest. The young men had already made him commit himself to a definite statement about the burning question of caste distinction in India; and the Guru's message, which they had printed in his own child-like autograph, was ready to be distributed in the afternoon. It ran as follows:

> Whatever may be the differences in men's creeds, dress, language, etc. — because they belong all to the same kind of creation, there is no harm at all in their dining together or having marital relations with one another.
>
> — Nārāyaṇa Guru

The Guru continued his conversation, contemplating man's manifold self-made troubles. As he sat and spoke, on one side of him stood fanning him an old man who disliked the youngsters and stoutly opposed, with all the influence he could command in his own village, the contagious spread of levelling philosophy preached by these 'hot-headed young men' — and on the other side stood the leaders of the youthful reformers themselves, as tame as lambs in the presence of this strange old man who 'puzzlingly' combined and represented the views of the hot-headed young reformers and those of the callous, conservative elders. The silent Guru stood between the two rival parties — who vied with one another in doing homage to him — as the personification of the principle of exalting Synthesis. His love of men made him the most artful and just peacemaker, whilst remaining himself most obstinately uncompromising when occasion demanded.

It was nearing midday. The Guru rose and wended his way to his river-side resting place. On the way he stopped, seeing some boys giving the last touches to the decoration of a triumphal arch through which the delegates were to enter. He suggested that the mystic syllable *AUṀ*[1] might be written 'as large as the head of an elephant' to decorate the top of the arch: and under it the words *sāhodaryam sarvatra,*

'*Auṁ,* Brotherhood Omnipresent Fills !'

---

1. *AUṀ,* a symbolic word made up of the elements *A*, *U* and *Ṁ*, supposed to refer to three aspects of reality, and together to constitute the essence of all mystical doctrines of the Upaniṣads, cf., *Māṇḍūkya Upaniṣad.*

5

Mystic Experience

IT is in a little-inhabited district of south Travancore, on the banks of a foaming mountain stream, where, roaring through rocks and pebbles, it passed into the plains, that our next scene is laid. The secluded valley resounded with the noise that rose from the river and the tall trees around looked as if imploring heaven incessantly. Except for the cowherds who followed the cattle into the woods or the goats leaping about among the rocks, there were scarcely any signs of human life in the vicinity. Such was the place in which, in the year 1886, a man of about thirty years of age emerged into public attention in the manner we are about to recount.

Leaving his home behind him, for years he had wandered from one man to another, from one centre to another, before he came to settle down, for the time being at least, at this spot. During this period of restless travelling he had sometimes walked three to four hundred miles with no better provision than that of a mere mendicant. Sometimes he had to swim across rivers or stretches of backwater on the coast line; but these barriers could not hinder the spirit of search that had awakened in him. Unknown to the millions, who only later began to adore him, he passed from one village to another sleeping at night on a cloth spread on the stone slabs of some wayside rest-house, with his stick as his only companion beside him. Other vesper hours found him perchance in a wayside verandah or some forsaken temple-yard where, with the leaves rustling in the gentle evening breeze and sometimes with the moon shining, he spent his night, famished perhaps, fatigued and forlorn, but at least apparently in slumber: in reality inwardly awake with the 'light of the silent tabernacle of the mind.'

Generally uneventful in the usual sense of the term, the life of the ascetic became more uneventful still, as his search made him turn more and more within himself for consolation. That search began to depend less on outside persons or things, and, as it became more pronounced, it was necessary for him to protect himself from the 'madding crowd's ignoble strife.' It was in the beautiful district we have referred to, that his search reached its final stages. Now established in his forest-abode, he was beginning to witness within himself an event of more import than the eruption of a volcano or the conquering of a kingdom. It was thus that the villagers of Neyyāttinkara had the opportunity of making continued contact with the ascetic, who sat by the river-side, his face shining with inner resolution, and who was none other than the Nārāyaṇa Guru beginning his life as a teacher of men.

One villager after another who went past him in the forest in pursuit of his daily occupations, began to wonder what the matter was with the man who was seen day after day not specially occupied in doing anything. He seemed to be busy over nothing, anxious over nothing, attached to nothing, and no events seemed to shake his calm. While the passer-by had slept and woken and fed his hunger and mixed with his mates and passed again, there the seeker sat with his calm yet resolute face; with his gaze showing complete wakefulness but seeming to see nothing in front of him. He was absorbed in some thought, the nature of which was a mystery. Thus day after day passed by.

As the villagers' curiosity became greater, they soon discovered that there were people in the neighbourhood who brought milk and fruits for the strange man, which they left beside him; but the birds and the squirrels were seen more often to partake of them than the man himself. A single banana and some clear water formed his sustenance from day-to-day, as he spent his time in introspective absorption.

His ways frightened some and served to keep them aloof. Others approached nearer and made bold to break the silence and tried to induce him to take more food. There was one elderly dame whose maternal instincts prompted her almost to compel him to take more food by putting rice into his mouth. To a vast majority of people who had not come near him, he remained merely an abnormal man. Some thought him an impostor trying to play on the religious sentiments of the credulous. Others thought him one whose virtue was only a cloak to hide laziness or even vice. Some of them blamed him openly even though the young seeker had asked for no favour of them whatever and was totally unrelated to them in any way. They blamed him and hated him and without apparent cause gave vent to their aversion in strong language. Indifferent alike to praise and blame, the young man sat neither loving less nor hating more but imploring God in the most supplicant terms to save him from his inner misery and lift him beyond blame. Some strange cosmic emotion was heaving within him and he was in the pangs of the birth of an inner life to which the life dictated by the senses was becoming more and more repulsive.

This state of self-absorption increased soon after. Human company of any sort became unbearable to him. When a curious passer-by stood and watched him as he would a curious animal in the zoo (so he himself described it), he would sometimes spring to his feet in resentment and walk off to the neighbouring hill-top on the summit of which, on a pile of stones for a seat, he would sit cross-legged, erect and silent, gazing at the vast panorama of hills that was visible from that point of vantage. He sank deeper and deeper into oblivion of the affairs of the world. The mind seemed to feed on itself and reap a strange happiness.

The emotional counterpart of this incessant search was so heavy as to make even a sturdy supporter groan under its trials. The torrential stream on the banks of which he sat was but an objective representation of the state of emotion in his heart. Nothing can describe adequately the trials he underwent. It would be vain to undertake the task.[1]

It was as if he was drunk. The red fire of knowledge was beginning to glow within him. It was as if his feelings were beginning

---

1. The description that follows is not an arbitrary one. It is taken from various passages of devotional poetry which he wrote for the sake of the village worshippers who gathered round him.

to melt. It was as if the ambrosial essence of his being was beginning to pervade his mental horizon. This emotion made him call upon God as his only refuge — God, 'whose tender feet dripped with the honey of compassion.' God was to him the pearl of perfection, the dancing centre of his life, the lotus that sprouted in the silence of his heart caught in the centre of which, buried among the petals, like a bumble bee having its fill of honey, his soul enjoyed uncoveted blessedness. It was as if his soul in the form of a radiant child, planting his foot in the centre of a glowing radiance, had devoured within his being the light of the sun and the moon. It was as if this radiant form was dancing and swaying at the centre of his being, mounted on the back of a peacock with outspread feathers of green and gold. It was as if a lamp shed its steady light in the silent house of the mind. . . .

It was an experience beyond words; and the volume and force with which images such as these surged up within his mind, richly breaking through barriers of rhyme and metre in some of his prayers written at this period, throw ample light on its nature.

This new experience was not in the nature of an event. It was an experience that changed for him the meaning and import of all events, so called. He waited no more for events that would bring him pleasure or pain. He inwardly smiled at the events that others round him attached so much importance to. The events that disturbed or frightened others round him, making them put on grave faces and speak to one another, with hidden hatred, seemed to him child's play. Death had lost its bitter meaning to him and the unknown had lost its mystery.

It was as if he had come into possession of a rich heritage. A veritable ball of radiance had come into his possession. Its light seemed to heave, with every breath, reaching beyond the bounds of the three worlds. Sounds seemed to fill the sky. The eye was filled with beauty. Music and rhyme burst forth unpremeditated in his voice. Tears of compassion and pity stood ready, at the least little demand, to overflow into action. He became a changed man with a strange silence in his ways, both the subject and the object of utmost compassion.

Undivided and uncramped with trivial events, Time to him became richer and richer in inner meaning, while the ponderable aspect of time became of less import. Past, present and future merged into a continuous whole and he forgot weeks and months as they glided freely by without affecting him. The joy of the state into which he had fallen was alluring him deeper and deeper into his own consciousness.

Controlling with an iron will the domination of one set of emotions over another, upright as a bolt, established firmly in that kind of reasoning which concerned itself with the most immediate realities of a simplified world, he soon entered a distinct phase in his life. The hunger of a simple villager who came to visit him, became a matter of greater concern to him than theological disputation or the establishment of a new religion. He began to live in a present which was the result of an endless and pure experience of the past and the most far-reaching expectation of the future. The result was that his duties became clear as daylight to him at every step. Philanthropy became a natural hobby to him. Philosophy gave his actions a detached motive, and poetry gave him the means of natural expression. His life and ambitions were simplified, and the foundations of a career of benevolence and prosperity were laid in his personality.

As days passed by, the crisis of the emotion connected with the breaking in of the new life was over. He became able once again to converse with the people who gathered around him, still keeping himself established in the state that he had made his own. While the great subjective events were taking place, the villagers had put up a roof for him to sleep in, when the weather happened to be bad. They had made special arrangements for his food. They had appointed office-bearers to be in charge of the different activities of the place. People arrived on foot and in bullock carts to see the *yogī*. Women and children constantly gathered round him, bathed in the river and brought simple presents of fruits or flowers which they placed as an offering before him. The crowds of such visitors had to be managed. They invariably partook of the hospitality of the place and returned to their normal business after a few days of comfort and consolation derived from ministering to the wants of a *yogī*. Fatigue, both physical and mental, was dispelled at this riverside hermitage, and the place grew into an institution, an *āśrama* as they call such in India.

The place, however, still lacked one feature of an *āśrama*, and that was a place of adoration. This became especially necessary as the *yogī* was beginning to move about again from this abode. On these occasions the atmosphere was lacking which his presence gave, and thus the need of a special place of worship was felt by the little community which had spontaneously established itself in connection with the new *āśrama*.

This new need raised a whole tangle of problems. What was to be the shape of the place of worship? What form of worship was to be adopted? Was it wise to depart completely from popular tradition, or was it better to respect tradition in its harmless aspects and point the way to reform? Agreement on these various problems seemed almost impossible. Under the encouraging guidance of the Guru the villagers progressed from one form of compromise to another until they reached a point which represented the farthest progressive step they could take. Uncouth formalities and customs handed down from time immemorial were mostly cut out, there being only retained some of the simpler harmless ones like the waving of camphor lights and the offering of flowers. The difficulties, that at first appeared Himālayan, dwindled into insignificance. There among the hills was to be established a temple of Śiva, the God of Renunciation. There the women and children could gather together. That would form the centre from which the children would begin to love the clean and the beautiful. The idea satisfied all concerned and the Guru instead of refusing to co-operate with the peasants and the villagers because he himself had risen above the need of formalities in worship, consented to consecrate the temple with his own hands. The necessary land was soon purchased and the date was fixed for the consecration of the temple.

On the appointed morning, long before the 'hunter of the east' began to throw his pink noose of light across the sky, the Guru was up to prepare himself for the duties of the day, bathing himself in the bubbling river. The spot for the installation of the stone altar had been selected and made ready. Thousands of people had gathered overnight to witness the event. The stars shone still when the young ascetic entered the enclosure.

What miracle was going to happen? This was the thought engaging the minds of the thousands of villagers who had gathered in eager expectation under the starlight. There in the centre of them stood the silent ascetic ready to perform the installation ceremony of the central stone of the altar. The darkness was lighted only by the golden flicker of a five-petalled brass lamp set among flowers.

To some present it all seemed strange and suspicious. Was the young ascetic fitted to perform such a serious ceremony? Was he orthodox enough for it? Had they not heard him talk of Śiva as a mere historical figure, some ancient hunter who lived in the Himālayas, who, because of his virtues as a leader of his people, was loved and began to be worshipped with godly attributes. Was he pretending to be a devotee? Would the wrath of God descend on the village for such breaking away from tradition? These were the thoughts that passed through the minds of some of the crowd as, standing nearer to him than the rest, they watched his features to find a reply to their doubt.

No answer to these separate questions seemed available. He stood in the centre, his face eloquent with expression, and with his eyes lifted in silent prayer.

> Let increased blessing come! Let the poor and needy be comforted! Let them prosper and let not their daily bread fail them from day-to-day! May they learn to be truthful and seek the ways of happiness each in co-operation with the other! May they learn to be cleaner day by day! Let all hatred and dissension vanish from among them! Let them learn to respect the feelings of the least little creature of God! Let at least a portion of the Great Truth dawn on them and bring them consolation!

These were the wishes with which he lifted up his eyes.

As he thus prepared himself for the act which was to be the living link, not only between the past and the future, but also between his deepest feelings and those of the ignorant millions for whose sake he was performing the act, in outward evidence as it were of his earnestness, the questioning villagers saw on his resolute features, rolling down in unceasing streams, just simple childish tears.

Silence prevailed while the crowd, moved by the same contagious emotion, looked one at another in the starlight. Soon the installation ceremony was over. The day had dawned. The clarion call of the conch rent the sky, and as the white-clad crowd began to disperse beyond the hills, each felt the petals of a new hope unfolding within; and victory seemed to reign.

6

Guru Role Begins

THE little white-walled institution, nestling among the hills, soon grew out of its infant struggle. The people of the locality formed themselves into a regular association to give continuity of life to the tradition started by the Guru, and the plant showed signs of growing into a useful tree. The Guru began the role of a gardener, not of plants but of a field of institutions scattered over the west coast of south India. Old ones he was obliged, in some cases, to uproot and establish anew. He was content to prune some, while he grafted others on the stock of ancient tradition. For the next thirty years of his life he travelled in annual cycles, watering and weeding them with the care and concern of a true husbandman. Calm as the seasonal changes, the reforms took root starting a new era for the people touched by them. Thus, his role as a Guru began.

All was not smooth on the course. Three thousand years of tradition, gone to seed, had covered over and shrivelled the life of the people. They held to the thin reed of traditional life with the tenacity of a drowning race. Deprive them of the be-all of life, they would call it their fate and meekly suffer it; but touch the nerve having its root in the traditions of their ancestors, and the hungry men rose to die for what they prized more than life. Not even the king could try to change tradition. The established religions could only continue the traditions that they inherited. The people were willing to carry their popes in golden palanquins as long as they respected the least little detail of tradition, but even a departure from a baneful practice was enough to dethrone them from *guru*-hood. Such were the forces.

There was a safety-valve which tradition itself afforded, and this consisted in the respect for renunciation. From time immemorial, the ruling kings rose from their seats to honour a holy man who entered the palace from the street. The people instinctively recognised such holiness. The books laid down the marks of such a one. It was traditional to think of a man of renunciation as a respresentative of God. Time and again in the story of that vast continent seething with population, a simple man of renunciation had led the people to the gates of safety. This tradition is still alive and is the silver lining of hope for the future.

The rare privilege of leadership in reform adorned the ascetic features of the Guru with a natural grace. His heroic qualities had been tested in fire. There came a night dedicated to the memory of Śiva, the ancient leader of the Hịmālayas, which kept a large crowd awake, hearing orators, musicians and lantern-lecturers and waiting for the elephant procession at midnight and the fireworks in the morning. They made the secluded river-side into a town for the night, and young and old gathered at the spot which was the seat of the ascetic life of the Guru. The Guru sat protected from the crowd at a distance, finding out from the by-standers all that was happening. He spoke of the vulgarity of elephant processions and the waste involved in fireworks. He made no speeches, but the crowd heard his views through the speedy medium of rumour; so that, while he pronounced no judgement, the people carried out his suggestions, as if responding to their inner voices.

At midnight the Guru came into the crowd. There was to be a meeting and the Guru was to preside. A deep unconcern sat on his features while he sat at the head of the crowd. Orator after orator rose to his feet and spoke on the ideals of the Guru as they understood him, as the Guru sat silent behind them. They moved the crowd, mixing their voices with the subtle emotional atmosphere of the midnight vigil.

A group of women and children, more sunburnt than the rest of the crowd, sat segregated from the others. They were poor peasants, who, after a day's hard work, had come in search of consolation to the festive scene. For ages these poor labourers and their ancestors had tilled the soil for the richer people who took advantage of their goodness. On the basis of their caste, these people had been condemned to age-long suffering, and were segregated and spurned. The Guru's watchful eyes lighted on the group. He asked the orators to wait a moment. He asked the crowd if these people should be segregated. Why should they not come and feel equality with the others? The Guru arranged that two of the boys from the crowd be brought on the platform, and seated them, after kind questions, one on either side of him. 'They are God's children as much as the others,' he murmured, and tears of compassion more eloquent than speeches carried home his silent message to the crowd. Even those who would have growled at such a departure from tradition, could not resist the winning power of the Guru's eyes. They crouched, innocent of the axe which the Guru aimed at the dead root of tradition. No statesmanship or subtle diplomacy was employed. It was the simplest manifestation of humanity, welling up in the heart of the Guru, that won the case for ever. Thus the first victory of the Guru was won. The boys were later admitted as members of the hermitage; and they and many such, remained near the Guru, wherever he went, until the day of his passing away. While others spoke and became excited over the past or the future, striving for hours to direct the popular mind, the Guru sat silent, and acted. His silence, when judged by its effect, marked the high-water-mark of oratory. In winding up the proceedings of this memorable day, the Guru had merely a few simple words to say. These he put in the form of a motto, which one of those present proclaimed to the crowd. It read:

> Devoid of dividing walls
> Of caste or race
> Or hatred of rival faith,
> We all live here
> In Brotherhood.
> Such, know this place to be!
> This Model Foundation!

Such, then, was the manner, and such the character he gave to his work. It soon overflowed the limits of the province, and spread its seeds far and wide. Let us follow him a step further in his silent task.

Let the reader imagine a village in Travancore in or about the year 1895. The sandy village-lane is untreadable in the midday heat. It is more than a hundred yards long and leads to the village temple and the pond. A poor villager, a hard working agriculturist, and his tired newly-wedded wife have traversed the hot sand on their way from afar. They meet the priest of the temple who enters the lane from the opposite direction. A new-comer to the village would have heard an angry shout raised by the priest, which was meant for the approaching couple to make way for him. He was the representative of God and had to be given the way. The harsh traditional shout was effective in making the tired couple retrace their steps all the way backwards till the priest could pass without distance-pollution from the poor workmen. Let the visitor pass on to the temple-yard, which is the centre of the village life. The white walls of the temple which once formed the canvas on which inspired artists tried to express the richness of their inner life, was now a place which the idle village-urchins scratched and defiled with ghastly figures in charcoal. The temple festival had degenerated into a drunken merry-making. Instead of the spirit of heroic sacrifice, society connived at the cowardice of ritual sacrifice of animals. The spirit had fled from the temples, leaving the shell of tradition behind. The unholy wand of degeneration had touched with its deadening touch the once luminous spirit that radiated from the village temple. Such and a hundred other such so-called places of worship were the canker at the core of a fallen society.

Not far from the temple stands the house of a trustee of the temple. The mistress of the house has finished the duties of the day. The children have retired to rest after their evening meal. The last visitor has arrived in the village, and this happens to be none other than the *yogī* of the river-side hermitage. A youthful follower is with him and conducts him through the slaty darkness beneath the palm trees, with the light of a torch. They partake of the last remnants of the meal and prefer to sleep in the open, under the starlight. At day-break the anxious housewife discovers that the bed, on which the Guru slept, is made, and the Guru departed. He is already on the scene of action. He has called the leaders together, and talks to them. Animal sacrifices must be stopped. The temple must be demolished. It is too dirty for a place of worship. Drinking must be discouraged. All are equal in the sight of God, so long as they are clean and moral. There is no harm in modern innovations in shaving or dressing. Such was his outlook and programme. Soon the task appeared to take on serious aspects. Hydra-headed tradition raised difficulties. Age-long precedents were quoted. Bloodshed was threatened. The wrath of the gods would descend on the race. The voice of a thousand years of convictions questioned the authority of anyone on the face of the earth to touch a hair in the accepted tradition of their forefathers. Some even trembled and gave vent to hysterical outburst, while the Guru sat on another side talking in his usual gentle way to the leaders. After hours of pitched battle, one by one the leaders yielded to reason. Demoniac feelings of ancient origin danced their last dance, exhausting themselves, and fell back before the gentle tear-filled features of the Guru. His voice sounded stronger than the shouts of vested interest. One by one the diverse elements melted into harmony.

Next morning the Guru began the demolition of the old temple. The stones were to be used for a new temple. An over-grown grove, untouched for generations out of superstition, was to be cut down by the Guru's mandate. The timber available therefrom was to be used for the school building that the Guru proposed for the education of the idle village-urchins.

Innumerable privations were involved in such a task of reform. Some of them were self-inflicted. Others took the form of protests, while still others were resorted to give a better example to the people. It sometimes meant that on entering the gates of a rich mansion where he was invited, he had to turn away in protest on seeing some poultry in the yard which made him mumble something about the cruelty of rearing a bird or animal with parental care until it was grown, and then on a fine morning applying the sharpened knife to its neck just to satisfy the wild desires of the palate. It meant at other times that he walked twenty miles on foot in protest against the ill-treatment of an animal drawing the vehicle in which he sat. It meant at other times still, that he walked all night disgusted with the heavy snoring of some of his followers who had feasted with him on a previous night. Once he spent a whole night sitting by the river-side refusing the requests of a rich landlord to come and sleep in a couch prepared for him in the house, just because he had seen a visitor spit on the ground within sight of his window. It meant starvation when he refused to take even milk on a day on which he had no supper, telling the bystanders that the milkmen were cruel to the calves and did not leave enough milk to satisfy their hunger. Such occurrences were constant events in his life, giving intensity and depth to his silent message, which he carried with him wherever he went.

For fifteen years he travelled incessantly, attempting to bring more cleanliness and light to the poor people of the country. He helped them to clean up the houses and streets. He helped them to have cleaner habits. He introduced and set an example in better diet. He gave an impetus to right moral standards. He pointed the right road to reform and more prosperity. He helped them to see clearly through maladjusted emotions. But these were only preliminaries to the real teaching that was to follow. This he left behind in the form of verses and writings for his future followers to learn and interpret.

As the honey in a flower attracts insects, so also the natural kindness that radiated from his person made him specially interesting to intelligent young men in the places that he visited. They gathered round him and followed him and were influenced by his ideas and ideals in various degress. He talked with them, unceasingly helping them to distinguish the higher duty from the lower and opening their inner eyes to the light of truth 'with the golden needle of knowledge.' With the care of a parent, alternately kind and harsh as the seasons of their mental unfoldment demanded, the Guru guided these men from one high pinnacle of thought to another. Some dropped off. Others lapsed into household life, where the training they received near the Guru made them shine in their self-chosen careers. Others developed the Guru-qualities themselves, and, filled with the spirit of the Guru's message, burst away from him as seeds burst to scatter themselves. It was a continuous task for the Guru.

After these fifteen years of wanderings, in which he was everywhere and nowhere in particular, he emerged into a more settled sort of public life again at a place forty miles north of the original *āśrama*. He had selected a neglected hill-top on which a poor peasant had built a shed for him out of coconut-palm leaves. The sea was visible as a silver gleam from here, and all the undulating country below. Visitors, when the more persevering of them had succeeded in discovering him in that secluded spot, found him once more absorbed in *tapas*.

He sat unconcerned. The perennial springs which gave rise to gurgling streams at the foot of the hill, had water as clear as tears, and represented objectively the inner state of peace within him. . . . As before, he wrote prayers for the people who were interested in him. This time he chose to address God as his Mother. The devotional language, instead of reminding one of the torrential stream, reflected the perennial flow of crystal water.

'O Mother,' he called, 'when will my spirit's fever be calm and mingle in the core of the radiant-petalled glory of the One Primordial Mind? When will the deceptive snare of hungry visions cease?. . .'

Such was the strain of his music at this period.

This place also soon began to grow into an institution by the same magic touch of his presence. He protected under his care a few of the poorest children he found round him. They did for him the odd jobs and lived with him. To one he taught weaving and how to earn his living thereby. Another was his personal attendant and read him books while he waited on him. He talked with each of them, directing their thoughts into purposeful channels. He simplified his philosophy for them, with the greatest consideration for their ignorance. In his attempts to explain to these poor children his religious attitude in simple language, he wrote the following verses for their daily meditation. Translated they read as follows:

God, protect us, and keep us ever away from harm!
Thou art the Great Captain,
And a mighty steamship on the ocean of being
Is Thy foot.

Counting all things here,
Touching them one by one,
We come at last to where
There is no more left;
Then, lo, the quest stops
In stillness.
In Thee, likewise, let the inner self
Attain its rest!

Food and clothes, and all things else we need,
Thou givest us unceasingly:
Ever saving us from want.
We thrive on Thy bounty, Lord !
Our only God Thou art.

To sea, and wave and wind and depth compared,
Let us within us see the plan, respectively
Of us ourselves, of *māyā,* Thy Power and Thou Thyself!

Thee we find in Creation;
The Creator, too, Thou didst become, and
Creation's myriad magic;
And the very Stuff of all created things.

Are You not *māyā*, the author of it,
As also the enjoying agent thereof?
Are You not even One who can cancel *māyā*
To grant us that state of Union Supreme?

Truth thou art,
And Knowledge and Bliss likewise.

The present Time art Thou;
Past and Future merge in unity in Thee.
Even the Spoken Word — a moment's thought reveals
As but of Thine own Self again.

That state which fills all, both inside as well as outside
Brimfully with Your Glory,
That We adore, O God of Goodness,
Victory be to You.

Victory to Thee, Great Master!
Ever-watchful Saviour,
All-knowing, bliss-filled Sea of Kindness, Hail!

In the deep deep ocean of Thy Glory,
Let us all together immersed be,
For ever and for ever —
There to dwell, everlastingly,
In Bliss.

AUṀ

7

Principle and Practice

THE Guru represented the principle which stands, as it were inactive and still, at the centre of practice, whose proper place is at the frontier or the circumference. Practice was concerned with particular events, while the principle was the dynamic centre which gave continuity and coherence to the separate events. The principle stood colourless and neutral in comparison to the particular act that was to be accomplished, but it was the silent and simple principle that lent support and benediction to every righteous cause. At Varkala, which was his new abode, the Guru became more and more the representative of the Principle with a capital *P*.

Varkala was not a populous place. The blackened rocks that cut into the greenness of the sloping hills, looked hard and unyielding. The seekers after ease and pleasure had therefore deserted this place and lived nearer the sea-coast where the abundance of fish, moisture and fertility favoured the proliferation of human life. Away from the competition and strife of daily life, the Guru sat on the hill-top, removed from the highways of business. To him the neglected spot had its aspects of sublime beauty. Hidden behind the apparently unchanging fixity of the rocks, the meditative eyes of the Guru could see the Principle of change and becoming. The ancient breezes that rose far away on the ocean's breast, greeted him where he sat. The starlit nights were rich with the distant murmur of the waves. At the foot of the barren rocks, hidden amongst the growth of fern, crystal springs perennially formed themselves into gurgling streams. The virgin beauty of the spot could not be discovered by the vulgar eye of haste or greed. To the Guru, as he himself used to say, it was the *puṇya bhūmi* (holy land), where the signs of human pettiness and greed were not in evidence.

A stranger would have thought that the Guru was inactive, or that he was resting without much work. A longer or shorter stay at the *āśrama* soon changed that notion. It was true that at early dawn, before even the contour of the hills became visible, the Guru, who had finished his morning ablutions, sat still on a raised couch while one of the *brahmacārī*s read, in musical tones, parts from an elevating scripture. His long staff and lantern with half-raised wick, and his sandals which he left on the threshold of his little dwelling room, seemed to add to the still picture of meditation. So did the morning shadows at the foot of the mango-grove. . . . It was true that most of the day he spent talking to various kinds of visitors, young and old, on topics that made a hasty man impatient while he stood listening to him. It was true that after his midday meal he shut himself up or sat under the shade of the mango tree. It was true that he retired soon after nightfall and lay down on his couch while someone read or sang to him. But the Guru was still wakeful. His voice would come unmistakably when the reader made a mistake that had to be corrected. Grammar and pronunciation were not neglected. The style was not left uncriticised. No sublime height was left unappreciated, while still he appeared to be lazy. Separate days mingled, thus, their boundaries, in a Peace that was ever active within him. It was a state of continued Yoga. It was a life of dedication to a principle which he shared with the sun and stars. The world of actions was only an outer zone of shadow compared to the brilliance of the light that burnt within him.

It was not that he did not engage in activity. The attitude of strenuous activity was a natural counterpart of the Yoga which he practised day and night. As a result of this ever-wakeful attitude, he always did what others forgot to do, and even this kind of activity generally kept him more occupied than most people. On a rainy morning, when all the inmates liked to stay longer indoors, he was already getting the waterways clear of the obstructing earth that the flood overnight had deposited. In the midday heat when the building-overseer who volunteered to supervise the erection of the new school building, was absent, he was there present himself to direct the stone-breaking and carting operations. He was at the timberyard at night to put away valuable timber that the workmen had neglected to store away in safety. The poor boys of the Sanskrit school had helped to wash the mossy greenness of the parapet wall that surrounded the temple of Śāradā, and he was there helping to make and distribute to the children milk-pudding with his own hands. It was a peaceful routine of activity, some strenuous, some calm, which the continuous Principle that he stood for, made him engage in without ado. Life was to him a continuous day of harmonised activity. It was not that he believed that all must work hard, but it was rather that man could not remain without activity. 'What can one do?' he used to say. 'Our hands and feet and finger-tips are all asking for work. They are like restless horses. We should be ill if we did not give enough work to them'. He would therefore stubbornly insist, saying he would cook his own food or wash his own clothes, when a devotee tried to deprive him of the chance. He would walk miles and miles to escape from some of the helpful attentions of his devotees.

Occasionally there came a visitor who was a knight-errant is some frontier cause connected with the principles that the Guru symbolised. Perhaps it was one coming from the ancient temple-city of Madurai, where, since the time of his breaking away from the leader, in the fashion we have referred to, several years before, he fought the slow but winning battle against popular superstition and darkness. Or he came from the island of Ceylon or from the Kanarese-speaking country of Mangalore on the coast towards Bombay (now Mumbai). Some others returned to the Master with fruits and flowers from Kāśī (modern Benāres), or, farther still, from Haridvār. They touched the feet of the Leader and remained with him imbibing afresh his Message before they travelled back to their chosen frontier. The spirit of reconciliation filled the atmosphere in the *āśrama* when any such came, and the inmates, young and old, rejoiced in the sense of life that came from the alternation of separation and return of the members of the great family of the Guru. The frontier was the real seat of activity. The Guru himself appeared inactive, and unconcerned with affairs as such.

Once came the poet Rabindranath Tagore, on one of his southern tours, to visit the Guru. In honour of the great poet of Bengal the people in the vicinity of the hermitage arranged a kingly reception. Elephants were requisitioned. He was to be brought in procession as far as the foot of the hill of the *āśrama*. Musical accompaniments were arranged. The Guru stood in the verandah of his rest-house and himself ordered the best carpets that the hermitage possessed, to be brought out to adorn the foot of the seat of the honoured guest. The people thronged with the guest, anxious to hear the conversation between the Guru and the seer of Śāntiniketan. Each of the crowd thought himself the chosen follower of the Guru, and as space was limited, it took some time to establish silence for the conversation. The two veteran leaders greeted with joined palms, and sat down facing one another. The seer of Bengal broke the deep silence that marked their meeting, and complimented the Guru on the 'great work' he was doing for the people. The Guru's reply was not delayed, 'Neither have we done anything in the past nor is it possible to do anything in the future. Powerlessness fills us with sorrow.' His words sounded an enigma to some. Others thought he was just joking. Still others examined the logic of the statement. A characteristic silence followed the remark. The crowd looked at one another for a meaning, but it was the Guru's face itself that gave the silent commentary to the words. Deep silence and earnestness sat on his features. Smiles of curiosity and the rival expectations of the people were drawn into the neutral depths of silence by the suggestion that was expressed on the features of the Guru. All was silent for a minute or two. The climax of the interview was reached in silence where all met in equality. Usual conversation followed and the poet and the crowd retired.

The apparently unproductive Principle which the Guru stood for, was all the time ripening fruitful results all round. Some were merely seasonal expressions of his message. Others had continuity beyond the limit of seasonal cycles. They began in the shape of reading rooms in the name of the Guru, which later developed into places of worhsip. The social and economic institutions were spontaneously aggregated round this central nucleus. Humble individuals, trained in persistent effort, once touched by the Guru, were at the bottom of each such new sprout. They carried the pictures of the Guru in procession. They arranged popular conferences in which men and women took part, and searched for the direction of progress at which the Guru pointed. Those who had special political or social disabilities, answered the rallying-call of the leaders more than others. Soon, hundreds of little nuclei of institutions were scattered all over the country in Travancore, Cochin and Malabār. Later, they spread into Ceylon (Sri Lanka) and the Madras Presidency (now Tamilnād).

Prominent among the permanent organisations that thus grew, as it were in the shade of the parent Principle, was one started in connection with the management of the original river-side temple of Śiva at Aruvippuram. The Guru sometimes sat at its annual deliberations, and he directed the course of its growth from year to year for more than thirty years of his life. Sometimes he protested and would have nothing to do with it. At other times he accepted its invitation and blessed its efforts. Its membership grew from a number of two digits to one of six. Although the Guru did not place much faith in big organisations which were obliged to work at the dull level of the popular mind, the voiceless people whose rights were trodden under the feet of special interests, found a powerful organisation here to voice their rights. Beneficial results accrued from year to year. This association still flourishes and its ponderous name signifies, 'The Association for the Propagation of the Dharma[1] of Śrī Nārāyaṇa.'

The peripheral limits of the Guru's influence were where his principles lashed in the form of waves against the rocks of die-hard conservatism and public opinion reflecting the dead formalities of traditional life. This was the region of actual conflict. This was the frontier where the cause advanced and receded in succession. This was the region where the leaders arose and became 'men of the hour.' They worked in the dust-clouds of controversy. They believed in mass meetings and demonstrations. They adopted tactics and made compromises. Youthful enthusiasts found food for imagination

1. The Law of Righteousness.

in this work. They joined in numbers the ranks of the older leaders. They used the name of the Guru and owed their leadership in varying degrees to his moral and intellectual guidance. He commended and ridiculed them as occasion demanded, and they visited him now and then to spend a day or two at the *āśrama*.

By this time the Guru had become a social force that could no more be neglected. He had the right to prescribe a deviation from customary practice. He could even alter marriage and funeral rites and enact forms. It was accepted that he was working for the good of the people. Protests and murmurs of dissent were raised, but the vital voice of truth and justice carried all before it. After a time, even these murmurs died in the silent victory that belonged to the Principle that burnt in his heart.

Once, a beautiful European girl stood by an Indian student who had not long before returned to India from his overseas studies. Intimacy had grown between them while in Europe, and, true to her word, she had crossed the ocean and come to the man of her choice. The father of the young man, who was much respected in the neighbourhood, had spent many a sleepless night thinking what would happen to the family traditions if his son married an 'imported' woman from a strange shore. The atmosphere of panic prevailed. Was the family to break away for ever from the rest of the relatives, whom they loved, by this mingling of blood? Debates were held in nooks and corners. The wise people shook their heads. Ill omens were imagined. The troubled father at last came to the Guru for advice. The Guru saw no harm. The wedding could take place in the *āśrama* itself. The public were invited. And there the couple stood, the brave girl, radiant in an Indian *sārī,* by the bridegroom who was then professor at a university. The Guru, who sat on a platform built at the base of a mango tree hung with jasmine festoons, surrounded by a crowd of several thousands of people of all religions, after a few simple formalities, consecrated the marriage. In the absence of a proper 'bride's party', the Guru specially asked an Englishman who was present to say a few words as a representative of the bride's people. Rival social and religious representatives met on that happy and significant occasion and feasted together. The clouds that seemed to threaten disaster, only brought joy in all hearts as they departed from the *āśrama*. It was the silent Principle which the Guru represented, that had again won a calm victory. This was only one of many smaller victories of the same kind which were almost of weekly occurrence at the *āśrama*.

Meanwhile, youthful enthusiasts were preparing the ground for a more serious clash with vested interests and conservative opinions. Events seemed to accumulate, as it were, underground, for a long time before they found characteristic expression in what is now a fairly famous event known as the *Vaikam Satyāgraha* struggle. In this, the Guru's efforts came into contact with those of Mahatma Gandhi. As the Guru's attitude in this campaign was not clearly understood,[2] we shall here give a brief account of the main happenings and circumstances with a view to studying his general attitude in relief.

As in many other parts of the world, some religious institutions, instead of being consecrated by a living symbol of justice and righteousness, had degenerated, and the temple walls had become the ramparts for the protection of vested interests. The traditional respect of the people for the name of God and religious duty began to be exploited by a minority. Public benefactions were being diverted into unlawful channels. Those who could not claim holiness, were reduced to the humility of waiting outside the institutions that their money supported, while those who were already not specially needy, feasted within the walls. Dirt and demoralisation spread its contagion. Myth and fiction having their justification in special circumstances in the past, overcovered simple realities beyond all recognition. Even some important roads were thus reserved for particular sections of the public, not to speak of the right share in the advantages of the public institutions.

With the general awakening to popular rights that followed in the wake of the nationalist movement in India, the nation was beginning to search its own conscience. Among the sore spots in

2. Cf. *Young India* by Mahatma Gandhi.

the national consciousness was the question of caste privileges which had been for a long time mixed up with social and religious duties. One seemed to lend justification to the other, until, in the dull background of the popular mind, one became confused with the other. Long lapses of time made them inseparable from the primitive stem of popular belief, and they came to be spoken of under the sonorous title of *varṇāśrama dharma*. Not only did the hereditary priests reserve to themselves the right to interpret this *dharma* or duty, but, what was more, they reserved the right to decide when they were right. Thus, by a vague sort of justification which was more felt than found reasonable, an unjust domination remained unaffected by the ebb and flow of popular opinion.

Dayānanda, Keshab Chandra, Vivekānanda and other pioneers of reform in India had for a long time protested in their own ways against this injustice, but it was Mahatma Gandhi to whom belongs the credit of inducing the nation as a whole to include items like 'the removal of untouchability' in the national programme, and trying to clean the national conscience. It was, however, from the point of view of all-India politics that the Mahatma looked at the question.

Some of the youthful followers of the Guru were impatient for results. It was some time since they had started a movement for the throwing open of Hindu temples to all sections irrespective of caste or birth. They linked their efforts with those of Mahatma Gandhi and the National Congress. They went to see the Mahatma who advised them to try the special method of fighting the situation, which he called *satyāgraha*. It was a kind of passive resistance with ethical principles and a philosophy which had evolved in connection with the personal life of the Mahatma in his work in South Africa and India. 'Soul Force' was its watch word, and it sought to obtain real results by the use of weapons which belonged purely to the emotional world. Even the nearest followers of the Mahatma were liable to be mistaken in their interpretation of this method which Gandhi's mind had conceived and perfected through various stages of trial and error in his life.

According to the Mahatma's advice a *satyāgraha* camp was

established at Vaikam, one of the ancient temple-towns of Travancore State, where the injustice was keenly felt. Volunteers arrived from various parts of south India. Constant directions came from the Mahatma, who was at Ahmedābād. The Guru's land and centre at Vaikam was placed at the disposal of the *satyāgraha* committee, and the Guru's followers supplied much of the manpower required for the campaign. The Guru encouraged and visited the camp, but as usual took no direct part in the campaign. More men and money poured in from all parts of India and the campaign, which was the first clear expression of the pent-up feelings of the people against a long-standing blot, soon took on grave proportions. Batches of volunteers went to the road that the Travancore Government reserved for the high-castes, and stood facing the police constables who were posted there to obstruct them from entering the road. Without retaliation the men suffered privations month after month, standing at their post in the heat and rain, hoping to raise the right emotion in the conservatives that would bring victory to the cause. The tension of public opinion grew from day-to-day, and still they kept on under keen provocation from the rival camp.

At last, Mahatma Gandhi himself came to Travancore to inspect, and, if possible, terminate the situation. He talked with all the parties interested in the question, and came to Varkala to speak to the Guru. It was thus that the silent sage of Varkala met for the first time the historic figure of Sābarmati.

The Mahatma represented a wave of reform that, starting in a political ideal, tried to make the people spiritual. He believed in *satyāgraha* as a special weapon of self-purification for the masses. They were, therefore, called upon to believe in this doctrine. The thought of the welfare of the masses haunted him day and night. He sought to serve their cause with all the earnestness that was at the command of his frail body. When his plans failed or produced a reaction, he took the blame on himself and confessed before the public that he had committed a 'Himālayan blunder', and implored the mercy of God in the most supplicant terms.

To the Guru, the elements of continuity of the Principle were more important than the particular extensive application of a doctrine or method to a given situation that arose. Rules served their purpose for a time and had to yield place to others. Each situation called for its own special intelligence and there was no one panacea. The mind was to be left free to tread its own way through the maze of situations that presented themselves before it, and rules were straight lines compared to the zig-zags and curves of the course of right action. He emphasised only two platforms of thought. One was that of the everyday world of facts, and the other that which belonged to the Reality beyond. He carefully avoided preaching or lending his assent to special philosophies or standpoints to serve temporary or temporal purposes, lest such creations should continue to haunt the minds of the ignorant after the creeds had ceased to serve an immediate cause, and thus add to the heavy load of superstitions with which the poor people confused their honest brains. Popular agreement in a course of action was not to be the result of faith in a doctrine or the appreciation of a special philosophy, but the natural outcome of tangible realities, of everyday life interpreted as simply as possible for the sake of the people.

The Mahatma saw special use in declaring himself a Hindu and a Vaiṣṇava, besides preaching the doctrines of *satyāgraha* and soul-force. He also believed in *varṇāśrama dharma* which he elaborated and interpreted in his speeches and writings. The Guru was content to call himself a man, and to call upon man to recognise God and the simple realities of life. One tried, as it were, to reach the heart of the masses from the circumference, with variety as the starting point; while, to the other, the starting point was the recognition of the One without a second. It was natural that the leader of all-India politics should differ from the solitary Guru in the point of view that he accepted as the basis of activity. One represented the peripheral and the other the central compromise of the same abstract Principle. The Mahatma emphasised and voiced the master sentiment of the nation, while the Guru stood for the neutral Principle.

The Mahatma represented the rare case in which the logic of

the emotions coincided in its essential aspects with the logic of pure reason. The test of both these kinds of logic was in action and this was the sure point of contact between the Guru and the Mahatma. As with the Guru at Varkala, Gandhi had 'untouchable' children with him at Sābaramati. The Mahatma still stood for Hindu-Muslim unity. Both of them were keenly interested in cottage industries; and the type of saintliness both represented, had marks of a common lineage. Although, therefore, in the interview with the Guru, the Mahatma seemed to differ from him in what concerned Hindu *dharma* and *varṇāśrama* and the dogmatic aspects of *satyāgraha,* theoretical differences converged until they met in practice. The Guru, for example, subscribed to the *khaddar campaign* (for popularising homespun cloth). After exchanges of mutual veneration the Mahatma took leave of the Guru.

The *satyāgraha* struggle terminated in a partial victory for the cause of the masses. On the land which was the scene of the historic event, the Guru erected a school for the poor children of the locality. It stands there to commemorate the noble efforts of many youthful souls who suffered.

The Guru liked to see continuity in human endeavour, and, as continuity is the essential factor in a principle, he discountenanced events which were mere expressions of seasonal enthusiasm. While the waves seemed to advance and recede at the circumference, the centre remained undisturbed. At Varkala the winds wafted their message as usual and the gurgling streams interpreted the continuity of the Guru's silent hours. The *brahmacārin* who read by the bed-side of the Guru, had his usual course on grammar and pronunciation. The inner brilliance kept the Guru self-absorbed, while his influence spread into action all round. He showed in his life that principle and practice, ends and means, were related to one another like the stem and branches of a great tree. Withdrawn into the central core of all practice, he remained silent. His life was a continuous commentary on the words of the *Bhagavad Gītā:*

> Mentally renouncing all actions, the sovereign dweller in the body resteth serenely in the nine-gated city, neither acting nor causing to act. — V.13

8

From the Past to the Future

THERE are two distinct orders of greatness. One of them expends itself in the region of contemporary life, while the other belongs to that order which leaves behind it 'footprints on the sands of Time.' It was to this second order that the Guru's life belonged more than the first. What such a type of greatness lost in the extent of its dominion, it gained by invading regions of Time, Thought, and Pure Reason. Surviving lightning-flashes that seem to efface it for a while, such greatness enters the horizon to stay there like a guiding star. The silent lustre of its message belongs as much to the past as to the future and links up the past and the future with one vital bond. We shall here take a short retrospective survey.

Imagine a great country, the vast continent of India, being subjected to constant waves of invasion during the course of several thousand years. The influx came mainly from the north-west. Imagine in this process a constant sifting and selecting of the population, one set of traditions giving way before another, a third gaining over a fourth, and so on, overcovering again and again the special sprouts of culture that protected leisure fostered here and there. Out of all the discordant sound which thus resulted, imagine one period when there seemed to be a pause and a rapid assimilation of the conflicting elements into the clear expression, of which the name of the Great Buddha was the inner symbol. This silent epoch was followed by a great pulsation of human endeavour. India united in the religion of kindness; and art, literature, science and philosophy put forth their finest blossoms.

Following the great unison that was thus attained, there arose a vast tidal wave of civilisation that swept the length of the land, carrying its seeds across to Ceylon and Siam, and along the chain of islands situated in the Indian and Pacific oceans; authorities have traced this influence as far away as the Hawaiian Islands. This tidal wave receded after a time, and shrank within India itself, leaving in various protected parts, on islands and in the seclusion of mountainous tracts, remnants of the days of expansion and growth. As flowers blossom in seclusion, these remnants of the past lay hidden from the public gaze.

The touch of the first adventurous mariner on the coast of India marked the beginning of a new order of things. From the sea-coast imported cultures of diverse qualities began to be absorbed rapidly. New models of greatness were before the public eye. Moral standards built up in the course of ages crumbled down into ruin, and the masses were face to face with new facts which required vision and re-adjustment. The rich traditions of old India began to be overcovered with the débris of its own greatness.

Saint after saint arose in different parts of India pained by the vision of the beautiful vessel, in which their forefathers withstood the waves, drifting helplessly away from their reach. Some stood on the foreshore imploring heaven, others were overwhelmed with emotion and gave vent to their feelings after the style of tragic heroes. Others went to martyrdom. Few had the courage and the presence of mind to plunge into the waters and do something practical to save the situation. Between the advancing and retreating waves of conflicting influences only a sturdy swimmer could survive. The task was difficult. To light the torch again from the dying embers of past glory and pass it on beyond the borders of the new, so that the best of the past could survive in the future — this was the primary task the Guru felt called upon to perform.

Of all the channels through which ancient thought reached the masses of India, the fountain source was the Sanskrit language. This was the tongue that had preserved, recorded in the form of inflections and sounds, and epitomised in symbol, the best thought of the ages. From the ancient chant that burst from the lips of our early ancestors, when the *disc of gold* that *hid the face of Truth* was removed to reveal to them their first surprise, Sanskrit culture had flowed through regions enriched by the writings of great minds like Vyāsa, Vālmīki and Kālidāsa, and at the present day it continues to kindle, in the heart of the modern votary of this mother of languages, rich and ancient emotions. Spurred by the sounds, the human spirit soared at its noblest and highest. Sanskrit combined the primitive and the pure into one magic spell.

This was the source to which the Guru turned to bring fresh life and reopen the weak eyelids of the poeple. At the time of his advent, this great river that had nourished the spiritual life of the whole population for many thousands of years was all but absorbed completely in the sand of its bed, like some of the holy rivers of south India. The once-rich tributaries of patronage that this culture enjoyed, stood overdrained. Sea-borne influences shook and distorted its quiet growth. It was more the shell or bark of the culture that remained, and the votaries of Sanskrit worshipped the forms and formalities of its dead relics rather than lived in the spirit of its culture. The Sanskrit schools, instead of reviving in the pupil the purest memories of the past, had become degraded into institutions where the ancient chants and formulae were repeated parrot-like. They turned out men to whom holiness was a profession and whose other-worldly absorption was strangely influenced by shining nickel or silver. Surface pools and stagnant waters of petty utilitarianism had contaminated the once pure and healthy springs which had their origin deep in the rock bottom of the past. The problem was to rid the nourishing source of the contaminating influences and to draw only the purest. The Guru showed how this could be done.

He had in fact prepared himself for this task from his early years. As a boy he had imbibed the best of the past both in the Sanskrit and in the Tamil writings. These were the two ancient languages which were connected with the history of thought among the masses of south India. In later years these two streams of culture approached until they united into one, like the confluence of two great rivers, and one thought became in essentials the same as the other. Saints like Tiruvalluvar and Tāyumānavar echoed the best in the Vedic culture. Long filtration and purification through centuries had made the essential characteristic of these cultures one and the same. The Guru had early bathed himself in these influences, and had made their spirit his own. He tried to impart to others what he himself had imbibed, so that, enriched in background, young men could advance to fresh fields of adventure and triumph. It was in this sense that the Guru fulfilled the role of a true educator.

The spiritual life of the Guru had never acted as a hindrance to the performance of such a task. It was true that while at Aruvippuram he was passing still through the agony of the birth of the mystic experiences which were constantly trying to break through stony obstacles. But even in those days he had preserved his role of educator intact. In fact, this was one of his personal occupations or hobbies that ran uninterrupted through his life. Wherever he was, there were a few young men who waited on him in the mornings to read and have passages elucidated. The Guru's voice fell on their ears in half-meditative, gently, musical tones as he put completely original interpretations and out-of-the-ordinary meanings into what they read. The result was an attitude of intellectual wakefulness in his pupils like that in his own mind. It was a subtle personal influence that he thus exercised constantly and continuously. Many young men were thus influenced.

Among their number was one, a poor lad of a village near Trivandrum, who came to the Guru to have certain doubts cleared. The Guru helped him and he became so attached to the master that he left his home and his relatives and went with the Guru as a *brahmacārin*. His name was Kumāran. After some years of training the Guru took him to Bangalore and later sent him to Calcutta to complete his course of advanced Sanskrit studies. On his return from his studies this young man was trained to organise the people, and for many years he filled the office of General Secretary to the big association started in the name of the Guru, which we have already had occasion to mention. What was more than this, he became a poet whose poems have become now a part of the literature of that part of the country, and mark a distinct literary epoch. Those who know the character and distinction of this poet, can trace unmistakably the subtle influence the Guru exerted on his writings, whose educational influence was thus subtle but fruitful.

It was a model attitude, a global expression, that the Guru was responsible for in his educational work. The technicalities and details did not concern him as directly as this attitude which he tried to impart. It was this which was his great secret, and it belonged as much to a synthesis of the past as to discriminative analysis of the future. It is a paradox to call this essential quality a 'secret,' for it was a secret only in one sense: in that all did not possess it at a given place and time. In the sense that essentially the same quality was possessed by individuals of divergent races and cultures at different epochs in the history of the world, this secret was nevertheless a 'public' one.

It was no other than the secret of religion, whose natural expression was in a certain stillness or silence. This was the same secret which gave the master-touch to the work of art. This was the secret of the professor and of the *puṇḍit*. This secret of stillness it was that filled thousands of temples with images of the Buddha in meditation, or again gave the touch of religion to the expression of a Madonna. This again was the secret into which Leonardo da Vinci dipped his brush to complete the features of his Jesus.

This secret of stillness is not merely the special possession of gifted individuals. It is the secret unconsciously shared by phenomena in the natural world. The fly-wheel of a giant machine appears motionless; a top sleeps while it spins in perfect poise. There is silence in the full flood. Even a heartbeat has a significant pause. All these belong to an inactivity which is only apparent but is always dynamic and positive. It was this secret of Stillness, Silence or Neutrality that the Guru possessed in rare abundance, and which made him the source of energy, physical, mental and spiritual. It was the secret of such a stillness or silence that made him the most successful educator and helper of men. This was the secret that made him the Guru.

The essential mystic experience of the Guru had passed through various phases by this time. It had taken the form of supplication and melting devotion of the most unconsolable type while he performed *tapas* on the banks of the torrential river at Aruvippuram. At Varkala the emotions had become softer and more tender. The kind Mother was the ideal of the soul, and he was the child seeking consolation in the thought of the Mother. As the pearly nautilus changes its shell, he had outgrown these earlier stages and left them behind.

By the year 1912 the Guru had again changed his headquarters. He wandered farther north. After several tours in which he became publicly recognised as a Guru, between the limits of Cape Comorin (Kanyā Kumāri) and Mangalore, he fixed on Alwaye as his abode. On the brink of the river under a simple roof made of dry palm leaves he again settled down, absorbed in meditation.

He was no more a devotee in the usual sense of the word. The silence of the full flood had entered his heart. He sat as it were idly watching the calm level of the winding river on whose surface were being traced without cessation varying patterns produced from the uneven bed of rock and sand over which the clear waters glided. He could see, far off, the river forking into two beyond the thin mist and the rich vegetation, as he sat with his mind feeding as it were on the nectar of his own heart. Only now and then a boat laden with bananas and vegetables, gently transported along the river to the weekly fair by some neighbouring cultivator, reminded one of the busy world of men. All else was calm at the *āśrama* and the Guru was the centre of this calmness.

It would be vain to attempt to record here even a little of the nature of the state which he thus again entered. As he sat in the calm strength gained through years of *tapas,* Time's narrow limits shrank within him, bringing to his ken the vast expanse of years. Ancient and immemorial truths, that have their being in regions far away, dawned upon him, making the present consciousness radiant with a brilliance beyond words. He thus describes the feeling:

The dawn of knowledge comes
Like the brilliance united
Of ten thousand suns.
This light it is
That, with its keen saw,
Can tear asunder the darkness,
Truth-hiding, impermanent,
Of *māyā*:
And victorious reigns !
Primordial Sun Supreme !

The roots of *māyā* had thus been *cut* in him and the dawn of Truth was now no ambition of the future. The luring vision of enlightenment had led him nearer and nearer the Truth. Now it had become part of his own experience, harmonised and united with the rest of his being. The thirsty traveller in a vast desert was, as it were, overtaken by an overwhelming flood. He had gained an entry into a world of sound, of music that, falling on his ears made his eyes open. He accomplished what he himself predicted for others:

The blue dome on high
Shall radiant resound !
And that day
Through its portals wide shall fly
All this visionary magic of the world.
Then too that still small voice,
That bridges the gulf between the known and the knower,
Shall cease its tiny trumpet
And . . . all sound absorbed,
Pure space remain
Self-radiant !

This was the vision that had come to him at this time. All thoughts of devotion vanished at this spot, self-effaced. Sin and evil and suffering had no place in the scheme to which the vision belonged. Good and bad, truth and falsehood, faded before the uniting principle. The visible world melted and formed part of the vision. It was not a vision that came to pass away. It was one into which one entered to live there for ever. Here was a state in which all colours and shades mingled into one white light.

It is like trying to describe the nature of light in terms of darkness, to try to state exactly the nature and character of this state. Some have tried to describe it as *nirvikalpa samādhi*. Others describe it as the state of the *paramahaṁsa*. The Buddhists have the word *nirvāṇa* and the conception of the Boundless Light or *amitābha* into which the individuality merges its identity. In more unsophisticated language some others call it the attainment of the Supreme Bliss or Happiness. Some attain this only after death, and then it is Salvation or Heaven. This corresponds to the conception of *mokṣa* in Sanskrit, and according to this conception a man can attain *mokṣa* while still living here on earth; this is called the state of *jīvan mukti*. By whatever special name this state is known, it is one same experience. This experience is in more modern language called *Cosmic Consciousness*. It may be described as the experience of the whole, which leaves no remainder. It is the vision of the Supreme Unity that characterises all the states referred to. There is a happy expression in Sanskrit which describes the essential nature of this state in the least controversial form, and that expression is *advaita*, which means the state in which there is no second to speak about. The Upaniṣads sum up in the boldest possible terms this conception of *advaita* when they state: *tat-tvam-asi* (That thou art). It was this same eternal and universal principle of which the Guru's life was an expression. His writings revealed the same philosophy. In the Guru's *One Hundred Verses to Self* (or *Ātman Centiloquy*) which he dictated to his followers at this time, he sounds the same note of the ancient discovery:

> Primordial Knowledge,
> Its own true nature seeking,
> Thus manifests Itself
> As earth and sky.

This state of *advaita* consciousness continued in the Guru, and, as before, expressed itself in the form of activities that bore the stamp of *advaita*. The Advaitāśrama at Alwaye was its first expression. Here was established a Sanskrit *Pāṭhaśāla*, a boarding-school where the children lived the life of *brahmacarya*[1] and learnt some Sanskrit and English and other subjects. The Guru himself took a keen interest in planning and constructing the new school building. Here, Christians and Mahommedans and *high* and *low* of the Hindus met and lived in unity. They bathed in the river in the morning, and grew brighter everyday under the spell of the broadening ideals that the institution represented. This was the way in which the Guru wished the peole to practise the principle of Advaita. The reader has already been introduced to this institution in a previous chapter.

The Guru's work had slowly broadened out all these years. Not a week passed without his being invited by a deputation from some village in the interior where the people had built a new temple or school under his guidance. Now it was a popular leader of the poor who desired his presence at a mass meeting; or, again, there was a longstanding dispute or faction over the formalities of a religious ceremony which divided the village into two bitter parties causing much bad blood, which the Guru was requested to come and settle. Possibly it was a family discussion, arising from an incapacity for impartial appreciation of points of justice which the Guru could alone supply and bridge. Manifold were the ways in which he became intimately related to the people. He was thus loved and respected as a leader within a growing circle of devotees. To come into touch with him was to be influenced by him for life.

1. Dedicated students who 'walk the path of *Brahman*' or the Absolute are called *brahmacārins* (*car* — to move).

9

Later Reminiscences

WE shall conclude this humble attempt to present the main attitude and happenings in the Guru's life with some simple personal reminiscences pertaining to his last years. It was at Trichur, in one of the *āśramas* he had founded, that the coming event of his passing seemed to cast its earliest shadow. As the writer of this narrative entered the enclosure of the little garden facing which he sat, the Guru was seen in a special state. It had been his habit on previous occasions to touch upon some philosophic theme. For many years he had thus kept up, with interruptions of months and even years, the chain of an argument he had begun. The writer remembered his last conversation in which he had treated of the problem of philosophy in simple language. Quite like a scientific philosopher he had said:

> Matter is divisible. Nothing has indicated anything to the contrary. Imagine a body subjected to division and subdivision *ad infinitum.* We can imagine that we thus reach what one would be tempted to conceive as 'nothing.' But it is something still. *This* is the primordial Substance, *This* is God or whatever you may choose to call it. This is one way of arguing the point.

Then he added:

> There are other ways of arriving at the same point. They appear more complicated and involve postulates less easily acceptable to the world, but there is nothing wonderful or secret or difficult about this knowledge. It is the simple essence of Vedānta.

Such or similar were his last words on a previous occasion. This time it was different. As the writer entered and stood by the Guru expecting the usual conversation for a few minutes, he witnessed something unusual. The Guru shut his eyes and sat self-absorbed without a word. Some inner vision caused a gentle glow of vitality to play about his face, venerable with all the outward marks of old age; it reminded one of a simple child's countenance, softly smiling, peaceful and absorbed.

To the mind of the present writer this was no mere accidental attitude. The Guru had purposely meant it to indicate the closing and the culmination of his long years of conversation. Silence expressed the secret of them all much better than words. This silence was the culminating point of his life. This silence was his joy. It was in the lotus-core of this silence that he wished to live. All murmur of message was absorbed in this silence. The emptiness of sights and sounds and sensations lay buried in degradation in its sublime presence.

Thus was the last lesson in Vedānta given by the Guru. He was then travelling in the Cochin State. The Sanskrit school that he had founded at Alwaye, stood in need of constant financial support and now he was thinking of providing a small endowment so that in the event of his passing away that part of his work could continue unhindered. The villagers of Cochin and Travancore everywhere received him with kindly honours. They decorated the streets, took him in processions sometimes miles long, and placed whatever money they could contribute at his feet. The Guru would accept willingly from some. To some others he would suggest the amount they could reasonably pay. A third person he would refuse or return part of his offering. In this tour he was evidently preparing for the coming event. The other institutions, the *āśrama* at Aruvippuram and the one at Varkala, with the big English School which he had founded, could stand on their own legs. It was his Sanskrit child that was rather weakly with bad days facing it, which was now holding his last attention.

Towards the end of the year 1927, when his labours had come to a sort of finish, the Guru was definitely unwell. His complaint was old-age, which laid its hands on him. The writer remembers meeting him at Pālghāṭ where he was under treatment. There were with him several doctors besides representatives of the various public and religious bodies that he had founded, from the various parts of Travancore, Cochin and Malabār. The time was early, and the Guru had a bad night's rest. As the writer stood before him, he was resting, seated on his bed and supporting himself erect with his now emaciated arms. His breathing was difficult and he could not speak except in monosyllables. 'These', he said, meaning the sounds of his obstructed breaths, 'have come as escort'. The people came to visit him and expected that, being superhuman as they believed him to be, he would not feel any pain when he was ill. As if to contradict this idea, the Guru was heard to cry like a child at every cause. While the crowd of villagers waited outside, they could hear the Guru's voice from inside murmuring like a distressed child, 'O Mother ! O Mother!', again and again conveying to them, through the tone in which it was uttered, a message that rang in their ears ever after, and containing the same attitude, the same essence of devotion and simplicity to which he had dedicated the rest of his life.

As the image of Jesus carrying his cross has served as a symbol of his love and service to humanity, so also great masters make even their sickness and suffering serviceable to their fellow beings. The life of the Guru was, in every detail of it, an example of the principle which he enunciated as follows:

> Acts that one performs
> For one's own sake,
> Should also aim the good
> Of other men.

In fact, this maxim may be said to form the key-stone of his whole life. By apparently trying to be selfish he on many an occasion impressed a useful principle or habit on the many who came in contact with him. He would insist that the barber who shaved him had the sharpest razor, and would see that the best methods were used in the art. He would complain of his chauffeur who did not gently put on his brakes when he came to an uneven part of the road. He would teach him to be proud of his car, and find fault with him if he had omitted to observe a new kind of car in which a visitor had come to see the Guru. He would say that he preferred a garland of gold to one of roses if, while on a tour, people greeted him with empty applause and theoretical loyalty and devotion. He would insist on good cooking, more with a view to reforming the food habits than for his own sake. He would insist on small details in building, and order an alteration in spite of expense, in order to set a better example in architecture. He would like to hear music in order that he could patronise musicians. Himself an adept in the art of healing, he missed no opportunities, whenever he was ill, to call together a little group of medical men of different schools of medicine in order to discuss with them the various bearings of the case and make them discuss the details. In the system of medicine called the *Āyurveda,* which is the ancient Sanskrit system, there lay, buried and forgotten, gems of ancient experience which he found valuable to unearth and apply, suffering himself to be the subject of the experiment.

His last illness was rich in such opportunities. He would find some point in which one system failed and in which some-one else knew better. Suffering and bed-ridden as he was, he would argue the minutest details with his doctors and those who attended on him. He went to Pālghāṭ and travelled about four hundred miles north-east to Madras, carried in stretchers and transported from place to place, from one doctor to another, from the care of one devotee, who loved to keep him under his care, to another. Then he came back to Travancore from where a strong deputation had arrived to take him to Varkala. One of the stations on the way was Alwaye, where on the platform were gathered all the students young and old of the Sanskrit School and *āśrama* for which he had given long labours. The coming event was still unknown to them but a deep emotion at the illness of the Guru sat on the features of each one.

He arrived at Varkala. Some of the symptoms of the illness which the experts of one school of medicine had declared incurable, were demonstrated to be curable by others of a different school. For some time the Guru seemed quite well. The radiant glow on his features had never disappeared. He still retained his good humour, and, although he was weak in body, he never yielded or compromised except where it was necessary. He guided the deliberations regarding his property and legal affairs with a perfect sense of justice and awareness of all shades of opinion. He regained a stage in which he took little walks on his own and, though highly emaciated, was still the same alert, radiant, and kind Guru. It was in this condition that the present writer left him on his voyage to Europe.

The 73rd birthday was celebrated by a select group of friends, representatives of different nations and religions, in September, 1928, in the beautiful city of Geneva. For the first time the Guru's message was proclaimed in the West. Strangers, united in worship, feasted together and discussed informally the significance of the ideals of universal appeal which the Guru's life had symbolised.

On the 20 September, 1928, about a week after this event, the Guru entered *mahā-samādhi* or the Great Silence, peacefully and silently at Varkala. In one of his last writings he wrote :

That Dispenser of Mercy — could
He not be that reality
That proclaiming words of supreme import the chariot
drives ?
Or Compassion's Ocean ever impatient
for all creation,
Or who in terms clear non-dual wisdom expounds, the
Guru?

Part-II

The Word of the Guru

10

The Dialectics of Advaita Vedānta

SILENCE, a silence filled with a certain content of kindliness — such was the note on which Part I, *The Way of the Guru,* came to a close. Both silence and kindliness are but aspects of a simpler, unitive and central human value. This value is not merely a philosophical abstraction, but a value that is liveable and realisable in actual terms.

Both existence and reality are comprised within the notion which, globally conceived in terms of human value, tends to abolish all shades of duality and consequent conflicts. To effect such a harmony in life, through contemplation, is our subject in the pages that follow.

'On the tree of Indian wisdom, there is no fairer flower than the Upaniṣads, and no finer fruit than the Vedānta philosophy'.[1] In these unmistakable terms, Dr. Paul Deussen, the eminent Western philosopher, recognised the place of a certain expression of Eastern wisdom more than half a century ago. He then undertook a visit to India, and on leaving its shores again said, 'Vedānta in its unfalsified form, is the strongest support of pure morality, is the greatest consolation in the sufferings of life and death — Indians, keep to it !'[2] Alluding further to the philosophies of Kant, Śaṅkara and Plato, he added characteristically, 'Here we have the same doctrine' (i.e., of the mental nature of the visible) 'in three different parts of the world'.[3] Since the scholar wrote these words, there has

1. See Preface, *Outline of the Vedanta System,* Dr.Paul Deussen of Kiel University, Wood's trans., Cambridge, Mass., USA.
2. See Appendix to *The Elements of Metaphysics,* Deussen: Address delivered at Bombay, 1893, Duff's trans., 1909.
3. See Appendix to *The Elements of Metaphysics,* Deussen: Address delivered at Bombay, 1893, Duff's trans., 1909.

been much recognition of Vedānta in the West. The Word of the Guru, as presented in the following pages, belongs to the same Vedāntic context.

Through Vedānta, especially the Advaita of the Vedānta (which is the formulation of non-dual wisdom) it is hoped that it will be possible to re-discover valid and universal human values in the terms of whatever is the dominant note in present-day world civilization. This implies a subtle interplay of dialectics between sets of values known or formulated hitherto in different epochs and contexts. Such a dialectical revaluation may help to regulate human relations and may offer a commoner or more generous basis for human conduct, one that is truer and stabler than ever before. With such a hope we have written these pages.

The Advaita Vedānta as formulated and presented in the writings of Śaṅkara was itself a revaluation of the Upaniṣadic and Buddhist wisdom which formed its background. Śaṅkara subjected the values held before and in his time to a critical and methodical scrutiny. His approach could even be said to be that of a 'positivist' since 'objective' rational norms entered into it, and because he did not try to *explain away* anything. That was over a thousand years ago; but, making due allowance for the conditions of his day, Śaṅkara may be said to have approached the subject in a fully scientific spirit, in so far as such an approach could apply to a subject in which much *a priori* reasoning has to be given its legitimate place.

More than a millennium after Śaṅkara, from almost the same part of India, there appears another Guru, the Guru Nārāyaṇa, who, as it were, is a representative of the same direct and vertical line of philosophical revaluators — a recognisable valuators-line which can be said also to connect Śaṅkara in his turn with the most ancient phase of human history. A series of dialectical restatements of human values have emerged and held the field in human history, and India has been a favoured soil where, for one reason or another, personalities have appeared time and again to influence the course of history and enrich human life generally.

In this last outstanding exponent of Vedāntic wisdom we have the same phenomenon repeating itself. Nārāyaṇa Guru, born of humble parents, among a peasant population of south India, once again emerges into world attention with his own formulation of perennial wisdom, but a formulation which none the less follows essentially the same lines of dialectically revalued Advaita Vedānta as his predecessor Śaṅkara. The voice of Nārāyaṇa Guru comes to us with a clarity and conviction all its own. Just those points in the original which needed more focussed critical scrutiny receive Nārāyaṇa Guru's corrective touch, his further elucidation or modification — while the message *as a whole* remains intact. His contemporaries instinctively recognised his authority and responded to him in the characteristic way that we have noted already in the first section of this book.

The best authority we have in thinking that the Guru Nārāyaṇa was a direct successor of Śaṅkara comes from the mouth of the Guru himself. 'What we have to say is what Śaṅkara said', he once informed the writer, as if to guide him directly in his enquiries about the correct place of the Guru's teaching. In the Guru Nārāyaṇa the same Advaita Vedānta is treated with a freshness often startlingly unique and simple, taking into its scope and purview more consciously and wakefully, not merely subjective idealistic verities but also all those secondary implications that Vedānta has, or can have, bearing on such human topics as equality and justice. He was for fair play between man and man, and, in his hands, this latest formulation of Advaita leads up to a natural programme of action belonging to Advaita, as its necessary corollary. What is more, his method and approach to the subject of non-dual wisdom, for the first time conforms not merely to 'objective' or 'critical' standards, but — and this is of epochal significance — even comes up to the requirements of a 'normative' or 'experimental' science, as far as that will probably ever be possible.

Thus revalued, contemplation, which uses a subtle dialectical method and touches both the actual and the ideological, becomes more than merely an art or an introspective mystery. Contemplation has wisdom for its 'result' and, in this renewed form, has a satisfactory and convincing content, worth or value, not only interesting to the dilettante but applicable to the welfare of the common man. Its simple, non-secretive, public, natural and central objective is to solve and reconcile duality in every phase and thus eliminate conflict at every step we take in life, throughout the entire range of human activity or interests, part by part and all in all, with immediate, conclusive finality. Such Word-wisdom, as herein denoted, is therefore to be regarded as the common heritage of all humanity, conceived as one whole, with no thought of time or clime. In human solidarity and human well-being is to be found its centre of gravity.

At this preliminary, indicative stage of our study and inquiry, the sweet delicacies or the subtle intricacies of the Advaita Vedānta must not lure us into any actual discussion of its various merits. Moreover, our intention here is to adhere as closely as possible to the living personality of Nārāyaṇa Guru himself. As his own words are to us the most reliable and direct sources needed for the elaboration of the non-dual wisdom of the Advaita Vedānta, here, in his own words, we present our basic starting point for all further detailed explanation:

> Beyond all count is One —
> Then the common reality here.
> Than these two besides — no form
> There can be, nor in memory, in sleep,
> In that city on high,
> Nor anywhere else, indeed ![4]

As we have remarked elsewhere, kindliness is that spiritual value which is essentially human, distinguishing our common human life. It is alluded to here as constituting one terminal reference or pole, as it were, of the real. It is the regulating principle of all human relations; its corollary being the brotherhood of man.

Kindliness necessarily exists as a primary condition of human life. Reaching out from the world of kindliness here and now, the

---

4. Verse 67 of *One Hundred Verses of Self-Instruction* (*Ātmopadeśa Śatakam*) of Nārāyaṇa Guru.

human spirit soars high into the freedom of unknown and absolute values through the exercise of a faculty higher than mere ratiocination, with its attention fixed on a form or value which is transcendental. The human spirit thus aims at perfection, fullness or freedom. In the hymn of dialectics which is the 'Word' of the Guru, one note after another is fingered on the scale of human values which stretches between the extremes of the polarities or terminals that are indicated here. The intensity or the volume of each value-productive note depends upon one or other of these two antipodal factors. This series of human values is lodged in the human personality, and human life is to be understood in terms of the blending of these two fundamental regulators — that is to say, on the fusion and coalescence of the unifying common kindliness in personal relations and the unitive supreme value, absolutely free and transcendent.

Such is the simple 'given' or a *priori* finality with which we wish to mark our starting point, in almost proverbial terms, as the basis for all further elucidation of the Word of the Guru. Even the two levels or extremes — the one, the outspreading world of kindliness and the other, the Absolute — indicated as the value-denominating factors, only seem to stand out as distinct due to the limitations of language whose very nature is disruptive, for finally, when consummated, non-dual wisdom is an inner, unitive awareness, beyond and without words. But here kindliness draws its meaning from the Absolute, while the Absolute itself becomes meaningless and insipid unless thought of in terms of 'the good' or 'the generous'. Contemplation alone can annul the distinction between these seemingly dual value-constituents. Here the duality is tentatively accepted only in order later to establish the non-duality that is really meant by Advaita. The actuality of existence here will be seen to lend reality to the ultimate that is beyond till, all duality dissolved, the light of the good life can prevail and triumph over all. How that is possible, the Word of the Guru is intended to make more explicit. Let us then journey together, as companions on a pilgrimage into the presence of the nouminous unknown.

• • •

Many are the teachers of mankind who have come and gone since the dawn of human history. In spite of them all, each of them in himself so great, human problems have remained unsolved to the present day. The need for fresh incarnations or *avatāra*s seems always to be there. The final victory of truth over falsehood, freedom over bondage, of brotherhood over egoism, seems always to be receding in spite of pride in a progress claiming to take forward strides.

The promised day should not be thought of statically. Instead, all such problems should be understood intuitively, inwardly, or contemplatively, as part of a process of dynamic becoming, avoiding mechanistic notions on the one side and mere mathematical abstractions on the other.

Even the redeeming task of the best of *avatāra*s has to be viewed realistically and factually, as being bound up with necessity, social, individual or human. Within these limitations even *guru*s come and go in our midst, fulfilling as best as they can their high role. Without such personalities, human life generally would be impoverished. Life would get out of joint as it were, in just the same way as the *avatāra* himself would be savourless, vapid, lacking all potency of message, if treated disjunctly away from the context to which he naturally belongs. Treated together with the historical and other dialectical counterparts accompanying them, each *avatāra* will be seen to hold up to view a high and laudable human value.

If this is true of *avatāra*s it is all the more so in the case of the *guru*s or teachers of mankind. Each *guru* should be viewed in his own dialectical environment, in historical terms as well as in the terms of the heritage of the Guru-Word of all time.

In the person of a *guru* — which includes his silence or his uttered Word — there is represented a dialectical revaluation of life-components which belong to his own epoch, while there also remains present, judged in its essence, almost a perennial mathematical constant, clearly given to the eye of contemplation, a constant which can equate and cancel out differences that are extraneous. All *guru*s have been thus representatives of the same

Guru-Word. They were all lovers of humanity and truth. They wanted freedom, with bread for all. Abundant kindliness was the seal set on their foreheads. Taking their stand on the platform of freedom and food for all, they pointed their silent fingers to the super abundant generosity and goodness of the Absolute Principle. Although human problems still remain to be solved, as they are bound to be for ever, the Way and the Word of the *guru*s of successive generations have helped to guide humanity in the past and shall do so evermore, as long as humanity here has a future.

This way of looking at great spiritual leaders of mankind, in the light of a central human value, expressed generally as kindliness, is the subject of a masterly composition from the pen of the Guru Nārāyaṇa. In this work, entitled *Scriptures of Mercy* (*Anukampā-Daśakam*)[5] grace, kindliness or compassion is referred to as 'the guiding star of life', and regarded as a universal correlative principle inherent in the spiritual teaching of many apparently different kinds.

Running through all such expressions is to be sought and found that golden thread of human value which gives unity and meaning to the whole of life. Such is kindliness as seen, for instance, in Kṛṣṇa who, out of his excessive love of justice and fair-play even condescends to become the driver of the chariot of his disciple Arjuna in the ancient war on Duty's Field (*dharma-kṣetra*), while speaking the Word of high wisdom, as seen in the chapters of the *Bhagavad Gītā*.

Again, the same kindliness is seen more directly in the Buddha who pleads before and converts half the world to his principle of non-hurting (*ahiṁsā*) of even animals and little creatures.

In the same spirit of exceeding kindliness Śaṅkara plays the part of a great *guru* and, with great effort, propounds Advaita's non-dual wisdom for the easy understanding of all men.

At another of the historical cross-roads there arrives Christ who baptises with the Holy Ghost in the capacity of both son of

5. See Part III, Chapter 27, for translation and comments.

Man and Son of God at once, mediating between the daily bread we need and the coming of God's kingdom.

Again, Mohammed, than whom there is none other more chosen of God, brings to man a sense of equality and justice revealing the same bounty or generosity of the Most High, in the example of His *nabī*, or Prophet, full of kindliness himself for suffering humanity, for widow or orphan.

In the personality of all these great leaders in wisdom, the two virtue-sources we have noted, the two fundamental poles of the axis of reality, come together in unity in various ways according to a principle implied in Advaitic teaching. To revert to our musical analogy, the notes may appear to sound differently, but they belong to the same ineffably uniate music. The strings of the violin of the human spirit can be fingered at various intervals of interest or necessity, but the music is common, the pleasant melodious harmony of kindliness which is in tune with 'the music of the spheres when the universe was born', and 'the morning stars sang together and all the Sons of God shouted for joy.'[6] Sometimes the music is deep and low and bends down to reach the earth. In the generosity of nature, which seems to imitate that of heaven on high, the poetic and mystically contemplative eye of the Guru sees the same principle of kindliness in the overladen fruit tree — a counterpart on earth of the wish-fulfilling tree which is said to be in Indra's heaven known to Indian mythology, or in that wonder-cow called Kāmadhenu dwelling in the regions of both fable and fact, unceasingly yielding the milk of human kindness. In all these varieties of expression we have a dialectical formula, in which the components are placed between two extremes, which are marked out for contemplative purposes. In their interaction, the polarities or extremes reveal the presence of the nouminous which can be called material or spiritual as we choose, while still, to the contemplative, it remains a unitive simple reality or a life-value.

Contemplation, as it is intended to be understood in these pages, may be said to oscillate between two terminal positions or

6. *Old Testament, Job,* xxxviii, 7.

extremities or poles, as it were, one implied by our common life here, and the other by the Absolute that is transcendent. All human values are necessarily an expression in ambivalent terms swinging now to one, now to another end of the life-shaft, so to say, and such human values must be capable of being validly thought of by the mind. It is in this sense that the truth of the Guru's verse is to be understood.

Although this double-charactered or basic dichotomy is bound to persist in all human beings, contemplation is expected to penetrate into the duality and resolve or reduce it into unitive understanding. In making such an attempt at synthetic understanding, it is possible for the mind to get lost in endless hypostatic fixations or hierophantic idolatries by conceiving reality asymmetrically in favour of one of these two extreme normative psychological principles.

By favouring the hypostatic, there is the unbalanced stress, for instance, on innumerable beings such as angels and spirits; while, by emphasising the counter-extreme, the hierophantic, inordinate value is attributed, for example, to stone images surviving from perhaps pre-historic times. These value-resultants can be good, bad or indifferent, depending on how they are treated or permitted to influence human relations or conduct. Inevitably they find a place, in one form or another, refined or etherealised though they may be, even in the most puritanically iconoclastic or 'imageless' of religions. All hypostatic ('other-worldly') forms have first to be reduced to terms of everyday values in human life, while hierophantic presences (animistically or otherwise conceived) have to be referred to the common norm of the Absolute, before these two categories can have the value proper to them assessed or related in the contemplative context of spiritual progress.

These are matters whose probable obscurity at the present stage of our discussion will be considered later. The inherent difficulties of our subject can only be dispelled piecemeal. Insight into matters which are elusive and subtle by their very nature will become stronger, and our vision clearer in the light of the Word of the Guru to which closer and more serious attention will be given as we proceed.

One further point may profitably be mentioned here in order to avoid initial misunderstandings. In the Guru's verse above there is a categorical denial of the reality of other forms — perceived or unperceived — than those coming within the scope of the dialectical interplay of human values. A promiscuous mixing and confusing of realities or values which belong to different planes, classes or systems, leads to absurdities and irrational situations in life.

In the first place the broad distinction must be made between the actual and the perceptual. As one Indian proverb puts it, 'a charm cannot make a mango fall,' and another says the same thing, 'Vedas will not stop a bull from butting.' Existence and reality have to be treated apart in a way that will still give unitive answers contemplatively, in the correct way known to the science proper to contemplation. Śaṅkara made this unequivocally clear in his treatment and approach to Advaita Vedānta. The method of the Advaita Vedānta, in order that it can yield clear-cut objective results, of any worthwhile applicability to life, has always been to keep these two aspects of the actual and the perceptual as distinct from and non-interfering with each other, as their intrinsic nature calls for. Caesar's domain is distinct from that of God's; or, as Śaṅkara would put it, the empirical or pragmatic (*vyāvahārika*) is to be understood and dealt with differently from the rational or idealistic reality (*pāramārthika*).

Philosophical speculations are largely determined by the profuse references of an ambivalent nature, to pairs or couples of antinomies such as the phenomena and noumena of Kant; likewise his practical and pure, while other pairs are the here and the hereafter, the ontological and the teleological, the immanent and the transcendent. Of all these dualities, one will always refer to the 'existent', while the other will apply to the 'real' or the 'true'.

Any error in referring to one or the other of these ambiva lence-pairs in a given context of contemplative wisdom will utterly compromise its value. Like milk in a dirty vessel (or, to use the analogy of Śaṅkara, like milk in a dog-skin bag), such a compromised wisdom becomes unfit for human consumption. It is in this way that endless confusion often results in regard to matters that ought to be taken either as permissive or mandatory. Likewise the necessary law of the world of the existent (*ṛtam*) is often confused with what should properly belong to the real (*satyam*), as it is to be rightly understood in Advaita Vedānta, i.e., as an attribute of the Absolute and ultimate value called *Brahman*.

At the present stage, however, as we have said, we shall avoid getting lost in further intricacies of the Word of the Guru. It is enough to remember here, in passing, that Nārāyaṇa Guru categorically denies all values here or hereafter other than the two normative formulations implied in this verse. Thus, according to the teaching given here, whatever does not yield meaning in terms of human understanding in the light of one or other of these two standard valuators or norms, must be dismissed to the limbo of the absurd, the erroneous, irrational, false, to the non-existing here as well as hereafter.

This no-man's-land between what is rational and what is within the laws of existence is the breeding place of all doubts and hesitations, full of disastrous portent. Irrational values which attract and repel the human spirit are the infernal elements productive of fear, maladjustments and even wars. This is the realm of counterfeit, delusion and self-deception at all levels, where pseudo-science, bogus spirituality, entangling pretended philosophical and religious theories and charlatanries thrive. In this twilight region of intelligence, the obscure, the occult and the absurd vie with one another. For its own sanity and survival, the clarified intelligence indeed must abolish this zone of deception and imposition from within and without. Such a region of doubt has been philosophically spoken of in India as *māyā,* in the terminology of Advaita Vedānta. It is a mistake to regard *māyā,* as some have done, as a doctrine of faith. *Māyā* is just a generic name for the possibility of error in consciousness, and, as long as error is possible, some such negative yet determinative term will have to be employed. For, before its avoidance can be observed, even error has to be systematically examined, analysed and classified.

And so the categoric denial of the absurd and the spurious has its place in this basic verse. The Word of the Guru is meant to disperse all dross and clear away all rubble so as to reveal the simple reality, with equally simple straightforwardness; to put order and sequence into human life; to bring intelligent understanding to bear upon human conduct here and now; and to give plain warnings of the pitfalls and dangers in the way of unitive understanding, so that disasters and calamities, big or small, can be safely avoided.

This guiding Word of the Guru has contemplation as its pivot, for contemplation alone clearly reveals how to fit the one end of reality (so to say) into its legitimate counterpart or apparent opposite to which it naturally belongs, and by this means enables us to harmonise our life practically as well as spiritually in relation to the three chief approaches to existence, namely, in the intimacy of functional metabolism within the limits of the body, in the larger domain of the whole cosmos and finally, in terms of reflexive self-realisation as a whole. It is in this sense that Nārāyaṇa Guru, like Śaṅkara, categorically denies any intermediacy, any 'third platform' (*tṛtīyam sthānam*).The fertile realm of the absurd is rigorously excluded.

But an equally grave source of error remains. Although religious, racial or cultural concepts have often involved these invalid third-feature luxuries, thus helping to divide the house of humanity against itself, that integral and unitive way of contemplative understanding which is called wisdom should never be treated as if it were an extra flourish, a luxury or appendage to life. Prejudices are often put on a pedestal and worshipped while fundamental human values are thrown away as useless lumber. Every closed integrated human group develops static modes of thought and behaviour which prepare that group for war against another. History has many such instances of large-scale brutality; hence those cherished values that hold humanity together as one family have to be restated. Man has need to be more truly ambitious in a more worthily human sense.

For this to come about, contemplation has to come to the aid of right thinking. Guru Nārāyaṇa's Words contain the seeds of such a freshly-integrated, wholehearted way of thinking. They have a direct bearing on individual or collective human happiness. In fact, it is to the extent that a Guru is concerned with the welfare of humanity as a whole, and in his primary role of enabling men to discover universal human values, that *guru*-hood itself may be said largely to consist. In this sense every Guru worth the name is a World Teacher (*jagad-guru*). Such a *jagad-guru* may seem humble to his contemporaries, and may be slighted by them while still alive, but he carries with him the secret of contemplation which, when understood, contains those dynamic life-principles which can help all closed groups to break open their frontiers and join hands with their neighbours and fellowmen everywhere in a spirit of forgiveness and willingness to start anew ever freely in the adventure of bold integral living as men among men — all differences abandoned. Advaita Vedānta, therefore, is not an apologetic escape symptomatic of weakness in confronting life, but rather a necessary aid and power for ensuring human welfare.

We take it for granted that all men are interested in their own happiness and, in what is the same thing generally, the happiness of humanity as a whole. The one cannot be exclusively contemplated without the other. When either individual or many are isolated the formula becomes misapplied and gives contrary results, which we call 'fatal irony,' Nemesis, or a travesty of providence. The strange factor of irony which is known as *māyā* melts and vanishes before the keen eye of contemplative science. Solutions to problems become simplified. The duality between the One and the Many must be abolished. Those 'open' human values which never come into conflict with others must be rediscovered and directed to the service of one and all.

This implies the discovery and application of a secret dialectical wisdom which has been taught by the *guru*s of humanity from time immemorial, but which tends again and again to be forgotten.

Without this cementing ingredient disclosed by contemplative wisdom, life would easily fall apart. Happiness would recede into the background of obscurity without that rare light of wisdom brought forth from time to time by *guru*s, for the consolation and strengthening of humanity. If such a prize is worth pursuit and attainment, then the contemplative way of solving human problems must be cultivated more and more. Without the crowning jewel of contemplative wisdom, which alone can make letters glow with dynamic word-import, libraries and universities are merely teaching the dead letter on mere paper.

Human interests, whether collective or individual, have their common centre in the Self. The Self is the secret key to those human values, most dear to the heart of man. From the time of Protagoras twenty-four centuries ago who held that 'Man is the measure of all things' and the oracular Delphic inscription of ancient Greece, 'Man, Know Thyself !' the same theme runs down the ages, echoed by poets like Pope who declare 'the proper study of mankind is Man.' Contemplation is the culminating science which resolves this theme, the science dealing with Self-knowledge through reflection, again and again discovering and rediscovering it with newer patterns and with purport and background suited to the varying stage of history, just those universally human and timeless values which can help man to dwell at peace with himself as well as in cordiality with his brothers. Religion itself has to be contemplatively understood as seeking to better man's relations with his fellows, endeavouring to raise him to a truly higher status as Man. Religion, therefore, cannot afford to be exclusive; neither should it tend to be orthodox or even heterodox. And this is where contemplative science has its virtue, for this superlative science is productive of that regulative principle or solvent of values without which religious or ideological rivalries can only spell disaster. It was in this sense that Nārāyaṇa Guru used to say:

> Whichever the religion,
> It suffices
> If it makes a better man.

In modern life religious and ideological rivalries assert themselves in various false garbs. Many are the new-fangled names employed by interested groups to label truth as a patent for private monopoly. Rivalry works the doom of the rivals, but the game goes on. The *guru*-contemplation, with touching concern, tries as much as possible to bring out a new attitude, establishing order where chaos has reigned. Guru Nārāyaṇa's kindly concern for universal welfare has been aptly expressed in the following lines, with which our preliminary remarks may fittingly conclude:

> To an outsider's view
> A certain faith is low;
> The cardinal doctrine of one
> In another's measure, lacks.
> Confusion in the world shall be
> While the unitive secret herein
> Remains undiscovered . . . .[7]

---

7. *Ātmopadeśa Śatakam*, (Verse 45).

11

The Word and the Silence

THE Word and the Silence are the same. It is the essence of a paradox. It is the everlasting mark of interrogation in the eternal present. It involves and implies the principle of contradiction, without any consequent conflict. It may be said to correspond to the middle term of the syllogism; and laws of thought have been so formulated as to accommodate the Word in a central and neutral position at their core. The Word has its place as a link between the thesis and the antithesis and is implied in the natural expression of the synthesis. It is self-evident and is sufficient reason unto itself without having to be propped up by ratiocination, cogitation or deduction. *A priori* and *a posteriori* thought-processes have, in the Word, their common point of departure. Inductive and deductive reasoning turn round it, their pivot. The particular and the general, cause and effect, species and genus, and all other apparent pairs of opposites, cancel each other out into the neutral zero or into the neutral nothingness of the Word.

If the Word is thought of in terms of the light of wisdom it will tend to be white or pure without any particular colour. With a dazzling effect its brilliance fills all space. Nothing is left outside the scope of this stunning experience. 'Observations', the 'observed' and the 'observer' — all three, fall into one straight line, one eclipsing or implying the other two, when contemplated in the light of the Word which is present in all three at once. The Word is not the predicate of another reality but all else can be predicated of it.

There is nothing to know beyond the Word. The known, knowledge and the knower meet in one presence in the Word. Outside itself it has no cause, and itself is innocent and oblivious of all question of cause and effect. Pure thought has to turn on itself before it can see its own nature. Failing accomplishment in the usual way, only by final contemplative effort is the nouminous Word left alone to represent reality and existence in one.[1] It thus stands for the subject and the object at once, glowing in single splendour in terms of a supreme value. In this sense it is both the *Logos*[2] and the *Nous* known to classical Greek philosophy. All things fall into the scope or influence of the Word and nothing can be said to be understood contemplatively without the Word presence implicit in each reality or entity, and all knowledge would become insipid and valueless without the weight that the Word lends to it. It is the keystone supporting the archway of the sentence, the verb of verbs, the sense and meaning which constructs the architecture of language. The unitive principle represented in the Word continuously transmutes mere opinion into knowledge which radiates the clear light of awareness or wisdom itself. All relative processes of becoming in time, all movements whether historical or cosmological tend to be purified into terms of pure being by the touch of the Word implicit in all being as such.[3]

It is often left to the combined faculties of guesswork and imagination to arrive at a correct concept of the Word which wisdom represents. The functioning of the higher intuitive faculty which contemplation induces is allied to poetic genius. Implied in this noesis, is a certain boldness of approach, a firmness of step which holds the head clearly above doubts in a certain characteristic manner, a firmness which is a distinguishing mark of the assured contemplative, recognisable behind the differentiating veils or formalities of languages and epochs. Yet, alas, when stated in cut and dried terms which may be logically or mechanistically correct, something vital seems to escape out of it. Its perfect beauty is poised

---

1. Cf., Plotinus: 'Our every act is an effort towards contemplation', *Enneads*, III, 8.
2. Cf., *Gospel of St John,* i. 1: 'In the beginning was the Word, and the Word was with God, and the Word was God'. (In the original Greek, *Word* is *Logos.*)
3. *The Māṇḍūkya Upaniṣad* uses *AUM* as *Logos,* declaring it to be the world, time, consciousness, knowledge, Self (*ātman*) and Absolute (*Brahman*).

on a strict neutrality and a delicate impartiality. Many-sided in its sympathy, million-headed and facing every way, with joy the Word omnipresently confronts the actual and the real. It is a wholehearted global sentiment which cannot be enjoyed piece-meal. It rises as a full-flooded surge of generosity within, utterly without petty distinctions between man and beast. Its bounty knows no bounds.

The wonder of the Word ! Add what may be wanting, subtract what is extra, strike the mean and balance or neutralise it once again. Turn it round and examine it from different angles, scrutinise it minutely or take a megascopic view; still it remains the same magic wonder. Install it, if you will, on a pedestal, ideologically or idolatrously, or remove it again in iconoclastic fervour to gaze into the vacancy where it was before — it is still a marvel, old or new. Rid it of all attributes and conditionings, and it will then loom large within consciousness, filling the three worlds to the limit, above, below, and at every point of the compass, multidimensionally, as though in radiant, omnipresent terms of electromagnetism. The light of the sun and stars is within the scheme of such a universal principle, at once attracting or repelling, or devouring all within the ambit of its all-embracing law.

Eluding all, reigning above all, exulting in its own ineffable enigma, it blows where it pleases within the expanse that is limitless. . . .

The Word can take wing and become a metaphor, a parable or a gaudy figure of speech. Allegory and the myth-making instinct must colour its soap-bubble till it bursts again, over-bloated. But the colours of paradise may play on it for a while before ever and anon all is again lost in the renewed wonder of bursting. Thus the alternating sport ever goes on, growing out, diverging fanwise . . . or expanding again from sheer nothingness. The twinkling nucleus ever shines on, bright or dim as its own fancy may dictate, indeterminate and undeter minable, following a rule that is one unto itself, the law never to be formulated entirely to include all contingencies. In the pursuit of the Word many a savant turns grey-haired and the eyes of loyal seekers of truth often grow dim, while the Word glows on for ever. In never-ending beats, it continues in quantum pulsations of energy, to be calculated in split seconds or in millions of light-years, while new and unknown galaxies leap within the ken adding to a wonder that is dumfounding.

All Platonic ideas of Justice, Courage, Truth or Beauty owe their initial capital letters to the Word element which enters their meanings. According to this contemplative approach to reality and existence together, we see that 'Good' already implies its own tail-end of 'Evil' which it can absorb into itself when it prevails in consciousness which is active or positive.[4] This is accomplished by a double negation of the unreal. Judas must belong to the twelve and sit at the same table whether he is good or not.[5] Ends and means must be conceived unitively in contemplative terms so that one can justify the other, for otherwise both would belong to the absurd. Word-contemplation can hold together opposites.[6] It is only when viewed horizontally, as it were, that opposites exist; when looked at vertically the duality vanishes. But this destruction of duality applies to the domain of contemplation and not to the field of action. A river may be thought of as touching its two banks alternately or as curving round in its course, but it can never, in principle, turn tail on itself and reverse its current.

---

4. Cf., *Tao Te Ching* Chap. 2: 'All in the world know the beauty of the beautiful, and in doing this they have (the idea of) what ugliness is; they all know the skill of the skilful, and in doing this they have (the idea of) what the want of skill is. So it is that existence and non-existence give birth the one to (the idea of) the other; that difficulty and ease produce the one (the idea of) the other; that length and shortness fashion out the one the figure of the other; that (the ideas of) height and lowness arise from the contrast of the one with the other. . . .'

   Also: *Bhagavad Gītā,* X, 25 '. . . of speech I am the one syllable . . .' i.e., the Word, called *Aum̐*, and Verse 36 'I am the gambling of the cheat . . . and the goodness of the good'.

5. Reference to Christ's last supper with his twelve disciples, which included Judas whom Christ knew would betray him. (see *Sts. Mathew* 26, *Mark* 14, *Luke* 22, *John* 13.)

6. Cf., *Bhagavad Gītā,* X, 32: Here in this chapter, Kr̥ṣṇa as *guru* utters the Word of the Absolute: 'Of creations I am the beginning, the end and also the middle, O Arjuna; of the sciences (I am) the science of the Self; of those who debate I am the dialectic'.

Contemplation likewise goes forward towards its final goal. Even cataclysms and disasters have to be understood in the natural light of the Word which itself represents an event of great magnitude in the eternal present. Other realistic answers are partial, and many such answers are possible, but the one given by the contemplative type of reason convinces and satisfies the innermost cravings for knowledge, while explaining away no actuality or evil as such, in the historical or the relative sense of everyday life. Headlines in journals may divert even intelligent minds for a moment away from contemplative verities, but it is on the background of the contemplative verity that even headline events must make a meaning. Whichever side it favours in a battle, the Word always wins and, often, from its viewpoint, the one who gains all, loses all. This is summed up in the proverb, 'Nothing fails like success.' It is the Word that makes the last the first. As the ocean includes and implies all the waves that rise upon it, the Word as the central reality draws all within its scope, abiding in its nature and ever implied in terms of self-realisation.

Justice is represented as blind. This refers only to the outward factors, while Justice weighs all in terms of a contemplative inner sense of *equity,* a more than merely mathematical or quantitative *equality.* Thus it is that in politics the Word principle underlies and regulates the connotation of slogans such as 'Liberty, Equality and Fraternity', or even mottos such as 'All for one and one for all', which contain the dialectical secret of the Word-formula. In literature and art, the Word is that 'thing of beauty' of Keats, which 'is a joy for ever:' and which 'will never pass into nothingness.'[7] In the integral personal experience of the *yogī* or the balanced mystic, the Word can be that bright radiant sphere which fills all, within and without, with a clear light of awareness. It is the stunning personal experience of the man who has attained cosmic consciousness, lit with the inner dawn of ten thousand suns rising together.

The man with the Word in his thoughts becomes holy, generous

---

7. *Endymion,* opening lines of Book I.

and loveable. Steeped in the perfection of the Word, he is poised between all points of view, to each one of which he seems to have the same assenting benediction which can accept all truth as pertaining to its own proper place or facet, and to each of which he has the same nouminous response of *Amen*, or *auṁ*, thus blessing them all from the particular standpoint proper to each. Established thus in its own calm, the Word, all-accepting, can bestow the peace that passeth understanding. Word-wisdom can make life more abundant, leaving no room for penury. It is Shakespeare's 'twice bless'd' mercy that 'droppeth as the gentle rain from heaven' — 'above this sceptred sway' and yet 'enthroned in the hearts of kings.'[8]

Its praise is beyond utterance — such is the glory of the silent Word. Although thus it would seem to call on its votary to hold his tongue, volumes of words flow out of the very mouths that try to be mute. The potent Word accumulates its force beneath the level of the open Word and bursts all barriers. The secret of the Word cannot be kept. It must at least be a wail in the wilderness or a shout from a high tower. It must burst into tears; otherwise the predicament of 'She must weep or she will die'[9] would hold true. Just those who have tried to be taciturn have given expression to most effective volumes of words. Why silence is golden has itself to be explained in words. Endless scrolls, filled with Word-wisdom, on silk, palm-leaves, papyri or parchment, or engraved on wood and stone, have thus come out in the past from persons filled with Word-content within. The *Mahābhārata,* the *Rāmāyaṇa* and the *Tiru-Kural* represent such oceans of Word-wisdom in the Indian context. The stream of words sometimes attains torrential proportions meeting all challenges of metre, syntax or prosody. The cryptic, gnomic, aphoristic or enigmatic sayings of the Chinese Lao Tzu, the Indian Bādarāyaṇa, the Greek Socrates or the Jewish Christ still blow with sharp mystical freshness wherever leisure for contemplation of the Word is found, from Peking to Pasadena, from New Delhi to New York, from Madura to Manchester. The Ganges must flow on, as the Euphrates or the Nile. Their waters find their way on the

8. *Merchant of Venice,* Act IV, Scene 1.

9. Tennyson's *The Princess.*

Rhine and the Seine, on the Cam at Cambridge, on the Hudson or even on some far-off tributary of the great Amazon. The car of Jagganāth must roll on by necessity. Such is the urge for the Word in human life.

In far away China, there was a wise man who began by saying that what could be named or put into words was not the real. In spite of this conviction, however, he filled a book of five thousand Chinese characters before he felt satisfied that he had explained what he really meant,[10] much in the same naive manner of the pilgrim woman in Chaucer's tales who went on enumerating the items of a feast she did not want to describe in detail. Whatever the literary device employed, words have their inevitable place in the understanding and in the sharing of ideas containing high human values. The Word itself is the highest of human values.

A strange law of opposites, of antinomies synergetically interdependent with a living reciprocity, seems to be regulating the subtler aspects of life itself. This is the ambivalent phenomenon known to modern psychology. Passionate longing is mixed with fear and disgust; attraction and repulsion are simultaneously present — a locking together of positive and negative vital charges. Whether sex or God, there is a combined love and fear, at once sacred and profane. A certain Nemesis seems here implied. Clip the shrub or shave a beard, it must grow again thicker than before. Break off the radial arm of a starfish, and it regenerates the broken ray with amazing rapidity. Even try to drive away a fly that wants to sit at the tip of your nose, while you try to rest on a summer's afternoon, and it persists in returning to the same spot. Challenge meets with

---

10. Lao Tzu's *Tao Te Ching* of 5,000 Chinese characters. The first chapter says, 'The name that can be named is not the enduring and unchanging name,' and Chapter 56 describing the contemplative, has the well-known saying, 'He who knows does not speak; he who speaks does not know.' Lao Tzu lived in the sixth century BC. The poet Po Chu-i (ninth century AD) with gentle irony wrote:

Who know speak not, who speak know naught,
Are words from Lao Tzu's lore.
What then becomes of Lao Tzu's own
Five thousand words and more ?

redoubled response.[11] A wilfulness or pressure seems to be behind all nature which is a categoric or necessary imperative urge to action whether individual or collective. Unitive life is expanded and displayed variously by this urge which pushes manifestation forward as if from nowhere. Raise your hand in front of a mirror and it reflects the same menacing attitude. Instruct a servant too particularly or order a child rudely: one reaps the familiar consequences. These are but a few of the familiar examples in nature which point at this same principle of polarity. And ever between the horns of this double-charactered principle of equal difficulties, the Word sits solving the dilemmas into neutral contemplative terms of a higher intelligence.

As a growing root can split a rock, the Word also is potent with power. The true Word spells freedom and happiness. Word-wisdom and consequent happiness cannot be enjoyed in exclusive isolation. It necessarily has to be conceived in terms of the greatest good for all. The secret of happiness needed for all political and other theories of our collective life here can be found in a recognition of the relation of the one to the many. As Plato has pointed out, in *Parmenides* and elsewhere, the one and the many are related dialectically as counterparts of a central reality. The happiness of the one depends on the happiness of the many and vice versa. This is an aspect of secret dialectics which is of imperative importance in everyday life. Necessity and obligation bind us at one end while the possibility of freedom is also present for the will to make its own. Life thus involves the taking of a contemplative decision between two alternatives, the choice always of surrender or sacrifice to a higher interest rather than to mere egoistically limited sense-pleasure. Necessary aspects of life have to be willingly faced, while the contingent must be given free play in a spontaneous self-confidence. When the two functions are properly partitioned, Word-wisdom shines with its own unborrowed light.

---

11. This is perhaps the chief theme of Prof. Arnold J. Toynbee's vast work, *A Study of History*. He classifies the challenges in two main divisions, physical (geographic and climatic) and social (the disintegration of a former society, or contact with a new one).

This is the way by which Word-wisdom leads us to tranquillity. In dealing here with the Word of the Guru, therefore, let us resign ourselves to play a humble and ordinary role, one that many great spirits have followed before with great distinction. As usual, let the muses be called upon to sing those heavenly songs in which Word-wisdom has been taught from most ancient times. Vyāsa invoked the aid of the elephant-headed god Gaṇeśa to write for him, with the tip of his broken tusk, long scrolls-ful of beauteous verse, describing the life of the humble mouse as well as praises of the highest, proudest gods of the Himālaya. So let there be an overflowing spate of the good Word like the discharging flood of the Ganges as it is said to descend from the matted locks of Śiva, as the earth is watered from the heavens. Or we can turn perhaps more appealingly to one more refined and favourable — the goddess Sarasvatī, patron of all the fine arts besides that of the Word itself — invoking her aid traditionally as many have done before, so that her approving smile may encourage the free flow of the Word.

Let the Word brighten our intelligence and set us free. Emancipated hence from the power of darkness let the liberating Word help the spirit to soar into the realms of pure light. Lazy automatic conditionings adhering and clinging to the spirit, and through memory affiliations withholding it in its onward flight, shall all be countered and sundered by the inarticulated potency of the Word of words.

Brooking no duality, the Word, as the eternal witness within us, suffers no change. All the wordy learning that has ever been uttered or written has to be burned away; and then, without being lost in the forest of words, the one Word, finally, will sum up all, representing all there is to be known. Such a Word will be the key to all knowledge. The mind with its rational, conceptual and perceptual powers will confront it, but will recoil vainly and frustrated in attempting to treat it as an intellectual problem posed for solution. From the bottom as well as from behind the Word fills the spirit while the focussed attention in bewilderment tries to clutch it. But to obtain the secret of the Word, to feel its presence, one has to become the Word, and then it is known to be inseparable from the Self that has mistakingly looked afar when all the time the Word was the gazing Self itself.

Within the womb of silence the Word lay dormant. In the intermediate stage the world was filled with mere words. Punditry and scribblings filled the libraries. Then it began to be recognised that analysis and research could go on endlessly. By analytical specialisation important human problems were by-passed. Words had to be reduced and raised into synthetical terms. Unitive integral thinking had to step in to save thought from branching out into infinite ramifications. Too much departmentalisation of knowledge in academic or scientific institutions means losing sight of the general perspective in the wholeness of which human values normally reside.

Rid of vain sophistry or eristic argumentation, the Word of the Guru again seeks to balance thought with synthesis. Dialectics is brought in again to relate and reconcile seeming oppositions and dualities. Thus the glare or the glamorous thunder of the Word is once more subdued and the Word which speaks in the still small voice of the silence within can be heard. As bees in the nectarine core of the lotus become silent, so the Self is sound-absorbed when fully fed on the Word within, joy intoxicated with the personal experience that remains. Such Word-content is both cosmological and psychological, and such is the Word of the Guru within his silence. . . .

Thus in the Guru-Word, both *Logos* and *Nous* (Absolute and personal intuitive Principles) are reconciled, the Word bringing together, in identical inseparability, the Guru's personality and the teaching. God and Guru so conceived are cohesive in the Word, a fact recognised by a long human tradition both in East and West.

This is the eloquent silence aglow on the features of that ancient model of a *guru* who was once approached by the Vedic *ṛṣis* who sought the highest wisdom. As legend holds, he sat on a raised stone-platform, under an overshadowing banyan (fig) tree facing southwards in the mute glory of the inarticulated Word. He has

Gaṇeśa, also known as Gaṇapati, eldest born of the Śiva-Pārvati family. Gaṇeśa represents contemplative contentment, with the mouse as his dialectical counterpart, both sharing in the global bounty of food, each having a handful of rice.

been the accepted model for all spiritual teachers for all time. Moreover his teaching, given in this way, was recognised to be fully satisfying, at least to his disciples. Śaṅkara, a *guru* of a period thousands of years afterwards, revived the memory of the silent teacher. And here we revive the picture again, in a modern tongue. This is what Śaṅkara wrote:

> A picture marvel. Lo !
> Under yon *bodhi*-tree, behold !
> Elders are the pupils
> And of tender years the Guru.
> The teaching, in silence mute it goes,
> And what is more, the learners
> In utter sundered doubts, remain ![12]

It is to a similar situation that the Word of the Guru dealt with here belongs. It fits clearly into its place in a general context of its own, a context in which the personality of the Guru and all the attendant circumstances that go with it have to be imagined together, so that the full living meaning of the Word may shine forth. Two distinct aspects of reality — the universal and the temporal, the general and the personal, wholeness and apparent separateness, Guru and man — can thus be made to meet and reveal in dialectical unison the full presence of the Word directly in a way that volumes cannot otherwise display or explain.

The symbol of the model *guru*, the southward-facing silent-tongued teacher of wisdom, tranquilly sitting under a tree, carved in stone or cast in metal, with many variations, sometimes with a gentle smile twisting the blissful corners of his lips, at other times profoundly serious, with eyes open or closed, has filled places of pilgrimage in the East and museums in the West, from Kāmakūra in Japan to the Musée Guimet in Paris, while still from time to time living *guru* models arise in ancient lands and far-flung corners of the globe who re-live and re-exemplify the timelessly old pattern,

---

12. *Dakṣiṇāmūrti-stotram* (*Hymn to the Lord Facing the South*) found, (p. 240) together with several other reputed works of Śaṅkara, in *Ātmabodha of Śrī Śaṅkarācārya* (Sri Ramakrishna Mutt, Mylapore, Madras, 1947).

and speak the same silent Word. Their seemingly enigmatic silence is a marvel indeed, a thread of gold which runs through all the aspects of worthwhile knowledge throughout the passage of history. Many are the rival schools of thought arising around them. Many are the *avatāras* and Messiahs appearing and disappearing on the bright stage of recorded history. Some speak in the stern voice of God, others beguile with gentle art and song — but the *guru*-witnesses simply look on with the silence of the unspoken Word.

The Guru Nārāyaṇa both consciously and unconsciously conformed to this *guru* model that has survived the tumults of time. He represented the Guru Word in its primary and pure form. Any uniqueness or originality in him consisted in a stricter adherence than ever to the requirements of the Guru-Word, as it is to be understood in its reiterated revaluation in a modern setting. Anything in the life of the Guru Nārāyaṇa which seemed to lend support to other than the pure Guru-Word, was but incidental or human, belonging to the setting and not to the principle. It is, therefore, as a *guru* who lived in recent years, fully alive to human affairs, most of which are still of current concern, while he yet conformed to the most ancient of Guru archetypes, that our interest in him lies.

Nārāyaṇa Guru's kindly ways, his silence and the Word implied in his personality, all have one reality. They point to a sublime or exalting human situation or value. All spirituality or morality consists of appreciation of personal human values. Like two-headed Janus, or the obverse and reverse of the same coin, oppposing aspects meet in the personality, thus yielding an intellectual ground on which moral or spiritual values can be appreciated. As the original and the image meet in the substance of the mirror's surface, so the central crystal within, which is the personality, is the meeting point of divergent facets. By meditation on this central living principle one becomes that crystalline substance oneself. The Word represents this focal point, and, with its own background of silence, it dwells in the lotus of the heart of man, as a pearl of price. The discovery of this value within constitutes bliss; while the Word is the key to this Self-discovery, the realisation that our own Self is the transparent jewel, colourless and pure.

Knowledge, the person and the Word are interchangeable terms. The correct elaboration of the Word is sometimes called *brahma-vidyā* (Science of the Absolute). The Word itself is said to be reduced to its simplest form in the three letters *A*, *U* and *Ṁ*; these being the open, the half-open and closed sounds, representative of the cosmos, the psyche and the Self, three aspects of the real. More subjective still is that nouminous aspect beyond expression which is named the 'fourth' state or stage. The spoken and the soundless Word meet and form the mystical syllable. This is constructed by equating the articulated trio to the inarticulated 'fourth' or vice versa. This takes us to some of the secret intricacies of Indian mysticism into whose depths we shall not enter further here. More can be found available to all in Upaniṣadic lore, especially in the smallest of all such works, the *Māṇḍūkya Upaniṣad.*

So far we have tried to fix as definitely as possible some answer to the natural question: 'What do you mean by the Word?' No answer is really possible to such a question, for as we said at the outset, the Word is an enigma and a wonder. Vedāntic contemplation only helps us in this matter in so far as it makes the wonder itself a doubtless one and deep. In such an attitude to the nouminous there is no superstition. Because it is a marvel, the reality only becomes an adorable one.

Before concluding this part of our work in which we have tried to express ourselves freely on the subject of the Word, it is fitting to address our adorations to all *guru*s who have come and gone, to all who had the strange, mysterious silence of the Word on their features. Known or unknown, they have lived in all climes and times. Sometimes derided or persecuted, they have been content themselves to live like simple men, mistaken even for simpletons, sometimes famous but many a time steeped in ignominy. The earth has been sanctified by the touch of some of the humblest of these *guru*s as they slept on the ground in their lonely purity of life away from all the comforts that collective life affords. Often the only pillows on which to rest their weary heads have been their hands. Each has tried hard to live up to the best standards of the *guru* tradition, adding their share to the accumulated wealth of Word-wisdom as a heritage for humanity. Praise be to all of them, those dauntless unperturbed spirits, representatives of the human race of whom we can never be too proud, those who were replete with wisdom's Word. They are the common fathers of humanity, with One High Absolute for ideal, one religion of commonweal to follow and one solid human fraternity to which all belong. Praise be to the *gurus*, known or unknown, who have consciously or unconsciously represented the glory of the articulated or inarticulated *AUṀ*.

12

Distant Drums and Word Enigmas

THE wonder or the enigma of the Guru-Word has to be studied in its natural setting. The physical and mental background, including geographical, historical, cultural and even including ante-historical ethnical features, is part of the whole scene and must be filled-in so that the Guru as a symbolic Word-person can have vital three-dimensional depth. So we return now to that river-side retreat of the Guru Nārāyaṇa at Alwaye in Travancore.[1]

Dusk had spread its slate-coloured velvety wings over the *āśrama* where Nārāyaṇa Guru was staying during the beginning of the hot summer months. Swiftly, as always in these low latitudes in the tropics, night had already come. The still heat of early summer was now and then relieved by gusts of cool air from the broad riverbed. But, in contrast to the lush green richness of the post-monsoon or rainy season, when we looked at the same scene before, now the river's course was partially uncovered, showing a wide expanse of sand, with only jewel-like streaks of star-reflecting water glistening here and there — the emaciated limbs of the languishing river-goddess gleaming through the heat-haze.

In the distance, where the water-ways could be seen spreading out, was a tall fig tree with wide spreading branches. The coconut, palm and the mango trees were comparatively recent additions mingling their dark umbrageous foliage to the characteristic vegetation of this Malaya region so well known to Sanskrit poetry.[2]

In silence, the Guru sat in front of the little white building of the *āśrama*. Only a few people were about, although the annual

---

1. See Part I, Chapter 2, *The Guru at Home.*
2. *Malaya* — now known as Malabār with Malayālam as the language.

festival in memory of the pre-historic God Śiva was again close at hand. No lights were visible except those coming from the flickering oil lamps in the prows of country canoes. Some way off, a number of these canoes huddled together, having brought parties of villagers from a distant part upstream, and these villagers cooked and ate their evening meal of rice in the boats, as they spent the time anticipating the annual *Śivarātri* (Night Festival of Śiva).

Not a word fell from the lips of the Guru as the humble listener who now sets down this record waited patiently for the usual favour. All was still dark, while the lamplight from the canoes made long streaks in the undulating waters as some late bathers splashed in the water, their gentle laughter breaking the monotony. The listener still waited for the word.

Under the tall tree where the waters parted, nearly a mile across from where the Guru sat, some people had gathered and started preliminary drummings evidently to propitiate the departed. There was an unusually large stone, more than half hidden by the sand of the riverbed, which came to view each year as the waters subsided in anticipation of the scorching summer time. Most probably this was one of those pre-historic monoliths, marking the spot where some ancient stalwart of the race was lying, for many such have come to the recognition of archaeologists in recent years in south India.

The crude rhythmic drum-beats went on and on into the night in never-ending manner, while at the same time a mysterious silence filled the air. The atmosphere was surcharged with ancient memories — as far as these could stretch backwards to the very dawn of human history. Memory became almost a clear intuition as it tried to visualise inwardly human life as it flourished around the same riverbed before the date of the civilization of the Susa excavations.[3] Life around this scene perhaps reached back to the beginnings of the Sumero- Babylonian civilizations or even further

3. Susa was the capital of the ancient country of Elam, north of the Persian Gulf and now part of Iran. Its civilization is considered to have been established between 4,000 and 5,000 BC.

beyond them. A span of time, at least six thousand years in its depth, is what even a scientific imagination would permit in connection with the origins of the archaic language of the continued drumming, or as it should have meant to a trained and attuned intelligent spirit.

This festival of the Night of Śiva, associated as it is with the worship of plain dressed-up stones, was evidently a characteristic group behaviour of antiquity when people wanted to honour those who had passed away. It was a custom both normal and necessary. Year after year on the same sandy bed of the river, through the centuries, people responded to the stimulation of habit coming from the distant ancestral past. And the custom in this way continued to the present day when tens of thousands came to bathe in the river, offering handfuls of rice-balls for support, as it were, with prayers and incantations, for the spiritual status of their forefathers in a symbolic act of gratitude. With ancient Vedic chants on their lips and with uplifted faces towards the sky, emotionally distorted in thanksgiving, the supplicants thus responded to pre-historic-based atavisms. This pattern of behaviour has persisted through the centuries, or rather millenniums, holding the soul of man relentlessly within the grip of *karma* or necessity. Archaic patterns have their way of asserting themselves through the ages, with an adamantine rigidity of expression.

Uninitiated as yet to the mysterious lispings of a language belonging to the cradle-phase (as it were) of humanity, these primitive drum-beats meant next to nothing to the present chronicler. The study of modern branches of learning filled him with a certain mistrust. Although he was familiar with geology and palaeontology, sciences also concerned with the remote past, they shed a different light, on aspects of life other than the human field revealed by archaeology and anthropology. His studies were concerned more with the dumb dawning of life, with the vital or mechanistic force which asserted itself over inert matter within the course of millions of years, while the cautious, conservative approach was also distinctive and alien to the understanding of the throbbing drums. Thermodynamics was even more generally disjunct from the situation, and its spokesmen theorised boldly about the origins of energy and its end with calculations involving billions of years. Science thus seemed either to stop short or to by-pass human values, while at the same time reading more fantastic than the wildest productions of fiction or fable. But in the domain of the Word, on the contrary, we confine ourselves to normal and natural human values, and in doing so keep in mind certain implicit methodological and epistemological considerations. One closed or over-specialised scientific system may seem to contradict or give an altogether different result from another. Each science has to be appraised within the framework of its own norms or values, and within such limits each remains a science, not absolute, but relatively exact in the world of its isolated facts. Another Science, the Master-science of the Word, has to step in to reconcile the contradictions, to resolve all the relatives in the one Fact of completion or wholeness, where all the strivings of individual questers towards exactitude can meet together in a final unity. It is this Science of sciences which gives meaning or value to both the scientist and his own particular science. It is the Light of lights of the aphoristic wisdom found in the textbooks of this Science in India.[4]

And so in this enlightening intelligence springing from unitive wisdom, consisting of the universal and perennial human values involved in that Word-language which extends back of and beyond the spoken and written languages, the sound of the pre-historic insistent drummings heard from across the river on this occasion ought to have had a meaning and a significance of its own. This thudding drum-beating itself revealed a state of mind with an implicit behaviour language which spoke across the gulf of time. Human memory when properly awakened or functioning naturally, can become lucidly awake to such a suggestive language of drums and ancient supplication, even without the artificial support found in archaeology, epigraphy or even philology. Instead of depending upon the evidences buried in the earth or recorded on stone, pure

4. Cf., 'Brilliant is It, the Light of lights . . . .' — *Muṇḍaka Upaniṣad,* II, ii, 9. '. . . . the Light of lights, said to be beyond darkness'. — *Bhagavad Gītā,* XIII.17.

Seal from Mohenjo Daro of the prehistoric Śiva as Paśupati, Lord of Beasts and Yogi. Compare with Gāndhāra Buddha sculpture for revaluation of this perennial contemplative image.

memory should be able to delve directly into the past by means of sympathy and insight. Thus an immediate contact with the remotest life-expression of the past can be established. The reasonable means here is not external digging into the débris of vanished civilizations, but by 'contemplative archaeology' or research by means of the light common within each of us, a light which vibrates responsively to every shade or expression of any real Word-import — even as in the case with electromagnetism, one can tune-in and gather the immediate echoing response when the right wave-length of frequency is touched. Listening in this way, these drummings legitimately suggested to the intuitive insight of the listener, something akin to the following imagery:

Śiva, the mighty hunter of ante-historic times, was a leader of his age. He was also a contemplative, a *yogī* who sat cross-legged under the spreading branches of a huge fig-tree or banyan. His hair was matted and bound up to a conical crest. Around him were gathered his favourite animals, tame or wild, who seemed to regard him with respect. The hunter's feminine counterpart was also there, represented within the forking of the tree, symbolic of the fecundity of the mother principle. The tree itself was a mysterious symbol of the Unknown and the Adorable. Śiva himself typified the virile male principle of the bull. He often forgot himself in the joy he felt within and danced in the forest lit with the light of the waxing crescent moon; while the goddess-companion often rode a tiger in awe-inspiring majesty suggestive of the potent, creative urge.

Such were a few of the dominant images that must have surged up within the minds of the people gathered together round the drummers. The antique Śiva hieroglyph of primeval memory, with all the associated trains of thought it brought up, steeped their minds in a joy that was intensely pleasureable and satisfying. Hence they kept up this festival habit, year after year, until it became an inseparable part of the necessary side of their personal lives.[5]

---

5. The seals of the Indus Valley excavations lend ample support to the picture we have tried to construct here. Ref: *Mohenjo-daro and the Indus Civilization* by Sir John Marshal; and many popular modern histories of India (e.g., p. 28 *et seq.* of *The Pageant of Indian History* by Mrs. Sen).

While the drumming went on, rhythmic and persistent, and night closed in on the land, the silence of the Guru remained unbroken. . . . The writer still waited for the Guru-Word to fall like a welcome drop of rain on the parched earth of his mind; and indeed the voice of the Guru at last did gently break the long period of suspense. He said little, but enough and of sufficient pregnancy to kindle a certain curiosity which, after more than a quarter of a century, has elaborated itself in the manner indicated above. But at the time the dead weight of concrete scientific impedimenta retarded the imaginative flight of free intuitive knowledge. On that occasion too, the Guru seemed to break the silence on purpose, as it were, in order to dispel a certain sterile indifference and mistrust towards knowledge in general, a condition then affecting the writer, particularly concerning the relevancy or value of ancient knowledge. It seemed to the writer then that modern science and contemplation had their faces irreconcilably turned away from each other. Time, however, has shown that this need not necessarily be so.

'Do you hear?' the melodious-ringing Guru-voice was heard to enquire, 'Do you hear that distant drumming? It has been like this not only for a few years; it has been like this for *ever* !'

A characteristic final intonation put its enigmatic and mysterious punctuation on the last word as he uttered the phrase: 'It has been like this for *ever* !' The Guru said no more on the subject, but deep within the listener the words 'for ever' made an impression impossible to erase, arousing a lingering curiosity and a strange sense of the unknown which the writer tried to explain to himself, half-heartedly, at that time. The Word worked its secret ferment in the form of a lingering question-mark, like a catalytic agent affecting doubts and opinions concerning scientific validities, rationalisms and values then strongly held. . . .

Nearly three decades have now passed but the strange enigmatic impressions have remained in their setting as bright jewels in the treasure-chest of memory. And although further study and meditation have helped to widen the wonder within, yet the enigmatic nature of the impression has not disappeared. This example of the Guru-Word has been revived here in detail on purpose as an illustration of the utter economy of the spoken Word he employed in his teaching. The Guru Nārāyaṇa always wielded his Word in such a way as to stimulate a certain type of curiosity about the unknown. Invariably the problems themselves, from a superficial point of view, were left unsolved or unanswered, but his response suggested the line of thought or meditation to be followed. Such meditation had the final result, not of solving mysteries, but rather of making the sense of the mysterious live in the heart of man for ever.

That Śiva picture which we have drawn from the pure-memory-approach to the drums with all their perennial associations, belongs to a dialectical situation which must be considered as a whole. The Guru's own personality also belonged to the Word context. For he too was a *yogī* who sat in meditation under a tree and the drums naturally revived in him pure memories which formed part and parcel of his own meditations. Here was an affinity with the far-off past to which the Guru responded in a direct and simple manner, uncluttered by those obstructive limitations and often beclouding assertions of science in its usual sense. The Guru in fact represented in his personality the dialectically revalued counterpart of the same pre-historic situation in which the Word nouminously evoked the result which we have attempted to interpret in terms of the Śiva pictograph. The same spiritual climate prevails now as it did then. At two points in time-everlasting, situations are marked by the same essential Word-value, so that the stimulus or emphasis of the one induces or recalls the other, in a subtle dialectical similarity of language, a clarion call heard across barriers of nothingness. One lends content to the form of the other, in mutual reciprocity, till, in each other's light they mean the same reality of the Word, as understood in terms of Self-knowledge. This will become increasingly evident as we follow further along the pilgrim path of the Word.

The engima of the Guru-Word provides us with many other examples. Nārāyaṇa Guru's early writings especially reflect this ancient atmosphere of the Śiva outlook. Bhadra-Kālī, Sarasvatī and other members of the sacred family of Śiva, such as the war-

God with six heads called Subrahmaṇya or Kārttikeya, and that other elephant-headed, pot-bellied God Gaṇeśa, whose vehicle is that dialectical counterpart, the field-mouse, all figure in his writings. Śiva himself is portrayed as a hunter or a beggar, half-naked in his radical individuality; while his markedly emphatic wild frenzy recalls vividly his Greek counterpart Dionysius. A whole world of antiquity is stored up in these primordial figures, and generations upon generations have utilised them to express mystical and philosophical doctrines of rare value to humanity. Thus conserved and considered, they all breath the same spiritual atmosphere of a subtle dialectical situation, containing a certain ineffable substance of mystery.

Geologically, the sandy expanse and the river must have been there from primordial ages. Right through a long period of prehistory down to the present, the drumming and characteristic group behaviour must have persisted. But beyond both these time-surviving elements, and transcending even the boldest hypotheses of thermodynamic theorists, pure human memory, like the clear waters of the river, must have preserved the same mystical Word, reflecting time and again through the human soul or spirit, its consoling message for all who could respond to its timeless presence.

Illumined by the starlight, like the gleam on the surface of the waters, the same mystical presence and message shines now as ever, for those who can see. Add the Guru-Word, and the meaning of a simple situation such as the one described becomes transmuted; but fill the mind and clog the memory with particular hard facts, harsh and insipid and, instead of the bread of life, there remains but a stone.

Supported by apt imagination and made transparent in the light of intuition, bold flights of memory are desirable qualifications for anyone who wishes to trace the Guru-Word back to its true sources where it emerges from its own stratum and background. Restrospective imagery, it is true, sometimes weakens the triumph of emancipating progressive thought but, even to reject what is extraneous or superfluous intelligently, and to reach the pure core of essential wisdom, a requisite clarification of memory-function becomes inevitable. The mind must be cleared, for if anything remains, it is likely to be the fanciful product of instinctive curiosity, myth or fable. Here the affinities of the Guru-Word are traced back to reveal its anterior implications first, so that its meaning with reference to the future may be made more realistically one's own.

This reaching out and linking up of prehistory with contemporary life may seem a far cry indeed. It might appear even impossible to throw a bridge between the two. But when we admit that the same sun shines now as it ever did before, or that the same vertical streak of mother's milk continues as milk uninterruptedly through generations, connecting each one of us materially with the remotest of our ancestors, the possibility of one enduring Word persisting through the vagaries of human language is, after all, not so absurd as it might at first sound. The perennial nature of the wisdom that comes to us through a symbolic, yet essentially human spiritual language, cannot therefore be too easily questioned. If we could abolish our prejudices in favour of what is non-contemplatively called 'objectivity,' many of the problems now considered insoluble by the sciences would yield new answers. Sayings like 'as it was in the beginning, is now, and ever shall be' would no longer sound as an apocryphal litany but rather as apodictic statements of law based on *a priori* reasoning.

As in linguistic symbolism, ideological and spiritual insignia with accompanying psychological attitudes and recognisable situations, persist through time and reveal a common human parentage. This is well established in the study of comparative iconography. Divergencies in the Word tend to vanish from faiths in the light of intuitive research into the deep recesses forming the racial past. It is in this sense that the picture-symbols of the Mohenjo-Dāro stamp-seals can be helpful to us. They are clear indicators of the original patterns of the earliest formulations of the Word of the Guru with which we are concerned in these pages.

As we have said, the *yogī* sitting on a stone under a tree is a familiar subject of these pre-historic Indus Valley seals. This figure of the man meditating under a tree has dominated the spiritual language of India persistently and continues to dominate it today as ever. Both literature and iconography are full of references to this archetypal emblem. It serves here as an ideogram denoting Word-wisdom.

Dakṣiṇāmūrti (which means the Divine Personality of the south) is Śiva when he plays the role of Guru to the Vedic Brāhmins of north India. In Śiva as Dakṣiṇāmūrti the pre-historic currents of thought meet, counteract and mingle with the spiritual Word-content which penetrated into India from the outside with the arrival of the proto-Vedic immigrants or invaders. The recognition of this dialectically revalued synthesis of the two apparently different spiritual traditions, that of the Śiva of pre-Vedic antiquity and that of the priest-preceptors of the wandering Āryans, is established throughout present-day India by the acceptance of Śiva as the Guru Dakṣiṇāmūrti.

As we have seen in the well-known verse of Śaṅkara quoted in our last chapter, Śaṅkara praises the glory of this model *guru*, Dakṣiṇāmūrti who is also represented as sitting under a fig tree. The cryptic formula, the archaic standard situation depicted and formalised in the Indus Valley seals, thus repeats itself here unmistakably. This 'picture-model' of a teacher of higher Vedāntic non-dual wisdom thus proves and establishes a revaluation of the ingressive early Vedas themselves in terms of Vedānta; and Śaṅkara, as a high authority in Advaita philosophy, here in this Dakṣiṇāmūrti poem, definitely puts his seal of approving recognition upon this revalued spiritual synthesis. And when we also remember that this mark of recognition is the dominating note even of contemporary Indian spiritual expression, the significance of this cryptic language of antiquity for the understanding of the message of Nārāyaṇa Guru must be sufficiently clear.

There are innumerable images of the Buddha, too, which intentionally or by traditional instinct, conform to the ancient Śiva-yogī pattern. A stone image of Dakṣiṇāmūrti could often be mistaken for that of Buddha, for both according to tradition, taught five learned brāhmaṇas under a sacred fig tree (the *Bo* or *ficus religiosa*), and both are often represented with that typical gesture of the thumb and forefinger forming a circle known as *jñāna-mudrā* (wisdom gesture), which is made by the Guru of tradition when he faces his disciples. In both cases, too, deer or goats may be seen carved on the pedestals of the stone seat, the one case interpreted to say that Buddha taught in a deer park, the other to inform us that Śiva was known as Paśupati, or Lord of all Beasts or created life.

The common people everywhere, and certainly in India, still instinctively understand the meaningful language thus transmitted from generation to generation through mute but nevertheless eloquent stones. In this way through the long course of history, written and unwritten, a cherished value exceedingly dear to the Indian mind has been preserved. In its descent through the ages, revalued and restated many times, the essential message has rid itself free of all angularities, and now gives us a simple formula of *guru*-hood in an epitomised form. The main purpose of this key-formula is not merely to enable us to enter the world of the ancient gods known to iconography, nor even to understand the accumulations of mystical lore, important side-issues though these may be. The paramount aim is to enable us to appreciate the constant language of dialectics which, in all contexts, archaic, historical, mediaeval and modern, becomes the recognisable master figure-of-speech peculiar but inevitable for expressing the secret of all Guru-Word wisdom. It is in this sense that the Guru-Word is an enigma or a paradox. In the Guru-Word both past and future, so apart elsewhere, are inviolably welded together in the unity of an eternal present. The apparent antagonism between anteriority and posteriority is neutralised when the Word prevails. Time as the old endless serpent at last is seen to swallow its own tail in the contemplative language of the Word. Thesis and antithesis disappear in the presence of the synthesis. But to delve into the enigma of the Guru-Word and move another step forward we shall now lapse into another illustrative anecdote. And if the enigma becomes only further underlined we shall be so much nearer to the heart of its mystery.[6]

---

6. Cf., *Tao Te Ching,* Chap.I. 'Where the mystery is the deepest is the gate of all that is subtle and wonderful.'

Once at Varkala[7] the writer was standing near Nārāyaṇa Guru. The days of the Guru's living presence among his disciples were beginning to be numbered with anxiety, for he was then old and suffering from a serious illness. In spite of this circumstance however, he had occasional spells of good health which encouraged all who could to gather round their beloved teacher to benefit by his Word as far as possible while he was still among them. And of those who were present the writer was one, likewise intent upon benefitting from the Guru-presence.

The Guru had spontaneously taught the writer many a subtle truth before, with kindliness. Never before had the disciple dared to put a direct question frontally as it were. But this time it was different and he had resolved to try the experiment while it was still possible. He thought that a definite answer from the lips of the Guru would be valuable. And so the writer decided to break the usual silence. His question concerned the meaning of one of the Guru's own verses which, translated, is as follows:

> With cares for its content,
> Five-petalled and with tiers two,
> Revolving and beginningless
> Is the lamp which, hung on high
> (Is) the Self. In shadow form it burns.
> Past habit tendencies its oil consists;
> As for the wick, functioning itself is.[8]

On hearing the verse the Guru turned and looked at the questioner. His eyes lighted kindly on him for a while, but he again lapsed into his silent mood. No answer came. Undeterred, the questioner passed on to another verse which at that time puzzled him:

> Eating of the fruits five
> Such as sound and the like,
> Perched the while on a shot-gun foul,

7. Varkala is a coastal town in southern Kerala, some 20 miles north of Trivandrum. It was here on Śivagiri (Hill of Śiva) that Nārāyaṇa Guru spent a great deal of his time.

8. *Ātmopadeśa-Śatakam* of Nārāyaṇa Guru, Verse 17.

Famous Daibutsu or Big Buddha at Kamakura, Japan,
Symbolic Guru-figure of the Far East.

Ever in wily changeful sport
Are those birds five; down what could turn
Shred to bits all these at once !
Such lucidity wielding — the inner Self
To brilliance — let it attain ![9]

Seconds and minutes passed but no answer came. Instead, one could notice, if well trained to discover such traits, a peculiar seriousness, which was associated characteristically with the same *jñāna-mudrā,* or wisdom-gesture which we have already described as the time-honoured secret dialectical password of the Guru attitude. One waited in vain for any further communication. As with the ancient model defined by Śaṅkara, the silence was meant to be self-explanatory. The very next verse following the one just quoted indicates to some extent the line of thought containing the significance of what the Guru meant by the silence:

Who spends his days
In contemplation beneath a tree, —
Climbing whereon, a blossomed creeper
Bears aloft on either side
The flowerings of the psychic states —
Verily, such a recluse remains
By inferno ever unapproached.[10]

The writings of the Guru Nārāyaṇa abound in enigmas of this type. These constitute a challenge to the modern man, a challenge coming from the past of India and the East. They have a psychology and a cosmology of their own whose validity may be doubted by those unfamiliar with the technique of ancient Eastern wisdom. Such crypto-symbolic verses involve major problems, questions to be answered, enigmatic paradoxes of a unique dialectical category which demand scrutiny in the light of the type of knowledge which dominates contemporary civilization. These writings must be understood again in a global context.

---

9. *Ātmopadeśa-Śatakam* of Nārāyaṇa Guru, verse 8.
10. *Ātmopadeśa-Śatakam,* verse 9.

These verses of the Guru that we have given here contain the solution to the silence of the Guru. That characteristic silence belongs to the general nature of Word-wisdom and must be incorporated into the wisdom-context to make the fully rounded meaning. As with the Guru Dakṣiṇāmūrti, this silence symbolises the negative way of the Word (the *via negativa*[11] of the Christian mystics), or the *neti neti* — 'not this! not this!' of the Upaniṣads. This can be compared with the Christian-Platonic method stated by the pseudonymous Dionysius the Areopagite.[12] In the language of Vedānta this Way of Withdrawal (*nivṛtti mārga*) is opposed to the Way of Forward Action (*pravṛtti mārga*). In the normal Guru-attitude, these contrary attitudes are neutralised, culminating in an unbiased central reality which is of the essence of non-duality (*advaita*).

It will be profitable to quote here another enigmatic verse found in one of the early poems of Nārāyaṇa Guru (*Śiva Śatakam*). It is addressed to Śiva. The theme of the prayer to this ancient God of the chase is at first apparently developed along traditional lines; but gradually the radical note is heard and a dialectically revalued mystical doctrine is eventually seen to be implied throughout. The work consists of one hundred verses, of which the 85th verse reads:

---

11. Philo the Jew (first century) was the first to stress the withdrawal of the senses as the way to Self-realisation; then the tradition was elaborated by Plotinus (third century), and in the meantime adopted into Christianity by St. Augustine, leading ultimately to the Quietist form of the great Mystics of the Middle Ages in Europe.

12. '*Neti ! Neti!*' occurs in the following passages in the *Bṛhadāraṇyaka Upaniṣad:* II, iii, 6; III, ix, 26; IV, ii, 4; IV, iv, 22; and IV, v, 15.

Dionysius the Areopagite was the title given to the author of mystical Platonic treatises introduced into Western Christianity in the ninth century by John Scotus (or Erigena) who translated them into Latin from the original Greek. They are given as of fifth century composition. In Book V. of Dionysius' *Mystical Theology* we find the following plain account of the Way of Negation: 'In the practice of mystic contemplation leave the senses and the activities of the intellect and all things sensible and intelligible, and things that are and things that are not. . . .' and in *The Celestial Hierarchy,* II.3: 'Divine things shall be honoured by the true negation.'

Viewing thee on a mountain top
Intent on beasts to slay,
And so their skins to flay for me,
If now, this one here, in turn,
Should think, 'Halt, halt'
And in worthy mien approach,
Wouldst thou then (O Śiva)
Filled with many a witty word,
Even into laughter break ?

Here we must note two counterbalancing factors. On the one hand we see the basic symbol of Śiva in its antique purity, depicted fully in its even gruesome actuality — while there is the antithetical Guru personality of a far far later epoch, the author of the poem — but both the Śiva image of the poem and the person of the poet have the dialectics in common, only in the latter case the spiritual Word is re-visioned and revalued. Nārāyaṇa Guru is the revaluating principle himself here, and all antecedent valuations occurring at different epochs, such as the Buddhist or the Jain, have been telescoped summarily in the new Guru assessment. The ancient *yogī*, like Socrates who offers a cock[13] is a killer of animals. This is the pre-historic element retained in the anterior dialectics of the Word. This is brought into close juxtaposition with the posterior Word content so that together they yield the synthetically revalued word, which represents the mystery of the Unknown itself.

This verse affords a typical example of what we have called here the enigma of the Word. Here for the time being we must leave the import of the subject. But before concluding this section of our discussion, there is one more short episode to relate which may help to bring out another aspect involved in dealing with Guru-wisdom.

On this occasion the place was a secluded village temple in Travancore, not far from the Varkala *āśrama*. The temple was founded by one of the Guru's humbler followers who came from this village. He had built a simple palm-thatched hut as a place of

13. See the death of Socrates in Plato's *Phaedo*.

worship and had also constructed a tiny white-walled room beside the temple, for meditation.

Villagers passed to and fro along a footpath through the wooded grove which surrounded the shrine. On the verandah of the room and turned away from the glare of the tropical sun, protected from the view of passers by, the Guru once sat, as the guest of his devotee. The traditionally familiar fig tree also happened to be there, while vesper prayers were announced by the note of a blown conch-shell. Bells, a metal trident and a plainly-dressed upright stone completed the furnishings of the most holy sanctum of Śiva worship, all that was essential for the simple believers in this virile Principle. As the Guru sat once again in an environment reminiscent of the simple primeval conditions, an ante-historical setting as it were projected into present times, like an outcropping of Archaean strata, one could observe on his features a certain spiritual glow of alert or positive wakefulness. His voice carried a resonance that was marked and his every movement unmistakably reflected the delicacy of his state of mind. He was a *yogī* who sat aloof in self-choosen loneliness in this neglected wayside temple. Clearly in this spot he felt at home and had decided to spend a week there with his follower.

A yellow-robed *saṁnyāsin* disciple of Nārāyaṇa Guru who was there with the writer, brought up the subject of a biography of the Guru, which, he intimated to the Guru, the present narrator was hoping to write.

The Guru expressed some interest in the idea. 'Biographies', he remarked, 'often degenerate to the discredit of human nature.' He referred to the autobiographical confessions of some great men who, in the name of veracity, had often put themselves at a lower level than was good for humanity. 'Such literature must raise up higher models to view', Nārāyaṇa Guru went on. 'Man must be made better one way or another — otherwise what is the use of biography?'

About his own biography he simply asked, 'Who is there to believe it?' It is possible to write the most admirable of biographies representing the highest human values. Yet it would still lack its other essential part — someone ready to read it and understand it in the intended light. Hence with characteristic wistfulness the Guru inquired, 'Where is the man who will believe?'

With the best of intentions Rousseau wrote his *Confessions*, and, given a Boswell, it would be possible to record every word of a Johnson; but despite these different styles, misunderstandings and wrong or distorted judgements about them still flourish, reflecting unintentional disrepute and humiliation on human nature generally and often too on the subject of the biography.

Even here two sides have to come to a dialectical agreement. A bipolar relation is inevitably implied, a relationship belonging to the same order that was the secret of the Socratic[14] and other discursive methods of ancient wisdom now gone into ill-favour and desuetude. It is in the harmonious interaction of counterparts coming into play together that values are thrown out. The soil is as important as the seed. Pearls have to be equated with the swine without any absurdity being implied in the situation. All vital relations, such as those between father and son or husband and wife imply the same bipolarity of relationship which is the secret of contemplative reasoning.[15] In so far as it is independent of the evidence of the senses, the true nature of this bipolarity is elusive. *A priori* knowledge has as much place in it as *a posteriori* knowledge. Our constant recognition of all values in everday life implies this secret of contemplative reasoning. When this secret which is so unique and yet at the same time so common, so present in every reasonable situation, is seen in this light, enigmas will lose their strangeness as such; remaining enigmas inasmuch as the wonder

14. Cf., Plato's definitions of dialectics in his work, *Sophist* (p. 262 D) where he takes the structure of the Greek sentence as his starting point. To make sense or have value, the sentence requires (implicitly at least) both subject and predicate. Even the exclamation, 'Oh !' implies '(I say) oh ! (to you or to myself)'. Disjunct words have no virtue, being merely like collections of stones, merely printer's marks or meaningless noises.

15. In Śaṅkara's *Dakṣiṇāmūrti* poem already referred to, in verse 8 this same set of dialectical pairs is stated, proving that Śaṅkara was fully aware of the fact of the dialectical Principle in dealing with the exposition of the Word.

will still be there, and will only declare the presence of the real which is the most common place and yet the most wonderful of wonders, the real which exists or subsists in and through all situations, and which can be seen in all things provided they are viewed correctly according to the disciplines of contemplative thought. It is in this way that the Guru becomes as important as the *śiṣya* (disciple), or vice versa, as we shall see in our further considerations of the Word.

13

Guru and Śiṣya

It is the Word which stands neutral and silent between the *guru* and the *śiṣya* (Master and Disciple).

Silence is the normal state of *guru*-hood. That normal *guru* state has no message to deliver — except that of the silent Word perhaps. Neither has it any gospel to spread, nor course of action to recommend on its own initiative. It is free from the sense of agency in the world of activities or works. These exist in the domain of necessity or restraint and take care of themselves according to natural laws of imperative urges, causal chains or obligation. Thus the *guru* rests in his heart's cave of tranquillity, locked in the secret of his silence, beyond all turmoil in the peace that passeth understanding.

Someone might approach a *guru* with a question. The best answer and the reply the *guru* wants to give is his silence. The indifference on the surface is only seeming. The *guru* really intends by his silence to honour the questioner. Indeed silence is a form of recognition given sometimes to the most intelligent of questioners. For the well-formulated question, fundamentally sound in its basic premiss, supplies in itself, half at least of the desirable question-answer situation which is a dialectical situation, like a subject seeking an object or predicate.

On hearing the question, the *guru* may open his eyes for a while, but presently relapses into his natural state of calm quietude, that being the most preferable of responses. Expressed in this way through his personality, his silence stands for all the reply needed. This very silence of attitude conveys the sense that the truth is so clear and simple that it needs no vocal evidence. Silence itself is the missing counterpart which covers the question like a benediction. The question can refer to one specifically possible answer, but the silence is an answer to all possible varieties of questions, even to those concerning the future. It is the crowning answer of answers, a finalised reply to the endlessness of questioning in an unexpected form which is itself paradoxically rhetorical.

We may say that the questioner must know the answer vaguely or roughly before he can ask a pertinent question; and the *guru*, in assenting to this propositional relevancy in question-form, meets him half-way with his neutral silence. Thus it is that a *guru* sometimes just witnesses the supposed helplessness of the disciple, but with a kindly look in his eyes. He wants no duality even between the question and the answer. At both beginning and end of the discourse there must be agreement. If the dialogue is not mere disputation but dialectically of the order of contemplation, then every question answers itself in terms of self-knowledge. Verities are equated intuitionally, and the problem is solved wihout burdening the answer with the extraneous.

Dialectics is said to be the coping stone of wisdom. It implies two sides of which Socrates is usually the common factor. Many are the questioners and varied the queries, but all the answers are already there as one answer in one Socrates. The silence of the *guru* goes even further in perfecting the dialectical approach to wisdom. It conforms to the simplest requirements of Self-contemplation and the question seems to stand still without swerving from its well-established selfhood in perfect symmetry and beauty.

In this manner the silence seems to take the disciple lovingly by the hand and conduct him into the realms of pure reason. It beckons from the tranquil heights where the *guru*s normally dwell, directing him into the glory of the light of wisdom. Thus the grace of the *guru* is manifested as the blessed look of silence, exalting the disciple and leading him even as Dante was conducted by the Master-poet till he came to the regions presided over by Beatrice, and was thence guided by her into the light of the highest wisdom in the spheres of glory and peace on high. Thus the disciple mounts from one Everest height of positive understanding to another till he wants to return no more.

The enticement of such a kindly glance is given only to some; others may receive only a nod of assent, or a recognising smile. In the Upaniṣads the Guru is known sometimes to say, 'Pleasing youth, you question well,' thus encouraging the seeker sympathetically.[1] In another mood when surrounded by inquirers of a more usual and ordinary type in a crowd, the *guru* may even explain a little. He may add a remark of his own to something said, but mostly, when in the midst of a multitude, if he does speak it is generally on topics of everyday interest or of fundamental human value.

The *guru* does not enter into anything secret or esoteric. Any stimulus generally suffices for him to begin, and like the murmur of a brook, the sound of the noontide bee or the chiming of distant bells, his words flow smoothly and gently into the ears of his hearers, as he seems to talk as much to himself as to all others at the same time, never anxious to convince anyone, but with a conviction welling from his own pure depths, as one interested in humanity. The lulling effect of such words on the hasty listener is often the same as his silence itself. In this manner the Word of the Guru is sometimes uttered for the sake of one or many questioners at a time. Both topic and treatment of the subject are such that it does not matter who listens. For it is of interest to one and all at once, and, although intimate matters may find a place in it, nothing that

---

1 The classical example is, of course, in the *Kaṭha Upaniṣad* (II.7-9). Here the Guru (Yama) after testing the young disciple, Naciketas, says 'Many do not even hear of this teaching, and many, even though hearing never know; hence the expounder is a rare wonder, and the attainer is gifted, and the knower who is properly taught is also a wonder ! This (Absolute) cannot be properly understood when taught by a person of inferior understanding, being then given a bias. Unless declared by another (i.e., a qualified Guru) there can be no realisation, for this is subtler than the subtle and beyond measurement (not arguable). Not by mere reasoning is this notion reached. But when it is taught by another (i.e., Guru) indeed, O dearest friend (*preṣṭa*), it is easy to know. This (relationship with a Guru) thou hast attained ! Ah, thou art of true steadfastness ! May there be for us a questioner (*praṣṭā*) the like of thee, O Naciketas !'

is not entirely open and just or in the interest of all will find a place in it. With Nārāyaṇa Guru it was humanity as a whole that interested him primarily, far and above all private ends or any unilateral personal good. A contemplative neutrality and stillness always characterised his attitude.

The Guru moods vary according to the situation implied in the attitude of the questioner. It is his consideration for others that induces the Guru to descend from that eminence where he sits clothed in the glory of his silence. Everlastingly he waits in this exalted loneliness, waiting for the right kind of disciple to approach him, almost like a lover for a beloved, waiting so that he can share with another the peace at the fountain-source from which he himself constantly drinks.[2] Although the market-place is not his favourite haunt, he may be seen even among publicans,[3] so as to be available to those who may need him most, and to wean them, if possible, to ways of peace and joy. Alternately human, alternately divine, in the light of grace that plays on his ever serene features, he patiently awaits thus the natural fulfilment of his purifying role. . . .

As the lambent glory of sunrise illumines one pinnacle of the Himālaya after another, so the Guru-silence glows gently and ineffbly on one general hypothesis after another, until finally all is included in the silent fullness of the risen sun of the Word. Or it may be likened to a softly played sonata, one note of music being struck after another, finally falling away in thematic completion with the last tinkling touch of the keyboard, a diminuendo of sound

---

2. Cf., the words of Christ, 'The water I give becomes a spring, welling up to eternal life'.

3. Christ was questioned as to why he had his meals with publicans (or state employees of the Romans). He replied, 'They that be whole need not a physician, but they that are sick'. and 'I will have mercy, and not sacrifice . . . .' (*Mathew,* IX, 10-13).

   There is also the classical case of Socrates who was always in the market-place. The word *agora* originally meant not a market-place, but assembly, but the meaning lingered. It was the *place* of assembly, then a place for trials and meetings, and finally a place for buying and selling. See Zimmern, *Greek Commonwealth* (Clarendon Press, Oxford, 3rd edn., 1922) p. 65.

which is the crescendo of silence, the crowning glory of the inexpressible Word. . . .

By the secret technique of negating involved in all this, the *guru* is not shirking or evading, but on the contrary ever bent on fulfilling his part of the necessary diacrasis, the dialectical situation arising from the presence of ideological inquiry, which demands, at its highest level, the transcendent unity of silence. What looks like reserve is only the underlining of the most effective method of conveying his meaning which is incapable of being given by the methods usual to other kinds of knowledge. The Guru-truth implies the negative approach. It is given *a priori,* and sounds as if it is 'dogmatic' and not reasoned in the modern sense. Induction, hypothesis, dialectics are some of its distinguishing features, as distinct from what is called discursive or 'eristic' logic or 'ratiocination'. The Guru-truth is invariably behind or implicit in what is explicitly stated in cut and dry terms. Again and again frustrated in their attempts to transmit their deepest affections, the *gurus* often subside into the most intensely expressive of silences. Such loneliness, such an 'orphanage in God', might be called their everlasting 'agony', 'crucifixion', or state of detached *nirvāṇa*, so great is the hunger of a *guru* for a true disciple. In 'the flight of the Alone to the Alone',[4] which constitutes the Guru-state, the sympathetic call arises for winging another into the joy of this *samādhi.* This constitutes the 'sad' element, for this *advaita* consciousness seeks expression, final consummation and fulfilment, and that can be only by transmission somehow to the right kind of disciple.

It is the possibility of questioners arising which transforms the lonely contemplative into the Guru. Every big library in the world is in existence in response to the need to answer questions. Every book is some sort of answer to a question, trivial or profound.

---

4. See Plotinus *Enneads* (VI, ix, II) by Stephen Mackenna (Medici Society, London, 1917). In his summary in the first volume, the translator, in rendering the passage, gave the words as quoted here; but in his final translation in the fourth volume, he gives the rendering: 'the passing of solitary to solitary'.

All the time we are teaching or learning, and each one insists on instructing or learning in his own way. Egoists insist on teaching when they should rather be listening, while the humble tend more to listen than to teach, though often better qualified than their would-be teachers.

The purpose of contemplation is often defeated by the pressures of necessary life, resulting in a travesty of *guru-śiṣya* dialectics. The delicate threads are snapped by misapplication. A catalectical situation replaces the dialectical. The tables are turned. For the disciple often consciously or unconsciously counters his own master. Again and again the rare blooms of wisdom wither at the hands of the gardeners in whose care they have been left, so that the accumulated wisdom resulting from the highest levels of human experience repeatedly suffers great losses. Aristotle thought he knew better than Plato and broke from his Academy to become a peripatetic philosopher. To the extent of that cleavage, the history of philosophic thought in the West wavered in its course down through the Dark and Middle Ages to the twilight dawn of the Age of Reason.

A true disciple is therefore an indispensable counterpart for the preservation and continuation of the heritage of a great master's wisdom. The histories and confusions, dissentions and schisms, that mark the course of many of the world's great religions and philosophies bear out the need for this continuous authenticity of wisdom descent. It is the main reason for the decline and fall of what was originally noble and of high value.[5]

---

5. Cf., *The Milinda Questions* (tr. of T.W. Rhys-Davids in vol. XXXV Sacred Books of the East) IV, i,61. Nāgasena, the Buddhist missionary tells king Milinda or Menander of the three ways by which a precious wisdom-teaching can disappear: '(1) The decline of attainment to an intellectual grasp of it, then even the man who conducts himself aright in it has no clear understanding of it. (2) The decline of conduct in accordance with it, hence the promulgation of the rules of the discipline ceases, only the outward form of the religion remains. (3) When the outward form ceases, the succession of the tradition is cut off'. This necessity for continuing the 'succession of the tradition' was recognised by the Buddha as the 'Ancient Way' in the same work, IV, v,12.

Guru and *śiṣya* are therefore the two vital links of that chain which, as it were, supports the lamp of wisdom which like a beacon lights up the world of humanity through the ages. Each link is as necessary and significant as the other, for between them, the dialectical torch of truth is transmitted down the narrow line of successive generations; and by this technique of conveyancing, the Word is handed down, enduring for all time, accumulating momentum until its value becomes a good and mighty heritage for all.

On the part of the disciple the Word of the *guru* demands a sympathetic understanding. The knowledge to be absorbed is global, unitive and integral and it is in the personality of the *guru* that these aspects are held together as one whole. The relation of the disciple to the *guru* is the important factor, and a process which is a kind of spiritual osmosis then occurs. It is an attuned communion of two who cease to be two in terms of the spirit, vivified beyond the personal by the dialectical lightning flash of the Word.

In our day philosophy itself has lost its purity. But the global attitude thus transmitted is a synthetic resumé of the gist of philosophy in its total sense. A historian of philosophy has to be a philosopher himself if he is to relate philosophic thought systematically. Likewise, a *guru* is an impartial witness of all that philosophy in general attests, rather than just a philosopher of any one school or system in either the academic or religious sense. He is thus a philosopher of philosophy, one who represents the Truth of truths, the Word above the wordiness, the All-in-all above the systems, the Fact beyond the data, Neutral Vision above intellectual speculation, dream, supposition, and outlook, as the Light of all intellectual illumination, endowed with an inner wisdom which has reached its term. As the Upaniṣad declares, a knower of *Brahman* becomes *Brahman* itself.[6] He is thus crowned with the Crest Jewel

---

6. Summed up in the *mahāvākya* (aphorism) *tat tvam asi* (That thou art), as repeated nine times with different examples, to the disciple Śvetaketu by his father-*guru* Uddālaka in the *Chāndogya Upaniṣad* (Chap. VI Khaṇḍas 8 to 16 inclusive).

of Discrimination.[7] He is the *sarvajña* (the All-knower) or the *sarva-vit* (the One aware of all). In him all the knots of doubt have been sundered. His personal value becomes exalted among men and his authority unquestionable. Such are the marks of *guru*-hood.

Without *śiṣya*-hood, which is the counterpart of *guru*-hood, the latter would be meaningless. As a king cannot be without subjects, so no *guru* can be without the typical *pūrva pakṣin* (the doubter, the one who is sceptical, who has the point of view which is anterior to finalised wisdom, the persistent critic found in all the texts of the Word-wisdom). He may be Arjuna to Kṛṣṇa the Chariot-Driver (in the *Bhagavad Gītā*), a whole group of illustrative critics, such as Gorgias or Theatetus contra Socrates (in the dialogues of Plato), a doubting Thomas querying Christ, a king Milinda questioning Nāgasena the Bhikṣu, the disciple Ānanda and the Buddha, or even a Boswell drawing out the worldly wisdom of a Johnson. Plato and Śaṅkara employed the situation as a necessary literary method, but one that was naturally taken from experience, far apart though they were in time and locality. In all such cases, the essential nature of the relation is the same. The humble camp-follower of the *guru*, often called the *ante-vāsī* (the dweller near at hand) or the poor *brahmacārin* (the treader of the path of *Brahman*) often in rags, serving his *guru* for decades for the sake of wisdom, are not really inferior in spiritual status to the *guru*. Indeed, on occasion, their feet deserve to be washed by the hands of the *guru*, even as Jesus washed his disciples' feet as a recognition of the contemplative ambivalent relationship.[8]

The bipolar *guru-śiṣya* relationship thus requires not only a genuine *Brahman*-knowing *guru*, but also an enthusiastic or earnest disciple. Only then can the Word of the *guru* be elaborated. And in conforming to this genuine relationship, the *śiṣya* on his part has to fulfil certain preliminary requirements.

---

7. 'The Crest Jewel of Discrimination' (*Vivekacūḍāmaṇi*) is the title of a Vedānta textbook by Śaṅkara.

8. See *John,* XIII, 4-17.

These, in the Vedānta context[9] are often referred to as the six graces or treasures (*ṣaṭ-sampatti*).[10] He must first of all be prepared to listen and not be in a hurry to teach himself. He has thus to submit himself to a self-imposed period of preliminary silence, similar to that imposed in the Pythagorean communities at Crotona (the 'Mystike Siote'). This patient waiting must be of a positive, alert and actively waking kind, and not just a sloppy succumbing into the torpor of laziness. The ego has to be held back, or encouraged, as required, stage by stage, to positive inner adjustments. Besides truthfulness, purity and love of wisdom for its own sake, which constitutes the pedestal or base upon which the statue of the seeker, the *brahmacārin* or *śiṣya*, is to be erected, there is also implied in these six qualities a certain rigorous immunity to hardships, an adaptability, and a stamina that is uncomplaining and capable of smiling under duress. In the unique

---

9. The qualifications of the disciple (and of the Master) are given in many other contexts, but all bear a close resemblance. The interested reader may refer to the following: for the Platonic qualifications Plato's *Republic,* Book V; for the Christian, instructions to the twelve disciples in *Mathew,* X, XXIII, as well as elsewhere, e.g., praise of Mary for sitting still and listening to the *guru*-Word *Luke,* X, 38-42; and for the Buddhist (twenty-five qualifications for the teacher and ten for the disciple — to begin with) in *The Milinda Questions,* IV, i, 8-9.

10. These qualifications will be found in Śaṅkara's important textbook, the *Vivekacūḍāmaṇi,* 19-30. They are (besides the longing for freedom, the intelligence to distinguish with reason between what is real and unreal, and the abandonment of self-will — *vairāgya* —) the following six attributes: the calm resting of the mind on the goal to be attained (*śama*); checking and turning the senses away from distractions (*dama*); refusing to allow the mind to be carried away by other interests than the global or unitive (*uparati*); endurance of the troubles incidental to the life of discipline without petulance or self-pity (*titikṣā*); intelligent confidence in the Words of the *gurus* of the past as preserved in their writings as well as full trust in the teachings of the present *guru* (*śraddhā:* this is often mistakenly called 'faith,' synonymous with 'blind belief.' Any discerning reader will at once note the vast distinction implicit here) and finally, constant firm remembrance of the fact of the Real or *Brahman,* but without curiosity, fancy or imagination, i.e., no hypostatic creations (*samādhāna*). In the last verse (30) referred to, Śaṅkara utters a warning note that without the true love of liberation from the unreal (*mumukṣutva*), and the surrendering of other diverting interests, these attributes are useless, as a mirage in the desert.

guru-śiṣya relationship which we are endeavouring to define, the *raison d'être* of which is the task of establishing wisdom, positive aspects of the personality of the one have to be grafted on to the radical or negative aspects of the other. Rare and wonderful and delicate is this transmission of the Word ![11]

The typical *śiṣya* of the Upaniṣads is often an interesting study himself. He is a Devadatta (God-given) or a Satyakāma (Passionate Lover of Truth), and usually of tender years. Even if he happens to be of questionable parentage, as with the latter, this is no drawback.[12] Only his honest zeal counts in the eyes of the Vedāntic *guru*. Śaṅkara recognises this in many places and quickly abolishes any pride there may be in a *śiṣya* of the Brāhmin caste.[13] Śvetaketu, twenty-four years old, the equivalent of our modern graduates, has his conceit broken by his father-*guru*.[14] His counterpart is the touchingly innocent boy Nachiketas. His greedy ruthless father Vajraśravasa drives him away, but Naciketas, in the allegory, receives the priceless Word from the lips of Death himself.[15] (Incidentally, there is another feature in this 'parable'. Vajraśravasa is the typical Vedic ritualist, sacrificing everything, even his son, for the sake of a reward from the gods; while the real boons are to be had from the Guru Yama — Death or Time — who is also known as the Dweller in the south, i.e., in the non-Vedic region of India. This has bearing on what we wrote in our last chapter on the Vedic-pre-historic synthesis of the Word.)

Traditionally, then, the aspiring youth arrives at the abode of the *guru* who generally lives away from society in a forest hermitage. The future *śiṣya* is expected to bring a token bundle of firewood as

11. Cf., *Bhagavad Gītā,* VII, 3: 'Among thousands of men, one perchance strives for perfection; and even among those who do strive and succeed, scarcely one knows Me in truth.'
12. See *Chāndogya Upaniṣad*, IV, iv, 1-5.
13. See for example, *Upadeśa-Sahasrī* (A Thousand Teachings of the Guru) Part I, 10-13, where the *śiṣya* is asked why he, as a *brahmacārī*, calls himself the son of a Brāhmin.
14. See *Chāndogya Upaniṣad*, VI, I *et seq.*
15. See *Kaṭha Upaniṣad*, Vallī, I.

Sculpture from Gāndhāra of Buddha giving his first sermon at Benares. This Buddhist sculpture has adopted all the symbols of the Mohenjo Daro Śiva and Dakṣiṇamūrti; e.g., the sacred fig-tree, the listening disciples, the pedestal, animals such as the two deer, and the right hand forming the wisdom gesture or *jñāna mudra*.

a sign of his willingness to submit to the household discipline required of him when he enters the *gurukula* (the family of the *guru*).[16] He proves in this way that he is one who has sacrificed all for the wisdom that he prizes more than family and friends. He is therefore a true orphan of God or humanity,[17] a stowaway on the cosmic ship, unwanted by society, a radical idealist by inclination. Even if he is of highly respectable parentage he is expected to take no pride in his family traditions. He has transcended and left behind that chapter in his life.

So, like a stray animal pleading for adoption, he appears of his own accord at the *guru*'s threshold. He is docile, of good manners and of pleasant mien. He is earnest enough and zealous to pay the utmost price for the wisdom he seeks; willing, if need be, to give the loyalty of a lifetime. He does not know wisdom in its completion, but he is aware that there is wisdom. He has, as it were, a foretaste of its value known in a vague way, and this inkling gives him the impetus, enabling him to take the ultimate step to discover it with whole-hearted aim, come what may. All this is understood and symbolically implied when he knocks at the *guru*'s door. Thus he is deeply sensitive, but neither timid nor hesitant.

The *brahmacārin* of tradition rises before the sun and usually has his morning dip in the nearest river or lake. There is nothing severe about this in a tropical climate. At early dawn he is ready for service at the *guru*'s bedside. Various kinds of service are exacted from him in keeping with his character as a student. Begging is not taboo provided it is just as much as is needed for elementary bodily needs. Competition with others in this connection is forbidden as may be seen from the story of Āruṇi who was reprimanded by the *guru* mentioned in the *Mahābhārata*. Extreme tests are sometimes applied,[18] till the mutual adoption between the *śiṣya* and the *guru*

---

16. Ref. ff. passages in the Upaniṣads; *Chāndogya,* IV, iv,5; V, xi,7 and VII, vii, 2; *Kauśītaki,* I, i; *Muṇḍaka,* I,ii,12; and *Praśna,* I,i.

17. Cf., *Tao Te Ching,* 20. 'I alone am like one without a home'. In ancient China the emperors were styled orphans because of their lonely position — the 'orphan sons of Heaven'.

18. But not so harsh as those employed by Zen Abbots.

becomes firmly established. It is an educative process, a drawing out, and, without the essential bipolar adoption recognised on both sides, it must fail.

Such in outline was the practice employed traditionally according to the sources at our disposal. The *śiṣya* was not to question the authority of the *guru*. It is clear also from the stories concerning Milarepa and others equally famous, whether from the Indian or Tibetan *guru-śiṣya* literature.[19] The testing period over, and adoption complete, proved by service to the *guru* or by other methods, all is ready for the instruction, which generally takes but a little time to give. The *mantra* (sacred syllable or word) is given to the disciple, the *mahā-vākyas* (Grand Aphorisms) are bestowed, and the climax of the relationship is reached.[20]

There is glory in being a *guru*, but by its own terms there is greater glory in being a *śiṣya*. The willingness, submission, discipline and extra good breeding implied in the tender strength of the personality of the *brahmacārin* is no less a marvel than that of *guru*-hood. The *brahmacārin* is at the beck and call of the *guru*. In the *guru*'s presence he never sits or plays pranks, but rises respectfully when the *guru* enters. In the presence of other elder *gurus* he is expected to be modest and only when asked shows off his knowledge. To be requested to sit in the *guru*'s presence is a rare recognition, gained only in the later period of discipleship.

---

19. Many of these accounts of *guru-śiṣya* relationships are now available for the Western reader, due to the patient scholarship of highly qualified translators like Max Muller, Paul Deussen, Rhys-Davids, Robert Ernest Hume and Dwight Goddard, etc. Milarepa was a Tibetan saint. See *Tibet's Great Yogi Milarepa,* by W.Y. Evans-Wentz, and *Tibetan Yoga* and *Secret Doctrines,* by the same author in collaboration with the late Lama Kazi Dawa-Samdup (both from Oxford University Press).

20. For examples of the tests in the Upaniṣads, see *Kaṭha.,* I, 20, ff; *Kauś.,* III, I: *Chānd.,* IV, 2; IV, x,2; V,iii,7 and VIII, viii, 4; *Bṛh.,* VI, ii, 6 and IV, iii, 1 ff: and *Maitr.,* I, 2.

    Śaṅkara sums up the situation in a verse (42) of his *Vivekacūḍāmaṇi.* 'To him who has sought his protection, who is thirsting for liberation, who duly obeys the injunctions of the scriptures (i.e., including the *śiṣya* duties, etc.), who is of a pacified mind, and endowed with calmness, (to such a one) the sage proceeds to teach out of sheer grace.'

The word 'Upaniṣad' which means 'to sit beside' (derived from the Sanskrit root *ṣad,* to sit, and *upa,* nearby),[21] indicates the privileged nature of the *guru-śiṣya* institution. It is an instruction to be given only when ritualistic services and works have been rightly performed or transcended. After these comes wisdom (*jñāna*) as a distinct chapter.

The understanding between the *guru* and *śiṣya* is like that of a knight errant who takes up the gauntlet. A tacit challenge is invoked. The *guru* may want something in the middle of the night. The *śiṣya* is not to be caught napping. When the *guru* speaks, the *śiṣya* is all ears. As in a well-bred domestic animal, his eyes follow the *guru*'s least movements. Subtle exchanges must be taken in good faith, and in the spirit of a chivalric code of honour. Dogged pursuit of truth is demanded. No retrospective glance of regret is permissible to the strict *brahmacārin*. He must gaze ever forwards. The peak has to be conquered, the citadel stormed. Moral courage dare not flag for even a minute. Ever listening, ever wakeful, ever willing to serve, and cut off from every situation irrelevant to the task in hand, the student treads the path. Such is the heroic nature of genuine *śiṣya*-hood.

This *śiṣya*-hood is in effect qualification for citizenship of the City of *Brahman,*[22] for admission to the mystical acropolis. This is the antithesis of the politics of everyday life. Between two citizenships the disciple must choose. Except in the final context of the highest contemplation, where there is no question of service at all, serving two masters is not possible. In this universal sense, when a pupil becomes a citizen of the *guru*-world he is no more bound by nationalisms or other distinctions. Artificial social, class,

21. Cf., Deussen on the meaning of the word Upaniṣad in his *Philosophy of the Upaniṣads* (Clark, Edinburgh, 1906), pp. 10-15. This work is considered by Hume and other scholars to be 'The most systematic and scholarly work on the subject yet produced, executed with a rare combination of linguistic and philosophic qualifications for such a task.' (tribute by Hume in *The Thirteen Principal Upaniṣads*, p. 499, Oxford University Press, 1934).

22. St. Augustine's City of God (in his *De Civitate Dei*) has parallels in other religions. The whole of Book V of the *Milinda Questions* deals with the City of God or Truth, entrance to which is made by surrendering *karma* (action, works).

or caste differences no longer affect his conduct. Neither is his racial background of any importance, and even when he does not know the name of his father, as in the case of Satyakāma the son of a maid-servant, he is accepted since he has all the qualifications that are needed, truthfulness and sincerity. He is as if reborn, taken into a new fold, baptised with water or by the holy spirit of wisdom, or the Holy Ghost, born into a group which transcends social systems, into the new society of the Word-wisdom, thenceforth dedicated, even as Vestal Virgins were dedicated in ancient Rome.

In such a personality the sacred thread of the twice-born is there, not in the social sense, of course, but truly implicit as a mark of grace for one who is treading the path to *Brahman*,[23] the Absolute. Birth here is irrelevant. He can be a Brāhmin merely by adoption of clean living and dedication of life. Generally he clips off the tuft of hair worn ceremonially by caste people on the crown of the head (known as the *śikhā*), or later, he may retain it so as to be able to assist at rituals of birth or death. But as far as possible he lets the dead bury their dead and avoids being involved in ritualism. By necessity he may be sometimes involved in religious ceremony, but he never affiliates himself consciously with the world of priestcraft. His ideal is pure wisdom only, and his path is the negative way (*nivṛtti mārga*), devoid of self-willed activity. Neither has he social duties to perform, for the same reason, as his personality is wholly dedicated with unswerving loyalty to the idealism of the Word-wisdom.

An experiment of such an extremely idealistic kind of 'negative education' may come up to the stage of positive fruition, or it may fail. Some detail may be overlooked. The *guru-śiṣya* relational technique has to conform minutely to a science of its own, to a code which is at the same time traditional — the result of long experience

23. *Brahman* in Sanskrit is neuter, and stands for the Absolute. The true Brāhmin (Anglicised version of Brāhmaṇa, is either a *brahma-jnānī* or knower of the Absolute, or one whose life is dedicated to *Brahman*.) The definition of the true Brāhmin has been made clear in the *Vajrasūci Upaniṣad* (pp. 110-12 of *Thirty Minor Upaniṣads,* tr. by K. Nārāyaṇaswāmī Aiyar, Vasanta Press, Adyar, 1914).

— and dialectically universal. All leakages to other interests have to be blocked and a constant pressure uniformly maintained until results accrue. The nervous system has to be trained to bear the strain of the psychological search. On some occasion, suddenly, the votary may relapse into regret. The soldier has to be removed to a rest-camp. He may have tried his best, but a freer flight into the alone, into the adventure of the unknown, may be too much for his moral stamina to sustain.

Hence the institutional device of the four *āśrama*s in India, as base-camps for the pilgrim-mountaineers. Camp IV would be the culmination of the *brahmacārin* stage, as taken in its full *saṁnyāsa* implications, one who has renounced everything else with the aim of making the last ascent to the freedom of the heights. Camp III would be the *vānaprastha* (literally forest-dweller), here signifying the climber who wants to make the attempt again but needs further recuperation. Camp II would be the *gṛhastha* (householder) who is still absorbed in the world of necessity, but who, at the same time, knows there is a mountain to be climbed, and is helpful to those who are on their way. Camp I is the starting-off base, the *brahmacārī* camp where all types meet together, some to go forward, others to halt at the different camps.

This *āśrama*-device was envisaged in view of this possible falling back of *brahmacārin*s. It should therefore be considered as a contingency-device, to be viewed from the top, from the *guru*-level, and not from the bottom, from the social ground-level, for, from the bottom viewpoint as some have interpreted it forgetting the *guru-śiṣya* intention, it might seem that the ascent to the top of the mountain of Self-realisation could only be attained by prolonged halts at each of these rest-camps or *āśrama*s. But the rest-camps have relevance only from the top-view, not from the bottom-view. Those who can, could and as in the case of Śaṅkara and the youths of the Upaniṣads, did, march right up the mountain, not halting at any of the camps. From being *brahmacārin*s they became full-fledged *saṁnyāsin*s and, in turn, *guru*s themselves.

The *brahmacārin*'s weaning from the anterior social background had to be cautiously graded to have healthy results, for otherwise maladjustments would easily set in. With the *āśrama* alternatives, viewed thus as merely recuperative rest-camps, no chances were lost, nothing became irretrievable, no career-chance was broken or personality distorted. The *brahmacārin* returned to the family life, enriched in spirit, where he could apply some of the values he had learned to appreciate while with the *guru*; and might in time bring up his children more in conformity with the *guru*-Word, so that they at least might succeed where he himself could not make the grade. A programme of continued assault on the heights was therefore charted, and nothing once gained was really lost, and ground once gained was owned for ever.

Guru and *śiṣya* form the two poles of a process of Self-realisation that is essentially an axial relationship. The disciple seeking knowledge at the cost of his life if need be, touches the foot of the *guru* who is already established in that high wisdom. In his turn, the *guru* blesses the *śiṣya* and touches him on his forehead in recognition of his aspiration. A mutual appreciation each of the other then begins which results in their further spiritual rapprochement. Finally, all distinctions vanish. The *guru* is the *śiṣya* and the *śiṣya* is the *guru*.[24] They are chips of the same block, sparks from the same anvil, poles of the same magnet, or beams of the same light. Image and original merge into the substance of one and the same integral awareness. All is absorbed again into the silence of the Word.[25]

24. Cf., Ramana Maharṣi, 'God takes the form of a *guru* and appears to the devotee, teaches him the Truth, and, moreover, purifies his mind by association. The devotee's mind gains strength and is then able to turn inward. By meditation it is further purified and it remains still without the least ripple. That calm Expanse is the Self.

'The Guru is both "external" and "internal". From the "exterior" he gives a push to the mind to turn inward; from the "interior" he pulls the mind towards the Self and helps in the quieting of the mind. That is Guru-Kripa (grace of the Guru). There is no difference between God, Guru and the Self.' (*Maharṣi's Gospel,* Sri Ramanashramam, Tiruvannamalai, South India. 1946, p. 38).

25. Cf., Faridu'd-Din-Attar (twelfth-century Persian Sūfī) *Speech of the Birds* (Mantiqu't Tayr), an allegorical poem of 4,600 couplets, where the pilgrims (typified by various birds) reach the light of the divine Presence and are astounded by realising that they are the Presence and the Presence their own Self, as in a mirror. They are struck dumb with amazement.

Thus we see how in the final stages of the relationship the tables are turned, the situation transposed. At first it was the disciple who stood at the entrance to the *guru*'s home, with his symbolical handful of faggots in his hand, and with formulated questions in his mind. With burning doubts, in great distress of mind, he was like the parched earth under the scorching heat of the sun. His position has often been likened to that of a trapped animal with a wild forest fire surrounding him on all sides. His youthful enthusiasm was caught within the ways of social life, all his radical idealism thwarted and bottled up. His state of mind has been compared also to that of a solitary mariner lost in mid-ocean, caught in adverse gales and rocked helplessly in fear and despair. In this nightmare of unknowing darkness he is unable to find the safe harbour on the further shore of life.[26]

No sooner is the right relation with the proper *guru* established than the weight of anxiety is lifted. The storm abates, the forest fires are extinguished by the cloudburst. The darkness is lifted and the welcome light reveals the longed-for shore and the safe harbour. Blessing from above, the *guru* calms the tumult in the breast of the disciple, and calls on him to rise. The *Guru* utters the *mahā-vākya*s: 'Thou art That; That Self of thine is one with Brahman; Knowledge is *Brahman* Itself; All is Brahman,' etc.

And thus, with eyes moist in compassionate understanding, they merge into the pure non-duality of That Word of Truth — *SAT AUṀ*.

26. See *Vivekacūḍāmaṇi* of Śaṅkara, Verses 35-42 inclusive.

14

The Far-Flung Affinities of the Word

To follow the Word-formula through its historical vicissitudes calls for a lucidity of imagination and a transparency of memory. Names like intuition, insight, guesswork intelligently undertaken, the yogic eye (or *uhā-pōha* as Śaṅkara terms this kind of intelligence),[1] all refer to that rare instrument of knowledge which is able to see reality, as it were multi-dimensionally. The contemporary setting of actualities is the resultant of generations of action and reaction, strife and counter-strife. Over and over through vast stretches of time, the opposing interests of humanity, like the drifting, shifting sand-dunes of the desert, silting up the wells and oases, choke the living waters of the formulated Word.

But the waters are there. For we have the surprising phenomenon in Nārāyaṇa Guru, of the possibility of a *guru* of the original type, giving utterance to the same perennial wisdom formula, in a modern context, in spite of all the adverse winds that have raged against the Word for ages, proving afresh, after thousands of years, that the Word can still endure and survive the counter-currents of hard history. Although driven backwards and forwards, throughout the more troubled times of history rather than prehistory, the Word has endured, unmistakably present by evidences from far-flung regions and in diverse environments, coursing hither and thither, but surviving, and

1. Śaṅkara's *Vivekacūḍāmaṇi*, 16 — *medhāvī puruṣo vidan-ūhā poha-vicakṣaṇaḥ; adhikāryātma-vidhāyām ukta-lakṣaṇa-lakṣitaḥ.*

'A superior man of wisdom, well-versed and fully specialised in intuitive understanding, endowed with the said qualifications and one competent for Self-knowledge.'

ever and again cropping up into the contemporary surface of human life. These varied contexts indicate the affinites of the living Word, the living waters bubbling up through the sands of history.

But the pure Word-strains have to be distinguished from the freakish accumulative details, often more misleading than illuminative, supplied by the objective disciplines of epigraphy, iconography, archaeology, anthropology, or even philology. For, in spite of these public and publicised methods of investigation, the field for study is teeming with controversy. Generations of devoted scholars have spent their lives labouring in this field where angels fear to tread, but the yogic eye of insight is superior even to that of conventional 'angels,' and its depth of penetration exceeds the acutest limits of scholastic vision, delving further into the mists of time.

By producing and joining lines in the *a priori* productions of their geometry, the ancient Greeks were able to make exact astronomical calculations.[2] The spectrum can reveal the composition of starlight and by its shift measure stellar distances; and the radio-compass and radar can steer aircraft and ships without landmarks through fog and darkness. In the world of pure thought, similar methods remain unexploited by human intelligence. It is here that contemplative insight has yet to develop its methods and norms. Inner disciplines make effective operational results simpler than is conceivable in so-called 'objective' fields. The possibility of error and consequent disaster being common to both 'insight-objective' science as well as

2. The theorems of the Greek mathematician Euclid (*c.* 300 BC) still constitute the basis of modern geometry. But he was only one of a band of famous Greeks who can be traced back to the Eleatic philosophers, to Zeno (fourth century BC) and Pythagoras (sixth century BC). Thales (sixth century BC) predicted the eclipse of the sun of May 28th, 585 BC. Eratosthenes (third century BC) was the Director of the famous Library at Alexandria, and he measured the circumference and axial tilt of the earth and the size and distance of the sun and moon. All these ancient geniuses based their daring scientific flights on *a priori* logic drawn by inheritance from the contemplative training of the Pythagorean-Zeno Eleatic School.

'outlook-objective' science, there is no reason why inner disciplines should not be properly developed, standing firmly upon their own *a priori* foundations. Without the support of sense-evidence, the science of dialectics was known in classical times, both in its ascending and descending modes. This same science of dialectics, contemplatively employed in terms of Self-knowledge, can also be applied, and it is here that the traditional methods and working procedures implicit in the Guru-Word become profitable for examination.

It was with this unsophisticatedly innocent clarity of insight that Nārāyaṇa Guru once, while conversing with one of his Mohammedan admirers, seemingly by way of a pleasantry, made the remark that the name of God in Islam, *Allāh*, must have some affinity with *allā* which in the Tamil and Malayālam languages of south India means 'not this.' Elaborating his meaning, the Guru continued, 'The Supreme is beyond and other than all that we see here.' According to him that was the common meaning to be derived from both *Allāh* and *allā*. The All-Merciful God of the proto-Semitic peoples was known by the same Word and this must have been retained in Islam by adoption from an old stratum of language. The Guru inquired of his Islamic friend if such an interpretation would be repugnant to the Mohammedan historians. His friend replied that he could not think of any objection, for, taken together with the main characteristics of Islam which emphasises belief in a true God, raised above all idolatrous, polytheistic taints, the interpretation of the *guru* seemed at least possible and even probable.[3]

---

3. In the Islamic world, the great Sūfī poets have made wide use of those verses in the Holy *Koran,* 'God was, and there was naught but He, and it is now even as it was then,' and 'He is Allāh beside whom there is none who should be served, the Knower of the unseen and seen; He is the Beneficent, the Merciful. He is Allāh beside whom there is no God, the King, the Holy, the Author of Peace, the Granter of Security, Guardian over all, the Mighty, the Restorer of every loss, the Possessor of every greatness; high is Allāh above what they set-up with Him. He is Allāh the Maker of all things, the Creator of all existence, the Fashioner of all images — His are the most excellent and beautiful attributes (that man could →

When the present writer heard of this conversation, his first impression was that the *guru* was laughing at some of the far-fetched constructions and facile obscurantisms indulged in by some philologists, as for example, the statement by some that Christ and Kṛṣṇa are the same, which is more improbable than impossible.

In his serio-lighthearted manner — according to the reaction of the listener, the Guru repeated this conversation. This time he explained that the difference between the two syllabic forms 'allā' in Malayālam and 'Allāh' in Arabic was really very slight phonetically, the variation only being around the consonant *L*, which after all was a very slight detail. 'Perhaps the man had a potato in his mouth' the Guru jocularly speculated. As the Guru never made jokes for the mere fun of wittiness, nor at the expense of anyone, his remark, though humorous, held a linguistic secret well known to those who study the shifts in speech.[4]

It was important for him to trace the affinity of the Word, with his lifetime of contemplation applied to the understanding of its mode of transmission. Hence his half serious and modest method of suggesting its parentage, indicating the common sources of the spiritual tradition, and how the Word could have

---

→ imagine); everything that exists in the heavens or in the earth declares His glory and His perfection, and He is the Mighty, the Wise.' (*Koran,* LIX, 22-24).

For an example of Sūfī poetry which introduces the non-duality implied, we give a quatrain from the works of Abu Sa'id ibn Abi'l-Khayr (967-1049): (tr. and ed. G.Browne).

The Gnostic who hath known the Mystery,
Is one with God, and from his Selfhood free:
Affirm God's Being and deny thine own:
This is the meaning of 'no god but He.'

4. Modern comparative philologists recognise that the doublings of vowel or consonant sounds can indicate deep-seated affinities between different ancient languages. Father W. Schmidt's works (*The Culture-Historical Method of Ethnology,* 1939; *Primitive Revelation,* 1939; etc.) show how affinities can be revealed 'through phonetic traits such as the distinctions between voiced and voiceless consonants' etc. (Cf. also articles in *Encyclopedia Britannica* under Philology).

been wafted across oceans and deserts even as the wind carries the perfume of flowers over the walls and fences of gardens.

The affinities of spiritual formulae reveal many mysteries of this order to ethnologists, Egyptologists and others, as is well known.[5] Here is the mysterious ground of the Word, where humanity becomes united with strands of invisible horizontal identity, even in the contemporary setting of human life, quite apart from those deep-rooted prehistoric links which represent the vertical affinity, as we endeavoured to trace in Chapter 12.

To be able to see not only affinity but equivalence and agreement where none is apparent to the ordinary non-contemplative vision, is one of the features of that yogic eye to which we have alluded. That clearly-focussed eye of rare intelligence discovers the evidences of affinities everywhere. This intellectual vision is a corollary of the integral consciousness of the man of wisdom, from whom, as from the mouths of babes and sucklings, words of wisdom flow in the natural crystalline clarity of truth. Here philosophical profundities agree with infantile prattlings and the naive proverb joins with apocryphal verities, as balanced apodictic equations stating factual truths. The luxury of bourgeois spirituality meets the down-to-earth common sense reasoning of the man in the street. The Word of the Guru speaks from this universally integrated and unitive zone of neutral wisdom. Even his casual remarks thus become pregnant with vital wisdom. A few examples that come to mind will not be out of place here.

Once when in Coimbatore, a district adjoining Malabār and falling within the Guru's natural orbit of travel, he called

5. According to D. Nielsen (see p. 5, vol.V, *Mythology of All Races:* Archaeological Institute of America, Boston, USA., 1931) the South Arabian deity ILAH or IL, which is also the common Semitic word for God and corresponds to the Hebrew and Aramaic deity EL or ELOHIM, is one of the names of the Moon God. The North Arabic ALILAH-ALLAH, who became the supreme and only God of the Mohammedan religion, and EL or ELOHIM of the northern Hebrew tribes, who became the deity of Hebrew monotheism would thus also originally denote the ancient pre-historic Moon God.

attention, while strolling along the countryside, to the panoramic view of the mile-high Blue Mountains (the Nīlgiris). 'Look at that trough-like depression', he said. 'You will find that same characteristic formation in many other places.' The Guru was no geologist, but this matter of contours, stratifications and formations was familiar to him in a general way. It was common sense but this typical remark illustrates how constantly intent he was on discovering and recognising similarities wherever they showed themselves. They spoke a language of universal affinities in the mysterious universe that surrounds us. Cosmology, whether appreciated through the medium of relativity, electro-magnetism, gravitational fields or thermodynamics, is mainly a problem of uniting separate observations, the problem of finding affinitive connection to weld all into one harmonious whole. It is the search for the universal agreements, the co-ordination through likeness, of the many into the one, the search for the unitive law in the universe. Thus the twinkling of the most distant visible star has its counterpart in the rods and cones of the retina of the human eye, proving that man can be sensitive to even the faintest tremor of light emitted on the periphery of the cosmos. Here is a fundamental affinity wherein mechanics and mysticism meet in a mysterious unity and closer to the real than many otherwise one-sided so-called real facts.

The writer also recalls how the Guru made a similar remark when he stayed at a traveller's rest-house outside the hill town of Kandy in Ceylon (Sri Lanka). Here there was a river descending to the plains, foaming and bubbling over rocks and pebbles. The sound of the little cascade made the Guru feel at home as he noted its resemblance to the scene at his *āśrama* at Aruvippuram, where as we have seen, he meditated during his early years. Places thus suggested to him the same eternal message as the words of scripture. There were teachings in brooks and sermons in the stones. Like a poet, he found himself at home in nature and he even tried to make others feel the same homeliness anywhere in the universe.

On another occasion while in the same island of Ceylon (Sri

Lanka), which has so many associations with the civilization of ancient India, Nārāyaṇa Guru was visited by an elderly lady of an old Tamil family long resident in Colombo. The present writer was also there and the Guru did not miss the opportunity of noting a resemblance between this old lady and a grandmother of the writer. 'She is just like that grandmother,' he said. It is in such casual remarks, and joking pleasantries, with their substratum of parallels and affinities, that the Word of the Guru is to be sought, revealing eternal verities of an intimate kind, as much as in the Guru's formal verses, for a seriousness of principle underlay his lighter sayings as well as his deeply philosophic writings. Even jesting Pilate would have had to wait if face to face with this subtle blend of the common place and the unique, the agreement amid apparent variety, the resultant of the Guru-Word in which reality was wed to existence in the Guru's arresting and convincing style.

The Mohammedan admirer we mentioned earlier once asked permission, which was readily given, to put the following hard theological question to the Guru:

'People say' he began, 'that human beings enter into salvation, but in spite of this there seems to be no decrease in human population.'

'Perhaps animals get promoted to human status', the Guru suggested.

'Even they do not decrease', the admirer replied and seemed to have won the point.

The Guru asked, 'Who created them?'

'God', the man replied.

'And has He now forgotten how to ply His trade?' asked the Guru.

It was in this half-joking, half-serious way that the Guru met all problems. The Guru-Word, by solving problems almost in a childish way, thus reduced the chances of ideological conflicts.

Dr. Johnson once said that poetry came into existence when a child told the story of 'Jack and the Beanstalk.' Naive childish prattle has the quality that truly enriches language, making it an instrument of happiness and Self-knowledge. It is in this sense that the Word of the Guru in the instance given should be taken.

Every literary device and figure of speech has to be used in the service of the Word, including wit and humour. Each has then its own high role. When employed consciously to exalt and extol the Word-wisdom, literature fulfils its best purpose for man. Without being interpreted too literally, all literary forms — paradox and parable, fable and metaphor, song, chant and magic spell, personification and apostrophe, dialogue and soliloquy — have to be pressed into the service of true Word-wisdom. To the contemplative mind everything is a figure of speech and can thus be reduced to a Word-formula. The perfect Word above is the same as the Word of words below, in which all words meet making the music of the spheres. Nominalism or phenomenalism are only words uttered loud or low. Some bang the piano in a tragic frenzy, while others caress the keys with the moth's kiss. Good musicians appreciate both phases, but to the unmusical all is conflicting discord. So with literary devices, innocent or exotic; they are incidental, it is the Word content that counts. In triumph it proclaims itself through blare of trumpet or by pounding of drum, marking the end of a tragedy. Not always need it be the slow sonorous measures of piety, for even the apparently opposite effect of abandon can stimulate the presence of the good when masterfully employed, as the Guru did when he seems to quarrel with Śiva himself in some of his prayers. He would even seem to be using swear words against this God as if challenging him in the language of pre-historic bluster. He thus took liberties in his own way, as a child would with a father; or like Lava and Kuśa of the *Rāmāyaṇa* epic who fight their father Rāma on the field of battle, even if he is the scion of the Raghu clan.[6] But supplication too has its place in the Guru-Word, every bit as

6. See *Uttara Kāṇḍa* of Vālmīki's *Rāmāyaṇa*.

much as the self-assertive *Eigensinn* (obstinate wilfulness) and the seeming arrogance of the *mahāvākya* (great formula) which says 'I am *Brahman*' (*aham brahma-asmi*), yet containing the ultimate figure of speech of the Word.

No device, no technique that could add to its effectiveness was outside the scope of the Word as employed by Nārāyaṇa Guru in his writings or speech. Every form of plea or persuasion, shock tactics or gentle suggestion, intimate familiarity or total abandonment, were alternately applied till the required introspection was induced in the subject. Prayer, supplication, adoration as well as philosophical discussion were all meant to develop a special state of mind favourable for the prevalence of truth, both intellectually and morally.

No style known in the development of Indian thought, whether of *śruti* (directly heard Word-wisdom), *smṛti* (indirectly heard, remembered wisdom, or wisdom applied to practical situations in life), *Purāṇa* (traditional lore), *Āraṇyaka* (forest of injunctions), or *Brāhmaṇas* (obligatory laws of ritualist life) is rejected in favour of another, by Nārāyaṇa Guru, but in accordance with a methodology and an epistemology of his own, all these literary forms have their place in his writings.

All the Guru's writings call for a contemplative approach, which can be an injunction, an admonition or a simple suggestion, according to context, but always for a better human life or understanding, for this is the motive coursing through his writings as a whole. And lest there should arise confusion of thought because of the many possible avenues of thought, his verses invariably end with an appeal to reason, memory, unity, vision, awareness or kindness. As against sophistry, hair-splitting doctrine, or eristic argument, he pleads for the avoidance of vain disputation and recommends the steady, generous way of contemplation. It represents a new approach to truth altogether. Instead of being lukewarm, the Guru's method is wholehearted, almost passionate, one-pointed, radical, fervent, intoxicating or heroic to the extreme. Uninterrupted, constant, faithful, ceaseless, and life-long are some of the other qualities outstandingly revealed in research on the Word of the Guru. In their cumulative effect, all these make of Guru-wisdom a field of knowledge all its own. And although at the same time there may seem nothing very original or altogether new, still there is a synthetic way which is new, an approach which is unique, a living and down-to-earth appeal, a breadth, confidence and bold atmosphere encompassing Nārāyaṇa Guru's writing which distinguishes it, making it of epochal value.

Nowhere does this uniqueness appear with greater force than when the Guru's method of thought is juxtaposed with notions current in the world today. Ever since the telescope became important, theology has receded into the background of general interest, while science, by way of the theory of evolution, may be said to have provided the means of distinguishing modern from mediaeval times. There are of course, also materialism and relativity as other ideologies, but there is little doubt that in place of theology, the master idea prevailing at present and influencing writers and thinkers, is still evolution. So for a typical example of the clash of contemplation with science let us pause for a moment and consider the reactions of Nārāyaṇa Guru to the theory of evolution.

The writer was then a student of zoology and had just sat for a degree on that subject in the university. During the summer holidays that followed, he happened to be standing in the presence of the Guru, discussing, as usual, some philosophical subject. This time it was zoology that was involved.

'What does that European pundit say?' the Guru inquired, referring to Darwin and his famous theory.'Does a monkey become a man?'

'Such at least is the theory,' the writer responded.

'Has anyone in the forest seen a monkey changing into a man?' the Guru continued, but went on, 'Perhaps he would say that the process was too slow, so that like the movement of the hands of the clock one could scarcely notice it.'

The conversation drifted to other examples of animal life. The writer mentioned the case of the hermit crab and described to the Guru how it would scoop out the flesh from the shell of a mollusc and then insert its own soft abdomen into it for protection, and thus live like a hermit, disappearing into the shell on approaching danger of any kind.

'But why not leave the hermit crab to be just like that? Why explain its natural history at all?' the Guru asked.

Facts, according to the Guru, had to be treated as facts plainly conceived from the phenomenal material point of view, and nothing more. When this strictly objective, experimental or empirical position of the scientist is rejected for any reason, what then is the next valid alternative? An endless series of compromises between extreme rationalism and empiricism becomes possible to an impartial thinker, and any one of these would have as much validity as any other.

The article of faith of the evolutionists has itself undergone much change since Darwin adumbrated it. He called it a theory to explain the origin of species, but his ultra-enthusiastic disciples went further. Some called it even the 'fact' of evolution. Most of them treat it as a corollary of natural philosophy. Being of the nature of a hypothesis it can even be called a credo, a cultus or doctrine. Then in the hands of Bergson evolution became almost like the *māyā* of the Vedānta, the principle underlying change or becoming. Add to these all the other possible variants, such as parallel, emergent, or mutatory evolution and we find that belief in the theory does not mean anything definitely fixed. It can only be said to be a position which denies the theory or doctrine implied in the Old Testament book of *Genesis.* Since its character has thus a negative derivation, it has the same status as the doctrine or view it opposes. Fossils and samples of comparative anatomies are found in the museums or biological laboratories as concrete facts but, whether because these samples are facts, the interpretation of the origin of different species of animals also becomes a fact of general agreement, is a matter upon which even authorities seem to be confused. Dogma persists in domains where we least expect it.

When Nārāyaṇa Guru asks a modern student of science the simple question: 'What is it that evolves, life or matter?' and goes on to say that if it is life that evolves, that is a truism, while if it is matter that evolves, that is impossible by very definition; we have a new way of reasoning which is neither that of the Age of Reason of Voltaire[7] nor of the Age of Theology of the Scholastics. The modern mind can hardly find a relevant answer to the objection when thus stated.

To find an answer to these questions demands an intellectual discipline of quite another kind. This is referred to as the higher reason, imaginative insight, and so on; but the nature of this kind of reasoning is still undefined, although many have recognised the need for it.[8]

---

7. The attitude implicit in what is called the Age of Reason can be seen from the following quotations. Writing on the earthquake in Lisbon in 1755 (*Poeme sur le Desastre de Lisbonne*) Voltaire said:

   Mais comment concevoir un Dieu, la bontê même,
   Qui prodigua ses biens à ses enfants qu'il aime,
   Et qui versa sur eux less maux à pleiness mains?

   • • •

   Un sophiste arrogant nous dit qu'il ne l'a pu:
   'll le pouvait, dit l'autre, et ne l'a point voulu:
   Il le voudra, sans doute;' et, tandis qu'on raisonne,
   Des foudres souterrains engloutissent Lisbonne,....

   (Can we conceive a God beneficent.
   Upon his children's happiness intent,
   Yet on them sorrows sparing not to heap?

   • • •

   His power to mend the sophist loud denies.
   'He wanted but the will,' another cries.
   And while the disputants their views proclaim,
   Lisbon is perishing in gulfs of flame.)

8. After the Age of Reason typified by Voltaire we find that scepticism itself changes its rigid adherence to mere facts. This can be gathered from the following taken from Tyndall (1820-93) who said: 'If you ask him (the materialist) whence this 'matter' of which we have been discoursing, who or what impressed upon this the necessity of →

Although with Bergson intuitive reasoning again got another lease of life, its place in the general scheme of philosophical methodology and epistemology remains as vague as ever to the modern mind. In the science of the Word, or the science of the Absolute, the contemplative or intuitive way is the only legitimate means to use. Although scientific theorising may serve a limited purpose, each supposition giving a more or less plausible answer according to practical requirements, no final answer comes by the use of this method. To be a sceptic and to know that there is a kind of natural boundary to reasoning is as far as this type of science dares to go. The schoolboy who sees a candle burn is allowed to ask 'how', but is discouraged from asking 'why' it burns. The schoolmaster has to refer the pupil to another teacher who may be confident enough to try to answer such questions. And generally, unless he is that rare being, the scientifically trained contemplative, such teachers degenerate into replying with the puerile forms of dogmatism that civilization has just outgrown.

Thus we see that our age of scientific reason is up against a dead end. A new and bolder form of reasoning is now called for, a form of reasoning admitting much more than just imagination, a form of reasoning that will touch the most concrete aspects of science, not omitting the field held by such theories as that of relativity. And if this is the case with regard to the future of

---

→ running into organic forms, he has no answer. Science is mute in reply to these questions. But if the materialist is confounded, who else is prepared with a solution? To whom has this arm of the Lord been revealed? Let us lower our heads and acknowledge our ignorance, priest and philosopher, one and all'. (see *Fragments of Science for Unscientific People,* 1871).

The same physicist, besides admitting the helplessness of science, believed in the need for 'imagination' (by which he could mean none other than what we have tried to establish above as the new contemplative way of envisaging verities). Of this 'imagination' he further says: 'There are Tories who regard imagination as a faculty to be feared rather than employed. They had observed its action in weak vessels and were duly impressed by its disasters. But they might with equal justice point to exploded boilers as an argument against the use of steam.'

scientific investigation, how much more so it must be in the pursuit of the affinities of the Word which we are trying to trace. Let us therefore proceed a step further in the direction we initiated at the beginning, exposing to view some of the axial routes of the dialectical reformulation of the Word in a bold, imaginative general way, but in so doing, not losing sight of actualities.

Prior to the age of the Tower of Babel, archaeologists begin to get lost in the haze of time. Objective evidence absorbs their energies and devotion. A larger view, a bolder flight, a living and open or transparent method of approach, is called for. Word-affinities have to be traced by form as well as by content. To take the example of heredity, we see that living organisms repeat themselves through a different mechanism than that of the formation of crystals in suitable solutions and other conditions. The crystalline growth is a purely quantitative material repetition of form, while the growth of life and its transmission from one living organism to another has to be conceived vitalistically in terms of qualitative factors which are subtler and elude measurement. Hence form and content both have to be considered in tracking the Word back through time.

A song once sung can remain recorded in celluloid or metal tape for years. It can be repeated mechanically. That is the form. But whether the music will appeal or not to the hearers is a different matter. That is the content, the quality factor. Hence mechanistic preservation alone of the Word does not suffice. And in tracing Word affinities, the living content of the Word-formula has to be kept in mind. The Word represents an ever-present personal value in life. It satisfies and liberate us. It is therefore with these main directives in our minds that we here enter into a survey of the Word-formula, to trace its history and affinities in far-flung and disjunct contexts.

* * *

Natural and impenetrable barriers have preserved India in such a way as to give the land a personality all its own. It is a strange compromise of vertical factors having profound Word-values, preserved through time and only moderately affected by factual cross-breezes of strife. This peculiarly personalised isolation applies all the more forcibly when we come to think of the extreme south-west of India, to that Malabār Coast where the Guru Nārāyaṇa, like Śaṅkara, lived and taught against a background of prehistoric Śiva worship.

We have already touched upon some of these aspects. Land invasions of India for the most part came from the north while the extreme southern limits of the country were connected with distant lands only by adventurous mariners. From time to time these bold visitors from afar had the effect of injecting new elements into the traditional social fabric. In this way, alternately stimulated and enriched in small effective doses, with intervening rest-periods during which the stimuli were absorbed, through long centuries, the West Coast remains to this day a zone of life-expression which contains the remnants of all the varied stratifications of history like out-croppings of rocks side by side as it were. Disturbances originating and affecting the north of the Indian land-mass were absorbed by the main bulk of the country long before their shocks reached the southern toe of Mother India; while sea-borne social influences were sufficiently gradual to be more or less negligible in the far south, leaving only small clotted ganglia of distinguishable social units. This was true of the main western coastal region of the south, while in the furthest south-east, over the high mountain barriers of the Western Ghāṭs, and also due to forest and climate, the social stability of the people for ages prior to written history, remained intact and unaffected by the turmoil and change taking place in the more exposed territory in the rest of India. For these reasons, as well as the psychological effect of a contemplation-inducive climate, certain Word-values linking the present to the most distant epochs of antiquity, have been preserved in these southern regions.

If one could revivify the spice-and-wine axial link connecting

Alexandria, Antioch, Athens and Rome with the ancient Malaya which is the modern Malabār Coast, many of the riddles of the Word and its affinities would leap into a new and surprising solution.

Some of the historico-philosophical puzzles would no longer be baffling. For example, the following would all find appropriate relationship; would no longer be isolated questions: the background of Socrates; the secret of the emergence of the Pythagorean communities who were both vegetarians and believers in metempsychosis; the sources of the ontological hylozoism of the Eleatic and Ionian philosophers from whom Plato drew so much of his doctrines; why Plato's dialectics had to be given a new turn by his own disciple Aristotle, to become once again matter-of-fact in the pre-Socratic way; and then the explanation of the amazing phenomenon of Plotinus whose personality and teachings are so characteristically those of an Indian *guru*, in whom all the philosophical waters of the Eastern Mediterranean seemed to meet as in a great calm sea — Plotinus who is so Indian in temperament and yet reflecting the cooler atmosphere of the Italian coast. One by one these puzzles would be solved if we imaginatively conjure up and re-establish the Mediterranean-Malabār trade axis along which, to and fro, much more than gold and wine, pepper and ivory, were transported. The clue to begin with might well be the *guru* of Plotinus, the mysterious Ammonius Saccus whose very name suggests the 'sack porter' who followed this great East-West trade route in the guise of a peddlar, or a carrier of bags of pepper.

If we could tread the thorny field of the Biblical landscape, we would discover how it is possible to reconstruct more imaginatively those events which can throw the necessary light on the dialectical process of the revaluation of the Word as it was wafted across desert sands and ocean billows; by the camel caravan routes to the meeting-place or *synodiai* at Antioch in

Syria on the shores of the Mediterranean, or by ships to Egypt via the Red Sea.[9]

Archaeologists, Assyriologists and Egyptologists study each piece of the jig-saw puzzle in isolation more or less, in almost nationalistic terms, relating finds to kings and dynasties. But even in the ancient times the world was one, and particularly so for the Word that knew no frontiers or monarchs. Archaeological specialists therefore miss the human dynamic or dialectical secret that fuses the many obsure separate facts into one living whole; for across the warring separate kingdoms, and independent of the political rivalries, life hummed intensely backwards and forwards across the spice-wine axis. Hence, it is only when this connecting welding axis is inserted into the picture of the ancient world that it leaps to life and the whole has relevant movement and meaning, thus solving the many conundrums of history, religion and philosophy, and disclosing what is important for us, namely the universalising of the Word.

For if the old Biblical world is fitted into the Indian counter-world, to that Eastern world which has changed comparatively little while the old Jewish world has perished as a living substance for direct evidences; and if at the same time the axial commercial link is kept in mind, then the darkness surrounding most of the Biblical records is to a large extent, if not totally, dispersed. We have to conjure up a world of courageous and adventurous travellers, sailors and caravan leaders, fond of making easy money by smuggling not only goods but people across difficult frontiers.

To take a few of these Biblical enigmas drawn from the *Old*

9. The name Red Sea was formerly the Erythraean Sea, and was applied to the whole Indian Ocean by the ancient European mariners. Then it was applied only to the Arabian Gulf, and finally it was restricted to its present limits. Great ports, like Berenike in Egypt on the Red Sea, and the port of Muziris (Kodungallūr) on the Malabār Coast may not find a place on the world map of to-day, and may have shrunk to the status of insignificant villages; but they were thriving world centres in the world of antiquity — *vide The Periplus of the Erythraean Sea,* tr. by W.H. Schoff (Longmans Green, New York, 1912).

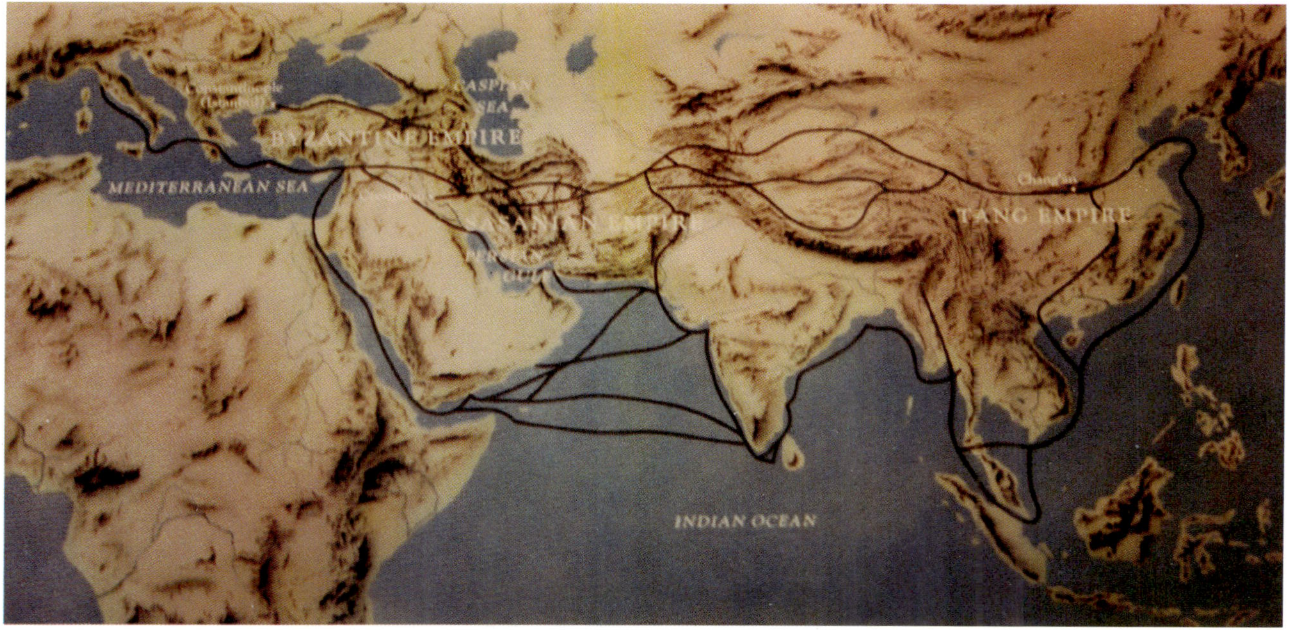

Mediterranean-Malabār Axis and the Silk Route

Between the first and the seventh centuries AD, there was a great dial of peaceful interaction between Asia and the Mediterranean world. Traders, ambassadors, artisans, and pilgrims travelled to and from the spice-coast of Malabār to the Mediterranean sea, as well as along the Silk Route from China, carrying with them spices, silk, gold, silver and religious artefacts.

and *New Testaments*, as for example, the myrrh and spices produced by Nicodemus and so easily available; that group of women, the Marthas and Marys who seem always so in fear of the Jews; the 'miraculous' production of barrels of wine; the Flight into Egypt, and how it was managed; the burning bush; the angels who differed from the prophets about commandments or idolatry; the Golden Calf; the 'resurrection' of Lazarus from a cave-tomb, later paralleled almost exactly in the case of Jesus himself; the Wise Men of the East, and the pillar of smoke by day and of fire by night — all of these illustrative riddles find a solution in the light of what we have said, and one which is at least theoretically as plausible and as valid in its own way as the theory of evolution whose status we have discussed.[10]

Without violating more or less accepted possibilities, the Healer himself can be imagined to have come and gone along this route or axis more than once at least. The doubting disciple Thomas is believed to have founded seven churches on the Malabār Coast as early as the first century of the Christian era.

---

10. The suggestive allusions in this paragraph should not be looked upon — at present at least — as any elaborate rival theory to existing and prevailing notions. When we read in the Bible (*Mathew*, IX, 6; *Mark*, II, 9-12) 'take up thy bed and walk,' it evidently fails to make sense in a Western context. In the warm climate of south India where it is usual to carry light matting beddings from place to place, this would make better sense. Prof. Max Muller is one of those experts who have been able to trace many modern fables from Europe to their sources in India. His philological insight and intuition were responsible for these epoch-making findings. The same kind of mental operation can be applied to the various mysteries of the Biblical context. Real piety would not suffer by such insight, but would rather be enhanced, since religion and philosophy must support one another rather than be at loggerheads. We have expressly left the mysteries unsolved in the above paragraph. In the light of the previous discussion it is for the reader to closely scrutinise the passages referred to and see if there is any better understanding of them in the light of the spice-wine axis against whose background we have placed these problems. It will serve no purpose here to enter into the merits of each of the enigmas listed, since each one would involve much preliminary discussion. Some student interested in this aspect of history may perhaps take this up for further investigation at a future date.

Whether this is true actually as claimed or not, some probabilities in the same direction are indisputable. Of all the coasts available to such a founder of churches, whoever it may have been in actual history, the simple fact remains that churches *were* founded on the Malabār Coast, which is sufficiently suggestive for our purposes here. Gnostic, Nestorian, Egyptian, Persian, Arab, Jewish, Greek and Manichean groups came to this coast and founded colonies here preserving contact with their motherlands. Their colonies and ethnological traits are impressed indelibly in the fabric of the population of Malabār.[11]

The hum of life across the Erythraean Sea must have endured through several centuries and, while wordly goods were being busily exchanged, the dialectical process of the revaluation of the Word must also have gone on apace, as revealed by the affinities such as the instance alluded to by Nārāyaṇa Guru. But phonetics was not the only factor involved; a variety of considerations have to be treated together imaginatively and impartially.

Authorities have found it quite reasonable to think that Jerusalem could have derived its name from 'Ūru' and 'Salem', both of which retain their original meaning in a suggestive manner as pertaining to a prehistoric context. Though the evidence is as yet disjunct and incomplete, the resemblance is at least curious and striking, considering that 'Ūru' in Tamil means 'City' and 'Salem' might very well apply to a temple city,

11. In passing, we might mention the existence of another commercial-cultural axis, linking up the Malabār Coast this time with China and the Far East. Chinese admirals in huge armadas of fifty ships have been known to visit Malabār. (Prof. Duyvendak, an eminent Sinologist of Leyden University gave a series of lectures in London in 1948, since published in book form *China's Discovery of Africa:* in which he mentions an expedition in the early fifteenth century, consisting of 62 ships bearing 37,000 men. Their motive was partly to exalt Chinese prestige, partly to acquire curiosities for the court, 'sent a-shopping for the ladies of the Imperial harem'. The Chinese too left their legacy on this trader's coast, and today one may see the *pagoḍā*-roofs, typical Chinese evidences in tiles, canoes, fishing-boats and fishing-nets, and unmistakable Mongolian faces amongst the people.

as in the case of the present-day city of that very name in south India. These and other matters of the same kind are rife with speculation.[12] Nevertheless, however, controversial the nature of the questions involved may be, this should not deter us from seeing the similarities that suggest affinites which, in the light of what we have said about the great Malabār-Mediterranean axis, does lend some plausibility to the existence of linguistic relations, and even to dialectical, spiritual or contemplative formulae belonging to the context of perennial wisdom. Hence, such study is interesting for its own sake.

However, probabilities become more than just possible when such facts as the evidence of diplomatic relations existing between the Roman Emperor Augustus and the Pāṇḍyan ruler of the south-west coast of India, as early as 20 BC are considered cumulatively.[13] Recent excavations in south India have unearthed

---

12. The following is a sample of the authoritative speculation employed in dealing with *Old Testament* linguistics:

    'Hosea (X, 14) in a hopelessly corrupt passage preserves the name of Shulman. Since Ishtar of Assur is called Shulmanitu, 'She is the city of Shulman,' it is obvious that the Assyrian god is identical with the name of the same city, as Adad was called Iluhallabu, after the city of Aleppo. Shulmanu and Shalman are probably identical with the ancient name of Jerusalem, Shalem where Melkizedek was king and priest of the god El, in the days of Abraham (twenty-first century BC). The name of the city was written 'Salem' in the correspondence of Abdihiba, King of Jerusalem, with Amenophis of Egypt in the fifteenth century, but with the Sumerian prefix Uru (city) and consequently U, ru, sa, lim replaced the older name before the age of Moses, and became Jerusalem of the later period.' — Cf. *Mythology of All Races,* vol. V. (London, Boston, 1931).

13. H.G. Rawlinson, the famous historian, quotes Strabo, the first-century Greek geographer who mentions the reception given to the Pāṇḍyan ambassador in Rome by the Emperor Augustus (Strabo, *Geography,* XV, 73).

    Rawlinson also quotes Pliny's *Natural History* (VI, 22) which 'tells us of a revenue ship of Annius Plocamus, in the reign of Claudius which was caught in the monsoon and covered the distance between Aden and Ceylon (Sri Lanka) in fifteen days. The usual time was about forty days. Rawlinson considers it 'highly probable that there were actually Roman colonies at Cranganore (Kodungallur) Muziris (where there seems to have been a Roman →

treasure-troves revealing unmistakably the intimate relations then existing between East and West.[14]

Research in south India will bring out many more surprises of this kind for the future historian who accepts and works on the basis of the hypothesis we have suggested, the underlying principle of which is the existence from of old of a reciprocal and subtly dialectical relationship between the head and tail ends of the dragon called civilization. But this must be conceived imaginatively through the Word affinities underlying all the given or yet to be uncovered evidence, for all such concrete facts will only lead us astray if unguided by the framework which is based on the Word-formula. The whole field of historical research needs re-examination, not merely in a truly scientific spirit, but with

---

→ temple), Madurā, Pukār at the mouth of the Cauvery, and other places. A Tamil poet sings of 'the thriving town of Muchiri, where the beautiful large ships of the Yavanas (the Ionians, generically applied to all Europeans) bringing gold, come splashing the waters of the Periyar, and return laden with pepper'.' (pp.16-17 of *The Legacy of India,* Oxford University Press, 1937 — In his essay on *India in European Literature and Thought* this careful historian summarises a great deal of highly interesting and relevant material.)

An account of the enormous volume of commerce is also quoted by Padmini Sengupta who gives the evidence of Pliny: 'In no year does India drain our Empire of less than 550 millions of sesterces (80 lakh of rupees, $3,000,000 or £600,000) giving back her own one hundred times their cost price'. (p.113, *Everyday Life in Ancient India,* Oxford University Press, 1950.)

14. 'Roman coins have been found buried under a tree in Calicut in Malabār. The merchants who left them there meant to return but evidently never did so.' (p.114, *Everyday Life in Ancient India,* P. Sengupta.)

'But in the early days, the Tamil south had little taste for anything Europe could offer in exchange, except gold, so gold had to pay for most of the Indian goods. Roman gold coins have turned up in astonishing quantities along the Malabār Coast, around Madurā and other places in the south. One such treasure trove consisted of 'five coolie loads.' Most of the coins belong to the reigns of the first Roman Emperors. A unique example among them is a coin of the Emperor Claudius (AD 41-54) struck to commemorate the Roman conquest of Britain.' (p. 202, *The Pageant of Indian History,* G.E. Sen, Longman's, 1948).

the light thrown upon history by the higher insight of contemplation.

Besides its double-filtered isolation by mountain ranges and a mighty ocean, the Malayālam-speaking coastal region of the south-west of India had — and to a great extent still has — other features which helped to maintain the calm cultivation and the preservation of vertical Word-values intact. These special features are of a cultural, climatic and sociological nature. They are of such special significance to the Word of the Guru that if they were omitted from reference, the Word would be like salt that had lost its savour.

In this South-Seas-like palm-beach part of the world, the temperature year in and year out, throughout the twenty-four hours, comes as near to that of body temperature as can be expected under natural conditions of rain and winds. The rain-fed crops upon which the population mostly thrive, such as the yams, and the coconuts and spices so cherished even in pre-historic times, such as pepper and cloves, supplemented with abundance of fish in the seas, inland lakes (the Backwaters) and rivers, have made luxury items meet the necessary ones in a beautifully blended compromise in the daily life of the people. As De Quincey was able to note, among his other subtle remarks in his opium dreams, man himself seemed to be a weed in these parts, as distinct from the cultivated plant that he tended to be in the West.

Exotic hothouse products were striking in the West, but the land-supported populace of the Malabār Coast could hold its own with almost nothing monetary to its credit at all. Buildings need no heating, while a palm-leaf hut was even better, in many respects, than a brick and tile structure. Half-nakedness was normal, and too many clothes made no sense either on women or children. The open air was better to sleep in than a luxury bedroom, just as the numerous pools and streams were better than well-fitted bathrooms. All could share in such nature-provided luxury without the question arising of dinars or dollars. Season after season the land supported the families and invading drums often meant nothing to them when in most places there was nothing to rob, no treasure to loot. Gardens grew the vegetables needed for the table. The pineapple gave its luscious fruit unwatered and untended, and even when one ate it and threw the top away on some soil, it would most likely strike root, survive and thus provide fruit for yet another human mouth, as if from the hands of the Supreme Goodness itself, as Nārāyaṇa Guru used to say.

Women were satisfied with ear ornaments of lac or palm-leaf. Gold was not even desired as embellishment. Palm-leaf umbrellas continue to be used today, in spite of a civilization thriving all round ready to encroach into the quiet precincts of this almost prehistoric self-sufficient simplicity. Even now the postman still has a hard time delivering a telegram to an anxious young wife whose husband may be on military service somewhere, for the postman would have to cross many a pool or muddy puddle, though rice fields and over narrow stiles to reach houses with no streets or serial numbers or any such mechanical distinguishing marks. The huts are often hidden because of clustering giant banana trees and palms of many kinds, nestling from view in the lush foliage through which sun-tanned children, clothed only in thin air, may be seen peeping out with innocent wide eyes. Life flourishes here by the bounty of nature, and in spite of all that is against it, the average man's life in this demi-paradise is thus equal to a prayer in a cathedral elsewhere. Such a picture is as true now as it ever was before, stretching back past the dawn of human history, and therefore the language that these people understand is the language of humanity. Such is the sociological, geographical and biological background of the Word of Nārāyaṇa Guru.

To complete this quiet idyllic picture where vertically growing human values were preserved through the sheer abundance of favourable circumstances, we must fit in another strand of the setting, a group of circumstances which now and then had the effect of a lancet opening up a tumour. Ships came from afar, bearing ruthless, strange and often greedy adventurers. But even a highway robber is good in his own way. If not to all the world, he is at least obliged to be true and loyal to his fellow ruffians. These were men fully alive to the value of commodities of all sorts. Gold was exchanged for spice, and wine and women were mixed up in their minds as they were exchanged or bartered the one for the other to satisfy the appetites of men on a large scale. Apart from other evidence, popular proverbs to this day preserve something of the atmosphere that must have prevailed. To weigh a man or a woman in gold was a familiar deal. A bag of spice when it reached a distant land, one to four months away in time, equated itself in terms of gold at the port of delivery. In Malabār 'To go to Kollam (the modern Quilon in Travancore)' was 'to lose one's Illam (i.e., family honour)', and 'To go to Kochi (as Cochin is called)' meant 'to forego one's Achi (Woman)'. Women seem to have been treated in terms of commodity value and included as an article of export or import with the connivance or for the pleasure of luxury-loving monarchs in different parts of the world.[15]

Artist and philosopher moved with buccaneers, pirates and prostitues in ships or caravans across these dialectical axes between the Mediterranean world and the Spice Coast of India. Monsoon winds did not deter them, nor did the dry desert sands where only manna (which some identify as a species of lichen) could keep them alive. Some women transported thus adorned distant harems, and often used their good offices to patronise and protect an intinerant philosopher of the type with which India then abounded, especially after the Buddhist period. Some went abroad as porters (as we have noted in the case of Ammonius Saccus the Guru of Plotinus); others probably were

15. In that classic of the spice-wine axis *Periplus Maris Erythraei* The Periplus of the Erythraean Sea, (A Guide-book to the Indian Ocean) written by an Alexandrian sea captain about the time of the Roman Emperor Nero, mention is made of the import of 'singing boys and choice girls for the royal harem'. These were, of course, imported Greeks. But there can be little doubt that human cargo was carried both ways, Greeks and others from the West to East, and Indians from East to West.

tent-menders or camel-keepers, or as clerks and storekeepers. Old medicine-men or healers like Nicodemus rubbed shoulders with merchant magnates or turbaned princes.

Coming and going in this way for centuries, a subtle Word-dialectics developed along the commercial axis, connecting the Ganges, Euphrates and Nile into one unit, as described by Dante. This dialectics has influenced the history of thought in mysteriously effective ways. Although this dialectical transmission can be traced also along the silk road across Tibet to the Pacific shores of China, and again from another aspect, across the wilderness of Central Asia to the plains of Europe and eventually to the Venice of the Doges in the Middle Ages of the West, as shown by the discoveries of explorers and scholars like Stein, Teichman, Lattimore and Yule,[16] its colour and complexion

---

16. Of these writers and scientists, perhaps the most valuable from the point of view of the tracking of Word-dialectics is Sir Aurel Stein, whose massive *Serindia,* an account of fieldwork in tracing the old Silk Road between China and India across the roof of the world, is the most interesting contribution from the evidential aspect. All along that route extending from the Pāmīrs across the wastes of the Gobi Desert to the Great Wall, this great explorer-archaeologist found ample remains, proving beyond doubt that the land route was in constant use for millenia. Finally, at Tunhwang (Blazing Beacon) on the very borders of China, where Kansu Province touches the Gobi, in 1908 he located a sealed library in the Caves of one Thousand Buddhas. Rolls and scrolls and paintings and all manner of manuscripts showed that Tunhwang was a kind of Central Asian Library of Alexandria, for besides the Buddhist relics, there were works in Sogdian, an Iranian dialect derived from Aramaic, and others in Sanskrit, in Asian Brāhmī, in Manichaean-Turkish, and in Tibetan. One large block-printed roll bore a date corresponding to AD 868 and was therefore the oldest specimen of a printed book so far known. But to us the chief interest lies in the fact that halting-places were so well organised that they developed into centres of learning and religious-philosophical study, linking up the wisdom of south India with parts of the world five thousand miles distant. And hence, aided by the commercial travellers, the Word passed on this trans-Himālayan axis to be re-kindled in the hearts of the Chinese-Mongolian peoples. The outstanding Indian visitors were from south India, and one can only mention that titanic figure, known as *bodhi-dharma* (in Chinese, Pu-ti Ta-mo), the founder of Ch'an (Japanese Zen) Buddhism in the fifth century, as typical of many who carried the Word abroad to the Far East.

→

there took on a more subdued and recessive character, although again, south Indians played a major role in carrying the Magi treasure of the Word.[17]

For at least during the historical context of the last three millennia, the head of the dialectical dragon of Word-wisdom seems to have been turning more and more westwards. The great rivers and seas formerly, and now the continents of the air are the backbones of this dragon-axis of the Word, whose head hides now under the very shadow of the tall buildings where modernism expresses itself most dominantly today.

How far have we to think back to take in the whole amplitude of the long process of the formulation of the Word? Here, to a large extent, we have to rely upon linguistic evidence. Prof. Max Muller and other authorities, since his time, have convincingly drawn the attention of the West to the fact that India, which gave the world the so-called Arabic numerals and the decimal value to the Zero, held also many philological secrets which made her a sort of elder sister to all others coming later. India was thus the key to open many locked doors in scientific and philosophic thought and in the light that India could shed, many

---

→ Marco Polo (thirteenth century) the amazing Venetian, proved that the Cambulac (Peking) and Kinsai (Hangchow) axial connexion with Constantinople and Venice was still open in his age, and for descriptions of the great trading cities of Malabār which Marco Polo visited on a mission from the Great Kubla Khan, and many other interesting features, one must refer to Sir Henry Yule's double volume *The Book of Ser Marco Polo the Venetian concerning the Kingdoms and Marvels of the East* (3rd edn., Hackluyt Society, 1903). The Word-wisdom also traversed this China-Italy axis, no doubt influencing many of the European mystics and probably Dante Alighieri who was exactly contemporaneous with Polo.

17. See para 1 of above note. In all the drawings of *bodhi-dharma* he is represented as a darkish heavy-featured individual, typical of the tough prehistoric strain which persists to this day in south India. Ostensibly Buddhist, his teaching, based on Sanskrit texts which are now only found from Chinese sources, consisted of the purely *jñāna* (Wisdom) works, those revealed by long lines of *gurus*. Hence the name for his 'School' of Buddhism, the Dhyāna (Contemplative) or Mahāyāna (Great Way).

problems could be solved or simplified.[18] This was true, Max Muller said, not only philologically, but by the style of expression of homely thoughts in a characteristic time-honoured way which was recognisable in the fables of Aesop and elsewhere.[19]

---

18. Speaking on 'What India can Teach us' before Cambridge University, Prof. Max Muller said: 'Sanskrit was the elder sister of them all and could tell of many things which the other members of the family had quite forgotten.' He continued to describe how the expression *I am* had behind it a long philological history, although it appears natural now. He traced this simple expression with its root *AS* (to breathe) and thence to *ASMI* (I am) and concluded that 'great efforts of our forefathers are to be found in such and other expressions originating in Proto-Aryan speech.'

    The same leading scholar declared: 'If I were asked what I considered the most important discovery of the nineteenth century with respect to the ancient history of mankind, I should answer by the following short line: Sanskrit *Dyaus Pitar* equals Greek *Zeus Pater* equals Latin *Juppiter* equals Old Norse *Tyr.*' And in his *Preface* to his Gifford Lectures before the University of Glasgow in 1892, he gives the clue to his imaginative-scientific genius. 'My endeavour has been', he said, 'to submit to facts only, such as we find them in the Sacred Books of the East, to try to decipher and understand them as we try to decipher and understand the geological annals of the earth, and to discover in them reason, cause and effect, and if possible, that close genealogical coherence which alone can change empirical into scientific knowledge. This genealogical method is no doubt the most perfect when we can follow the growth of religious ideas, as it were, from son to father, from pupil to teacher, from the negative to the positive stage' and again: 'My object was to show that there is a constant action and reaction in the growth of religious ideas. . . . It has been my chief object to show that this reaction was produced or at least accelerated by the historical contact between Semitic and Aryan thought chiefly at Alexandria. . . .' and 'I have tried to show that the doctrine of the Logos, the very life-blood of Christianity, is exclusively Aryan.'

19. See Max Müller: *On the Migration of Fables,* in *Chips* from *a German Workshop,* iv, 412. *Selected Essays,* i.500. The oldest folk-stories, woven into the web of European literature (as Rawlinson tells us) may be traced to those great Indian collections of tales, the Buddhist *Jātakas* or Birth-stories, the *Pañcatantra* and the *Hitopadeśa* or Book of Useful Counsels. (These include not only Aesop's Fables, but such common tales as the Judgement of Solomon, Sindbad the Sailor, the Fables of Pilpay, the Welsh story of Llewellyn and Gelert, and most remarkable of all, the story of Josaphat [a concealed Bodhisat!] etc.).

If this is true of India as a whole, it is all the more true of the extreme south. The affinities of the Word if thus traced, would help us to see how the joking remark of Nārāyaṇa Guru to which we alluded at the beginning assumes a more and more reasonable light of probability. The languages of south India, collectively known as the Dravidian group (including Tamil, Malayālam, Kannaḍa, Tulu, Kota, Toda, Telugu), as well as the central Dravidian group (consisting of Gondhi, Kurukh, Mālṭo, Bhīl, Kolamī and Naiki), and also inclusive of an ancient Dravidian remnant in Baluchistan known as Brahui, have all unmistakable prehistoric affinities which take us back from four to eight thousand years before Christ.[20] There are in language peculiar interjections, maintained especially by peasantry, with vowel or consonant intonations, doublings and other features, all having a homely personality of their own which subtly flavour a living langauge and elude exact definitive research based only on outward evidences.[21] It is akin to the memory-recognition of tone and sound whereby a dog knows its master's voice. Pure memory, as we have tried to show, thereby supports itself on such *a priori* elements, and when such pure memory is given attention it conveys convincing meanings and indicates kinships all charged with depth of understanding, concerning puzzling relationships otherwise inexplicable.

The unique approach to matters of historical affinities that

---

20. R. Narasimhacharya writes: 'The Sumerian or Accadian language which was non-Semitic and earlier than Assyrian and Babylonian, was beginning to be a dead language as early as 2000 BC. The Sumerian civilization must have been an old-established one long before 3800 BC, which is about the date of the earliest of their written documents that have yet been discovered. . . .The language has, like the Dravidian group, the characteristic of agglutination and vowel harmony' (p.13, *History of the Kannada Language,* University of Mysore, 1934. Cf. also Sweet's *History of Language.*)

21. The Kings of Judah were bewailed at their death with the phrase, *Hoi Adon,* 'Alas ! O Lord !' (Jeremiah XXXIV,5): so says Langdon on pp.76-77 of his *Mythology of All Races,* vol. V., and adds that this custom 'belongs to the sphere of Semitic religion profoundly influenced by Babylonia. In its development it was essentially of the Tammuz cult transplanted to Phoenicia', etc.

we have recommended and developed in this chapter of our work, will enable us to discover what evidence is relevant amid the many varied and miscellaneous items, as a magnet can quickly find the iron filings in a huge mass of sawdust; and in this way we can now perhaps see clearly the evergreen nature of the Word-formula as it has expressed itself in the naturally favourable environment of south India.

Traced backwards to its pristine, natural source, such evidence gains in volume of convincing character as we approach the essential Word in its purity and simplicity. In later periods philosophy is of the nature of an elaboration of a fundamental human truth, a human truth known to the humblest members of the race from time immemorial.[22] The south Indian contemplative matrix, the soil of spirituality, once again repeats the same simple Word-formula through its representative Guru Nārāyaṇa, in whom many aspects of philosophical speculation from widely dispersed regions of the world come together focally to neutralise themselves in the simplicity of a brilliant zero.

Many are the problems that in this way become simplified. Let us, for example, take Dionysius, around which name veil upon veil of mystery is enshrouded. It is the name of the nature-god of the ancients. The same name continues to be applied to various divinities or semi-human heroes or mystical personalities. The very fact that a cultured Greek, Megasthenes, who came to India as an Ambassador in 302 BC at once recognised the affinities between this ancient Greek divinity and Śiva, although discredited by many writers, holds out a challenging

---

22. Cf., that wonderful chapter, called *Ma Thi* or *Horses' Hoofs,* written by the third century BC. Tao Guru, Chuang Tzu, in south China, in which, from the Word-Way or Tao-Teh, the earliest so-called primitives who were without class, caste and the knowledge of differences, are shown to have had their own natural integrity and happiness, and man lived at ease and friendship with nature, naturally virtuous.

    Cf., also chapters in the *Tao Te Ching* of Lao Tzu, especially Nos. 37, 40 and 80. (*Sacred Books of the East,* vols. XXXIX & XL).

suggestion.[23] Dionysius was variously called the Divine Bacchus, the Young Tyonee, Evan, Iacchus and Lenee.[24] The elephant, tiger, bull and tree are associated with this divinity as with Śiva. His relations with women votaries and the manner of his espousal with Ariadne, the daughter of the snake and bull worshipping Minos of Crete,[25] his visit to India and the mystery-plays at Eleusis near Athens,[26] from where the name seems to have passed on

---

23. Dr. Jane Harrison, a noted anthropologist, writing of Dionysius, says: 'Another trait marks Dionysos off from the Olympians. They are wholly human; He keeps about him some vestiges of plant and animal shape. He is tree-god (dendrites), and at will he can change himself back into plant or animal form. When the Bacchantes in extreme peril call upon Dionysos for vengeance, his ancient incarnations loom in upon their maddened minds:

    Appear, appear, whatso thy shape or name,
    O Mountain Bull, Snake of the Hundred Heads,
    Lion of the Burning Flame !
    O God, Beast, Mystery, come !

    (The poem quoted is from Prof. Gilbert Murray's Euripides *Bacchantes,* see pp.76-77 *Myths of Greece and Rome* by Jane Harrison, Benn, London, 1928.) The similarities between Dionysos and Śiva, quite apart from the many-headed Snake are patent, likewise the (fig?) tree motif.

24. See *Etudes et fragments* of the French poet André Marie de Chénier (1762-94), in which the lines occur:

    Viens, O divin Bacchus, ô jeune Thyonée,
    O Dionyse, Évan, Iacchus et Lénée......

25. See *Palace of Minos,* by Sir Arthur Evans (4 vols. 1921-35).

26. Nielsen traces the Dionysian religion to the ancient Bull and Snake religion of the Minoan civilization of Crete (3000 BC) and says it had 'to be hidden underground' in Greece at the time when Attica was overrun by the Doric invasions. (See his *The Minoan-Mycenean Religion and its Survival in Greek Religion.*) Later, a compromise was made with the Appolonian Sun religion, and Delphi the ancient centre of Greek faith, was actually shared between the sky-dwelling Olympians and the earthy Dionysius.

    From the inscriptions and wall-paintings in the so-called tombs or underground chambers in Central Italy, in Etruria, which have so far baffled all efforts to decipher or fit into the setting of European history, it might be suggested that here is another Dionysian-Śiva link. The tree, the bull, the fish motifs and the spirit of frenzy are prominent and resemble the pictographs of far-off Mohenjo-Dāro in India. (See Phaidon *Etruscans,* and *Etruscan Places* by D.H. Lawrence, Penguin Books, 1950.)

into the closed Christian preserves, through Dionysius the Areopagite, sometimes mistaken for Dionysius the theologian, (called pseudo or true)[27] — all these offer interesting titbits for thinkers in tracking the Word-affinities too complicated to enter into here.

To turn to another part of what is the same mystery, we find in the *New Testament*, John the Baptist wearing 'camel's hair, and with a girdle of a skin about his loins'[28] or even the Prophet Elias or Elijah, who was another hermit and 'a hairy man dressed in skins',[29] both apparently belonging to the pre-historic context of the Word. St. Denis the patron saint of France and Bishop of Paris who is also Dionysius (in Latin), honoured by the earliest kings of France, must also be considered as belonging to the same potent influence of the Word with its affinities reaching far into modern spirituality itself.

Our object here is not to prove anything or to displace any view that may now be accepted. It is rather to look at the same facts from a new angle, in a more contemplative manner which involves and employs pure memory factors dynamically rather than by the more usual way of viewing them statically or mechanistically. What are called proofs often prove nothing of any value, whereas integrative affinities understood generously, with the contemplative imagination can only strengthen bonds

---

27. Evelyn Underhill, well-known writer on Christian mysticism, says: 'To Dionysius the Areopagite (probably a Syrian monk who lived between AD 475 and 525), Christian literature owes the paradoxical concept of the Absolute Godhead as the 'Divine Dark', the unconditioned, the negation of all that *is*, i.e., of all that surface consciousness perceives — and of the soul's attainment of the Absolute as a 'divine ignorance,' a way of negation. The idea is common to Greek and Indian philosophy. With Dionysius it enters the Catholic World' (p.457 of *Mysticism,* Evelyn Underhill, 1930).

28. *St. Mark,* i.6.

29. See *Old Testament II Kings,* i,8: also *I Kings,* xvii-xix. Elijah (Elias) is treated as a venerable *guru*, with *śiṣya*s such as Obadiah who falls on his face at his feet, and Elisha, etc., who apparently lives with fifty 'sons' of the prophets, i.e., spiritual sons, disciples of some other *guru*.

between one race and another, between one tradition and another. The spiritual treasures for which some are willing to lay down their lives must be recognised in common human terms. And if approached humanly with common understanding as the aim in view, our manner of studying the Word affinities as indicated here, may be helpful. Until we discover that we are of one true blood, we may see brightnesses because of divergencies in the actual factual conditions, but with greater inward light we shall see the common one Word factor lighting up all the modes, only varying in given situations.

If a common sense proof was insisted upon we could think of no more valid one than the average south Indian peasant. Imagine a Christian missionary approaching him with the Bible, intent on preaching the Gospel of Christ. To the peasant the language, the style, the phraseology and the figures of speech would present no problems. Indeed they would all seem homely and would ring familiarly in his ears. And this applies not only to the texture of the *Old Testament* but also to the dialectical subtleties of the Christian scriptures, such as the almost Vedāntic-sounding chapters of *St John's Gospel.*

The opening lines of *St.John,* 'In the beginning was the Word and the Word was with God and the Word was God' would have the same authentically familiar ring as his own time-honoured spiritual language.

Even the parables and figures of speech have the same homely note. Although it sounds unfinished and queer in the English version, 'Blessed are the poor in spirit'[30] speaks a home-truth when translated into any Indian language. Add to these the innumerable other suggestive features of a miscellaneous nature, such as baptising with water, anointing with oils and spices, eating loaves and fishes, speaking to a woman at the well, rolling up one's bed and walking away with it, washing the feet of guests and out of faith wiping them with one's hair, and such items as burnt offerings, the anointing of dressed-up stones,

30. *St. Mathew,* v.3.

the pillar of light, the fig-free under which Jesus met John and the parable of a fig-tree and that of the mustard-seed, the offering of fruits, and vinegar drinking and even living on locusts and wild honey, in caves, in the hills and wildernesses. All these sound not at all out of place or exotic to the ears of the Indian peasant.

And so is that 'Kill not' commandment, so often explained away in the West, rightly received by him.[31] The preaching of Christianity to the country people of India gives rise to a situation which is not without its humorous side, an aspect which is not missed by the shrewd common man or woman who listens to the fervent preacher of a 'true religion' who wants to save the souls of the audience by teaching them what they already accept almost instinctively without question. The 'message' after going the rounds of time and space, returns to its original home where it has always been part of the mental climate.

As the elder sister — or mother — in the preservation of the Word, in its pure Vedānta form, India and particularly south India, in her great Word-representative, the Guru Nārāyaṇa, accepts all reality implicit in the holy Word, as *Brahman* or Logos, silently assenting in the all-embracing formula of *Auṁ* or *Amen*.

---

31. *St. Matthew,* xxii, 37-39: 'Thou shalt love the Lord thy God with all thy heart, and with all thy soul, and with all thy mind. This is the first and great commandment. And the second is like unto it, Thou shalt love thy neighbour as thyself'.

15

The Ascending Dialectics of Stone-Language

In the East, more than elsewhere perhaps, wisdom often enshrines itself in images. Iconology in India becomes as important as theology is in the West. In its own way it speaks the profound and secret language of dialectics. Although the simple Śiva *liṅgam* (mark) is just a round upright stone which is decorated and annointed, it becomes an eloquent presence, an inspiring noumenal hierophany.

But as we travel westwards, away from the primeval or primitive centre of the Word in the heart of south India, the originally pure hierophany begins to be discredited, until finally it is only a fugitive radial thread, almost entirely overwhelmed and almost invisible in the midst of environing doctrines, prophecies and rigid commandments.[1] Historically, as soon as the Word in its transmission down through the ages and across the oceans, attains a certain recognition, it is revalued. This revaluation frequently manifests through statues, idols or images, crude or refined as works of 'art,' and these are often epitomes of all the Word-value hitherto recognised by the parent symbol; but nevertheless, at each stage in

1. The noumenal is, however, irrepressible and often assumes other forms which are less recognisably iconic: some growing from a reasonable stem, others parastitic on the tree of sentiment, and others plainly absurd. Thus the Bible, fresh from the press with the printer's ink half dried, becomes iconic. A nouminous aura surrounds old landmarks, historical sites, national flags, etc. Then there are private relics endowed with the noumenal, such as the manuscripts of poets and kings; and then the descent to the purely sentimental, the locks of hair of dead parents or personal bric-a-brac from infancy, etc., — all of which have the power of recollecting presences imbued with greater or lesser affectiveness. For the evocative presence and not for the often trifling item itself, individuals or nations even are willing to fight to the death.

passage of the Word, its revalued iconological expression proclaims itself to suit the 'novelty' in which its votaries live out their daily lives, and they feel its renewed significance both through memory and intuitive imagination.

However, as with a verbal doctrine, its comprehension is limited to the intelligence and understanding of the subject, and hence, even with the same symbol, the individual response may be a dull subdued lambency or it may be a radiant blaze. For our part here, because the earlier writings of Nārāyaṇa Guru contain much of this subtle popular image-language-dialectics incorporating Word-verities of rare mystical value, it seems profitable for us to pass in quick review over some of the implications of Indian iconography.

On the Indian soil one of the distinctive features of this Word-iconography is that it synthesises both doctrine and sacred presence, both the teaching and the noumenous feeling. In the prophetic religions — Judaism, Islam and Calvinism — sacred presences tend to be discarded in favour of legalistic doctrines, and where this tendency has come about suddenly, encouraged by social circumstances (as in the case of the Reformation in Germany), it has often developed an iconoclastic turn. Yet in spite of this hatred of idols and idolatry, sacred objects still persist within the body of such protestant religions. Mecca has its Kāba and the Bible even in severely Protestant Christian countries, is regarded with a kind of invested noumenical awe, and regularly used in courts of justice as a silent powerful witness to the truthfulness of the attestants.

The icon treated as a symbol belongs to language, but considered as an object, it is stone, wood, metal, paper, etc., — just matter. But not even the simplest idolator in India takes the idol to be 'just matter.' It says something to him, however vague or crude that may be.

Some sort of sacred object, whether in the form of a marble statue or wooden totem, persists among human beings, whether known as cultured or primitive. The 'primitive' is one poor enough to be laughed at while the 'cultured' idolator is called a dilettante, a *connoisseur des objets d'art.* The difference is not at all mutual exclusion but relative or even reciprocal. The uncultured African Negro carves what has been called his 'god machines', while the often puritanical collector looks down on the carver but takes pride in exhibiting the carvings themselves. Thus a certain type of dilettanteism goes with its own counterpart of puritanism or iconoclasm; but when toted up in the arithmetic of values, both together constitute the sum of what human nature demands by way of spiritual appetites and satisfactions.

If we hope to follow the implicit dialectics of Indian iconology, there are some primary notions which must be borne in mind. We have to note the existence of an old order of values, then additions to the old order; crystallisations and constant revaluations as hardening processes set in during the unravelling of the panorama of history; submergence almost, then resuscitation and fresh recognition under revaluation, each revaluation being for the general good, the fluid Word spreading like a benediction over the affective territory.[2]

The dumb stones require a traditionally trained or dialectically contemplative ear attuned to the message of their secret sermons. The enigmatic Sphinx and the tranquil majesty of the Kāmakūra Buddha whisper the same secret to the initiates of each Word-culture, whether they are dedicated Egyptian hierophants or Zen *brahmacārīs*.

If the tracing of the Word through history was like sailing in a fog, then our present task is like exploring in the Stygian gloom of

---

2. In *Traite d'Histoire des Religions* by Prof. Mircea Eliade of the University of Bucarest (Payot, Paris, 1949), confirmation of what is implied here is elaborately worked out by an authority of high academic status. It is to the author of this work that the present writer owes the expression 'dialectical revaluation of hierophanies.' One sentence by way of a sample may be quoted from this book. Prof. Eliade writes: *'Nous recontrerons un nombre considerable de telles revalorisations des hièrophanies primordiales, l'histoire des religions étant, en grande partie, l'histoire de devalorisations et des revalorisations du proces de manifestation du sacré'.* ('We find a considerable number of such revaluations among primordial hierophanies, the history of religions being for the most part the history of devaluations and revaluations of the process of representing the holy.') pp.35-36, *ibid.*

the Catacombs. To follow the intricacies of the Word across the multi-textured entanglements of the forest of Indian icons and myths where the Word, like some rare bird flitting from tree, to tree is forever moving from one revaluation to another, needs very special equipment, an inner sagacity to discover the evidence that what we seek is here and not there. Indeed, to use a simile common to Vedāntic literature, it is like tracking the musk deer by its scent. Both a certain naive simplicity and an innocent yogic eye of honesty must be our main guides, and we must abandon the leadership of both loud erudition and pontifical authority, even as simple jungle-dwellers wearing a dress of leaves and bark can follow where uniformed and heavily equipped hunters have to be left behind. For the quest of the Word we require *Simplicitas Dei* — the simplicity of God.

The key to the dialectics of the Word may be said to be that resultant synthesis and fusion of values uniting from the opposite ends of a central nouminous Absolute Verity. The Word in its endurance through time may be compared to the formation of the white limestone pillars found in deep caverns, where the icicle-like stalactites pendant from the roof meet the conical stalagmites from below, but both due to the same imperceptible drippings and tricklings of calcium bicarbonate solution percolating slowly through the centuries. Stalagmite needs stalctite to form the pillar. Time does not count here. The common solution of lime ignores the difference between the downward and the upward movements. At last, after layer upon layer has been deposited, they meet in an eternal present. Thus ambivalance cancels itself out gradually. The common value-factor is always there. From the prehistoric drummings throbbing in the antique darkness far from civilization, to the modern orchestral concert played in a fashionable city hall, the basic value of rhythm and melody remains the same. What has been there primordially, in the 'for ever' that is the essence of the eternal present, is music that was and is pleasing to the hearers. In every case of music, old or new, however varied the instruments or strange the sounds, there has been someone to compose and produce the melodies and someone to respond appreciatively. Sound-form and formless happiness of hearing thus come together. In the same way the simple Indian peasant who took a plain dark stone and made it holy and sacred, dialectically related form and idea so that they met in the central Word, thus bypassing the danger of 'the letter that killeth,' and ever revealing to the inner eye the white marble pillar of pure vision.

At the ancient temple-city of Cidambaram (literally: *Mind-space*) there is a famous bronze statue of Śiva which is worshipped by hundreds of thousands of persons each year. The temple is dedicated to that aspect of Śiva as Naṭarāja (the Dancing King). The towers of this temple scrape the skies with rows of golden spires. The votaries here are undoubted survivals of an ethnic group who have defied the ravages of time. Their remote ancestors traded with far-off lands when India's glory was renowned and with characteristic devotion they built these fabulous monuments to represent their own iconologic formulation of divinity.

And still today as ever, festivals in temples such as these in south India attract enormous crowds, absorbing a lavish expenditure of flowers and incense. Drummers and clarinet-players come from far-off corners of this ancient land. Tradition survives with the wilful necessity of the car of Jagannātha. Again, as millennia before, it is the prehistoric Śiva whose glory is celebrated in contemporary India. This bronze dancing image marks the culmination, as it were, of a certain genealogical line of iconographic dialectics. The potent, primitive, fecund and animistic presence of double power for divine protection and at the same time ominous destruction, to which we drew attention in writing of the early Mohenjo-Dāro seals, offers essentially the same enigma in this frenzied abandon of Śiva as the King of Dionysiac dance.

With these two examples in our minds of the prehistoric Śiva as the jungle hunter-*yogī* and as the triumphant Dancer of Cidambaram, it is possible for us to examine how the language of stones is employed to explain perennial wisdom or mystical doctrine. We have already noted how the Indus Valley seals often represent a spiritual truth or value around the personality of Śiva. As

Nārāyaṇa Guru used to say, Śiva was a simple hunter of prehistory who, because of his goodness, was loved by his contemporaries and later became sanctified.

The Śiva imagery has had various lines of growth as it has been transmitted from land to land, the original imagery modified, transformed and grafted on to many different bodies of thought and religions. Within the bounds of India itself where idolatry was accepted as a recognised mode dialectically familiar to the genius of the south Indian villager especially, the Śiva tradition enriched mythology and supplied many archetypal foundations for later iconographic elaborations of the spiritual formula.

Here we must try to give a few explanations of the chief usage of the Śiva-Word-formula as it found expression through the development of this imagery-language. Each member of the sacred family of Śiva became representative of some aspect or other of the applied spiritual formula.

Thus Gaṇeśa, the child-god of elephant-head and satisfied appetite, the eldest son of Śiva and his consort Pārvatī the huntress, was the personification of relaxation, contentment and calm contemplation. This induced the same qualities and attitude in the votary or seeker after wisdom. Good could only accrue when Gaṇeśa (or Gaṇapati as he is sometimes called) had been duly worshipped and propitiated. Wholeness (or holiness) normality, health, balance and all the other middle qualities, including a global sympathy, dwell together in the mind of the devotee when he meditates on this Gaṇeśa-symbol of the Śiva tradition.

In the Śiva hierogeny another iconomorph is Subrahmaṇya, also called Kārttikeya, the younger brother of Gaṇeśa. As the war-god, Kārttikeya provides a more positive note, the power to counter evil effectively. In glorious lightness of body he rides a peacock. He was born of light from the contemplative middle eye of Śiva. He has six heads, luminous like brilliant suns or stars. To sing his hymn of praise meant to emancipate oneself from the thraldom of evil and suffering. Thus many emphatic psychological and cosmological images were telescoped together in a single divine personality created for the mass mind, by the mystical votary of wisdom or self-realisation.

Pārvatī, goddess, wife and mother, also typified a number of grades of nouminous feeling, each with its own iconographic representation. She could be the personification of the tragic power of creative becoming, the great irresistible urge that dominates phenomenal nature. This is the consort-counterpart of Śiva as Mother Kālī, the Terrible as well as the Beneficent.

Pārvatī-Kālī is thus the correlating principle of all manifestation both in its positive and negative modes. She becomes good or evil depending upon the requirements of the worshipper, for consolation or correction. This ambivalence is true of all sacred presences whether represented physically or conceived mentally. God is to be feared and loved, at the same time an object of attraction and repulsion, both hated and adored. And so from this one multi-personal feminine principle many symbolical characters have emerged, as Umā, Kārtyāyanī, Gaurī, Kālī, Haimavatīśvarī, etc., each successively portraying some one aspect in varying degree of divine tragedy or delight.

Into the positive reality thus visualised the idea of negative *māyā* (phenomenal becoming) has to be understood. When traced to its emergent source it is united to the head of Śiva, as the primal cosmic principle. This transcendent source is invisible but from there arise all beneficent creative principles. Iconologically, the Ganges, the greatest river in India, source of existence to millions of people, is therefore symbolically the greatest of human values or goods; and it is appropriate also, that the cornucopious Mother Gaṅgā should be imagined as gushing from the head of Śiva.

When intimately associated with wisdom, the tragic modes of Kālī are superseded by the gracious mode of the gentle goddess Sarasvatī, who is always clothed in radiant white and born of a pure lotus as the first of creation. Tender-hearted as the Madonna, her Indian lyre, the *vīṇā*, glorifies art, while the book she carries extols the contemplative search for wisdom. In Sarasvatī the *brahmacārī* and the Vedāntic novice have a saintly or divine Mother, who, like the Sophia of the Greek and Christian records, ever inspires and elevates the seeker, sublimating all instinctive weaknesses into the courageous conquest of repressions and weaknesses, constantly weaning him from the old habitual ways, until as a spiritual athlete he attains full rank in the inner courts of this Indian Queen of Wisdom and *rāja-yoga*.

The image-language of the Śiva iconographic family has elaborate ramifications. The peasant devotee can sing endlessly rich and meaningful lyrics intended to stimulate his nouminous understanding in the ascending dialectics till the light of wisdom triumphs. From the pedestal step represented by the virile power of the bull (Nandī) upon which Śiva rides, step by step upwards through all the degrees of the symbolical *scala perfectionis* or spiritual ladder to perfection, the Śiva imagery inwardly supports the aspirant, towering higher and higher until there is attainment by likeness contemplatively with that sacred central eye of wisdom's fire before whose eruptive glance all doubts and ignorances are withered and consumed never more to rise. Thus is attained the terminus of all spiritual travail in that pure and holy domain of Absolute Goodness and Kindly Abundance.

Through this long ascent, the statue of Naṭarāja, God of the Cosmic Dance, represents a culminating station in the graded formulation of the Śiva Word-principle.

The virtue of the simple round Śiva-stone consists in this, that it suffices to recall all these associations. This is the language it speaks, while to those who are unaware of its eloquence it is just a dull dumb rock. And what this nouminous object by its natural limitations cannot do, is supplemented by the stanzas of adoration sung with instrumental accompaniment in the great and venerable temples of south India whose foundations were laid in the times of antiquity.

The stone of Śiva is sometimes a pillar, to be 'read' in the dialectical language as an endless column of light, a shining presence of verticality, typifying the Absolute Principle which is neither matter nor mind, but neutrally supersessive, solvent and

Śiva and Pārvati on Nandi, the bull (Thanjavur painting)

reconciliatory of all antinomies and oppositions implicit in existence and truth. This pillar of light, effulgent and haloed with glory, reaches from heaven to earth. Viṣṇu as the boar in the icon-language could not dig out the bottom of this pillar without end, nor could Brahmā (the highest of the gods of existence) as a swan fly to its top. Such is the greatness of the Śiva pillar of light, illustrative of the mystery of the unknown, as defined in later supplementary accounts.

In almost endless variety artists have interpreted the glory and light of the Śiva presence. Readers will remember that Śiva form known as Dakṣiṇāmūrti, the *guru* who sits on a raised stone platform facing the south — perhaps in recognition of the ancient mother-source of his wisdom, just as Mohammedans turn devotedly towards Meccā. We have already noted elsewhere the Word-idea accompanying this *guru* model. In iconology Dakṣiṇāmūrti is seen as the luminous *guru* with his fingers forming the *jñāna-mudrā* (gesture of wisdom) either facing the disciple or the supplicant. Jaina and Buddhist images must also be said to belong 'linguistically' to the same icon-context. Later exponents of the icon-language used more eloquent 'phrases,' exercising their ingenuity and creative imagination ultimately in the Cosmic Śiva of the mystical dance, the Naṭarāja or Tāṇḍava. Nowadays this figure is recognised all over the world as a masterpiece of significant form. In some degree or other this striking creation of Indian mystical art speaks a direct language outside the dictionaries of diverse peoples. Scholars have elaborated its meaning fairly minutely, but in the light of the suggestions developed in these pages we must add some relevant remarks.

The positive majesty of the protective blessing Śiva is expressed in a cosmic dance over the inert body, whose recumbancy signifies the negative aspect. For the glory of truth to shine it requires its own anterior background of weakness, negation and falsehood. The achievement of wisdom is of the nature of a triumph of a certain personal value, a victory that discards its elephant and tiger-skin crudeness or lethargy — as Śiva is supposed to have done when he frenziedly danced in ecstasy in the forest by the light of the crescent moon. Although awe-inspiring, he really meant to be kind to all. In the same dramatic image-language, it was he who drank the poison, which is so disastrous for humanity, during the churning of the milk-ocean, thus making him the saviour of humanity. In the eternal conflict between good and evil, that poison represents the middle region of doubt and uncertainty. The virile Śiva principle, rational and assertive, absorbs and digests this third factor of absurdity. Hence in the legend Śiva drinks the poison, and forever afterwards has the honoured title of Blue-Throated (Nīla-kaṇṭha).

These and many other associated ideas are familiar to the common man in India, conveying immense content of doctrinal meaning in applied psychological and cosmological wisdom, which, to be grasped or used properly in everyday practice requires direct imaginative intuition.

Śiva's dance, known to the art-world of India, has the special name of Tāṇḍava. It is the full manifestation of masculine vigour, and adds special character to the language of the Naṭarāja image. Thus to the intuitive mind of India the single Śiva-Naṭarāja dancing the Tāṇḍava equals, what in the West would take centuries of sermonizing to accomplish. Locked up in one expressive symbol is the material for volumes of religion and philosophy, epitomised and telescoped.

Nurtured in the traditional spiritual climate of Śiva adoration, the common people of India are familiar with all the implications of this effective compact compendium in bronze. Meaning is aided by the stories and songs related or sung under the village trees or in temple courtyards by peripatetic minstrel *puṇḍita*s. Although considered illiterate, there are many homely grandmothers in rural households who know well the secret mystical doctrines in their own unacademic or unofficial way. Thus the hidden or ignored domestic or country life of India enables Wisdom to survive through generations. The wisdom heritage is cultivated further by being incorporated into the institution of the *āśrama*, which often combines temple, monastery and community life. Here the *guru* and *śiṣya*s live with the co-operation of idealistic members in a natural, unconventional commune of common unlimited liability, open to all to whom the pure ideal appeals. These institutions empha-sise the wisdom more or less consciously, and more or less secretly, according to the immemorial traditions of perennial wisdom, handed down from Master to Disciple. Some of these traditionally-inherited *āśramas* may have degenerated, which is natural, but this does not prevent new ones from emerging, and endeavouring to sustain the original aims and high ideals.

Within the scope of our remarks here it is impossible to do any justice to these subjects, even in outline. Only long familiarity with the image-language can disclose the unitive scheme of Word-wisdom which is the alpha-omega of this whole subject. The key to this strange stony linguistics is the enigma of the Word with its double-values or ambivalence. Every image seeks to clarify or draw attention to the nouminous Absolute essence, and hence icon stands upon icon, in vertical procession and successive transcendence, re-affirming the prime purpose in revalued terms, preserving the wisdom-aim, conserving the past expressions, but adapting the theme of imagery to suit the advancing transformations of new generations both religiously and socially. But all manifestations or elaborations speak the secret of the Guru-Word which remains ever the same, and which is ultimately best expressed in the full-flooded silence beyond all imagery of language or stone. After the crashing thunder of the musical symphony comes the still silence of heaven when all the vibratory waves of sound and thought are calmed and in that absolute tranquillity only the pure Word itself floods all with the cool splendour of moonlight. If our words too seem strained and hurtled impetuously at the reader, it is to one end only, the inducing of the after-silence where our words cannot go.

Contemporary India, particularly in the south, is still steeped in this image-ideology of the adoration of the Śiva of prehistoric times. The language of icon and myth is in everyday use and is instinctively understood by the poeple. Once in a modern part of the city of Madras the present writer was waiting for a bus. He then heard some children of an adjoining primary school singing in chorus some popular song just before achieving their freedom from the boredom of school-hours. As the words of the song struck the ear of the listener, he felt a conflict, for at that time a dichotomy or ambivalence of sentiment was in his mind, the desire for decent standards of education for citizenship alternately struggling with an appreciation of the rich heritage of India. But as the verses from an ancient bard came from the lips of these innocent boys and girls he was aware that they were too young to be either shocked or profoundly moved by them. Translated, the following are some of the words of this old song:

O Madman, Crescent-wearer,
Mighty Master, mercy-filled,
To Thy thraldom to demur
How can I ever ! O Father mine . . . . .?

The song then stopped, but soon again the little voices renewed the refrain. Again it was to the ancient Śiva. It rang out:

O Thou of radiant golden form
With tiger-pelt around Thy waist,
And bronzed hair and middle eye;
Except of Thee, O Father dear,
How can I for a moment even think !

This slight sketch of the relation of the dialectics of the *guru*-formula would be incomplete without some reference to our main theme; hence before concluding our examination of icon and myth we must refer to that living image which was the personal aspect of Guru Nārāyaṇa himself.

Both Sanskrit and Tamil-Malayālam traditions, both north and south India, accept the principle of identity of *guru* and God. To unite the two currents of theology and mystical teaching is the task of *guru*-hood. In such an equation of *guru* with God, every movement, posture, attitude or gesture in the actual person of the *guru* is as important as the abstract teaching. All the time he is under the limelight of a devout and watchful public and hence there must not and cannot be any withdrawal from the stage of teaching, even by the flickering of an eyelid. The form is only the anterior half of the idea (or name) which is the posterior half; while both together combined give a central unitive totality as when similar correlations are expressed either by geometrical or algebraic methods in modern mathematics. The same fundamental relation is revealed by either. Similarly the form which preserves the past is the pedestal for the idea which is the abstract doctrine. These meet, extremes are cancelled and the result is a central non-dual unity which is the Silence and the Word.

And so it was once in the same city of Madras in 1925 that the Guru was one day missing since the early hours of the morning. As was habitual with him, he had left his bed without being seen, and had gone out for a long early-morning walk by himself, leaving behind a group of *brahmacārins*, *saṁnyāsins* and laymen who comprised his entourage. All of them, bewildered, set out to find the missing Guru. They went to his favourite haunts, one of which was a scheduled spot on the sea beach, where a cluster of shady trees, a bridge and a river, broke the sandy monotony of the sea front. A horse and carriage had also been sent by one of his hosts.

After hours of vain search, when the disc of the sun had already risen over the eastern horizon, making the sweeping billows of the Bay of Bengal gleam like a drawn sword, from under the dark shade of a tree the Guru made his appearance. Without ado or speech he got into the waiting carriage. Fisherfolk living nearby were still asleep as the horse trotted along. Some, including the writer, sat in the carriage with him while the rest followed on foot. The Guru then chatted on the importance of names in giving a sense of reality to an existent thing. The name, he said, when coupled with form, finalised a notion, and therefore to destroy a false notion, the abolishing of the name went a long way. He said that thus caste prejudices could be avoided.

We arrived at the host's house. After the fatigue of the early morning's 'chase' had somewhat abated, it was arranged that the Guru would be photographed. The cameraman had already arrived, but Nārāyaṇa Guru raised his usual objections. On the insistence of all, he sat on a leopard-skin spread on a raised seat, on the sunny terrace of the house. Murmuring protests about something or other that was not just right, he was at last prevailed upon to sit in the usual cross-legged posture of repose, confronting the camera.

Across the Guru's features there appeared an expression which the writer had never noticed so clearly marked at any time before. His casual countenance dropped its former mild indifference and became deep and clear. The eyes seemed to be looking into pure space. The corners of the lips curved downwards a little, in an expression which was neither a smile nor a serious frown, but connected, it seemed, with something unrelated to the events that went on around him, something which absorbed him to its very depths. A mild form of 'ecstasy' must have been there, but this was almost imperceptible to all but the trained eye of one familiar with such effects of the yogic tradition. One had to look carefully to discover in the clear-eyed features of the Guru the secret gesture or *mudrā*. Evidently, on merely being asked to assume the posture of the *yogī*, sensitive as he was to each little suggestion in the air, Nārāyaṇa Guru had lapsed into the traditional *yogī* state.

A *saṁnyāsin* standing by seemed to disturb the calm repose into which the Guru had fallen, by holding out to him a small silk pouch of holy ashes. Thus disturbed, the Guru questioned its need and for a minute seemed to object. 'Is it necessary?' he asked. 'Yes,' was the response in almost insistent tone. Thoughtfully, the Guru dipped three of his fingers delicately into the grey ashes, and with the tips of the three fingers made the orthodox triple streaks of ash on his forehead. But the quantity of ashes he had thus taken was barely sufficient to make the beginnings of the lines visible and then only half-way across the forehead. Thus the lines were both visible and invisible, present and fugitive at the same time, a subtle display perhaps half-consciously implied revealing how, under the dialectics of chance or occasionalism, the Guru wished to be both orthodox and heterodox at the same time.

This fuss and detail seems almost futile, banal and moody if it is not understood as part of the unique language of *guru*-hood, when known as it is in India and elsewhere in its esoteric significance. Every odd situation provides an opportunity for the exhibition of the teaching. The Guru himself has to express, as a *guru*, the Guru-Word through behaviour of personality, as well as through posture, gesture, passing expressions, signs, subtle hints, indications, in addition to speech and other methods of communication. Behaviour-teaching becomes as essential as the spoken instruction. To those who stood around him, the actions of the Guru spoke the Word-language while he himself remained neutrally withdrawn within his own sphere of inner meditation. He was the *yogī* and had no objection to the animal skin on which he sat; because for one reason, the leopard was no longer alive, and for another reason, it was part of the recognised paraphernalia or traditionally fixed appointments of the *yogī*, adopted as essential and inherited from the days of the prehistoric Śiva, belonging to what had become, through ages of association and habit, part of the necessary being of people's lives. In this case the Guru's objections would have been unavailing. Helpless to abolish the past, he therefore accepted it with graceful resignation, while using it as a pedestal from which to declare his revalued Guru-Śiva message, one of the principles of which was a strong disapproval of killing. But to break totally with the past under these circumstances would have made him a destroyer who could not fulfil.

The Guru message has thus to use even dead letters to express its living truth. Some entrance has to be effected into the receptive heart of mankind, hidden though it may be within an age-old crust of immoveable fixtures of habit and custom. The living Word is therefore established on the existing platfom of the effete and archaically defunct anterior structure. On such a platform it is then possible to keep the back-benchers in their place as an audience, and to win their consent to changes and corrections which they would otherwise resent and would not listen to, but on the contrary, would dive underground and become a powerful opposition.

Like any other person born in this world, Nārāyaṇa Guru could not escape his own background, and therefore he consciously recognised this instead of falling into the mistake of escapism and vainly protesting against it. He thus willingly played the role he had accepted with all it necessarily implied. If a tiger was killed unjustly in the past, kill it justly, or do not kill it at all if possible, in the future. In the meantime be free and reasonable, basing conduct on common sense. Keep the teaching to the domain proper to it, keep it where it belongs and keep necessary action within its field of the inevitable and the incidental. Never let a good doctrine become a fetish of blind faith, or a fixed dogmatic idea; both being productive of suffering and anguish. Let the Sabbath be for man and man for the Sabbath intelligently, and not just by blind obligation or superstition. Only those who love might chastise; only a certain degree of conforming could reform effectively. Breaking with the past entirely would create a rival camp, and it was precisely this which the Guru wished to avoid.

Indeed the bane of human life is the formation of closed and static groups who are organised on a basis of rivalry and competition. The role of the Guru is to find points of agreement and reconciliation, something far more than mere patchwork compromise. Here it is the contemplative Word-message which contains that synthesising medium which acts like a cement on dialectical pairs of opposites bringing such dualities together into single unitive comprehension.

The three lines that the Guru smeared on his forehead belong to the prehistoric context of Śiva adoration. As we have said, Śiva dances the dance of the victory of the radical, tragic, uncompromising destruction of the old in favour of the new contemplative value. Śiva thus represents the positive principle in self-realisation, that will which transcends *māyā* and becomes the pure Absolute. This will when sublimated in this way burns to ashes all that is of the materially relative, or the vitalistic aspect of the personality. Madana, the Eros of the Indian myth, is burnt to cinders by the fire emitted from the central eye of Śiva.[3] And so, having by heavenly fire from the Self within, burnt up all instinctive

3. Compare the following passage from Plotinus: 'That our good is There is shown by the very love inborn with the Soul; hence the constant linking of the Love-God with the Psyche in story and picture. The Soul, other than God, but sprung of Him, must needs love. So long as it is There, it holds the heavenly love; here its love is the baser. There the soul is Aphrodite of the heavens; here, turned harlot, Aphrodite of the public ways: yet the soul is always an Aphrodite. This is the intention of the myth which tells of Aphrodite's birth and Eros born with her.' (*Enneads,* VI, ix, 9)

conditionings, the Self triumphs in positive freedom, revels and dances in its own joy.

Three instinctive levels are envisaged in this refining process. These are known as *sattva* (pure, rational), *rajas* (active, passionate), and *tamas* (inert, negative or dark). These three, even the pure and rational, have to be transcended by the intuitive will, so that Word-content may manifest itself.

Such is the theory implied in the wearing of the holy Śiva-ashes. Conquest of these instinctive vital levels is indicated by the three lines on the brow of the *yogī*. In all probability, with this kind of interpretation in his mind, Nārāyaṇa Guru agreed to conform to the wish of the *saṁnyāsī* regarding the usage of the holy ashes. By maintaining a strict neutrality between the former and the revalued positions, between what was anterior and what came later, between the orthodox and the revolutionary, the Guru-function of fulfilment was accomplished without disruptive commitment.

We shall see in a later place how the Guru was not partial to the Śiva cult. He moved amidst Viṣṇu worshippers and adopted their form of orthodoxy also for expressing the same dialectical neutrality of the living Word, a neutrality which accepts the necessary and yet announces the freedom of the contingent will at once in each act, attitude or utterance.[4] From the figure of the ancient hunter and *yogī* of the prehistoric Mohenjo-Dāro seals, through the Buddha images and the dancing figure of Naṭarāja in bronze, we have therefore witness of the same Guru-language persisting in varied ways, revalued in the Dakṣiṇāmūrti model-*guru* and reaching right into the present, to be given further revaluation by the Way and Word of the Guru Nārāyaṇa.

4. Cf., the passage in the Upaniṣad: 'For just as men here below pursue the aim after which each aspires, as though it were done at command, whether it be a kingdom or an estate, and live only for that (so in their aspiration for heavenly reward they are the slaves of their desires). Therefore he who departs from this world without having known the *ātman* or those true desires (*satya kāma*), his part in all worlds is a life of constraint; but he who departs from this world after having known the *ātman* and those true desires, his part in all worlds is a life of freedom.' (*Chāndogya Upaniṣad:* VIII, 5-6).

16

Blast and Counterblast

THE *Bhagavad Gītā* opens with two armies facing each other in battle array. The well-known scene is laid on the Field of Kuru which is at the same time the Field of Free Exalted Duty (i.e., both Kurukṣetra and Dharmakṣetra). The impending conflict between right and wrong, higher spirituality and its anterior version, is to be announced. It is the beginning of an historically dialectical revaluation, stated in terms of a heritage preserved from antiquity, which is to take place again on the Indian soil. Both parties in the struggle are ready to lay down their lives for what they prize more dearly than life. The great warriors are named and distinguished and their might and prowess declared openly in the barbaric but pure setting of a prehistoric epic.

Here therefore we have the essence of the formulation of the Word of wisdom in a typical situation of opposition. The hour strikes. Pipes, bugles, trumpets, drums and conch-shells tumultuously echo and re-echo in blast and counter-blast. Between these bellowing challenges the Word is again formulated. One hears its silent, still voice. In subtle reciprocity, one shrill blast evokes and implies its counter-blast, and in that delicate relationship is the secret of silence, of the Word-wisdom of the *guru*. We have seen what it implied in the context of hieratic imagery. We shall now pass on to its manifestation in noetic literature.

In the first place, we have to distinguish between the two sets of writings of Nārāyṇa guru himself. His earlier works were more related to the Indian scene than the later ones which were free, as far as this was possible, of all special background. The earlier compositions abound in references to Indian myth and legend, and generally speak the language of iconology. Here we find Kālī the tragic Mother of timeless becoming, Gaṇeśa the baby-god with the head of an elephant, Bahuleya the son of Śiva who is nursed by six mothers, and Sarasvatī that lustrous deity of the Word. Vāsudeva or Viṣṇu, Lakṣmī the goddess of normal human values in life, and all the associated galaxy of heroic or godly conceptualisations and personifications of virtues associated with India's long traditions, entered these early works of the Guru in a simple natural form.

These early writings fulfilled a fundamental need; they were written for those who really wanted them; for those who had to be taken by the hand in a kindly manner. For such people the given imagery of god-forms had rich nouminous meaning: hence from this starting point, through their own accepted language, they could be trustfully guided to hitherto unknown and subtler domains of reason or wisdom. The Guru's method could not omit any intermediate stage in the educative process of conveying the Word. Nothing might be skipped. But the weaning from old to new had to be gentle and in conformity with the primary formulation of the Word, as it had appeared in the ancient context of primeval Indian life.

Hence the role of the Guru consisted mainly in clearing away the impediments rather than in changing or interfering with the basic structure of Word-expression. Like a midwife he had to see that the healthy child of wisdom was born in safety to the satisfaction of the mother. At the birth of the Word the Guru was also a foster mother, for as a mother he had to know the nature of the child; and as opposing tendencies are involved in every process of weaning or emancipation, the problem here was one of incessant adjustment of ambivalent factors, of protection and education going on simultaneously.[1]

1. This analogy of the Guru as a midwife is not far-fetched, for we find it elaborately worked out in Plato's *Theaetetus*. Here, in the mouth of Socrates, we are told how the spiritual midwife has a difficult task 'for women', he says 'do not bring into the world at one time real children, and at another time counterfeits which are with

→

Once while sitting under the spreading branches of a mango tree which the Guru planted near the temple of the goddess Sarasvatī at Varkala, a bystander alluded to one of the Guru's early compositions whose verses were rich with all the imagery of poetry, with rhythm, melody and rhyme. Commenting, Nārāyaṇa Guru gave evidence of the way he meant these early productions to be looked upon. 'They happened to have been written once upon a time,' he remarked, as if half disowning them and seeming to infer that he did not consider them as containing his fully finalised or formulated Word. In the light of his later writings, which were more impersonal, and adjusted to standards of a more publicly positive critical order, it was clear that here the Guru wished to draw attention to the esoteric nature and individualised personal mysticism contained in these earlier productions. Even these earlier works, however, when closely examined by the critical eye of Vedānta, reveal the same fundamental principles of Advaita (non-dualism), but they have the addition of poetry or mystical music, using the keyboard of deistic imagery. It is the electric current of Vedānta lighting up the variously shaped lamps. The wisdom-light is the same throughout all the Guru's works. There is nothing in the older poems to reject or revise, but he was addressing a more intimate and smaller circle of devotees. Later, as the numbers increased, he stated the same message in terms of universal impersonal applicability — his circle of admirers becoming wider and wider, including all, without even India as a limiting factor.

→ difficulty distinguished from them; if they did, then the discernment of the true and false birth would be the crowning achievement of the art of midwifery' and he continues: 'I attend men and not women, and I look after their souls when they are in labour, and not after their bodies: and the triumph of my art is in thoroughly examining whether the thought which the mind of the young man brings forth is a false idol or a noble and true birth. . . . Some of them (the young men) appear dull enough at first, but afterwards, as our acquaintance ripens, if the god is gracious to them, they all make astonishing progress; and this in the opinion of others as well as in their own.' (see *Theaetetus,* Jowett tr., *Works of Plato,* Modern Library Series, pp.490-93.)

Nārāyaṇa Guru further clarified his position and defined his attitude to spiritual or mystical literature on another occasion, when someone read out to him some verses from Tagore's *Gītāñjalī* which at that time was making its début before the English-speaking world.[2] 'The verses sound like conundrums,' the Guru remarked. Such a style, he seemed to say, was natural to poetry but positive teaching had to be critically conceived without these naive musical forms. True, suggestive riddles have always been employed to reveal secret doctrines from olden times. Ornate and figurative language, using allegory and fable or puzzles are familiar to all in esoteric literature, as myth has also been used. But the Guru thought teaching should be more consciously overt or public. A method and a theory of knowledge with a well-defined scale of values ought to be used or implicit at least with consistency and in a doubt-dispelling conclusive style. Where laws can be enunciated, they have to be clearly formulated. Where laws do not or cannot prevail, this should be explicitly understood. Knowledge has to be more than merely an intellectual luxury. Besides the sweets there has to be the substantial curry and rice. Vaguenesses lead to dogma and the confusion of doctrines. Spiritual statement has to come to close grips with actuality, with existence, reality or truth in crystalline, unambiguous language.[3]

---

2. *Gītāñjalī* was first published in English in 1912. In 1913 Rabindranath Tagore (1861-1941) was awarded the Nobel Prize in Literature.

3. Western critics of Śaṅkara and of the Advaita Vedānta generally, level two main objections, even when they are sympathetic to the wisdom-teaching. One objection is that it is impractical, that nothing concessional or of daily use is done for the problems of ordinary life; the second is (in the words of Dr. Paul Deussen) that the spiritual teaching is accommodated in the wrong way, what is called 'the practice of clothing metaphysical intuitions in the forms of empirical knowledge,' which 'is met with not only in India, but also in Europe from the earliest times.' (see Deussen, Preface to *Philosophy of the Upanishads,* Clark, Edinburgh, 1906, p. ix.) Guru Nārāyaṇa, as we shall see, by the use of Word-dialectics, avoided both these errors, the error of retreat to an Ivory Tower of Spiritual or philosophical isolation on the one hand, and the error of hypostatic fixations on the other hand.

It was in order to emphasise the same distinction between the two classes of mystical literature — the private and public as it were — that Nārāyaṇa Guru once asked a *saṁnyāsī* who was a Tamil scholar, which mystical Tamil writer he most admired, Tayumānavar or Tiruvalluvar. The former was an ancient Tamil Bard full of mystical loneliness who poured his soul out, as it were, in strains of philosophical and poetic fancy. He employed an ornately suggestive and figurative style. The mystical message was essentially that of Vedānta, but the treatment resembled Sūfī or Christian-Plotinian poetry, in its flights of 'the alone to the Alone.' The other sage, Tiruvalluvar, belonged to a prehistoric Śiva background. Sixty three other saints belonging to the hierarchy of his days are honoured once a year, even now, at the temple at Mylapore, in Chennai. This saint was not of Āryan origin, but came from an earlier Indian stratum, and was therefore approximately designated as of an aboriginal 'Caste' or 'untouchable,' in the dull statistical language of modernism which has lost its memory in regard to its own heritage. He was untouchable because he was proto-Āryan, but he was also worshipped by all because he was unmistakably related to Word-dialectics from its very inception. Thus he has an everlasting place in the life of the people and presents one of those enigmas of south Indian life in being both respected and despised at one and the same time. Tiruvalluvar was a reply as well as a riddle, a 'yes' as well as a 'no'. And so every year in the month of April a festival is celebrated in his honour and he is worshipped as a divine Guru.[4]

Tiruvalluvar's fame rests upon the *Kural*.[5] In 1,330 metrical

4. H.A.Popley, *The Sacred Kural,* p.16 Oxford University Press, 1931.

5. There are many books with translations in English and other languages on the *Kural*. Popley (*ibid*) lists 26. By far the most compendious, but not literal because it was forced into English rhyme, is Dr. G.U. Pope's pub.1886 when the great Tamil scholar was eighty. One of the latest, and fairly accurate translations in English, is *Tiruvalluvar's Tirukural* in Tamil with English Translation by Prof. M.R. Rajagopala Aiyangar, (pub. S. Viswanathan, 56, Broadway, Madras, 1950,).

→

couplets, this ethical and mystical work deals in a pungent homely style with the great questions of life and death.

We have dwelt at some length on these two ancient poets of the Tamil land because of the bearing it has on our present subject where we are concerned with understanding the nature of the blast and counterblast, the thesis and antithesis, in the process of the formulation of the Word in its Indian 'home.' We have seen how the Śiva tradition, far from being overcovered during the five thousand years and more from its earliest visible appearance in Mohenjo-Dāro, still survives as the dominant spiritual note in common Indian life to the present day. The key to the time-honoured spirituality of south India is to be sought in the Sacred *Kural* of Tiruvalluvar. This ancient sage, mystic, moral and spiritual philosopher, as well as gifted genius in poetry, at once shrewdly poky and also dialectically true to the Word, commanded great respect at the hands of Guru Nārāyaṇa, as may be gathered from a composition he wrote apostrophising the Lord of Mercy in which he said:

→ Mrs. Sen says rightly, 'The *Kural* is the most beloved and the most widely read book in the whole of south India. Tamil children begin their education by memorising its verses.' (p. 200, *The Pageant of India's History.*)

The precise date of Tiruvalluvar is uncertain, but it lies between 1500 and 2000 years ago according to scholars.

M. Ariel, a French scholar in Tamil, has written: 'That which above all is wonderful in the *Kural* is the fact that the author addresses himself without regard to castes, peoples or beliefs, to the whole community of mankind: the fact that he formulated sovereign morality and absolute reason: that he proclaims in their essence, in their eternal abstractedness, virtue and truth; he presents, as it were, in one group the highest laws of domestic and social life; he is equally perfect in thought, in language and in poetry, in the austere metaphysical contemplation of the great mysteries of the Divine nature, as in the easy and graceful analysis of the tenderest emotions of the heart.' There is little doubt that the *Kural* gives a strong clue to the deep practical mysticism of the proto-Āryan south, and the fact that it is having a quasi-political revival at the moment of writing these lines adds some passing interest to the powerful hold it has had on the south for centuries.

Or else is he that sage
Of crowning fame so great
Who ministered anew that holy script
Of wisdom antique
Already then well-known
And writ in Hara's name?[6]

In the far-off background of south Indian history, hidden away and forgotten, overlaid by later formulations, was a valuable heritage of wisdom which the Guru's keen eye and clear memory recognised and revived. In this we touch a stratum of universal values and a form of Word-wisdom which was the antecedent blast to the counterblast of post-Āryan spirituality. Between the proto-and post-Āryan formulations of the Word was to be sought the neutral ground of synthetic and comprehensive understanding of which the *Kural* accords an antique example of a masterpiece of perennial wisdom.

All this brings us naturally to a consideration here of the two main currents of spiritual as well as social history, without which understanding the whole import of Indian spirituality would lose much of its importance. Historians and scholars have so far touched on this aspect with somewhat hesitant hands. But now any further hesitancy can only damage a cause equally dear to a lover of India or of its best heritage.

'The Foreign North' and 'The Indian South' are titles of distinct chapters in a recent book on Indian history by an able American lady.[7] Although it is not our intention here to inflame

6. Hara is a name for Śiva.

7. Mrs. Gertrude Emerson Sen. Chapter VIII of her book *The Pageant of India's History* (Longman's 1948) dealing with 'Indian South' begins with the following paragraph: 'Histories of India nearly always have a peculiar northern bias, and it is to be feared that the present one is no exception. South India and the great Deccan Plateau are sadly neglected, and the distinctive contributions of the Dravidian south to Hindu civilization as a whole are overlooked or given scant attention. This neglect of the historian is due to no fault of his own, but to a series of circumstances over which he has no control. . . . Mohenjo-Daro itself may possibly represent a mainly Dravidian type of civilization.' (p.173)

Śiva Liṅgas, Śiva Liṅgodbhavamūrti (Chola 13th *c.*)

local sentiments or rivalries around the question of Āryan and non-Āryan, it has to be recognised that without an understanding of the principle or process of blast and counterblast, of challenge and response, of attack and retaliation, in the dialectical formulation of the Word-Wisdom, much of the spiritual expression and literature would remain a closed book full of enigmas and riddles. What is called Dravidian should be taken in a wholesale integral sense as meaning pre-Āryan and what is called Āryan should be understood as including all that vast literature of the Sanskrit language, put out age after age in the centuries following the settling of the Āryan people in India as a result of their contact with the pre-Āryan (or Dravidian) people. Pre-Āryan and Āryan therefore belong together as the obverse and reverse of the same coin — the India of today.

The Indo-European or Āryan centre often referred to by historians was somewhere in the Asian north, possibly beyond the north-west frontiers of India. From this reservoir of human life certain forces and influences penetrated into the closed matrix of proto-Āryan life in India itself, which extended far beyond the south and included the Indus Valley civilization along with others. The influx could be put at from three to four thousand years ago.[8]

---

8. Prof. Arnold J. Toynbee discusses the origin of the Āryans and the reason for their wandering into and occupation of India as well as Europe in his gigantic *Study of History* (Oxford University Press have published a one volume abridgement compiled in Toynbee's own words by D.C. Somervell. 1947,) His theory is that the Aryas were living as 'an external proletariat' of outlanders to the universal society called the Sumeric, whose territory culturally at least extended from ancient Egypt to south India, and covered the valleys of the Euphrates, Tigris, Indus, etc. 'The break-up of this empire after Hammurabai, (1947 BC) ushered in the period of the Āryan Völkerwanderung,' Toynbee says. 'While some', he also writes, 'entered India, others overran Iran, Iraq, Syria and finally Egypt, where they established in the seventeenth century BC a rule of barbarian war-lords known to Egyptian history as the Hyksos'.

   These invading peoples from the Eurasian Steppes had horses, and the very close correspondence between the chariots which appear in literature, carvings, etc., all over the same wide region mentioned above, and gradually extending even to such remote places as Ireland

This penetration of peoples from the Steppes of Asia into India must have been slow and continuous over several centuries; and it is not important for us here to say whether it was one steady flow of the same Āryan group or whether there were waves of immigrants of different layers at different times. The chief point to remember is that two distinct currents of thought met and neutralised each other for a long period of time.

Imagine the vast sub-continent then in a state of super-saturation with its own Word-content. The mass of humanity therein was an amorphous matrix. The invading groups on the other hand, were organised pyramidal theocratic units. They had the ritualistic Brāhmin priest as the apex of each formation and with the fire-sacrifice or 'burnt offerings' to the sky-gods of nature, accompanied by Vedic chants and a phenomenal cosmology as distinct features.

The spearhead of these rebel groups on the north-western fringes of the prehistoric Indian society was evidently round the leader-types such as Droṇa of the *Mahābhārata* epic war. This invading spearhead at once started a disturbance in the socio-religious society of pre-Āryan Proto-Dravidian India. This challenge constituted the blast we have mentioned, to which there came the responsive counterblast from the hitherto stabilised proto-Dravidians, thus converting what was a prehistoric into an historic situation. Stalwarts like Bhīma in the same epic who were polyandrous and related to the dark-skinned Yādava (cowherd) leader Kṛṣṇa, belonged to the remote times of prehistory, while the priest-leaders such as Droṇa of the Kauravas, monogamous and of fair skin, constituted the then modern socio-ethical beginnings of Vedic history, recorded conveniently in the *Mahābhārata*.

→ confirms the tentative theory of the original Āryan homeland being 'somewhere between the Danube and the Oxus.' The evidence from Ireland is 'that elements of the curious and complicated ritual of the ancient Indian (Vedic) horse-sacrifice . . . survived until the twelfth century AD in Ireland, etc.' (see Chapter VII 'Conquerors from the West — the Āryans and the Rigveda' discussed in the *Prehistoric India* by the Prehistoric Archaeologist Prof. Stuart Piggott, Penguin Books, 1950.)

The other great Indian epic which poetises another historical effect is the *Rāmāyaṇa*; and it can also be examined in the light of the same blast and counterblast. Here the geographical movement is plainly from the north to the south, from the Himālaya to Ceylon (Laṅkā of those days). This is the Āryan challenge, the 'blast' of our metaphor.

But the southern counterblast is evident in the *Mahābhārata* — as for example in the closing scenes, where the epic narrative moves northwards, to the Himālayan gateway to heaven; and there, one of the principal characters, the chief of the Pāṇḍavas, who is depicted as a man of well-recognised renunciation and spirituality hard-won by battle, refuses the Āryan heaven (which is justly rewarded to him) because it debars admission to his dog. Thus a universal sentiment or value is introduced into this otherwise Āryan tale, revealing the infiltration of higher values which must have been derived from a different and contemplative society which can only have been the proto-Dravidian.

In the *Rāmāyaṇa,* on the other hand, a contrary position is depicted. A heavy legalism predominates over the higher laws of the less positive but more contemplative society being overrun. Rāma in his southward march is known to have killed a sage called Ṛṣyaśṛṅga because he claimed spirituality without being a Brāhmin by family stock as the Āryans understood it. Again the 'monkeys' who co-operated with the hero Rāma in all likelihood were the proto-Dravidians he had won over to his side.

When examined from the standpoint of social virtues such as monogamy and other latter-day refinements at present accepted by Hindu society, Āryan morals were of a higher order; but against that it must be understood that the intensely spiritual content of the conquered proto-Dravidians, non-social and amoral from the viewpoint of a fixed society, and working out from an individual rather than a group level, was in many respects of a superior moral character. But in the *Rāmāyaṇa* the coded group morality of the victors though inferior, won a victory over the uncoded individually free morality of the prehistoric contemplative wisdom-appreciating southerners. Rāvaṇa, the King of Ceylon (Lanka) was the last of the southern heroes of antiquity to resist the power of the northern conquerors. This stalwart giant had to be made into an Āryan civilised man through the moral standards personified in Rāma.

Such is the implicit nature of the blast and counterblast as evidenced from the ancient epics, and within whose opposing orders of values the spiritual Word achieved restatement and a reorientation which had terms of agreement with both the forces involved.

Apart from evidence from the epics there is a large quantity of miscellaneous literary evidence which could be gathered together to strengthen the double-sided picture we have tried to present above. For example, allusion is often made to dark-coloured *r̥ṣis* (sages) as against fair-hued ones. The fair ones were often called *brahmar̥ṣis* while the dark ones, who adhered neither to the fire-sacrifice (the *agnihotra)* nor to the Vedic ritual, were sometimes included in this order by sheer force of merit; their worth could be suppressed or ignored. Parāśara the father of Vyāsa, the author of the *Mahābhārata,* was a dark-skinned outcaste, while Vyāsa himself had to be granted *brahmar̥ṣi*-hood by sheer force of his superiority. In the *Mahābhārata* it is Kr̥ṣṇa the dark-complexioned man of the cowherd caste who is the hero and *guru*, and Kr̥ṣṇa is related by marriage to Arjuna, his pupil, who is one of the Pāṇḍavas who uphold caste and Āryan sociology. Droṇa, Vasiṣṭha, as well as Vālmīki the author of the *Rāmāyaṇa,* all belonged to the Vedic Āryan social context. The suggestions we have put forward as well as the dialectics of the situation alone can explain this co-mingling of values, and must shed much light on features of Indian literary and spiritual history which are otherwise inexplicable.

All the legends connected with Śiva add weight to the view presented here. In spite of Br̥haspati being the teacher of the Vedic gods, he is displaced by Dakṣiṇāmūrti who is the accepted *guru* of the other *brahmar̥ṣi*s, and, as we have explained, the latter is none other than a revalued Śiva of the south, model *guru* for India. The same clash of rival values is found in the hierography describing the various marriages of Śiva. Thus although labelled an outcaste (an *akula*) by her father, Dakṣa's daughter weds Śiva by sheer wilful prayer, while Dakṣa disapproves of the marriage. Śiva is said to have disturbed sacrifices many times; one such striking instance being when the same daughter of Dakṣa, married to Śiva by a miracle from the air finally gives up her life, at another sacrificial ceremony, to prove her loyalty to her husband, Śiva, and counter to the wishes of her father who happens to be the officiating ceremonialist.

Agastya, a Vedic *guru*, is accepted in the south only after the mediation of the god Subrahmaṇya (the son of Śiva), who becomes his *guru*. Then there is the case of Droṇa and Ekalavya. The Āryan Droṇa refuses to permit Ekalavya learn archery because the latter was only a proto-Draviḍian chief. But Ekalavya does learn by the device of substituting a dummy Droṇa for his *guru*, and according to legend, this inanimate presence was sufficient (by telepathic sympathy) for him to learn the art of archery well enough to become an exact marksman. However, this displeased the Vedic *guru* Droṇa, who insisted on having his dues as a *guru* repaid by cutting off Ekalavya's thumb.

The Āryan heroes excelled in political standards of a very rigid and exacting kind, as we see in that part of the *Rāmāyaṇa* called the *Uttara-Rāmacarita* (the Later History of Rāma) where the whole tragedy consists in putting the personality of Sītā, Rāma's queen, under and not above politics. The code was ruthless, the law inexorable, even when Caesar's wife was involved and proved innocent.[9]

---

9. Padmini Sengupta writes: 'Rama, for instance, against his own conscience had to exile Sita for no fault of hers because it was the custom that no wife who had stayed for any length of time in another man's house, whether willingly or under force, could be received back into her husband's house no matter how innocent she was. Despite Sita's proving her purity and despite Rama's great →

Today the bugling conch-shell of controversy still resounds in India, echoing and re-echoing over plains and hills in everlasting challenge and response. There is an axial movement of pilgrims, subtly dialectical in its nature, still passing to and fro, as of old, from north to south and south to north, between the two poles of Indian socio-spiritual life, between Mount Kailās in the Himālaya and the *Ultima Thule* of Cape Comorin (Kanyā Kumāri) at the far southernmost tip. Between these two termini, one of snow and rock and the other of burning sands washed by warm seas, a dialectical interplay of ancient inherited values and legacies, moves, meets and mingles, all interfused, a jostling mixture of Āryan-derived and proto-Draviḍian peoples and patterns, while through and through, the bellowing conch-shell still rends the air.

Subrahmaṇya (son of Śiva) is the god of the Palni Hills in the south where he still receives much popular homage. At Palni he is seen as the ascetic with only the loincloth and ashes, understood from time immemorial as the typical expression of renunciation and spirituality in the Śiva language of the Word-wisdom. But in other temples Subrahmaṇya is worshipped in the form of a married man and then his wife invariably belongs to a pre-Āryan tribe, as for example, his spouse Vallī who is of the aboriginal hunting caste. Even Kālidāsa[10] describes the goddess Sarasvatī, notwithstanding all her refinement of learning and Vedic wisdom and symbolised by the book and the *vīṇā* she

→ love for her and his belief in her chastity she had to be sent away, until finally Mother Earth opened her arms and Sita was carried into the Furrow from which she had been born. One feels today that it was a blot on the otherwise perfect character of Rama that he should have treated his faithful wife so cruelly, but his subjects demanded it, and in his time no alternative course of action was open to him as a king.' pp. 51-52, *Everyday Life in Ancient India* (Oxford University Press, 1950).

10. Kālidāsa, considered by some to be the greatst Sanskrit dramatist and poet, lived about the fifth century AD in Malwa. His *Śakuntalā* is well known outside India. His *Kumārasambhava* tells the story of Śiva's austerities and his wedding, nevertheless, to the daughter of the Himālaya.

carries, as a *mātaṅga-kanyā* (a maid of the un-touchables). The poet thus recognised the subtle Word-dialectics in so alluding even to the purest presiding deity of all art and wisdom.

The point of fusion in the caste antagonism as between the extremes of Brāhmin and pariah, as it obtains to the present day, must also be considered in the light of the same Word dialectics if it is not to continue as an unpleasant enigma for ever. Even to this day the untouchable pariah has strongly-rooted spiritual objections to intercourse with the Brāhmin who is unwelcome in the *cheri* reserve where the 'untouchable' tribes live. This again is related to the bilateral development of untouchability itself in the social context where the Āryan pattern of life prevails.

The enigma of Brāhmin and pariah therefore belongs to a certain secret of dialectics and without which it can never be understood. Any philosophy that aims at touching the life of the people must have as part of its task the bringing together of these two ends of society into unitive terms of sympathy and comprehension. It is here that the Word of the Guru Nārāyaṇa has been a potent factor in the recent history of south India. It is in this field that the Guru's value as a representative of the silent model of the Guru-Word gains fresh point and importance.

Buddhist and Jaina solutions to socio-religious evils failed to succeed, although they did leave colouring traces which are still valid in Indian life today. Their failure was due to the extreme or unilateral or asymmetrical emphasis laid upon them by political groups from time to time, producing a grotesque exegesis. But certain valuable ingredients from each were assimilated into the dialectical content of Indian spiritual life. Thus the prehistoric Śiva's element of cruelty in hunting was modified by the *ahiṁsā* (non-hurting) doctrine coming into and dominating Indian life for sometime under the teaching of Vardhamāna Mahāvīra (the Prosperous Great and Brave One) of the Jains and the similar teaching of the Buddha, and his followers.[11]

---

11. Mahāvīra (599-527 BC) was the founder of the Jain religion.

Modernised Vaiṣṇava cults that once flourished all over India during the post-Pallava[12] period (after seventh century AD) also made their contributions of social refinements and virtues, adding an overlying pattern of equality, emphasising justice and other values, more apparent in some parts of the country than in others, so that life was maintained at a more reasonable level than before.

The Guru Nārāyaṇa strove to revaluate all these contributory factors in the life of the country, conserving all former revaluations in a supremely generous synthesis of Advaitic vision.

Mahatma Gandhi described his ideal India as a *rāma-rājya* or Regime Based on Rāma-Rule. Rāma personified the social virtues of the Āryans. A Vaiṣṇava sense of equality was noticeably implied in this Gandhian outlook to which India responded characteristically, particularly adopting it in the struggle for emancipation as an integrated political unit.

But political unification is not the end. Integration has to be deeper still. It needs to touch both root and branch. Hence the value, we believe, of the understanding of Word dialectics in the light we have tried to throw on both social and spiritual effects, and especially through the medium of the original contribution of the Guru Nārāyaṇa to the subject.

For in spite of the fact of political integration and emancipation, problems of a communal and social nature still remain unsolved. Strife between Hindu and Muslim offers difficulties which come from sources deeper than mere surface differences, and therefore solutions for such problems have to be also deeper, more radical and thorough. Here also the Word

---

12. The Pallavas ruled in south India during the third to ninth centuries of the Christian Era. Their centre was Kāñcī or Kāñcīpuram. They used a Prākṛt (Sanskrit variant), performed the *aśvamedha* or Vedic horse-sacrifice, but were also worshippers of Śiva. They were tolerant of other religions, and the Chinese traveller Hiuen Tsang in the seventh century found 10,000 Buddhist priests and a number of monasteries at Kāñcī.

of the Guru is of direct and practical importance. Dayānanda stressed the importance of the Vedic and Āryan virtues of equality; Vivekānanda defended Hinduism primarily in the name of mother-worship of Kālī; Gandhi stressed Vaiṣṇava democratic notions in public life; and Tagore sang songs breathing something of the freedom of the Upaniṣads across modern India — all of them aiming at raising the status of India in the world.

The silent Guru of Varkala, sitting on a hill-top at the southern extremity of Mother India, steeped in the silence of non-dual unitive vision, integrated all the contributory views and visions into one whole, brought all within the scope of one contemplative Word-Wisdom, by which human dignity could be held high everywhere and all mankind become free.

17

The Guru-Trio of South India

BUDDHISM'S divergence or at least superficial appearance of breaking away from the main body of the line of descent of the Word-formula as we have traced it — a heterodoxy which is implied in the Buddhist religion — was the reason for its displacement on the soil of its birth by fresh formulations of the Word which, while being new revaluations, were at the same time not severed from older formulations.[1]

---

1. Many passages from the writings of Buddhism make it clear that Buddhism's revolt was only superficial. The following may be quoted as an example. King Milinda was the Greek Menander of the second century BC. He was converted to Buddhism by the teacher Nāgasena, who visited Menander's capital Sakala (present-day Siālkoṭ in the Punjab). The *Milinda-Pañha* is believed to have been written in the first century AD and it is in the form of a *guru-śiṣya* dialogue.

   '*King Milinda:* Venerable Nāgasena, it has been said by the Blessed One: "The Tathāgata, O Brethren, the Arhat, the Buddha Supreme, is the discoverer of a way that was known." But on the other hand he said: "Now I perceived, O Brethren, the ancient way, the ancient path, along which the previous Buddhas walked." If, Nāgasena, the Tathāgata be the discoverer of a way not previously found out, then it must be wrong that it was an ancient way that he perceived, an ancient path along which previous Buddhas walked. But if the way he perceived were an ancient way, then the statement that it was unknown must be wrong.

   Nāgasena: Both the quotations you make, O King, are accurate. And both the statements so made are correct. When the previous Tathāgatas, O King, had disappeared, then, there being no teacher left, their way too disappeared. And it was that way, though then broken up, crumbled away, gone to ruin, closed in, no longer possible, quite lost to view, that the Tathāgata, having gained a thorough knowledge of it, saw it by the eye of his wisdom (and knew it) as the way that previous Buddhas trod. (IV, v, 12-13, *The Questions of King Milinda,* tr. Prof. T.W.Rhys-Davids: Vol. XXXVI Sacred Books of the East.)

From the study of biology we learn that over-specialisation leads to the extinction of a species, and that organisms survive by the conservation of their original simplicity, as in the case of the immortal amoeba.[2] Too good, too perfect, simply means not true, as proverbial wisdom puts it. A goodly apple is often rotten at the core, and painted tombs do worms unfold. Languages become dead when their grammar becomes too exacting. To modern society and politics Sanskrit is a dead language, although its exactitude makes it ideal for the survival of the wisdom which still lives within it. The heavily armoured species of gigantic animals of past geological ages leave nothing more behind them than their fossil bones, or the impressions of their huge bodies. So too with mankind; jungle primitives can survive under conditions of adversity which would mean death to the civilised man in the bowler hat, softened by socks and shoes and modern ways of life.

It is the same with the wisdom-Word. The growth of the Word in many mouths for collective action is different from its simple survival through time as a trickle of perennial wisdom. That is why the rich man cannot enter the kingdom of heaven, and why the world cannot be gained at the cost of one's own soul. A Constantine[3] or an Aśoka[4] can make whole empires follow a faith, but there is something in the faith itself which is needed in addition to all the efforts of well-meaning reformers, something

2. The amoeba is the simplest animal, about 1/100th of an inch in diameter, a tiny mass of protoplasm. New amoebae are formed by a cleavage of the body, by simple division in two. Thus there are neither parents nor offspring, neither birth nor death, but plainly immortality. See *The Standard Natural History*, pp. 5-8, ed. W.P. Pycraft, Warne & Co.1931.

3. Constantine I (AD 288?-337), Roman emperor and founder of the Holy Roman (Christian) Empire at Byzantium which he renamed Constantinople, where he forbade any 'pagan' religion.

4. Aśoka, India's greatest king. For forty years he ruled over a vast empire extending from what is now the N.W. Frontier to the borders of Mysore. After a period of war and conquest he was converted to Buddhism, introducing Buddhist morality, *ahiṁsā* and tolerance into his empire with missionary zeal. He died in 237 BC.

which alone gives stability and permanence to the good after which men strive. Dynamic and living aspects are deep-seated under the visible surface, while the static and closing-in tendencies in each religion defeat their own ends by using means which are contradictory to the dynamic or living principles.

And so, bearing the above in mind, after having traced the formulations of the Word from ancient times, we shall now follow three of its modalities as they were manifested in south India in those *gurus* of more recent times — Śaṅkara, Rāmānuja and Madhva — a trio whose Word-formulae still prevails and regulates the lives of people in contemporary India. It is not because we want to be partial to south India that we select these three, but rather because they are sufficiently representative for our purpose and what we have to say of them would apply to others *mutatis mutandis.*

Buddhism and Jainism were repulses against the first blast of the Āryan conch-shell. Later they themselves became too good, too etheralised in an intimate personal sense, to be existent or real. Theory and rarified argument of a kind comparable to the hairsplitting dogmatics of the Christian theologians of the European Middle Ages, became for religion an end in itself. Thus over-specialised, raised above and escaping from human needs in the day by day sense, these two religious expressions evaporated into the peripheral fringes, while new revalued formulae once again grew out from the centre, near to the source of Word-wisdom, and by their intimacy with the old but undying roots, prevailed in India. It might be said that Buddhism and Jainism were not ousted, but rather that they ousted themselves by spectral unsubstantialisation, something too rarified for the masses. And so the simplest and the lowliest held the secret that could make the last the first, by the renewal of the inner sap of wisdom from the deep fountains buried within the humanity of India, and when the wisdom spring was tapped properly it could be applied again to whatever situation was present in a way that was ever fresh and rich in its content of common human values.

Śaṅkara[5] effected the necessary synthesis and link with the past. He opened the old wells of wisdom. On the one side the conventionalist *paṇḍitas* and priests of the Āryan heritage suspected him of heterodoxy and called him a 'Buddhist in disguise' (*pracchanna bauddha*); while, on the other side, his attitude to and respect for Āryan patterns of life, such as taking caste distinctions for granted, made him suspect as a 'revivalist' by the Buddhists and Jains of his time. The fact is that he balanced his attitude delicately between both heterodoxy and orthodoxy. On the one hand he rid religion of its tendency towards over-abstraction and vain theorising; and on the other hand, he endeavoured to breath into it the fresh air of a vitally rational and imaginative interest. In spite of the boldness of the Upaniṣads, the Vedic tradition had entered a blind alley. The thread of the Word was almost snapped. Śaṅkara led the Upaniṣad message again into the open, strengthened the old cords, and even brought and bound Buddhism within its scope, despite the latter's seemingly atheistic expressions. Śaṅkara did this with a forceful sweep of unitive thought, arguing at enormous length, in a war that he decided must end all wars.

Śaṅkara himself conformed to a *saṁnyāsin guru* model of the Dakṣiṇāmūrti-Śiva tradition that we have already described in Chapter 11; but he proclaimed a new, revalued Word-formula in which stern renunciation and tearful devotion met and neutralised each other. Without the spearhead of the fire-sacrificing Vedic priest the Āryan-turned section could not think. This could not be by-passed. It was part of the necessary background of the Word as it had been formulated from the most ancient historical times. Śaṅkara made the best of the situation and of the caste notion which followed as a corollary to the Vedic priesthood, treating it all as a necessary background for Advaita Vedānta. Philosophically, caste notions and Vedic priestcraft were abolished, but in practical life actually accepted apologetically as can be seen from his composition called *Manīṣā*

---

5. The date of Śaṅkara's birth is generally accepted as AD 788.

Pañcakam which is a dialogue, actual or imaginary, between Śaṅkara and an 'untouchable' in Kāśī (Benāres). In these verses Śaṅkara admits and accepts defeat on Advaitic grounds from the outcaste whose reasoning is so apodictically final. But in his many great commentaries on the canons of Vedāntic thought, Śaṅkara fails to exercise his *guru* role effectively, excusing or glossing over caste and indeed seems to be its apologist.

Whenever the Guru Nārāyaṇa came across a *saṁnyāsin* of the Śaṅkara tradition he rarely missed an opportunity of referring to this question. The *Bhagavad Gītā* explains caste in its own way, reducing and confining it as necessarily part of human society, part of the limitations of a world of necessity and restraint, upheld by the God of nature.[6] It is also shown however that this condition is dissolved by the 'God' of freedom who emancipates by wisdom when the devotee turns towards the goal of Self-realisation.

Wherever reference to the question of the duties and obligations of caste is made in the various commentaries of Śaṅkara we find that he is seemingly excusing the orthodox attitude, without however supporting it philosophically.[7] Injustice in the name of this vestige of the historical conflict therefore remains unrectified in Śaṅkara. His zeal for toeing the line of orthodoxy and also for absorbing the wisdom-values that Buddhism had brought to the surface, left him a *saṁnyāsin* more or less like a Buddhist *bhikṣu* (monk), a pure votary of

---

6. The relevant verse in the *Bhagavad Gītā* is IV.13: 'The fourfold caste was created by Me by the different distributions of energies (*guṇa*) and actions; though I am the author thereof, know Me to be actionless and immutable.'

7. The method adopted by Śaṅkara is apparent in his *Thousand Teachings* (*Upadeśa-Sāhasrī*) Ramakrishna Math, Madras 1949, which begins by a *guru-śiṣya* dialogue, the *śiṣya* being a Brāhmin. The *guru* tells the *śiṣya* that in the context of Self-wisdom it is wrong to think 'I am the son of a Brāhmin belonging to such and such a family line,' and that there must be renunciation of any idea of difference such as implied in the Vedic ritual, castes, etc. Caste is only rejected on the contemplative level, but not on the level of society where it is treated as something belonging to the body.

wisdom which he personifed again as Sarasvatī of the prehistoric Śiva tradition. Piety, faith, devotion and uncompromising rational wakefulness to reality combined with imagination and insight — these made Śaṅkara the last of the great *guru*s of ancient India.

He could not have effected any more perfectly synthetic or revalued restatement at that historical period when the heterodoxy that Buddhism spelled had still to be more symmetrically poised. India was more self-contained at that time.

We find therefore in Nārāyaṇa Guru a more finalised version of the Advaitic Word-wisdom. In fact, he stated his affiliation to Śaṅkara when he once called the present writer and said: 'Śaṅkara's point of view is our own.' This had to be taken with his further remark that if there was anything that he, the *guru* Nārāyaṇa, came to teach it was that there was no room or justification for caste distinctions like Brāhmin and Pariah.[8] The revision of the position by the Guru was thus unequivocal.

Taken all together, perhaps beginning with the ancient Śiva-Yogī model or symbol from prehistoric Mohenjo-Dāro times, modified or revised by the tradition established by Buddhism (an anti-ritualist monastic system of shaven-headed, yellow-robed monks with begging-bowls) as well as the ideal of renunciation prevalent, Śaṅkara added his touch of devotion to the wisdom-goddess Sarasvatī and combined this with the Dakṣiṇāmūrti model of the Śiva-Guru, thus offering at that critical phase of Indian history, a pattern of ethico-religious life consistently in line with what was then currently accepted as well as with the most ancient patterns of Indian Word-wisdom. Śaṅkara also revalued atheistic Sâṅkhya rationalism and even put in something of Cārvāka epicureanism (the so-called materialism[9]), adding a note of Stoical severity. Thus the prehistoric god Śiva was re-established with deeper significance in view of maturer thought from these various sources; but Śaṅkara also linked

8. Detailed discussion of this subject is postponed at this juncture.

9. The name Cārvāka literally means 'sweet-tongued' (*cāru-vāka*).

Śiva cosmologically with the more ancient Pañcarātra legend where God is said to have slept on the primordial waters, by calling Śiva 'Nārāyaṇa Priya' (the Beloved of Nārāyaṇa).[10] Śiva is made the first-born man, the *yogī*, recluse, ecstatic dancer and Guru by Śaṅkara, identified with the supplicant and *yogī* who approaches him in the meditative prayers composed by Śaṅkara in the words, '*śivo-' ham, śivo-' ham*!' ('I am Śiva ! I am Śiva !').[11]

Among the numerous hymns attributed to Śaṅkara there occur the following well-known words of a popular prayer, which will help to confirm the views we have expressed regarding his place in the ancient tradition of perennial Word-wisdom.

Worship Govinda ! Worship Govinda !
Worship Govinda, muddle-headed boy !
When death takes you, grammar won't save you,
No matter how many rules you employ.[12]

---

10. See footnote 22 below. The title occurs, in Śaṅkara's 'Hymn to the Great God', *Śiva-nāmāvalyāṣṭakam*), Verse 7 (see *Self-Knowledge — Ātmabodhaḥ*, p. 274, Sw. Nikhilānanda, Ramakrishna Math, Madras, 1947).

11. See 'Six Stanzas on Nirvāṇa' (*Nirvāṇāṣṭakam*) each verse of which ends with the refrain '*śivo-'ham, śivo-'ham*!' *ibid.*, pp.302-4.

12. The hymn is called *Dvādaśa-mañjārikā-Stotram*, and consists of twelve verses, each ending with the refrain quoted, which in the original Sanskrit reads:

    bhaja govindam, bhaja govindam, govindam bhaja, mūḍhamate, ।
    samprāpte sannihite kāle, nahi nahi rakṣati dukṛñ-karaṇe ।।
    — *Ibid.*, pp. 287-97.

    In his day Śaṅkara founded several institutions — four of which are still extant — known as *maṭhas*, with semi-monastic rules; and with successors who hold the title of 'Śaṅkara' generically or hierarchically. Few have come up to the Vedāntic height attained by the founder, and a great many of the hymns and works attributed to the original Śaṅkara are obviously, from the internal evidence and departure in content from the Advaitic standpoint of the founder, not the founder's at all, hence our qualification 'attributed'.

    A similar attribution of what are very often inferior writings to the canonical original author is found in the case of scriptures elsewhere, Christian, Buddhist, etc.

The reference to Govinda here would apply both to Śaṅkara's *guru* who was known as Govinda, or equally well, as some think, to the pastoral Kṛṣṇa who is also known by that name. Simple piety, faith and devotion found their place side by side with uncompromising support of the primacy of wisdom, as in the opening verses of the *Crest Jewel of Wisdom* (*Vivekacūḍāmaṇi*), one of Śaṅkara's immortal monuments to rational religion.[13] In this work wisdom is extolled as the only medicine for true freedom, while yogic and other practices, *pūjā* (ritual), etc., are ridiculed in a way that Voltaire could not have bettered. Śaṅkara, indeed, seems to combine the tearful sentiment of a J.J.Rousseau with the pride in reason of a Voltaire. In this way he reconciled opposites, from ordinary standards a baffling figure, only to be understood in the light of his work as a *guru*, conforming to the ancient model, and taking on himself the neutrality of the non-dual or Advaitic attitude.

This neutral Word-formula referring to the Absolute has its corollary in what is known as the doctrine of *māyā*, as put forward by Śaṅkara. Any factor impeding unitive comprehension of the Absolute contemplatively (whether because of vital energies or other effects disturbing the restful, unconditioned consciousness) is taken in its totality of double-charactered expression as of *māyā*. *Māyā* is both good and bad, existent and non-existent. Nothing definitely can be predicated of it. It is, however, the supreme generic category of 'possibility of error'. It is *māyā*'s 'double negation' implicit in its nature that leads to the triumph

---

13. For example, 'Let people quote scriptures and sacrifice to the gods, let them perform rituals and worship the deities, there is no liberation for anyone without the realisation of one's identity with the Ātman, no, not even in the lifetime of a hundred Brahmas put together.' — Verse 6.

'Work is for the purification of the mind, not for the perception of the Real. The realisation of Truth is brought about by wisdom-discriminisation alone and not in the least by ten millions of acts.' — verse 11.

There are several English editions of the *Vivekacūḍāmaṇi*. A fairly reliable one is published by the Advaita Āshram, Almora, Himalaya.

of non-dual vision. *Māyā* is a necessary stepping stone, a final diving-board to spring from firmly before plunging into the depths of the challenging unknowable.

The *māyā* of the Buddhists was like the Bergsonian cinematographic function of thought which sees stills of life, cross-section views of universes in static terms of Euclidean space. It was highly psychological in its approach. Śaṅkara added the personal touch of piety, devotion, theology and orthodox correctness and consistency, while holding firmly to the position gained in the form of pure wisdom. In matters of devotion the Śiva-imagery was his natural point of departure.

By his uncompromising love of philosophical precision, Śaṅkara suffered the disadvantage of being considered too theoretical in his attitude. To theologically pious minds God or *Īśvara* was a necessity, and they could not understand the error or the duality implied in such a concept which was as high as piety could go. And, therefore, in the rallying of people round Word-values, other formulae than Śaṅkara's came into vogue. But without Śaṅkara's initial labours these variants could not have had their genesis. To Śaṅkara is due the high honour of giving the initially impelling revaluation of the Word.

Hence there were variants in method of approach, diverging according to actual social needs, adaptations of the original non-dual position of Śaṅkara which was implied in the philosophical silence of the Buddha himself,[14] who refused to commit himself either by denial or affirmation, thus allowing a neutral ground for the Word, not only through Śaṅkara but others as well. And therefore, in the vast matrix of amorphous Indian life there were aggregations of people around variations of the Word-formula,

14. The Buddha refused to speak when asked about the existence or non-existence of God and Soul (*ātman*) by the Bhikku Vachagotta, thus taking the time-honoured stand of the great *gurus* of the past which Śaṅkara used as an illustration in his *Dakṣiṇāmūrti-Stotram* (Verse 12) and to which we have already referred in Chapter 11. See *Saṁyutta Nikāya* for the silence of the Buddha.

with varying degrees of orthodoxy in that theocratic political setting of the post-Pallava period.

These variants in the Word formulation took their point of departure from the concept of Ādi Nārāyaṇa (the Original cosmological person later identified with Viṣṇu and Vāsudeva, the consort of Lakṣmī), basing their philosophic structure on Vaiṣṇavite forms of worship. Temples were more important to them than *maṭhas* or monasteries. Although Rāmānuja[15] took to monastic robes, the severe touch of Buddhist monkhood and renunciation was transformed by degrees to suit the requirements of family or social life. While the theory of salvation through Brahman still remained the common doctrine of the Absolute, yet the Vedas were to be accepted and the Upaniṣads permitted interpretations of the mystical teachings because of their charmingly sublime but vague paradoxes, enigmas and compression into aphorisms. The effect of the spearhead shock of ritualistic priestcraft and the strain of its exclusive severity had to be mitigated somehow; and Rāmānuja and Madhva[16] therefore formulated suitable variations of the Word which accorded favourably with the needs of those who integrated themselves under them.

Any detailed discussion here of the philosophical implications of the positions taken by these three *ācārya*s or Teachers of south India would take us into the core of the methodology and epistemology of the Vedānta. This must be left for treatment when we come to the translations of the writings of Guru Nārāyaṇa. It must suffice here to indicate first, that any primacy given to *māyā* relatively minimises the need for a personal deity

15. Rāmānuja (AD 1017 ?) inherited the *bhakti* (devotional) background of a long line of Tamil saints known as the Ālvars. His philosophy is known as Viśiṣṭādvaita (the Non-duality of the Qualified, Special or Attributed) and emergent evolution (*pariṇāma*) is preferred to *māyā*.

16. Madhva (C. AD 1199-1300) played a Christ-like role in which his monotheistic 'Father in Heaven' was Viṣṇu. His philosophy or religion is known as Dvaita-Vedānta (Dualistic Vedānta). Madhva was born near Uḍuppi on the northernmost fringe of modern Malabār, in what is now south Kanārā of Karnatak State.

or *Īśvara*. But the theological requirements of society (i.e., religion as ordinarily understood with its injunctions and rules, etc.) are not met by mere critical philosophy. The primal source of 'creation' itself being *māyā* (and its consequent evils), all the determinative creative necessities (God monotheist or gods many) or demi-urges theologically desired, are comprised under the general title of *māyā*-effect; while the negation of *māyā* which is the aim of Yoga as understood in Vedānta brings us to pure Advaita or Non-duality without even the need for God(s).[17]

When the *māyā*-effect is stressed, even in terms of the most precious of human values in a personal God, in which duality is implicit as between a worshipper and a worshipped, it is known in the technical language of India as the *satkārya-vāda* (the theory of the primacy of effect). This is opposed to the position of Advaita Vedānta where the duality of worshipper and worshipped is abolished and the *satkāraṇa-vāda* (the theory of the primacy of cause) declared.

Giving primacy to the *māyā*-effect leads to the supreme Effect which is God as the object of meditation or adoration. The personalised God is thus none other than *māyā* conceived positively (known as *Īśvara*). Two of the main recognitions of such a Supreme God, within the Viṣṇu cosmology rather than in the Śiva psychology, are represented by the teachings of Rāmānuja and Madhva. The names Viśiṣṭādvaita (Non-duality of the Specialised) and Dvaita (Duality) which are applied to these religio-philosophic schools, further indicate their gradation or variation in relation to the original neutral Word-formula as we have traced it and demonstrated on earlier pages. Our aim in showing these

17. Cf., Plotinus: 'Think of The One as Mind or as God, you think too meanly: use all the resources of understanding to conceive this Unity and, again It is more authentically one than God, even though you reach for God's unity beyond the unity the most perfect you can conceive. For this is utterly a self-existent, with no concomitant whatever. This self-sufficing is the essence of Its unity. Something there must be supremely adequate, autonomous, all-transcending, most utterly without need.' *Enneads,* VI. ix.6 (tr. Mackenna and B.S. Page).

variations is merely explanatory. The history of Western philosophy could likewise be graded with reference to Plato or Aristotle as expressions of complementary dialectics. Similarly, these Indian philosophical expressions depend the one upon the other and can all be strung together into one single necklace of visions or insights (*darśana:*German: *Anschauung*) as the Guru Nārāyaṇa has done (in his *Darśana-Mālā* — 'Garland of Visions') or as in the earlier attempts of Śaṅkara's followers (the *Sarva Darśana Siddhānta Saṁgraha* — 'The Epitome of all Possible Visions of Truth').[18]

Madhava also compiled a summarisation.[19]

In the works of all who take up the study of comparative philosophy the acceptance of a common substratum of values is implied as in the able histories of philosophy in the West, such as those of Victor Cousin[20] and others. A tacitly understood scale of values joining all together is present in all such critical histories, depending upon how pragmatic or idealistic each writer is willing to be. Because no one escapes being human, the golden thread of precious human values stringing together all the possible philosophical aspects or visions, remains common to all

---

18. Although attributed to Śaṅkara, the *Sarva Darśana Siddānta Saṁgraha* by internal evidence is really to be traced to one of his school. A study based on this work which contains valuable critical remarks on the lines we have adopted above, is to be found in the University of Paris thesis of Iswar Dayal Tawakley (pub. Jouve et Cie., Paris, 1927).

    Prof. Lacombe's *'L' Absolu Selon le Vedanta'* (Les notions de Brahman et d'Atman dans les systemes de Cankara et Ramanoudja — Librairie Orientaliste Paul Geuthner, Paris, 1937) analyses the theoretical aspects in a thorough-going manner which will further confirm what we have stated.

19. This Madhavācārya was elected in AD 1331 the head of the Smārta order in the maṭha (monastery) or Śṛṅgerī in Mysore territory, founded by Śaṅkara. *The Sarva Darśana Saṁgraha* of Madhavācārya has been translated into English by E.B. Cowell and A.E. Gough (Trübner, London, 1882).

20. Victor Cousin (1792-1867) celebrated French educational leader and founder of the eclectic school of philosophy.

humanity. It thus becomes possible for the Guru Nārāyaṇa to sympathise with all philosophers, and even to be at one with all the *gurus* who ever spoke in the subtle dialectics of Word-wisdom, without the slightest duplicity or lukewarm weakness being involved. Faith and reason are treated as complementaries, and the one is meaningless without the other.[21]

Kāñcī (modern Kāñcīpuram) near Madras, was the capital of the Northern Pallavas after the third century AD and was dominated by them up to the ninth century. Formerly it had been the centre of the Cola kingdom, a city of ancient Śiva temples and with contacts spreading to the Mediterranean as far back as the times of King Solomon, at least 1000 BC. Kāñcī has been one of the focal centres not only for the emanation of the Word but for its revaluation in historic times. Like Ujjain of the golden age of the Guptas, celebrated by the great Kālidāsa and other geniuses, Kāñcī was a city of immense significance in the spiritual dialectics of India. Its temple towers, paved courtyards and broad streets survive to this day, still reflecting a glory that reaches back to prehistory. A cultural history is remembered and kept alive here as in some other world centres such as Paris or Beijing. Kāñcī is a landmark in the historical process of the formulation of the Word-wisdom, a glowing focal centre in the south. As in Alexandria in Greek-ruled Egypt two thousand years ago, where Greek Dionysians, Platonists, Egyptians, Jews, Persians and Christians resided together and debated and mingled philosophically; so too at Kāñcī, right through the centuries of Pallava occupation.

---

21. Faith must always accompany reason and reason, faith. Cf., 'Weakness of faith combined with strength of intellect are apt to lead to the error of talkativeness. Strength of faith combined with weakness of intellect are apt to lead to the error of narrow-minded dogmatism.' from *The Supreme Path, The Rosary of Precious Gems,* X, 1-2: (tr. from the Tibetan of Gampopa in *A Buddhist Bible,* ed. Dwight Goddard, USA), and 'As the text (*grantha*) is completed by reason, (*yukti*), so is reason revealed by the text; therefore let there be reason and the text.' from *The Laṅkāvatāra Sūtra,* Sagathakam, Verse 883, tr. from the Sanskrit by Prof.D.T. Suzuki (Routledge, London, 1932).

All this has relevance when we come to consider the age in which our south Indian *guru*-trio lived. This was a major part of their field and constituted an important background to their roles as *gurus*.

Śaṅkara was born probably in the village of Kālāḍi in north Travancore near Alwaye where the Guru Nārāyaṇa had his *āśrama*, in the year AD 788. Rāmānuja was born in AD 1017 at Srīperambudūr near Kāñcī. It was a region of temples including Śrī-Raṅgam (further south) where purer philosophical and monastic trends aided the work of giving Vedāntic formulations of Viṣṇu worship. Those followers of Rāmānuja who gave primacy to the northern-originating Vedas were called *Vada-galais,* while those who identified themselves with southern or Tamil revelatory sources were known as *Then-galais* — the two prefixes indicating 'north' and 'south' respectively.

Madhva was born in AD 1199 in the village of Pajakakṣetra six miles south of modern Uḍuppi on the West Coast. Although worshippers of Viṣṇu, the worship of Śiva was allowed in the temples of the Madhva followers. The affiliations of the Madhva cult extended in the form of temples and monasteries from Uḍuppi in the south to Dvārakā in the north and the followers traced their faith to the historical personage of Kṛṣṇa of the *Bhagavad Gītā.* South India is pervaded by the influence of this group today.

Śaṅkara, Rāmānuja and Madhva each commented on the *Brahma-Sūtras* (terse aphorisms summing up Upaniṣadic wisdom on *Brahman* or the Absolute) of Bādarāyaṇa. The West Coast of south India was the home of two of these *gurus*, Śaṅkara and Madhva, and the temple city of the East Coast of south India, where the south was gripped by the domination of the north, was the place where the third of the *guru*-trio, Rāmānuja, lived and evolved his Word-formula. Thus in the religious expression of these three great *gurus*, might be seen, as if in a cross section, the dominant trends of south Indian orthodoxy.

In order to see how the Guru Nārāyaṇa related himself to

these expressions we shall lapse here once more into intimate personal anecdotes.

It was in the same city of Rāmānuja, now called Kāñcīpuram, the ancient renowned Kāñcī, that the *guru* Nārāyaṇa was residing in quiet retirement in the Sevāśrama (Home of Service) founded there by his disciple Govindānanda. Hundreds of temples still burned incense both to the Śiva symbol of prehistory as well as to the Viṣṇu of a later age, in this town of antiquity, where priest, soldier, philosopher and courtesan had passed and repassed across the scene, through a drama of many centuries, filling the atmosphere with mellowed old memories dear to the mind of the devout Indian.

Once again the present writer was standing in the presence of the Guru listening to the stimulating conversation that constantly went on around the Guru wherever he happened to be. The company consisted, as was often the case, of yellow-robbed disciples, but there were also present this time white-robed holy men wearing the distinguishing religious marks of both Viṣṇu and Śiva groups. *Then-galai* Rāmānujas and *Veda-galai* Rāmānujas rubbed shoulders with Madhvas as well as with Smārtas of the Śaṅkara school. Such holy men were called Brāhmins, whether or not they had actually descended from the original Āryan priests of the time of Droṇa, Viśvāmitra and other patriarchs or *ṛṣis* of the Vedic epoch. At present such Brāhmins comprised all ethnic groups, united only by common loyalty to the heritage of the Word-wisdom through the *Bhagavad Gītā,* the various Upaniṣads and the *Brahma-Sūtras.* These wisdom-writings, and the extensive commentaries on them, formed the background of all these group configurations of 'Brāhmins' — and when considered together with other members of prehistoric ethnical groups, such as the merchant communities of all these south Indian temple towns, united to form a completely representative cross section of the socio-religious life of south India today.

The Guru sat amidst this motely crowd surrounded by a garden of equally varied shrubs neatly arranged round the edges of a fenced-in, sand-strewn, open courtyard. The air was filled with incense burned in his honour, and despite the modernist age, an atmosphere of old-time reverence and veneration for a *guru* prevailed. The scent of rose and jasmine mingled with the fragrant incense-smoke. Here religious atmospheres of far-flung contexts and memories met in the unitive presence of the serene and silent *guru*, whose characteristic mystical composure once again distilled all into a common blend radiating an ineffable sense of peace.

As was usual with the Guru, he avoided the use of the first person singular pronoun 'I', but using the collective 'we', he began to speak to the writer, recognising him with a kindly eye, from the many of whom he was the last or the first, accordingly as the Guru's glance lighted on him or not.

'They took us inside', he declared. 'They took us into the very holy of holies of the temple of Sri-Perambudur of the Viṣṇu worshippers. Though very orthodox, they showed no indication of caste prejudice. Full temple honours were bestowed on us and we were received with full ceremonial pomp with all its usual accompaniments.' The Guru seemed touched by the recognition thus instinctively extended to him by the latest descendants of the Rāmānuja school of wisdom-adoration. They had heard of the Guru's arrival at Kāñcīpuram and had been impressed by his erudition and saintliness. His humbler and more common origin among a peasant population was no bar to the recognition of the type of spirituality that sat so clearly on his features, unmistakable for the trained eye of south Indian religious experts to see at once.

Here was another *guru* who represented the time-honoured *guru*-model which was at the back of their memories as a priceless archetypal heritage — another *guru*, in the repeated phenomena of history whose voice and presence the flock recognised. The Guru Nārāyaṇa too declared, as Rāmānuja himself had done, the equality of all in God, and it was remembered that Rāmānuja's first disciples were men of humble callings in life. The masses had reformulated the Word through Rāmānuja, and the Guru

Nārāyaṇa was also one such who was neither orthodox nor heterodox, although incidentally, if it would stimulate goodness in man, he could behave like either.

'Then', the Guru continued, 'they took us to an anteroom in the temple precincts where the priests put on their marks of piety or holiness on their foreheads.'

Traditional orthodoxy was exacting to the minutest detail even in this matter of forehead decoration, using sandalwood and other pastes and ashes. The mark shaped like the letter U or Y with a red or orange streak in the middle and carefully applied to the forehead, had to have its limbs carved in a specially formal way as the stroke was drawn up with a pencil-like tracer. It took long years of practice before this could be done with full satisfaction, probably one of the precautionary measures of orthodoxy.

'We tried to respect their feelings by conforming to this requirement. The result was surprising to ourselves,' the Guru explained.

Through sheer sympathy he astonished all the orthodox followers by conforming with precise exactitude of detail to their customs. He became one of them, even in conforming to outward requirements of orthodoxy.

As related in his own words, this incident gives us the key to the Guru's personal attitude to the various religious groups in south India which it will be important for posterity to know, in as direct a manner as possible, so that no cleavage can develop between the Advaita Vedānta he represented and those other schools which are supposed to be different or opposed, by those less familiar with the true nature of the Guru-wisdom as understood and explained in these pages.

On another occasion the Guru Nārāyaṇa was walking along a street in Cochin with a number of his admirers. It was in the Jewish quarter of the town. The Jews had been there since the Fall of Jerusalem. Someone expressed the view that the Jews were peculiar people. As if in protest to this attitude the Guru walked into the house of a wealthy Jewish merchant, well known in Cochin. He was received with kindness by a respectable looking lady of the house and he spent a day or two there as her guest. Many years later an American Jewish friend of the present writer visited the family and the story of the Guru's informal visit was repeated to him at the table, with that strange sense of appreciation which was characteristic of the understanding evoked by this simple gesture. The lady had become old but had treasured the incident in her memory as a valued souvenir.

The Guru thus fitted himself into the contemporary context of the spiritual life of the people in a simple, human and natural manner without frontiers or barriers of any kind. He belonged to all contexts without partiality or preference, but he carried his own proper background with him by sheer necessity as the incidental aspect of his universal outlook. Such a reconciliation of seemingly conflicting aspects was his mission in life, if there could be said to be any 'mission' at all for a *yogī*.

His attitude to the Madhva background needs no further explanation in the light of these incidents. In Mangalore, not far from Uḍuppi, near which place Madhva was born, the Guru established temples which followed the Madhva tradition. He called one temple Gokarṇanātha, affiliating it to that of Madhva; and one of his last disciples who came from that part of India was named Ānanda Tīrtha which was Madhva's name also when he took to the monastic order. Apart from these evidences there is a prayer to Vāsudeva written by the Guru in his early years, which breathes the Madhva atmosphere of Śrī, the Goddess Lakṣmī, and Vāsudeva or Viṣṇu of the Conch, Discus, Mace and Lotus-holding hands, radiantly shedding the grace which the pious devotee (the *bhakta*) can drink as he worships at his lotus feet.

The Guru's name itself — Nārāyaṇa — means Viṣṇu rather than Śiva; although prehistorically and originally it refers to the primordial spirit which sleeps on the Waters of Creation, as the etymology of the name indicates. The name really refers back cosmologically to creation itself, where all traditions, whether of Brahmā, Viṣṇu or Śiva, meet and efface themselves. The Absolute has been alternately known by one or other of these names, and hence as names, and in the light of the Word-wisdom with which we are here concerned, they should be regarded as interchangeable terms and nothing more.[22]

Orthodoxy in itself meant nothing to the Guru. Nor could he commend heterodoxy. Between or above the positions there is a point of accordance, an agreement which is of the essence of the contemplative way of seeking truth. The progress of spirituality has to be conceived in living dynamic terms of a conquest of the new and a relinquishing of the old; but in terms of pure transcendentalism there is nothing to win or to discard; for the eternal present is the meeting-place of becoming and being. These and other matters have been touched upon by us in their various aspects and bearings, and in the discussions that follow we shall have occasion to return to this dynamic formula of progress in spirituality many more times before its full implications can be exhasutively brought into view.

---

22. Besides the coincidence in name, we can go deeper into the source of the Nārāyaṇa tradition. *Nāra,* water, and *āyaṇa,* suggesting inclining, refer to the cosmic man as the first principle of Creation. This name later became identified with Viṣṇu. The *Śatapatha Brāhmaṇa* (XIII.6-1) alludes to *Puruṣa Nārāyaṇa* attaining to Godhood by virtue of a series of sacrifices lasting five nights called the *Pañcarātra satra;* and the Vaiṣṇavite religious expression known under the name of *Pañcarātra* having the *ekāntika bhakti dharma* of Vāsudeva or Kṛṣṇa, has been linked later with *Puruṣa Nārāyaṇa.* The reference here to the Vedic sacrifice, used as a test, must mark the point where the Śiva tradition of prehistoric times terminated, to be revalued in terms of Vedic ritual, especially of sacrifice. Śaṅkara, whose background is Śaivite, in his *Śiva Nāmāvalī-aṣṭakam* apostrophising *Candra-cūḍa* (the Wearer of the Moon) i.e., Śiva, refers to Śiva himself as being *Nārāyaṇa Priya* (Verse 7), i.e., the One Beloved of Nārāyaṇa, which appellation gains added meaning in the light of the tradition anteriorly accepted. As Prof. O. Lacombe points out: 'Viṣṇu also passes from his subordinate position in the Vedic texts to a supreme rank. His identification with Nārāyaṇa and with Vāsudeva takes place at the epic period, posteriorly to the composition of the *Gītā.*' — *L'Absolu selon le Vedānta* (translated), p. 26.

We shall here conclude by referring to the relapse into lazy attitudes of complacency which marked the religious atmosphere in India after the decline of Buddhism. In trying to find normal human values, the pendulum began to swing in the opposite direction from the Stoic asceticism of the earlier days. The naive episode of the churning of the ocean of milk is a typical example of belief reflecting the atmosphere that began to prevail after the age of the Pallavas. Śrī, the Goddess of Prosperity, Plenty and Beauty was the personification of the value that all sought. Śrī or Lakṣmī is indeed the first prize that emerges from the lacteal ocean of good, in the well-known allegory wherein Śiva and Kṛṣṇa figure equally. Kṛṣṇa grabs the prize for marriage while Śiva drinks the poison as the god of tragic frenzy. The various other factors involved in the allegory reflect utilitarian values. A static and comfort-loving form of mysticism thus existed in India for several centuries (at least in the south) after the Pallava era, until the rude shocks of invasions from outside again acted as a spiritual eye-opener. Huns and Khans did the work of again awakening India to deeper-seated more virile values. Later we again see how the leaders of India such as Dayānanda, Vivekānanda, Tagore, Gandhi and others contributed to the deepening of the same value-potency into a supreme synthesis of living idealism.

Whatever may be the doctrine or philosophy accepted by a people, it is for them to make it alive so that it serves mankind. By themselves, doctrines do not effect good results. Merely to belong to a religion does not automatically save man. Whether in the form of faith, piety, renunciation, truth or reason, contemplation has to come in. The mind has to consent to look upon the face of truth. The weight of tradition or memory has to be lifted and purified. Finally, an intuitive vision has to be developed, which will ultimately triumph in terms of Self-realisation. These three laws of spiritual progress are voiced in the following three verses from the Guru Nārāyaṇa's work '*One Hundred Verses of Self-Instruction*' (*Ātmopadeśa Śatakam*) which we give in translation. A willing and neutral attitude in reaching Self-realisation is stressed:

This which prevails by overcoming the hindrance
Of each object of sense cognition
One's own memory alone
Can counteract.
Yet retrospection most lucid
Can with all reason be expected
To discover and to bring to light
All-transcending wisdom's treasure trove. (64)

Mere orthodoxy that bans with insistence
As heretical all other doctrines of the ultimate,
How can it knowledge ever bring ?
Lip service will never do,
The status of the Supreme
Has to be contemplated upon. (62)

That same knowledge, which from this knowledge here
Is not other, and than to know which
Immediately, there is nothing else here,
That by heterodox disadoption, to know,
Such, the secret supreme of the well-informed,
Who is here alas ! to know ? (63)

18

The Duality of Ends and Means

HITHERTO, in order to place the Guru-Word in its proper perspective and background or context, we have delved deep into the past and traced its course through history, iconography, myth and forms of faith, and brought it up to the surface in its setting in contemporary India. But essentially the Word is not concerned with institutions or social life, neither with the altar nor the pulpit. By implication these may be there in the background as a matter of necessity, but the Word itself rises above petty utility to the lofty status of a sublime treasure of a supreme human value.

The Word reconciles 'ends' with 'means' without being either of them. From the one side all ends are reduced to 'Reality', while the means come to meet them from another side. These 'means' are sometimes called *karma* — 'works', or ritualistic, pious actions with a view to attaining Self-realisation or final emancipation.

Self-realisation being non-dual belongs to neither ends nor means, but in itself is a full-flooded silence beyond the reach of mind and word. In the Word which represents this kind of silence, the positive and negative ways of mysticism or philosophy meet. As the *Bhagavad Gītā* says (Chapter 13), the field (*kṣetra*) and the Knower-of-the-field (*kṣetrajña*) have to be distinguished the one from the other, even as in the case of 'knowledge' and the 'Self', in order that, by abolishing the duality between them, or by bringing them together as dual aspects of the same silence, one may gain a globally integrated and immediate awareness of truth without being subject to synergic or ambivalent antinomies or rival conditionings of uncertainty or conflict. The duality in all ends and means has to be abolished systematically. There is no place at all for chance of any kind; and no amount of fortuitous, haphazard, mere non-chalant gambler's daring, radicalism, nor even free-lance bohemianism will by itself suffice.

Systematic abolishing of duality therefore requires a methodology and an epistemology. These are found in Advaita Vedānta. Indeed, without them Advaita Vedānta would be at best only a variety of personal dogmatism, a luxury or hobby. The Word is a personal appreciation of value in life in a very real sense, and this might excuse or condone dogmatism, but even in doing so a strict acceptance of first principles, of method and theory of knowledge is necessarily involved. The state of mere ecstasy or bliss, or mystical travail or agony, in vague, varied and often picturesque terms, such as 'practice of the presence of God',[1] will take us but less than half way in formulating an exact science in regard to Word-wisdom.

In the Indian legend, Kṛṣṇa has to steal the nectar from the hands of the evil forces (*asuras*) for the benefit of righteous humans. Or, to use another parable, Prometheus has to be unbound by a strong Hercules from his Caucasian rock where an angry Zeus had chained him for stealing the fire of the Olympian gods to light the life of men of clay. Whether called nectar or the life-fire, Word-wisdom is an end in itself, and all means meet the end indifferently when used for the sake of the Word. Self-knowledge is sufficient to itself and the Word is what induces self-knowledge to find peace and joy in itself, which is oneself. Perfection prevails before, perfection prevails after and, taking the one away from other, the same perfection remains over. Such is the ancient formula of Word-wisdom.

Word-wisdom can make use of cryptic esoteric language wherein doctrines of rare personal value for emancipation or salvation in a private sense can be enshrined. Then it relies upon metaphor, allegory or other figures of speech. Myth itself is but an elaborated figure of speech. Apocryphal or dogmatic expressions of reality

1. A phrase much in use by Christian mystics, especially by the Quietists and sometimes by members of religious bodies who have no liturgy or theology but who follow the 'Imitation' of Christ.

appeal to the masses and remain recorded in localised traditions. Sometimes a certain language (Hebrew, Arabic, Sanskrit, Pāli, Greek and Latin) or a civilization's remnant, is able to make use of these forms of expression for current usage within a circle large or small. Parochial variations still make such a language inadequate for general use.

Then the Word itself, in its triumph over limitations, speaks without theology, myth and even without dogma. Through a living and workable framework of reasoning, the Word emerges into public view as a value that is for the *general good*, while it remains for the *good of all* treated individually too. Then it rids itself of its own weight of traditional memories. The hitherto dark background becomes transparently clear as the higher reasoning or intuition penetrates into all that confronts the intelligence.

Through the acceptance of an epistemological frame of reference, using method, criticism, with freedom of the will to live for all and for oneself too without conflict of any private egotisms, the Word again triumphs in another sense. Bold spirits, bards, giants of wisdom or supermen arising from time to time, also declare the freedom of the Word in terms of pure Self-awareness or Self-realisation, in which again ends and means coincide. Laws take the place of dogma, and the necessity aspect is dealt with separately from the contingent aspect of Word-wisdom. Existence and reality are correctly related to a truth that makes all free.

Word-wisdom thus conceived as a human value is then common property, a genuine commonwealth of and for all. The frontiers of closed communities and civilizations can then be abolished or they wither away, while imaginary iron curtains are seen to consist of merely thin air, penetrated easily and effortlessly by the clear vision brought by Word-wisdom.

We have seen how the Guru Nārāyaṇa drew the line of demarcation between his earlier and later writings. Having completed the background setting of the Word, we shall now concern ourselves with a more direct examination of the implied method, of the frame of reference employed *vis-a-vis* the various aspects of knowledge and of the scale of higher human values disclosed in the triumph of Self-realisation when it is positively finalised.

The first axiom of the methodology of the Vedānta is one that we have referred to in Chapter 1. The *Īśa Upaniṣad* has the expression *satya-dharman* which means that the person who is the truth-seeker is also a man of righteousness, a follower of the true.[2] In the man envisaged by this expression moral values meet the mystical or philosophical truth. When the Sabbath is made for man, inner integrity is given primacy; and when man is made for the Sabbath outer standards prevail.[3] The secret of Word-wisdom is where the *Logos* and *Nous*[4] meet and cancel each other out in terms of Self-realisation. Intellectual enthusiasm for truth which, as some say, was Hellenic, meets the Hebraic enthusiasm for morality, and so again truth prevails. Both the pure and the practical aspects of wisdom have to come together in unity. *Vidyā* and *avidyā* (reason and nescience) have to be treated together, so that by transcending ignorance, positive wisdom shall emerge victorious. The same formula applies to the notion of being and non-being (*sambhūti*

---

2. *Īśa Up.*, v.,15:

   hiraṇmayena pātreṇa satyasyāpihitam mukham,
   tattvam pūṣaṇn apāvṛṇu satyadharmāya dṛṣṭāye.

   The face of Truth is covered with a golden disc;
   Remove, O Sun, the covering for one whose law is Truth's to see.

3. Christ and his disciples were hungry and plucked corn on the Jewish Sabbath, thus breaking the religious law. The Pharisees (one class of priets) questioned Christ who declared that when a man was hungry he had every right to eat and concluded, 'The Sabbath was made for man, and not man for the Sabbath.' (see *St. Mark,* II, 23-28; *Mathew*, XII, 1-8; *Luke,* VI, 1-5)

4. These two Greek words are very difficult to translate, because of the cosmological, psychological and mystical meanings woven around them. *Logos* is the Word itself, the creative unitive Word before the thought is expressed, the Word of God. *Nous* is pure *buddhi,* the divine Mind reflected in man, his 'soul' or 'spirit' or 'higher reason.' These and other Platonic terms were introduced into Christianity during the first centuries in Alexandria in Egypt when the Word-wisdom was being formulated by the Christian sages.

and *vināśa*) as subtly and finally alluded to in the same *Īśa Upaniṣad*.[5]

Pure being is synonymous with 'emancipation', 'freedom', 'gaining immortality', 'attaining salvation', *nirvāṇa* or *mokṣa*. When reduced to terms of Word-wisdom there is no duality; but examined from the angle of the method, i.e., the practice of the aspirant, the duality in treatment becomes inevitable. Electricity is a single energy, yet its positive and negative have to be recognised by the practising electrician. The real nature of the energy remains the same; it does not become two, but the supposition helps the initial understanding of the practitioner or apprentice.

So it was with Madhva. If he seemed to stress duality, it was not because he did not realise the unity of *Brahman*, but plainly because he was interested in the methodology and epistemology of Vedānta and had a programme of institutional life attached to the movement he started. Śaṅkara had enough to do arranging the theoretical aspects. His polemics were directed against the previous schools who had failed in various degress to satisfy the aspirations of aspirants, by being either too good or without high aims. Vaiṣṇavite love of luxury and excesses of ritual and imagery marked other schools, while what they wanted to say remained the same.

Thus *satya* (Truth) and *dharma* (what is held to be right) have to meet, but not in such a way that both would be annihilated, as so often happens when they are treated together; but rather in a manner that enables freedom of reason to triumph, finally abolishing all taint of duality in the consciousness of the *satya-dharman,* the Truth-natured. Hercules can kill the ravenous avenging vultures gnawing at the flesh of the imprisoned, struggling Prometheus, but it is the fire of pure wisdom that finally gives him

---

5. *Īśa Up.*, 14:

   sambhūtim ca vināśam ca yastad vedobhayaum saha, ।
   vināśena mṛtyum tīrtvā sambhūtyāmṛtam aśnute ॥

   Those who understand becoming and non-being together
   Get over death through knowing non-being
   and win immortality through knowing being.

spiritual freedom. The nectar must be worth stealing from the *asuras* (the demons) by Kṛṣṇa for the *devas* (the gods).

It is therefore in Word-wisdom that ends and means become reconciled, and the conflict is over between *jñāna* (wisdom) and *karma* (works). Thus the bipolar reciprocity between, the synergic antinomy or ambivalence underlying, action and wisdom, the existent and the subsistent, the actual and the perceptual, and many other pairs of seeming contradictions, is no longer puzzling, but, consequent on the axiomatic position indicated above, methodological corollaries follow and a unitive understanding prevents all conflict arising.

Satya or Truth has to be approached with the full freedom of the intelligence, as a part of the contingent in human life, while *dharma* or Duty is seen as belonging to the necessary, to the prior, relative, obligatory, social or traditional context of the Word. Any mixing of these axiomatic fundamentals, any confusion of the one with the other, makes all method, criticism, logic, reason or ratiocination give wrong results. The calculation will go away because the essential constant is left out. As in mathematics, functions and operations of contemplation have to be based on fundamental premisses which are at the root of Advaita or *brahma-vidyā* as conceived as an exact discipline. The high human value of *Brahman* is revealed both by the *a priori* and the *a posteriori* methods of reasoning operating hand in hand, regulated by epistemological and methodological axioms or laws, and this brings about Self-realisation.

More than any other philosopher of India, Śaṅkara brought out this subtlety in regard to the understanding of the Upaniṣads and the *Brahma Sūtras*. He never mixes up religious duties with wisdom, under the vague intermediate title of *dharma*, which is often a no-man's-land between the existent and the real, the necessary and the contingent. Over and over again, wherever the occasion presents itself in his various *bhāṣyas* (commentaries), we find him pointing out the absurdity of what is called *jñāna-karma-*

samuccaya (treatment of wisdom and works in combination).[6]

Dharma involving *vidhi* (obligatory injunctions — as for example, the Ten Commandments of Moses, all the 'thou shalt' portions of scripture) referring to social duty of a conformist orthodoxy is one thing, and the dedicated life to wisdom is another. It is the distinction between Christ dedicating his life to the Father and others to Caesar and the Mosaic laws. *Dharma* is relative within time and history. The life devoted to wisdom through speech transcends action, reaching to the perceptual through the actual, reaching the *satyam,* the Real through the *ṛtam,* the Existent. This involves a double negation — of ignorance, evil, darkness, sin or concupiscence. Whatever the name, it is the negating of the negative factor which is opposed to Self-realisation — hence a negation of a negation, the negation of *māyā,* the *negativitat* of Hegel.[7]

The positive result of wisdom is indicated by the reality of *Brahman* which is existent reality perceptually or conceptually implied in the Word. The Absolute (*Brahman*) is not a mere abstraction, but a value, not a nothingness or darkness, but a good, not an absence of awareness, but a bliss given to pure contemplation.

---

6. The distinction is made particularly clear between the two sections of the Vedas as scripture, the 'works' section (*karma-kāṇḍa*) and the 'wisdom' section (*jñāna-kāṇḍa*) or in general terms, between Veda and Vedānta. See Śaṅkara's *Svātmanirūpaṇam* (One's Own Self Defined):

   aṁśadvayavatī nigame sādhayati dvaitameva ko-apyaṁśaḥ:
   advaitameva vastu pratipādayati prasidvamaparom-āśaḥ
   — Verse 50

   'Of the Vedas consisting of the parts, one part enunciates duality and the other plainly expounds the non-dual reality.'
   — from *Select Works of Śrī Śaṅkarācārya* (Natesan, Madras).

   The division is in most scriptures, between the *Old* and *New Testament*, between *Tao* and *Teh* in China; or even between Lao Tzu and Confucius; clearer still in the case of the *dharma* spoken of by the Buddha in its mystical sense and the *dharma* of an Aśoka, purely social in meaning. All teachers have used this division, but have generally made confusion by using the same terms, using the word *dharma* for both man's will and God's. Only with Śaṅkara is the division made clear between wisdom and *karma*, with *dharma* as part of *karma*.

7. Hegel (1770-1831) famous German philosopher.

Sat (existence), *cit* (idea) and *ānanda* (supreme value) meet in *Brahman*, the Absolute thus conceived.

Advaita Vedānta is essentially a *sat-kāraṇa-vāda,* a philosophic insight built on a primacy of cause over effect. The cause is more real than the effect, and, starting strictly in an apodictic, ontological, realist and common sense manner, avoiding dogma or theological belief of any teleological nature, Advaita constructs a monumental edifice of knowledge leading up to the Absolute notions of value covering the triad of aspects just mentioned (*sat-cit-ānanda*).

Even in the matter of seeking a cause, Vedānta has its own norms of validity. There is the *nimitta kāraṇa* (the incidental or immediate cause) which is of the nature of a secondary agent; and there is the *upādāna-kāraṇa* (the cause that draws out into being something out of itself). There is therefore a vertical as well as a horizontal set of cause-effect series. The horizontal series is that of physics, while the vertical is that of more fundamental ways of seeking knowledge, beginning from matter considered intrinsically as in the modern hypotheses of matter as energy, dynamic, etc., or the values emergent from chemistry, etc. Aristotle's philosophy of *entelechia* and *prius*[8] recognised this way of seeking causes, ontologically, as opposed to other and teleological approaches which as it were, put the cart before the horse, by postulating far-off ends hidden away from present actualities.

The pot and the clay is the cherished, classical example of the Vedāntin here. The potter is incidental and secondary. His instruments may be many and his art is a nebulous item, but the clay is real and is the basis of the search for the real, for the essential substance behind the many pots. In the clay lies the true value. Another favourite Vedāntic example is the wave and water. The wave is but water with a certain conditioning of name and form. The resulting wave has no existence apart from the cause which is

---

8. Aristotle (384-322 BC) the pupil of Plato, coined the word entelechy from the Greek words *en telei ekhein* meaning 'to have in perfection', i.e., the perfection attained by anything by reason of which it actually exists and realises its true function — its self-existent value. Prius is from the Latin, meaning what is *previously* there, the 'given' in life or nature.

water. One can eliminate or change the incidental causes, but the primary substantial cause is the basis of the pot or the wave itself, and the search stops there with the ultimate. The Self is its own cause, and, as Spinoza[9] perhaps would put it, the *natura naturans* of the Self is the cause of the *natura naturata*[10] of the world of nature, *karma* and *dharma,* society and necessary duties. In seeking the 'thing in itself' (*Ding an sich*) we seek the substantial, natural prime cause, the substratum, and thus pass from the merely phenomenal to the noumenal, to use Kant's possible explanation.[11] The descending dialectical process of Plato envisages the recognition of the real and the actual too, in the general context of his approach to truth in terms of goodness and beauty, etc., which are effects rather than causes.[12] Ideal beauty is a perfected effect in the vague world of the intelligibles postulated by Plato. Propped on hypothesis after hypothesis, the term of high wisdom is attained in such an effect; but this transcendent teleological tendency has to attain simple existence by a reversal of hypotheses, referring back to ontological immanent aspects of the real which are here below on earth.

Thus some of the secrets of the methodology of the Vedānta are: that primacy in seeking the real must be given to cause rather than to effect; that an ontological approach be made at the beginning, without transcendentalism coming at that stage at least;

---

9. Spinoza: 'The Euclid of metaphysicians', born in 1632 in Amsterdam of Portuguese Jewish parents. Died 1677.

10. *natura naturans* is the *a priori* or God-given in nature, *natura naturata* is the *a posteriori* modes by which the God-given appears.

    Both Latin terms were Spinoza's own.

11. Kant (1724-1804) German philosopher: reduced phenomena to his categories of understanding, and used logic to prove the *Ding-an-sich* as quoted above.

12. There is the well-known passage from Plato's *Symposium* (211) 'Such is the true order of going — to use the beauties of earth as steps along which one mounts upwards for the sake of that other Beauty, going from one to two, and from two to all fair forms, and from fair forms to fair actions, and from fair actions to fair notions, until from fair notions he arrives at the notion of Absolute Beauty, and at last knows what the essence of Beauty is.' (Jowett's tr. 1871)

and that an appeal be made always to the immanent existent and simple reality of public common sense. This methodology seeks reality first through its own existent aspect, then passes on to its rational aspect and finally conceives reality as a human value.

These two poles of truth which meet as *satya-dharman* in a person and are thus expressed as a unitive human value, become more and more distinguishable when we turn to functional or intellectual aspects. According to the *Bhagavad Gītā:* 'Wisdom as to the field and the Knower of the field; that in my opinion is *the* wisdom'.[13] Unequivocally, this states the need of recognising the distinction between the perceptual and the actual aspects of wisdom, which together make what we have tried to designate as Word-wisdom.

Many are the unvarnished examples that philosophers and mystics have used to drive home this truth. There is a popular proverb in Malabār which says, 'Magic won't make a mango fall,' and another 'The Vedic chant is useless against a maddened buffalo.' Sri Ramakrishna used to say that if you shake a calendar which forecasts rain, no water will fall down. Śaṅkara has the same when he says that while one can carry a burden for another, there is no use in drinking his medicine for him. Vicarious suffering and other theological doctrines of grace and sin contain the same antinomian principles.[14] Discussions round these antinomies such as 'grace' and 'nature'[15] are endless because philosophers do not go to the root of the matter which involves the double-facing principle, in the truth

13. *kṣetrakṣetrajñayor jñānam*
yat taj jñānam matam mama. — *Bhagavad Gītā,* XIII, 2.

14. When Luther nailed his 95 theses on the church door at Wittemberg in Germany in 1517, which was the critical act that led to the great Protestant Reformation, he was really pointing out the absurdity of vicarious suffering, although it was the sale of indulgences by priests which was the immediate cause of his protest.

15. In Christian writing one of the best of these discussions on the aspects of nature and grace is found in *De Imitatione Christi* of Thomas á Kempis (1380-1471) e.g: 'My son, mark diligently the motions of Nature and of Grace, for in a very contrary and subtle manner do they move, and can hardly be distinguished but by him that is spiritually and inwardly enlightened.' Book IV, Chapter 54, v.1.

we all seek. Good and evil, the one and the many, genus and species, indeterminism and predestination, nurture and nature, free-will and fate, the general and the private good, unity and diversity — all these are pairs held together in reciprocal ambivalent relationship by a central value, grounded in the Absolute (*Brahman*) in terms of Self-realisation.

Every school of philosophy could be studied profitably with reference to its historically or ideologically anterior counterpart. The Stoic has the Epicurean, the idealist has the materialist, the mechanist has the vitalist, the empiricist the rationalist, and so on. The Christian *New Testament* is similarly built on the basis of the *Old Testament,* the Vedānta Upaniṣads on the Veda, the later Sūfis' works on the Koran, the *Tao Te Ching* on the *Shu-Khing, Yi-Khing, Shi-Khing* and *Li-Khi,* etc. The Pūrva-Mīmāṁsā (earlier inquiry) which is related to religious obligations in Vedic ritual, discussed critically, has always to be strictly distinguished from the Uttara-Mīmāṁsā (later inquiry) which is a posterior critique or philosophy as in the Upaniṣads. The Śruti (literally, what is heard) which pertains to pure knowledge as heard directly from the mouth of the original guru or *ṛṣi,* is to be understood as distinct from the Smṛti or Smārtta literature which pertain to duties arising from the original teachings in the form of various recommendations, directions, injunctions or obligations which recognise laws of existence or of certain necessary aspects of reality. The latter comprise all the Dharma Śāstras (Scriptures on Law), covering commandments and codes for social or individual life, in an everyday practical sense.

Any Indian *paṇḍita* or scholar who fails to make these lines of demarcation clear is treated with as scant respect as the medicine man of the ancient Āyurvedic school who did not know which names applied to chemicals and which to herbs. The anterior knowledge was always to be distinguished as the *pūrva-pakṣa* (the former position) and what the *guru* added on the basis of such an anterior position which would be taken by the disciple or implied from a previous school, would be the *siddhānta pakṣa* (the attained conclusion). The dialectical process of revaluation of old truth in new terms thus goes on between the *guru* and *śiṣya*, between the man of wisdom and the sceptic. A prophet speaks with his authority coming from a deep conviction.[16] His oration is sanctioned by God's truth or Self-knowledge, and then he speaks out in the unmistakable accents of a *guru*, as an oracle, a prophet or a messiah. Supermen or *avatāras* have the authority of conviction, earnest truth or love of humanity. They do not hesitate to call others 'people of little understanding,' or 'generations of vipers,' while such words as 'Verily, verily, I say unto you' mark out the superior distinction of their utterances when they depart from the hitherto-accepted to the re-valued statement of truth.[17]

The *Bhagavad Gītā* has the expressions *me matam idam* (my firm opinion is this)[18] and *niścitam matam-uktam* (my certain and highest opinion);[19] words uttered by Kṛṣṇa as the Guru of the *guru-śiṣya* dialectics (or *guru-śiṣya-saṁvāda* as it is called in Sanskrit) to his disciple Arjuna. Many are the references in the *Bhagavad Gītā* to the intrinsic difference between *karma* (action) and *buddhi-yoga* (a spiritual discipline of wisdom); indeed the *Gītā* itself as a whole fails to make any cogent meaning if not examined in the light of the implicit dialectics in its method of *pūrva-pakṣa-siddhānta-pakṣas* (the attained conclusion after discussion with the sceptic representing the old way of knowing), through a literary device which permits a *saṁvāda* (dialogue) as between a *guru* and a *śiṣya*. Implicitly or explicitly, all Vedāntic literature has to recognise this distinction.

When examining a Dharma Śāstra (code belonging to ritual commandments, injunctions and prohibitions) one has to look for the *vidhi* or rules to be unquestionably followed. As with the soldier

16. The word 'prophet' (*prophetes* in Greek) means 'one who speaks out,' not 'one who predicts'. In the *Bible* it was used to translate the Hebrew *nabī*, 'announcer,' and *roeh*, 'a seer,' which is too close to the Sanskrit word *ṛṣi* to escape significance. (see Wyld's *Universal English Dictionary* and Zimmern's *Greek Commonwealth*, p.124 fn.)
17. These phases are found in *Old* and *New Testaments* of the Christian *Bible*.
18. See *Bhagavad Gītā*, III.31-32; VII.18.
19. *Ibid.*, XVIII.6.

on the battlefield — 'their's not to question why, their's but to do or die,' — it is final. But the obligatory nature of the Śāstra changes in the Uttara (later) Mīmāṁsā (critique) where one can discuss and question with the *guru*. *Arthavāda* (discussion of implications) becomes not only permissible, but something encouraged by the *guru*.

Imagine a disciple of the ancient Upaniṣadic period arriving at the door of a *guru* with a bundle of firewood in his arms, willing to serve the *guru* round the sacrificial fire. He can be a forlorn Devadatta, a gentle Śvetaketu, an abandoned Naciketas or a sincere Satyakāma of humble birth, whose acquaintance we made in a previous chapter. He has to hold his breath in silence in the presence of those who have known the nature of the *Brahman*. He has to respect them in the light of the indications given by other wise men who render them homage. In silence and submission he has to wait his turn and has, in the meanwhile, to be engaged in the *nitya* and *naimittika* (daily or incidental) duties, following the life of a *brahmacārin* (one who is willing to tread the path of *Brahman*-wisdom). The *smārta karma* or obligatory aspects of duty have to be complied with first, whatever they may happen to be according to the context or tradition to which the disciple belongs. By traditional or social upbringing Satyakāma was not a Brāhmin, but that was no hindrance. He had to serve the necessary term, accepting the necessary side of the discipline in one form or another. After sometimes years of trial and patient suffering, when this period is over, the *guru* asks the *brahmacārin* to sit down by his side for the free discussion with him of the Vedānta, the subsequent aspects of free contingent wisdom. Then that other transcendent reality begins to be discussed, but only after the time-honoured distinction has been well-recognised by teacher and pupil.

The Upaniṣads themselves, however cryptic or ambiguous their contents may be as described by modern philosophers, never fail to make unequivocally clear the fundamental distinction between *karma* and *jñāna,* work and wisdom, the distinction which is so important methodologically. Invariably this is done at the very commencement of the Upaniṣad. Either the distinction is directly broached, or else is included in a preliminary literary device. The pupil Naciketas is accorded his first two boons easily, but when as the third boon the Spirit of Death is asked for the clearing of a doubt which shifts the subject into the domain of pure higher knowledge, he wails piteously, and puts forward apologetic excuses and objections, because it is rare and unattainable by ordinary people who have not come to seek it wholly. Death asks Naciketas to choose another boon, one less difficult to bestow, and even tries to fob off the young questioner by giving him an extra boon as a bonus.[20]

In another Upaniṣad, Umā Haimavatī, the resplendent daughter of the Himālaya, has herself to come down to explain to the Vedic gods Indra and others the nature of the Absolute which is only a mystery in the form of a *yakṣa* (semi-divine being) to them. Here Umā who is the personification of higher wisdom, is the consort of Śiva; and in the light of what we have said earlier regarding the historical blast and counterblast of Word-wisdom, this meeting of the two traditions in allegorical form in an Upaniṣad should not be without its significance to the reader.[21]

In other places distinction is made between *parā vidyā* and *aparā vidyā* (Ultimate and non-Ultimate knowledge). Nārada, who is a *brahmarṣi* of the Vedic context, frequently affords the dialectical link needed to make these aspects of knowledge clear. Although a *ṛṣi* himself, he has to learn the difference between *mantra-vidyā* (Knowledge of Chanting) and *ātma-vidyā* (Knowledge of the Self) from Sanatkumāra who was wise before him.[22]

The *pravṛtti mārga* (forward and active path) and the *nivṛtti mārga* (the way of negation, the *via negativa* of European mysticism), are also constantly distinguished in all Vedāntic literature. In his *Bhagavad Gītā Bhāṣya* (commentary) and also in his commentary on the opening *sūtra* (aphorism) of the *Brahma Sūtras* which expressly uses the words 'therefore or then' or 'hereafter or now' (*atha ato*) as a kind of double protection against

20. See *Kaṭha Upaniṣad,* Vallī I.

21. See *Kena Upaniṣad,* Khaṇḍa III, 1 *et seq.*

22. See *Chandogya Upaniṣad,* whole of VII Prapāṭhaka.

the anterior doctrines of a different nature, Śaṅkara underlines again how important it is to differentiate and recognise the gulf between these two aspects of wisdom which are variously named in their different contexts.

In concluding our present discussion, there are many other features of the Advaita Vedānta, but they require more detailed treatment since they involve subtleties not to be dealt with summarily. Incidentally, we have referred already to one of the peculiarities of the Vedānta, which belongs to its methodology and epistemology. *Nirviśeṣa* (absence of specialisation) sums up what we mean. In Vedānta high thinking is part of plain living. This is the touch of renunciation, or abnegation, a refusal to be lured away by luxuries or by over-specialisation in life. Ceremonial elaborations are therefore also repugnant to the Vedāntin's way of life. Without being too severe with himself he stresses natural and normal daily values. Clean-shaven plainness is inseparably associated with a man of the Vedāntic tradition on the Indian scene; and, while it is true that this is a matter of outside appearance only, what it implies is valid to the general outlook of Advaita Vedānta.

Vedānta also tends to stress a certain inwardness in thinking. Outer events and actions lose their importance in the Vedāntic context. The central, the subtle living core or kernel of our being, interests the Vedāntin more than even the cosmos. Although cosmology may enter the field of Vedānta, incidentally accepted in a form modified to suit its dialectical, contemplative, inward approach, Vedānta is more psychological in its subject-matter and approach. Contemplation thus undertaken from the interior of each Self or 'thing-in-itself' tends to become solipsist in its outlook of aloneness, and the extreme idealism which results might also be mistaken for sceptic phenomenalism of the Hume pattern or for Berkeleyan one-sided noumenalism — which, when closely examined, in the light of the two-sided nature of Word-wisdom, are really complementary.[23]

---

23. David Hume (1711-76): noted for his philosophy of complete scepticism.

George Berkeley (1685-1753): Irish Bishop whose philosophy is known as Subjective Idealism.

Utilitarianism and pragmatism, in so far as they stress unnatural and complicated or mechanistic values in modern civilization, tend to be discredited, as also materialism and empiricism.

In thus accepting many schools of philosophy hitherto considered distinct in the West, the modern mind might even label Vedānta as a form of syncretism, but this, instead of being objectionable, should rather be taken to be the good point about Vedānta. Strict Vedānta admits of no eclecticism. It is a distinct, contemplative or mystical discipline, understood and employed at all times and climes by those who have kept the traditional torch of perennial wisdom burning irrespective of all the outward differences of history and geography.

We must also note that Śaṅkara often stresses the distinction between what he calls *lakṣaṇārtha* (the figurative sense) and *vācyārtha* (the actual, literal sense). For example, when *Brahman* is said to be *sat-cit-ānanda* (Existent-Rational-Value) he is never tired of pointing out that when *Brahman* is described in words we have to take the inner meaning and not the outward, dead or literal sense, which seems to exclude one adjective from another. The same unitive *Brahman* is described as *sat, cit* and *ānanda,* and it is for the intuitive mind of the seeker to put these three together into one complete unitive whole of global awareness in terms of Self-realisation.

In this plea of Śaṅkara we see the affinity of Vedānta with Abelard's conceptualism.[24] The Idea and the intelligibles of Plato were brought down to meet actualities in Plotinus[25] and the Neo-

24. Peter Abelard (1079-1142). French philosopher and teacher. Had a tragic romance with Heloise. He emphasised Aristotle's dialectic as opposed to the devotionalism current in his time.

25. Plotinus (*c*.205-70) revalued the whole Greek philosophic tradition at his school outside Rome. His works survive as the famous *Enneads.* He was an Alexandrian.

The Neo-Platonists had their chief school at Alexandria in Egypt during the era just before and after the beginning of the Christian period. They revived and revalued the teachings of Plato and his successors like Aristotle.

Platonists. Abelard and other theologians of Paris, from this synthesis, derived a 'conceptualism', or what is sometimes also called nominalism. The doctrine of the Word (*Logos*) of St. John's Gospel comes near to this, lends weight to this view and brings our own point of view here in treating the Word of the Guru as close as could be expected to an ancient line of thought. Cartesianism[26] itself, although named dualistic is only mistakenly thought to be so. It attempts to refer valid reasoning to inner rather than outer norms, and thus it lays the foundation for later rationalism which paves the way to all the later idealistic traditions in modern philosophy. Through later idealists in Germany[27] dialectics was rediscovered, while intuition was again given its place by Bergson[28] bringing us back to a position in which the discussion of mysticism and Vedānta in a systematic way becomes possible in a modern context.

Finally, it might also be pointed out here that Vedānta, at least Advaita Vedānta, aims at proving or solving nothing. As Eddington[29] said, the proof is the idol the mathematician worships, and final solutions in the matter of the Absolute is an impossibility. The word Absolute has no definite meaning unless interpreted in terms of some human value, high or low or ordinary. It is to be understood in a nouminous presence of the Good that we recognise within ourselves, or in some dear object or idea that we conceive within.

---

26. Cartesianism derives its name from Rene Descartes (Latin *Renatus Cartesius*) (1596-1650). French philosopher and scientist. Famous as a mathematician (originated Cartesian co-ordinates and Cartesian curves), and in philosophy 'doubts everything but the existence of doubt itself', which he expressed in the famous saying '*Cogito ergo sum*', (I think, therefore I am). God is to him the link between noumenal and phenomenal.

27. Such as Kant, Schopenhauer, etc.

28. Henri Bergson (1859-1941). French philosopher and author of brilliant and imaginative but precise philosophical works (winning him the 1927 Nobel Prize in Literature), such as *The Two Sources of Morality and Religion* (1935), *Introduction to Metaphysics* (1903) and *Creative Evolution* (1907).

29. Sir Arthur Stanley Eddington (1882-1944). British astronomer and physicist, but more famous as a popular expositor of scientific subjects, and author of a number of books such as *Nature of the Physical World* (1928); *The Expanding Universe* (1933), etc.

The very fact that people are prepared to lay down their lives for ideas which they prize, shows that such values do exist, and they exist in an endless possible series, all of which could be arranged along the rungs of a Jacob's Ladder or scale of values reaching from earth to heaven. All visions of ultimate values could be strung together under the presiding Crest Jewel of Wisdom which is the brightest ornament on the crown worn by Sarasvatī, who, though a lowly-born goddess of pre-Vedic times, still reigns on the Indian scene as the representative of the Guru-Word.

19

The Living Method

In Guru Nārāyaṇa the critical and methodical standards used in gaining insight into Word-wisdom were employed so perfectly as to make this a Science of sciences. We have used the simple title of Word-wisdom in our writing, but it would be equally correct to use the Sanskrit terms *ātma-vidyā* (Self-knowledge) or *brahma-vidyā* (knowledge of the Absolute). Methodology, epistemology and a certain theory of human values which are normative, are all present in this Science, and clearly evident in the writings of the Guru, more implicit in the earlier works and in a particularly positive explicit manner in his later productions.

Word-wisdom deals with inner human values and therefore cannot be impersonal. The human personality is an integral part of its very scope of enquiry. Cosmology and psychology are treated in an intuitive and intimate manner with a special metaphysics peculiar to this Science and derived from contemplation rather than from merely external objectivity.

Avoiding the indirect approach through lifeless symbols, the science of Word-wisdom aims at establishing a *rapport* between subject and object, so that by impartially neutralising all possible prejudices a universally valid wisdom can be achieved in integral, unitive or global terms. While myth, allegory and all other forms of speech and literary devices can be (and have been) employed by the masters of this science, these usages are never to be understood in their literal sense, but always in that synthetic spirit which leads to attunement to or awareness of a high human good or value, in accordance with Self-knowledge.

Empirical philosophy postulates subject and object as real; rationalism places these within the mind; pragmatism sobers down the excesses of idealism and brings values within the scope of human needs; naturalism seeks to establish norms in accord with nature and natural laws; utilitarianism aims at satisfying one and all with something positively worth while; and idealism stresses freedom as a precious value. In all these systems of philosophic thought there is an implied 'self' and 'non-self'; a knowledge and an ignorance; a *Logos* or a *Nous*. In them all there is the attempt to reconcile, find agreement, explain, equate or cancel one view of reality or truth in terms of the other. In doing so their interest lies in revealing a motive for human relations or conduct with oneself or with something in one's environment. They seek norms of value which belong to the various levels of possible contexts in human life.

The common centre, the clearing-house where all these apparently different expressions of philosophy meet, is the human personality or the Self. The teleological approach will give certain answers, the ontological will supply others. Immanent aspects have their corresponding transcendental counterparts. All these are understood by the various terminologies of different schools of thought, but underlying them all there is an implicit unitive epistemology, and when this is understood by means of the laws of thought or of contemplation, with axioms or corollaries which cling together systematically, they are all found to be grounded in the Self. Such a study, when strictly conceived, will be found to fulfil all that is required of a science.

Sociology and economics, which are considered to be sciences, are based on statistical evidence. Though meant to be normative thay are often open to prejudiced data with subsequent wrong conclusions and findings. All the same, these are accepted as 'sciences' in modern life. The *a priori* basis is gaining more headway in the preserves of scientific thought, so that laws and doctrines tend to mean the same, to be more or less synonymous.

In view, therefore, of these modern developments in science, there remains no more valid reason for excluding Self-knowledge from the status of a science; especially when the subject is treated with strict 'objectivity,' with critical reasoning, positive recognition of laws and norms of human value, as the Guru Nārāyaṇa has done. This is particularly manifest in his various later writings, such as the *Advaita Dīpikā* (Lamp of Non-Duality), *Ātmopadeśa Śatakam* (One Hundred Verses of Self-Instruction), and the *Darśana-Mālā* (Garland of Visions).

In many of his miscellaneous works too, some of them written quite early in his career, such as the *Brahma-Vidyā Pañcakam* (Five Strophes to Brahman-Knowledge), and even in his compositions clothed in the conventional figurative language of south Indian Śiva worship, there is a completely elaborated and coherent presentation of scientific knowledge of great value.

What is known as scientific method today consists of what Bacon[1] called experiment, observation and inference. In the normative sciences, where strict laboratory experiments as in the case of the study of simple phenomena in nature, become difficult or impossible, statistical evidence based on questionaires or 'mass observation' are commonly employed. Variation experiments under controlled conditions, and the comparing of results obtained — eliminating some and retaining others — are the familiar ways of science today. These ways have become fashionable. The intrinsic merits of the method employed in a particular case are not seriously questioned. Much passes for science which at best is but quasi-science. Charlatans can quote scientific scripture in the form of graphs, charts or schematic representations. The letters of the Greek alphabet are freely employed in equations which are reduceable to common sense statements, but which the scientists prefer to present in their own almost secret codified mathematical language. Cases have been known of differences between physical and chemical calculations involving the same initial factors. Geological results vary from thermodynamical conclusions. According to one such set of data, the history of the earth will be

---

1. Francis Bacon (1561-1626): English philosopher, statesman and litterateur. Formulated and introduced inductive method of modern science as opposed to the *a priori* method of scholasticism. Among his most famous works are *The Advancement of Learning, Novum Organum Scientiarum, Essays,* and *The New Atlantis.*

quite a different picture from that painted by another who speaks in terms of the 'entropy' of the universe. There are *paṇḍita*s and theologians of science who are just as vague and sentimental as in other fields of human knowledge. Wherever higher subjective values are involved, fool-proof methods seem difficult.

But, as Tyndall pointed out, burst boilers need not deter us from continuing to make use of steam. In able hands, and in the essential rules of its discipline, the scientific method can be applied to any section or field of knowledge. Perennial philosophers of all ages and climes have had this objectivity, this apodictic common sense realism, a love of fact and down-to-earth public actuality, a 'coming down to brass tacks' and 'hitting the nail on the head' and 'calling a spade a spade' as the vulgar might say. These popular expressions however, do mark a point where the actual living language recognises a certain agreement or accord, a consolidation of facets of reality, bringing out to view tangible results of value in everyday life. Common speech, proverbs and adages often enshrine this attitude, bringing out a certain kind of conviction which interests and satisfies the man of intelligence as well as the man in the street. Such ought to be the quality of a scientific truth. It must be of a general public nature so as to induce that well-known sense of certitude in all impartial minds, whether *a priori* or *a posteriori* reasoning enters into the proving of such convictions.

From time immemorial our intelligence or reasoning faculty has been compared to vision or the eye that sees light.[2] The light is the objective counterpart of vision which is subjectively implied in

2. Cf., Plato: 'In every man there is an eye of the soul which, when by other pursuits lost and dimmed, is by these (philosophic) studies purified and re-illumined, and is more worthy of preservation than ten thousand bodily eyes, for by it alone is Truth seen.' — *Republic,* 527 E

'And so we have at last arrived at the hymn of Dialectic. This is that strain which is of the intellect only, but which the faculty of sight will nevertheless be found to imitate. When a person starts on the discovery of the Absolute by the light of the reason only, without the assistance of the senses, and never desists until by pure intelligence he arrives at the perception of the Absolute Good, he at last finds himself at the end of the intellectual world, as in the case of sight at the end of the visible.' — *Republic,* 532 A

→

the eye. Sun, eye and vision — all refer to the same central phenomenon in consciousness, although each gives primacy to one or the other of the three aspects of subject, object, or central reality that is suggested. These three are called *tripuṭi* (tri-basic) in Vedānta.

Apart from these distinctions which are incidental and not fundamental as far as reflexive Self-knowledge is concerned, the eye, sun and vision have essentialy the same content which, contemplatively conceived, is a relation, a situation, an accordance, an agreement or an equation. The eye sees an object and, with the help of sunlight removes or eliminates the possibility of error with reference to that object. The error is a kind of veil or darkness which the eye with the help of light is able to penetrate. A certain veiling (*āvaraṇa*) is removed and reality directly apprehended. This is called *pratyakṣa* (given to sense).

This process of penetration into reality 'as such' is pushed forward by science. As science proceeds with such a task, the primacy of objective light becomes inevitably transformed, either by slow degrees or at once, into a primacy of the inner light. We can *know* the true nature of an object only *by something prior to the object* itself. There is a memory factor which is prior to the sensation, and with which it must tally to make any meaning or sense. Sensation has therefore to depend upon an innate sense. This innate sense being of the nature of knowing or awareness, resembles light, having a similar essential value, and this, contemplatively, can be equated with light such as that of the sun. This light within when theoretically conceived after the manner of the *prius nobis* of Aristotle, has its reality in oneself. The supreme idea of the world

---

→ Also Plotinus: 'Never did the eye see the sun unless it had first become sunlike, and never can the soul have vision of the First Beauty unless itself be beautiful.' — *Enneads,* I, vi.9

And Goethe:

'Wär' nicht das Auge sonnenhaft
Wie könnten wir das Licht erblicken ?
Lebt' nicht in uns des Gottes eigne Kraft,
Wie könnt' uns Göttliches entzücken?'
— *Entwurf einer Farbenlehre*

of the intelligibles of Plato is also a factor that is grounded in the Self. Just as the eye cannot see itself, so the subjective aspect is not known objectively, while conversely the objective aspect is not known subjectively. Contemplation reduces the difference that separates these two — as between light and the eye, or Self and knowledge.

Intense meditation on the intrinsic verity of these two forms of knowledge abolishes the difference between them, merging both in a central, neutral, non-dual awareness which is both transcendental and immanent, 'positive' as well as 'negative'. This awareness remains a final thing of joy, a rare human value much coveted by human beings from the most ancient times. It holds interest both for public and private life.

Socratic wisdom is summed up in 'Know Thyself'.[3] The entire devious course of speculation since his days is but the further elaboration of this central problem, finding, reference or dictum. The Self is on one side and 'objective' knowledge on the other. All the mystical formulae such as 'Thou art That', 'I am *Brahman* (or Śiva) ', or 'This Self is Knowledge', known as the *mahāvākyas* (*dicta magnus*) of Vedānta, are neutral statements wherein positive and negative wisdom cancel each other out, in terms of a central personal experience of value.

Words can go no further to explain this simple situation, and yet in seeking for an explanation of this Word-wisdom, men have travelled far and wide in all times and climes. Śaṅkara discusses this simple position of the Advaita Vedānta in his *Dṛk-Dṛśya-Viveka* (Wisdom

3. 'Know Thyself' (*Gnothi Seauton*) was the inscription at the entrance to the oracle-temple at Delphi, a town at the foot of Mount Parnassus in Ancient Greece. It was known as the Navel (i.e., the centre) of the World, because it was an international spiritual centre of advice, holding otherwise fragmented Greece together and not only Greece but other states as well. Originally a temple of Dionysius (the Greek Śiva), it was later shared with Apollo (the Greek Sūrya), by the former during the winter and by the latter in summer. When the Greek philosopher Socrates (469-399 BC) was 30, the Delphic oracle pronounced him the wisest man in Greece, and accordingly he took on the role of a *guru*, questioning everyone to discover the truth of the oracle.

of Seer and Spectacle), a work which follows the methodology and epistemology that we have indicated. Other schools, calling themselves and distinguished by other names, have given primacy to one or the other of the aspects of being and becoming. In 'neutral monism', as Bertrand Russell would call it, all the contributions of speculation gain unitive correlation.[4] The two categories remain always at the basis of all knowing, whether based on laws of thought, or parts of speech. Mathematics knows of positive and negative quantities and infinities, and of rational and irrational numbers. It also knows functions, operations and correlations through algebra, geometry, or Cartesian correlates.

Employing like methods and the same underlying epistemology, it is possible to discover, round the simple formula of Self-knowledge, a series of graded personal values which will suit every major situation in life or which will answer the major questions of human quest. As there is a strange agreement between water and thirst, the central experience of knowledge remains the same, whether satisfactions are simple or complex. It is of course possible to erect more and more complicated superstructures round the simple nucleus of Self-knowledge, as an answer to all the possible situations that are likely to arise in the complications of human life. Such further elaborations of Advaita Vedānta are without any end in scope or possibility, but the innermost nuclear

4. In Russell's own words: 'The philosophy appropriate to quantum theory, however, has not yet been adequately developed. I suspect that it will demand even more radical departures from the traditional doctrine of space and time than those demanded by the theory of relativity. . . . While physics has been making matter less material, psychology has been making mind less mental. . . . Thus from both ends physics and psychology have been approaching each other, and making more possible the doctrine of 'neutral monism' suggested by William James's criticism of 'consciousness.' The distinction of mind and matter came into philosophy from religion, although, for a long time, it seemed to have valid grounds. I think that both mind and matter are merely convenient ways of grouping events. Some single events, I should admit, belong only to material groups, but others belong to both kinds of groups, and are therefore at once mental and material. This doctrine effects a great simplifiction in our picture of the structure of the World.' —*History of Western Philosophy, p.861,* Allen and Unwin, 1946.

knowledge remains ever the same simple Word-wisdom.[5]

However, in spite of this verity, we find much vain disputation tearing asunder large sections of humanity. Frontiers are marked out, endlessly dividing man from brother man. Hence in the task of reconciliation the emergence of a new and exact science which will help to establish the greatest consensus of opinion, through proper methods of reasoning, by a sound epistemology and by normal appreciation and arrangement of values, becomes a matter of great import.

The method arising from the contemplative discipline of Word-wisdom is based on an inherent dialectics where two reciprocally ambivalent and synergic antinomies, or double-charactered aspects, or poles of quality, phase or sign, have their interplay in a tacitly understood relation, an operation or function as in mathematics, each counteracting, cancelling and revaluating the other opposite twin. What results or emerges out of such a contemplation effects a symmetrical view of reality, a resultant or value slanting neither to the objective nor the subjective prejudice into which the mind is naturally prone to swing.

Contemplation therefore strikes a true balance and, blind-fold to externality, arrives at the resultant plummet line along which all true central points of human value lie. Glamour, exaggeration of ego, or attachments to persons or places due to habits, memories, or external or extraneous considerations, are avoided. When the

5. Cf., Chuang Tzu, (*c.* BC 300): 'Infinite, unceasing, there is no room for words about the Tao (Brahman). To regard it as in the category of things is the origin of the language that it is *caused* or that it is the result of *doing nothing*; but it would end as it began with things. . . . . The name Tao is a metaphor, used for the purpose of description. To say that it causes or does nothing is but to speak of one phase of things, and has nothing to do with the great subject. If words were sufficient for the purpose, in a day's time we might exhaust it; since they are not sufficient, we may speak all day and only exhaust the subject of things. The Tao is the extreme to which things conduct us. Neither by speech nor by silence can our thoughts about it have their highest expression.' — *Writings of Chuang Tzu*, p. 130, tr. James Legge, vol. XL, *Sacred Books of the East*, Oxford, 1891.

counterparts are determined the intelligence discovers equations, and finds accords, points of continuity and agreement. A synthetic global attitude brings the 'existent', 'real' and 'dear' aspects of a situation into one unitive appraising whole. This is then reduced into terms of the Self so that the final fusion of *apperceptive* wisdom may result.

This kind of direct or immediate awareness attains wisdom's centre without difficulty or fuss. There is nothing in this wisdom about which to lose one's head. One's own Self becomes convinced and satisfied with the elimination of doubts and conflicts. Virtues shine by themselves when the extraneous aspects clinging to the surface of the mirror of the Self are 'wiped off.' Conditionings vanish from consciousness and errors of judgement decrease till, for all practical purposes, they may be said to exist no more. One says 'And so that's that!' or attains *yātā-tathya* (the-way-it-ought-to-be). A new matter-of-fact attitude is attained in which everything is reduced to a natural simplicity where the necessary and the contingent meet to make life a harmonious flux. This in Vedānta, is known as *anubhava* (realising).[6] The man who comes to this

---

6. This free and easy attitude comes out emphatically in the teaching of Zen Buddhism (introduced into China by the South Indian Bodhi-Dharma sixth century AD). *Zen* is Japanese for *Ch'an* in Chinese, from *dhyāna* in Sanskrit, meaning contemplation. Zen stresses the crystalline state achieved by resolving the dialectical counterparts arising from the adoption of individualisation or egoism.

For example,
No offence offered, and no ten thousand things;
No disturbance going, and no mind set up to work:
The subject is quieted when the object ceases,
The object ceases when the subject is quieted.

× × ×

Obey the nature of things, and you are in accord with the Way,
Calm and easy and free from annoyance;
But when your thoughts are tied, you turn away from the truth
They grow heavier and duller and you are not at all sound.

× × ×

One in all,
All in One —
If only this is realised,
No more worry about your not being perfect !

→

attains detachment and unconcerned harmony. His flight is from the 'alone to the Alone,' or he is the *yogī* who holds the prize like a gooseberry within the palm; of free will, an emancipated person. Various degrees of such detachment cause rarer and rarer values to be represented in such persons. He is knowledge and, thus equated, he becomes holy, adorable, kind, good or divine. He begins to live according to the Guru Word-wisdom. Beauty, joy and love wait upon such a man, who lives for himself and for all others at one and the same time.

The theory of knowledge or the methodology of Word-wisdom can be elaborated or stated simply and succinctly. Always it has to be grasped by a certain grace or blessing of a *guru*. Nature itself in very rare cases can play the role of a *guru*, and many *gurus* can represent the fruition of one result of Word-wisdom in a person. Whatever way it comes about, wisdom is the mercy or grace that 'blesseth him that gives and him that takes,' like that quality which is synthetically spoken of by Shakespeare. It always takes two sides to bring it about. In all wisdom of the kind spoken about here the *śiṣya*-relationship is implied. He comes to the *guru* with his typical doubts such as 'Who am I?', 'How does this phenomenal world come to be?', etc. The burning quest is a thirst which has to be quenched by its corresponding counterpart of the consoling water of wisdom which a veritable *guru* carries always with him. Baptism implies this situation. The disciple then rises to his feet, and, conversely, may be waited on by the *guru*. They attain unity of status in the context of the pure contemplative life. Thenceforward they are fellow pilgrims in life's journey.

We shall have occasion, later, with individual specimens of the

---

→ — from *On Believing in Mind*, by Seng-T'san who died AD 606 (from *The Bible of the World,* ed. Robert O. Ballou in collaboration with F. Spiegelberg, Columbia University, Kegan Paul, London, 1946.25s.)

Perhaps the nearest of the Advaita Vedānta texts to Zen is the *Aṣṭāvakra Gītā* (English tr. Swami Nityasvarūpānanda, published by Advaita Ashrama, Mayavati, Almora, Himalaya, 1940) where the happy state is extolled, e.g., 'Equanimous in practical life as well, the wise one sits happily, sleeps happily, speaks happily and eats happily'. Chapter 18, Verse 59.

guru's writings before us, to enter into further aspects of the approach to Word-wisdom. Many aspects are necessarily implied by hoary custom and tacitly understood in the *guru-śiṣya* relationship in India. The willing disciple in India fits into a certain rigidity of framework given by tradition. This, however, needs some revision in the light of modern notions of self-respect and dignity, without however spoiling its essential purity, its bipolar intensity and directness. Thus the *guru* and *śiṣya* belong intrinsically to the methodology and epistemology of the Advaita. They are the inevitable counterparts of its vital contemplative dialectics.

Rare indeed is that philosophy which can speak of scientific fact in terms of human values and of human values in terms of simple scientific reality. The *Śvetāśvatara Upaniṣad* which is one of the later productions according to scholars, accomplishes this synthesis of wisdom and value in lines such as the following:

> Transcending the world-tree, time and forms
> Is He from whom this universe emerges;
> The Source of righteousness, the Destroyer of Sin, the Lord of Glory,
> Know Him as the Immortal, the Abode of all, as seated in one's own Self.[7]

The *Bhagavad Gītā* too, sets before the reader this ideal of an apodictic common sense finality of easy and convincing public discipline underlying its mystical teachings which it praises thus:

> Royal Science, Royal Secret, Pure, of high value is this
> Which by direct awareness is sensed;
> Ever conducive to right living, easy of practical application,
> And knowing no decrease ever.[8]

7. *sa vṛkṣakālakṛtibhiḥ paro-anyo*
yasmāt prapañcaḥ parivartate-ayam;
dharmāvaham pāpanudam bhageṣam
jñatvā-ātmasthānamṛtam viśvadhāma.
— *Svetāśvatara Upaniṣad*, VI.6.

8. *rājavidyā rājaguhyam*
pavitram idam uttamam
pratyakṣāvagamam dharmyam
susukham kartum avyayam. — *Bhagavad Gītā,* IX.2

Although it is true to some extent that Indian mysticism tends to stress individualised values sometimes at the expense of public virtues of a social order, often subjecting the latter to neglect and distortion,[9] there are valuable lines of thought suggested like the above which bring secrets out of their hiding places into common public view for general benefaction. Esotericism can meet openly-declared truths, and orthodoxy unite equally well satisfied and convinced with heterodoxy, in the light of a Self-realised, reflective, yet public discipline supporting universally valid norms which a new Science of the Word can employ.

It is precisely in this content that the unique quality of the writings of the Guru Nārāyaṇa consists. A strange agreement of matter and method underlies his treatment of mystical contemplation. He includes all within its scope. What has been the object of endless discussion, of hairsplitting, non-contemplative, blind, unsound, or feeble understanding, is most ably brought by him under unitive dialectical scrutiny. Counterparts are determined by a certain inherent theory of knowledge which distinguishes between actualities, realities and truths. Absurd entities are put as it were into the wastepaper basket and the rest reasonably arranged into orderly pigeon-holes, till there is no jumble of paper remaining on the desk; so that the simple work of meeting any situation squarely may proceed unhampered. When all that has no value has been rejected, and the remainder sorted out tidily, each essential in its place, the result is a harmonised life. Vain beatings about the bush are avoided and much human energy conserved for ever better uses.

Let us take one example from the Guru's writings to show how he simplifies all questions in the light of a contemplative method

---

9. Cf., J.M. Nallaswami Pillai: 'Amongst the ancient Indians, whose consciousness of human solidarity, of common needs and common interests was but slightly developed, the sense of the objective worth of moral action (that is, the worth it possesses for others), is very inferior to ours, while their estimate of its subjective worth (that is, its significance for the actor himself) was advanced to a degree from which we may learn much.' — *Madras Review,* Vol.6, 1900, pp. 364-65 quoted by Hume, *Thirteen Principal Upanishads*, 1934, p. 505.

which one can say goes to the extent even of resembling a modern style scientific laboratory experiment. Exact thinking is therefore introduced into problems hitherto considered belonging properly to the domain of mere speculation or some vague spiritual doctrine, left in the hands of various philosophers and men of religion, of East or West.

Such a problem is that of the nature of the 'Soul' or the 'Self'. The *jīvātmā* (individual or living Self) and the *paramātmā* (the ultimate or universal all-Self) have been for centuries but vaguely defined in books. Buddhists are supposed not to believe in the Soul or the Self; and in the case of Western theology we know how many battles have been fought round pluralism, genus or species as applied to souls or other hypostatic entities, such as the Persons of the Trinity, Angels, Arch-angels, etc. Although Kant[10] and Comte[11] attempted the critical examination or positive classification of such concepts under categories or universal laws, the problem has been generally considered unfit for any kind of

---

10. Immanuel Kant (1724-1804) the first and greatest of the line of modern German philosophers; author of the *Kritik der reinen Vernunft* (Critique of Pure Reason). To Kant, 'things-in-themselves' or noumena, are unknowable. His 12 categories of *a priori* concepts are as follows: of Quantity (unity, plurality, totality), of Quality (reality, negation, limitation), of Relation (substance and accident, cause and effect, reciprocity), and of Modality (possibility, existence, necessity). Moral concepts, he affirmed, originate *a priori,* hence the famous Categorical Imperative (a certain action is right because it is so), and its corollary, the Hypothetical Imperative (i.e., acts *with* a motive).

    Schopenhauer (1788-1860) was the real successor of Kant and by a reading of a Latin translation of the Upaniṣads, modified Kant's views in the light of Vedānta. One of the best textbooks of the Kant-Schopenhauer school is Dr. P. Deussen's *The Elements of Metaphysics* (tr. C.M.Duff, Macmillan, 1909).

11. Auguste Comte (1798-1857), French philosopher, founder of the positivist school. Saw the history of philosophy in three stages, (1) Theological (where phenomena is explained by the supernatural); (2) metaphysical (cause is abstractions); and (3) Positive (where observation, hypotheses and experimentation explain phenomena). He further classified the sciences hierarchically, beginning with mathematics as the most general, followed by astronomy, general physics, chemistry, biology (including psychology) and ending with sociology (a word he invented) which he placed at the head of the hierarchy. Each later science depended upon the last one.

treatment other than in poetry, mystical effusion, speculation, philosophical theorisation and hypothetical postulations. It was certainly never brought into the field of laboratory science.

Yet the problem has to be tackled somehow in keeping with the conditions of everyday living; and whether *a priori* or *a posteriori* reasoning is employed, it has also to be valid in terms of one's own inner experience which alone supplies final conviction. Here the scientific method need not be ruled out; experimental conditions can easily be imagined for controlling and regulating the result to ensure the certainty that is sought. And although not based on sense objectivity or actuality in the gross meaning of the term, still the certainty has to be immediate. At the same time, although this immediate awareness is of an inner order, this does not mean that it is a private domain of closed esotericism. All men generally being equally endowed with common sense, the validity of the certainty thus achieved is as sound as in an actual experiment in the laboratory. Statistical evidence need be gathered only when some residue of doubt is possible, but here in the experiment we are coming to, as arranged by the Guru from a matter-of-fact position of reality, the whole problem becomes simple and self-evident and needing no statistical support.

Contemplation tallies here with the common sense everyday experience of one and all, and there is no fear either of heresy or of speculation entering the scene, and no room for the easy lazy luxury or dream of a private heaven to be accessible by undeserved grace. Irrespective of sin and absolution, we have the matter discussed in a truly scientific and even 'experimental' spirit. The self of man is demonstrated to be not a mystery but an existing and subsisting everyday reality, and one capable of being studied in the same way as other 'facts' or problems in science are capable of being examined.

The same strictness of approach characterises the Guru-writings throughout, while his witty conversation was filled with humour and always carried that touch of apodictic finality which ever marks the utterances of great men of all times and places. The Self or the Soul, or the *paramātmā* together with the *jīvātmā* of Vedāntic lore, are brought under close and related scrutiny by the Guru as follows:

> Who sits there in the dark ? — Speak !
> Says one, which the other, hearing,
> To know in turn asks:
> 'And you there, who may you even be?'
> To both of these but unitive remains
> The word of response.
>
> The ever-repeated 'I', 'I'
> All contemplated from within
> Is not many — it is one;
> Divergent egoity being plural
> With the total of such
> The substance of the Self
> Continuity it assumes.[12]

In conclusion we may summarise the discipline of Vedānta as follows: first, great reliance on common sense and *a priori* Self-realisation; second, abolition of duality in such reciprocal ambivalences as the one and the many, subject versus object; third, elimination of the prejudices of what is called in Vedānta *tripuṭi* (i.e., threefold points of view, the giving of primacy to one or other of these three as 'the subjective', 'the objective' or 'the meaning'); fourth, reference to a principle of continuity understood as an eternal 'now' or as *being* rather than *becoming;* fifth, non-acceptance or rejection of creative specialisation (*nir-viśeṣa*); sixth, giving primacy to cause rather than effect (*satkāraṇa-vāda*); seventh and lastly, viewing the whole situation contemplatively and realistically.

These are some of the time-honoured methods and basic principles of knowing kept in mind by the Guru Nārāyaṇa in his writings which may be found in this and other examples; but, at the same time, the whole treatment is revised by him to suit the requirements of the modern scientific outlook and the modern method. The two men in a dark room speak of an ultimately unitive

12. From the Guru Nārāyaṇa's *Ātmopadeśa Śatakam* (Centiloquy to Self-Wisdom), Verses 10-11.

but undeniably existent ego, which nobody *can* deny, an ego that is common and the same to all and therefore a universal real. Moreover this Self is one which sits neutrally in the dark, knowing its own side as well as the side of the questioner. What he is meets what he is not in a neutral or undifferentiated consciousness of the Self. In this neutral Self the silence is again reached, the silent detachment of full freedom of the Absolute Witness of all.

Typical country homestead in Malabār where “Man and nature blend in harmony without conflict”

20

More Intimate Jottings

ŚAṄKARA'S opening verse in his *Vivekacūḍāmaṇi* (Crest Jewel of Wisdom) offers the usual adoration to his own *guru* called Govinda.[1] This is also the name of the pastoral Kṛṣṇa of the Viṣṇu tradition. The name Govinda occurs again in the refrain of a hymn by Śaṅkara beginning *Bhaja Govindam*! (Worship Govinda!) which we have already quoted in translation.[2] Some hold to the interpretation that it is the pastoral god Kṛṣṇa who is referred to; while others, more cogently it would appear, consider that the reference is to the person of the *guru* of Śaṅkara. In that case, the Guru Govinda must have come to Malabār with a Vaiṣṇava Vedic outlook, to which Śaṅkara's own mind reacted, throwing up a revalued Guru-Word representing a new synthesis. In both these instances, therefore, the reference would be to the person of the same Guru. It is unlikely that Śaṅkara would recommend Kṛṣṇa worship, at least in the usual sense for salvation, considering that Śaṅkara was so well known for being uncompromisingly in favour of reason, as well as one who gave primacy so wholeheartedly to the contemplative wisdom of non-dual Vedānta. Whatever the theory, there is an enigma here, especially when we know that Śaṅkara adhered to the Śiva tradition in all his writings. Although lukewarm critics may mix everything up, it is worthwhile for us to linger here to discover the underlying principle uniting this intimate personal devotion (*bhakti*) with the pitched polemical battles that Śaṅkara always fought in the name of the primacy of reason (*jñāna*).

---

1. *sarva vedānta sidhānta gocaram tam agocgaram,*
   govindam paramānandam sadgurum praṇato-smyaham.
   — *Vivekacūḍāmaṇi,* 1

   'Visible to one of finalised total Vedāntic wisdom, but not seen;
   I bow to the true Guru Govinda whose nature is supreme bliss.'

2. See chapter 17, *The Guru-Trio of South India.*

The opening lines of the *Vivekacūḍāmaṇi* themselves afford the key. Govinda the Guru is apostrophised both as one who is visible and invisible. He is said to be visible to the eye of one of finalised Vedāntic wisdom, but invisible otherwise, although to Śaṅkara he was a living Guru. Here we witness a delicate dialectical interplay between aspects of reality. Existence and Subsistence meet, as if from opposite poles, neutralising each other in one central presence which thus comes to represent the Absolute, not in merely one-sided abstraction, but in a manner by which the Absolute becomes adorable also. The dualism inherent in the methods of *bhakti* (devotional worship) and *jñāna* (pure reason) thus tend to be abolished.

This way of approaching reality from two opposite yet reciprocal ends is also the secret of the contemplative mysticism of the Upaniṣads. The *Īśa Upaniṣad* has an invocation to the Supreme Sun as Pūṣan which has the fairest of forms as seen by the adoring supplicant.[3] The form is seen in the Sun but soon the worshipper also says, as if on second thoughts: 'He who is yonder — yonder Person — I myself am He!' By mutual recognition the Cosmic Person is thus equated to the Psychic Person within. Śaṅkara therefore only continues this ancient way of wisdom when he makes the Guru Govinda the meeting point of two distinct aspects of reality as if from opposite sides. The subjective and the objective aspects of the personality, the noumenal and phenomenal, thus fuse and blend in the Guru-Presence which is both visible and invisible. There is no *guru* apart from the essential high human value called *guru*-hood. The actual visible appearance of the *guru* as given to the gross senses is incidental or secondary in the presence of this neutral or central *guru* personality which represents non-duality itself as it is to be understood in Advaita Vedānta.

---

3. *pūṣannekarṣe yama sūrya*
prājāpatya vyūha raśmin samūha;
tejo yatte rūpam kalyāṇatamam tatte
paśyāmi yo'sāvasau puruṣaḥ so'hamasmi.
—*Īśa Upaniṣad*, 16

O Universal Nourisher (Pūṣan), solitary Seer ! O Controller! O Sun! Son of Prajāpati! Put away Thy rays! Gather up Thy over-brilliant light! I behold Thy glorious form — He who is yonder — yonder Person — I myself am He!'

The life and teachings of a *guru* have thus to be considered as the further elaborations of *guru*-hood. The second Person of the Trinity in Christianity has been treated exactly in conformity with this system of *guru*-hood. In India there are popularly known devotional verses in Sanskrit which proclaim 'Guru is Brahma', 'Guru is Viṣṇu' and 'Guru is Maheśvara (Śiva)'. Theology and ritual flow together in a single river of this Master-Tradition. Mystical doctrine and contemplative philosophy are in the same stream of perennial wisdom, with their implicit methodology and epistemology. Equating *guru* with God is recognised in various disconnected contexts the world over, but the common source of this pattern of thinking is to be traced to the East, to India of the far south in that protected area at the tip of the Peninsula, that coastland where the world made contact with India, and whereas in Valencia 'the earth is water and men women', the land of milk and honey where nature has been kind to human life for millennia. The ocean's surf washes the feet of Mother India here where the formula of Word-wisdom is preserved and strangely manifests itself repeatedly millennium after millennium.

Doubly protected and preserved by the high mountain ranges of the *ghāṭs*, the Vindhyas and the far-off Himālaya, this ancient 'Malaya' region of the Sanskrit poets gave birth to simple yet true bards and philosophers such as Śaṅkara, Govinda and Nārāyaṇa, who all belong to a signle line which links prehistoric Śiva with the latest revaluator and perfect expositor of the Guru Word. Ancient drummings, extending far behind recorded history, beat out a perennial message which is transmuted and scientifically restated, after passing through the vicissitudes of history, through *guru* after *guru*, while the wonder and simplicity of the healing unitive Word rises triumphantly out of its own ashes, phoenix-like, in its natural Malaya-home, where the contemplative science can flourish, unmolested by the strivings and disturbances going on in less protected lands.[4]

---

4. Cf., Lao Tzu (sixth century BC) 'When we can lay hold of the Tao (the Word) of old in order to manage the affairs of the Now, and are able to know it as it was in its prehistoric beginnings, this is called the 'clue' of

The personality of the *guru* is the meeting-place of the Word and its own wisdom. As the central principle of correlation can be expressed in mathematical language in terms of functions and operations, all of which become possible round the neutral point of a zero (which is an Indian invention), so it is also possible with a simple neutral Word-formula to reconcile sacred objects and supreme ideas (both hierophanies and hypostasies — as with the reconciliation of geometry and algebra) into harmony with a central neutral verity which is of the core of Word-wisdom. This is the hub of the wheel.[5] This is the radiant centre. This is the seed. Every *guru* carries this secret of the *guru* Seed-Word (*bīja-akṣara*). This is the milk of human kindness which is life itself. All meet in the silence of this adorable high value.

* * * *

A biography of the Guru Nārāyaṇa on usual lines and giving primacy to factual items has been hitherto consciously avoided in these pages. But now that we have been able to explain to some extent the position involved; now that we can see facts in the simple light of *guru*-hood, and will therefore be able to assess such facts as they ought to be treated, we shall be able to enter, in a rambling and intimate way into some of the details pertaining to the life of the Guru Nārāyaṇa. Without some such rounding-off all our previous remarks might seem truncated or incomplete in the eyes of the general reader who might chance on what we have written,

---

→ the Tao.' (*note* the word 'clue' in Chinese is *Chi,* meaning, according to Lin Yutang, 'main body of tradition', 'system', and 'discipline'.) — *Tao Te Ching,* Chapter XIV. (rendered from James Legge's translation in *Sacred Books of the East*, Vol. XXXIX, and Lin Yutang's in his *Wisdom of China,* Michael Joseph, London, 1948).

5. Cf., 'That which is the Self (*ātman*) is a hub', *Bṛhadāraṇyaka Upaniṣad* I.v.16.

'Verily the Self is the Overlord of all things, the King of all things. As the spokes are held together in the hub and felly of a wheel, just so in the Self all things, all gods, all worlds, all breathing things, all these selves are held together'. *ibid.,* II., v.15.

Also *Praśna Upaniṣad,* VI.6., and *Śvetāśvatara Upaniṣad*, I.4 and VI.1.

Also: 'The thirty spokes unite in the one nave; but it is on the empty space for the axle that the use of the wheel depends.' *Tao Te Ching,* Chapter XI (Legge's translation).

and who might not be acquainted at first-hand with the background and particular context of the Word of the Guru as we have studied it in these pages. And so, without attempting orderliness or sequence, as if we were jay-walking along trafficless cross-roads, we shall here dispose of some of these miscellaneous matters belonging to biography.

A *guru* who consciously or unconsciously conforms to the values or patterns of *guru*-hood does not get involved in actualities as such. He refuses to live in a bloated and sensational world of newspaper headlines. Contemporary actualities interest him only in so far as they are related to normal human happiness against a *lasting* background, a background that survives the shifting acts and figures of history. He avoids the lure of mere glamour. Tinsel and glittering trash does not hold his interest except as part of a passing show before him.

This attitude implies a certain detachment and abnegation. It is a state of retirement, withdrawal or calm self-possession. He seeks no happiness outside himself and thus attains peace.[6] The relation with that aspect of the Absolute which is not immediately implied in his actual person is sought in the Ultimate, the Supreme, the transcendent 'That' beyond, which is 'the Most High God', or the *puruṣottamaḥ*.[7] This supreme value meets the ontological everyday existent aspect in the *guru*'s own person, and together

---

6. *yas-tv-ātmaratir-eva syād ātmatr̥ptaś-ca mānavaḥ,*
   ātmany-eva ca samtuṣṭas tasya kāryam na vidyate.

   nai'va tasya kr̥tena'rtho nā-kr̥tene'ha kaścana,
   na-cā-'sya sarvabhūteṣu kaścid-arthavyapāśrayaḥ

   But the man whose delight is in the Self only, who is satisfied by the Self, for him there is no work to be done.

   For him there is no interest in what is done or not done; nor is there dependence or interest in any creature or being.

   — *Bhagavad Gītā:* III.17-18

7. Cf. *yasmāt-kṣaram-atīto'ham akṣarād-api co-'ttamaḥ, ato 'smi loka vede ca prathitaḥ puruṣottamah.*

   — *Bhagavad Gītā,* XV.18

   As I transcend the perishable and am higher also than the imperishable, therefore in the world and in the Veda (scripture) I am declared the Supreme-Person.

they give synthetic unity and virtue to *guru*-hood.

Nothing that pleases or pampers the senses can give this dialectical counterpart which is needed for a life of elevated human value. Wealth and fame, family and friends, are not ends in themselves. They serve a higher end which is Self-knowledge or the other pole of reality. This is the sacrifice mentioned in the *Bhagavad Gītā* where this second or transcendental pole of cherished value is marked out to maintain purificatory interest in an ever Self-fulfilling and Self-realising process.[8] All normal interests can be stepping-stones to the next higher interest, when properly taken advantage of as 'a tide in the affairs of men'.[9] Adversity itself, as Shakespeare says, can be put to its 'sweet uses.'[10]

When these two poles of the immanent and the transcendent are brought together into interplay in everyday life, we have what is called the dedicated life of the *guru*, whose value is finalised and grounded in the Self — that Self which is to be realised by the given Self itself which is already there by necessity. This is the gist of the doctrine of *niṣkāma karma* (non-greedy action) of the *Bhagavad Gītā*.[11] Although each stage of such dedicated living can have an individual complexion of its own, the underlying technique or principle is the same. The dialectical counterparts of a given situation have to be treated together, contemplatively, for a naturally dedicated action to result. This involves a normal amount

---

8. *saha yajñāḥ prajāh sṛṣṭivā puro-'vāca prajâpatiḥ,*
anena prasaviṣyadhvam eṣa vo 'stv-iṣṭakāmadhuk.
— *Bhagavad Gītā*, III.10

Having created mankind in ancient times together with sacrifice, the Lord of creatures (Prajāpati) said, By this shall ye propagate; be this to you the yielder of the milk of your desires (Kāmadhuk).

9. *Julius Caesar*, I, iii, 218.

10. *As You Like It*, II, i, 1.

11. *aśaktabuddhiḥ sarvatra jītātmā vigataspṛhaḥ,*
naiṣkarmyasiddhim paramām samnyāsenā-'dhigacchati.
— *Bhagavad Gītā*, XVIII.49

He whose pure Reason is everywhere unattached, who has conquered himself and from whom desire has fled, he attains by renunciation the supreme perfection of freedom transcending all action.

of detachment which yet does not become so Stoical, puritanical or austere as to be of the nature of self-immolation or torture. In such a mystical discipline agony is not lived for its own sake (as it is by some persons); instead, every situation is made to yeild its own maximum interest which is legitimate in the contemplative context.

Thus, a Kṛṣṇa's love for the *gopīs* (cow-herding girls) finds its place as well as the destruction wrought by Śiva when he makes Rati (the Spring Goddess — Kore-Persephone) bewail her lover Kāmadeva (Eros, God of Desire), who is reduced to cinders by one glancing shaft from Śiva's fiery middle eye.

All normal human values find their place and arrange themselves in an orderly way in the light of the *guru*-presence. All natural and normal interests have the *guru*'s blessing, whether in child, woman or in the mature, positively awakened man of wisdom. Woman's wisdom too is given its legitimate place without insisting that it should conform to asymmetrically distorted standards often demanded of it by agitated or greedy manhood. A sanctioning, presiding, neutral, subdued and finalised value is ever represented in the just vision of *guru*-hood as it ought to be understood in the context of the *Guru*-Word-wisdom.

All is viewed by the *guru* from his calm, contemplative, central or symmetrical position. As the *Bhagavad Gītā* puts it, he makes no distinction between a holy, pious Brāhmin of great learning, a cow, elephant, a dog, or even a dog-eater.[12] Representing himself a finalised value, the *guru* makes no comparisons, he passes no judgements, but views all with the same eye of a just and equal mystical catholicity, characterised by boundless generosity and kindliness.

Closed loyalties in the name of the *guru* are not, therefore, in order. Every *guru* worthy of the name is a *jagad-guru* (World-Teacher), whether he be humble or well known. Pontifical paraphernalia and cavalcades of camels, elephants and footmen, do not add anything to *guru*-hood in its essence, although they may add to social status or authority, which is a different thing. Between

12. *Bhagavad Gītā*, V.18.

these two sources of virtue or ethics the *guru* exercises his higher judgement as each situation presents itself. Generally speaking, he leads a life of plain living and high thinking.

Clean-shaven, with no ornamental things about him, the Guru Nārāyaṇa avoided even any stripes or colours in his clothing. He dressed in two seamless pieces of white cloth (in later years tinged orange at the request of his ochre-robed disciples of the *saṁnyāsin* tradition). He would sip clean pure water as if drinking a rich beverage, and extol simple foods like fruits or roots. Often he preferred to sleep on a cloth spread on stone for a couch under the clear starlight, with his own arms alone for a pillow; and likewise he preferred bathing in rivers and walking on foot; and he would eat any kind of food from the devoted hands that offered it in village homes as he moved among the people.

To the Guru Nārāyaṇa, peasant or proletarian was the same, while priest and publican received from him equality of treatment. Born of humble parents himself, the Guru Nārāyaṇa lived in conformity with the highest traditions of *guru*-hood. He recognised no exclusive disciples for himself. 'All or none' was his position in this matter. He avoided the division arising from the terminology of a narrow way where a camel could not pass, in which those 'not against' were 'with', and those 'not with' were 'against', with its pattern of a flock closed to humanity in general. The Guru's sheep were found in all folds, and no folds were without the Guru's sheep. Such was the open character of his attitude. For himself, he had no programme of action, although all worthy programmes of action started by others received his blessing if sought. The blessing would be of the nature of a silent assent to all that had any value in a human context.

We have traced the history of the Word of the Guru in our own way from antiquity, making no great distinction between immense antiquity and eternity or timelessness. When an origin is removed to a vast degree from the normal extent of human perception or interest, it tends to have an indifferent meaning. Endless antiquity means nothing, just as an endless future cannot have a definite meaning either, in relative terms. Thus we have to accept both retrospective and prospective life-values in the light of a simple present, in an eternal Now. Whatever the antiquity (or, conversely, the futurity) of humanity may be, that same humanity is distinguished by those essential spiritual qualities which give it its human nature.

The personality of a *guru* has to be looked upon in an eternal context. There are peculiarities of temperament or character which distinguish one person from another. There are light-hearted people who carry with them an easy and pleasant atmosphere and there are others who are heavily weighted down by emotions. A balancing of these ambivalent tendencies comes from an equable climate and those kindly natural conditions in which man can live at peace with his environment. Egyptian deserts are said to have been favourable for the wisdom that has come down to us from Abraham and Moses; and from the early Christian Fathers; and certain temperamental peculiarities have also been fostered in Malabār for the nurture and preservation through time of a certain Word-wisdom and patterns of Word-value, shown in the personalities of *guru*s such as Śaṅkara and Nārāyaṇa.

Malabār life beyond the *ghāṭ*s to the West, in that long strip that lies so close to the ocean, is populated by a light-hearted, plain-living people who (hitherto at least) eat of the simplest of foods and clothe themselves with the least ornament or luxury. From year to year the land supports the people evenly, while invading war-drums have no meaning here as nature cannot be robbed too much in advance. No clothes are needed for the sake of warmth, as there is no winter at all, while body temperature prevails with only negligible variations between day and night. Man and nature blend in harmony without conflict.

When foreign economies did not percolate like water into this domain, all was self-sufficient and easy, and spiritual life, like a flame untouched by breeze, burnt on steadily through time. This had its effect on the temperament. The Malabār man had simple, human, almost prosaic, emotions. Effusions were foreign to his nature, and *bhakti* or devotion was not overladen with flourishes, elaborations, or heavy ornamentations. All remained simple, as with the Polynesians before the arrival of Captain Cook and other explorers. Indeed, the comparison in every respect between these two antipodian peoples has been remarked upon by many writers, and Malabār has been described as the South Seas of India.[13] Sea-fish and rice and the seasonal fruits and spices kept the masses alive from age to age. Simple Word-wisdom lay deeply buried under this calm and steadily peaceful pace of life. Śaṅkara and Nārāyaṇa were typical products of such a soil. Wisdom was there, with wit and humour, simply conceived, as even the Zero was conceived by the simple Indian mind with whom simplicity itself constituted his high genius. A down-to-earth matter-of-fact realism was also a part of the social environment of the Malabār people.

Travancore is the remotest of the monarchies of antiquity that has survived to the present day. Pre-Pallava Travancore was essentially Śaivite (i.e., prior to AD 300). There was an intermediate period of Buddhism and Jainism, which, having spread its influence as far as Ceylon (Sri Lanka) where it still flourishes, gives us the clue to the state of affairs that prevailed in Travancore till it was overcovered by Viṣṇu temples.

It was about the Pāṇḍyan and Gupta periods (*c.* AD 300-600) that Vaiṣṇavism penetrated into Kerala, displacing Buddhist

13. There are many scholars who consider that the Polynesians of the Pacific originated in south India. As an example here is what W.J. Perry the anthropologist says: 'India is of peculiar importance in the study of movements of early culture, for it was the original home to which Polynesian tradition harks back. In south India the caste of the Paravas, the pearl-fishers of the Gulf of Manaar, is composed of folk of pure Polynesian type, who, together with their fellow-castes, like the Pariahs, belong to the dual grouping of society. The importance of these Polynesian pearl-fishers lies in the fact that, on every pearl bed from Ceylon to the shores of America, and, again, in America itself, there are distinct traces of a form of civilization closely akin to that of Egypt in the Pyramid Age. The Polynesians are also of great interest in one more important particular — they are partly of the same physical type as the Phoenicians, who were, as Elliot Smith claims, formed of a mixture of peoples in the Persian Gulf, again the seat of an important pearl-fishery. . . . The carriers of this archaic civilization started from India, and went out by way of Indonesia to the Pacific, leaving behind them traces that still are to be detected. . . .' — *W. J. Perry, The Growth of Civilization,* pp. 109-11, Pelican Books, 1937.

remnants; and when this process was complete the triumph of religious reformers such as Madhva and Rāmānuja (eleventh and twelfth centuries AD) was also completed. A Travancore ruler became attached to these new movements and went as a recluse to Śrī Raṅgam in the Tamil country, while another became a Mohammedan and went to Mecca. Two Nambūdiri (Brāhmin) families of Malabār became custodians of the Christian religion in the earliest years of its history. There is one day set apart for the Syrian Christians of Malabār to observe some Hindu orthodox customs, and after the marriage ceremony among the orthodox Nambūdiri Brāhmins, on the fifth day the couple are expected ceremonially to catch fish in a pond, perhaps in reminiscence of their ancient origins among the fisher-folk. These are some of the miscellaneous enigmas that Malabār still presents to the modern sociologist.

The infiltration of Vaiṣṇavism brought with it a theocratic form of government. The older Śaivite stratum was submerged and became more or less inarticulate. The Buddhist remnants were either effaced or absorbed. Theocracy further introduced a complicated hierarchy of castes, on the topmost rung of which hierarchical ladder was the priest, especially of the Vaiṣṇavite temples. A form of the feudal system became established round the theocratic authority which kept the monarchs under its power. In the place of serfs in this pyramidal formation, the masses became 'untouchables,' at first ceremonially in the context of the temple, and later by dint of the economic and other disadvantages that this system brought upon them. The little kingdoms that still survived here and there, ruled by the archaic masses, were annexed one by one and brought under the suzerainty of the Vaiṣṇavite temple theocrats.

Iconography unmistakably reveals how King Mahābali, who must have been a remnant of the Buddhist period, was cheated of his empire by the Vāmana *avatāra* (Pigmy Incarnation) of Viṣṇu. The Malabār people, in spite of this overcovering of the antecedent conditions, to this day celebrate the glory of the ancient days of Mahābali. The yellow cloth is worn by all, and girls sit on swings in the harvest season, singing ancient songs which speak of Mahābali — 'When Mavali ruled the land, men were equals, one and all; no cheating then, no falsehood too!;' such are the words of their familiar refrain. And so theocracy came to stay. Temples that were part of the government could only be entered by those who were within the theocratic fold. All others, comprising more than half the population of petit-bourgeoisie, medical men, astrologers, fishermen and coconut-climbers, not to mention all those who gained a livelihood like Śiva himself of antiquity, from hunting, from the gathering of natural products, or from harvesting, etc., all in fact who belonged to the vast-amorphous matrix of prehistory, comprising both proletarian and peasant groups, within a vast, inarticulate but persisting social stratum, were excluded from the theocratic caste, religious and social system.

Let the reader now imagine an undulating country prospect about twelve miles to the north-east of Trivandrum, which is the Englishman's version of the original name *Tiru-Ananta-Puram* (the City of the Holy and Prosperous Ananta, i.e., the many-headed snake representing eternity, upon whom Viṣṇu reclines on the Ocean of Milk). The temple of Śrī Padmanābha (which is another name of Viṣṇu, from whose navel a lotus came, and which later gave birth to Brahmā and all creation), this temple is the central institution in this capital city of the theocratic state.

In this rolling countryside, then, imagine also a little palm-leaf-roofed house, standing at the edge of rice-fields, with tall coconut palms raising their heads high into the air. The tender green of the rice-fields, the clear vibrant blue of the sky, a flock of white cranes startled by the passerby — these perhaps give the necessary touches to this self-sufficing tranquil picture of peaceful domestic life. The straggling pepper-vine, the big generous jack-fruits, and the mango trees add to the variety and colour of vegetation.

An agricultural family lived at this country-place about the year 1855. The father, Māḍan Āśān, was more than a mere farmer. He was versed in astronomy and Āyurvedic medicine, and was a teacher, as his name Āśān (or Ācāryan) would show. He was respected by his fellow-villagers and he guided them in matters of agriculture, land surveying, revenue questions, and so on. He walked into the temple City of Trivandrum to pay his taxes, dressed in two pieces of white cloth and carrying a simple (non-folding) palm-leaf umbrella, such as one can see even to-day being carried by villagers in these rural parts. Once a week the villagers assembled in the verandah of his house to hear him expound the *Rāmāyaṇa* or the *Mahābhārata,* the two ancient epics of India. His son Nānu was the Guru Nārāyaṇa of later days. We have to fit the son into this picture, dressed in similar simple attire, as an assistant to the father, and in the exposition of the epics, sometimes deputising for his father. In later years, when the son became more learned, the father looked upon the youth to do better than he himself had done.

The village had the name Chempazhanti and had its own wayside Śiva temple, in a state of much neglect, where the ancient trident and the Śiva stone are still dressed-up and anointed, with the inevitable religious fig-tree (*Ficus religiosa*) — the entire environment being evocative and reminiscent of prehistoric Śiva days.

It was in the rice-harvesting season, soon after the festivities in memory of the King Mahābali of the days of the yellow robe, in the Indian month of the Lion (*Siṁha* or *Chingam*) that Nānu, which is a contraction for Nārāyaṇa, was born, about AD1854.[14]

The simple and pleasant young wife of Māḍan Āśān, the mother of Nānu, was a sensitive and pretty woman known as Kuṭṭy. This simple name which means 'child', fitted the basic simplicity of her nature and social status. She just happened to be there, as if by nature's own conspiracy, and neither titles, sophistry, nor any extra embellishments of dress or ornament happened to be superposed on her. Nature itself had given her grace and kindliness, which the son inherited, with wisdom. The sensibility of the Guru Nārāyaṇa has to be acknowledged as drawn from this simple woman who gave him birth, and who in her quiet ways seemed to merge into

14. The actual date is still under dispute. The Malayalam month of Chingam occurs mid-August to mid-September.

the background of nature itself and seemed hardly to exist at all. Her personality did not make itself felt on the surroundings with any loudness or gaudiness. Neither trimmings nor frills were added to it. Her ancestry and that of her husband belonged to a simple human context, to that same human simplicity which we have tried to trace in earlier pages.

Here was a gentleman farmer, instructed in Sanskrit, Astrology and Āyurvedic medicine (medical science coming from Vedic times), belonging to the context of ancient Śiva worship, outside the Viṣṇu fold of later days, living the life of a 'mute inglorious Milton' as the poet Gray would put it, with a simple, unpretentious but pretty wife who gave ample evidence that nature had endowed her with beauty and sensibility. The son was known to be a slender, agile little boy full of pranks and fond of acrobatic tricks. With a single stone he could make a mango fall from the tall village tree near which he grazed cattle with other village lads, even like a pastoral Kṛṣṇa. He was good at his lessons and had a clear calligraphy free from the need of corrections. The neatness of a scholar went with him from his earliest days. His alphabets included the ancient hybrid script called *Malayālma* which was neither Malayālam nor Sanskrit. For all we know, this alphabet could easily have had affinities with ancient Akkadian and Sumerian scripts.

The boy Nānu lost his mother when he was fifteen or so, and his father too passed away when Nānu Āsān (Teacher Nāṇu or Nārāyaṇa) which he had become in the meanwhile, was about thirty years of age. He had already started his life as an intinerant teacher by this time, and came to the parental home only once in many months. He taught Sanskrit to a group of disciples who came to him. Some of them occasionally accompanied Nānu Āśān to neighbouring places within about fifty miles, a distance from his house which in those days formed the natural orbit of his wanderings.

This transition from a farmer's assistant to the status of a teacher, took place by imperceptible stages within the period of his mother's passing away at his fifteenth year and his father's passing away at about his twenty-eighth year. He once left his home without telling anyone, leaving a letter and a gift of cloth to a friend, and was sought and found by his uncle thirty miles north, where he had begun to live and teach. On the occasion of the father's passing away it is told, according to graphic accounts given by villagers of sufficient age to have been eye-witnesses, that Nānu Āśān arrived in time by some strange coincidence. He did not enter his family house straight away, but sat in a neighbouring house.

He entered the room where the father lay, with other village neighbours sitting by the bedside. The father referred to the son as 'a well-instructed teacher (*vidvān*)' and alluded also to a significant circumstance, saying: 'He eats food from many hands' and added a request that his son should hand him some nourishment with his own sanctified hands, which, as he put it 'themselves were nourished at the hands of many.' Nānu Āśān had thus attained a pattern of life of a *bhikṣu* or *saṁnyāsin* who supported himself by *madhukara bhikṣā* (i.e., a 'honey-bee-like livelihood') and this was already recognised by his father on his deathbed, and by his accepting the presence of his son as a last blessing.

The years between his childhood and the death of his parents has to be filled in by his days of more advanced Sanskrit education which he went to seek at a place fifty miles north called Karunagapalli. Here a traditional teacher belonging to the orthodox theocratic context admitted Nānu and several others to sit and have lessons. The name of this teacher was Rāman Pillay Āśān. Although orthodox rules demanded the segregation of the non-theocratic class children from those more within the fold of the Malabār theocracy, the teacher treated all his pupils with kindly consideration.

Here the Guru became more than a mere Sanskrit scholar, more, that is to say, than was required for the purposes of *Āyurveda* or Astrology, which was the level attained in his own village. He was now a dilettante instructed in *kāvya, nāṭaka* and *alaṅkāra* (Poetry, Drama and Literary Criticism with Rhetoric). He soon went beyond even this stage by himself and the secrets of the Vedāntic and Upaniṣadic wisdom became an open book to him by sheer dint of his straightforward simplicity, his purity of life, and with his alert positiveness of mental outlook and discipline. The lad Nānu thus became Nānu Āśān, known to a circle of admirers within a radius of about fifty miles.

Soon even this imaginary shell was opened out still wider as the Guru Nārāyaṇa began to gain a reputation through his life of high value to all, by his writing of prayers of great appeal and charm and in connection with the renovation and cleaning of various neglected Śiva temples — a work that he naturally undertook for the sake of the villagers outside the fold of the new theocracy of Malabār. Soon he was in demand from one end of Malabār to the other, from the southernmost point at Cape Comorin (Kanyākumāri) to Mangalore in Kanara, four hundred miles to the north up the coast. He helped to integrate two million people through a movement which naturally opened out, breaking through later overcoverings and stratifications, to proclaim again the ancient perennial *guru*-wisdom that lay dormant underneath. Soon all limits were broken off and a revalued and restated Guru-Word-wisdom was proclaimed by the Guru Nārāyaṇa in terms unmistakable to anyone who could recognise the voice of a *guru*.

His Sanskrit education helped the Guru to formulate the Guru-Word in perfect relation to the past heritage of the Word. This was but one circumstance. After his education he disappeared into the mountainous region near Cape Comorin (Kanyākumāri) and lived in caves, eating from the hands of surrounding villagers. Here he practised most intense introspection. His father died in 1884 — if astrological calculations that have been made in this matter may be finally relied upon.

About the year 1890 a holy man, recluse, a *yogī* of silent ways, haunted the caverns of the rocky hills near Kanyā Kumārī (the Virgin Daughter) which is the name of a temple at the Cape. Here is the last southernmost stone of India, where Vivekānanda of Bengal sought the same prehistoric Mother and sat meditating on the blackened rocks which rise out of the multi-coloured sands by the everlasting sea. The caverns in the nearby hills, and the lotus

The parental home of Guru Nārāyaṇa at Chempazhanty, Trivandrum.

ponds abounding in the locality, where the great seas meet from east and west, and pure oceanic breezes sweep forever across the land, unhindered and uncontaminated, were favourable to the formation of the pearl of the potent Word-formula in the Guru Nārāyaṇa. The personality of the Guru matured here and attained to its full stature of *guru*-value.

Thus was the Guru Nārāyaṇa born. From Nānu, a village boy of humble birth we have to imagine the birth of a *guru*, having the full stature of *guru*-hood in every respect. His silence, his voice, and his kindly harmonised values expressed in his life's work, all point to a personality of rare value for a long time to come. His visible aspects are only incidental to the value which arose, mature and finalised, as the culmination of non-dual Word-wisdom, in his personality.

Later, the Guru's wanderings were not confined to the regions round about Cape Comorin (Kanyākumāri). He was known to have lived in a Mohammedan house mixing with fisher-folk in *Anchu-Thengu,* now called Anjengo, which has an old fort established by mariners who came from the West hundreds of years ago. He soon got involved in the temple reformation and renovation movement which began to grow round him spontaneously. Old and overgrown temple-groves and prehistoric snake-worship sanctuaries were uprooted, renovated, altered or abolished, sometimes in favour of schools, or refined into better shrines. A plain mirror and lamp was installed by him at one place, so that idolatry might come into line with Self-knowledge, for at least one's own image in a mirror told no distorted lie in any hysterical terms.

And so the movement which began at the toe of India spread enthusiastically as far distant as Gokarṇam which was the northern limit of the ancient Malaya region. By the time of the Guru's passing away, all limits, whether geographical or traditional, were transcended, while philosophy and mysticism supplemented former aspects of doctrine to convert it into a Word-wisdom to be understood as a science in universal terms.

In his early wanderings, the Guru was influenced by two

personalities who deserve mention here. One of these was called Kunjan Pillay. He was a *Chattambi,* senior or monitor of the Sanskrit school where the Guru went for his finishing course in Sanskrit rhetoric. Later he became an elder brother and companion in the wanderings of the Guru. In fact, round the person of this senior companion who represented the solid native wisdom of the soil was noticed a kind of renaissance, literary, cultural and spiritual, in the Travancore of the early nineties. A group including poets, grammarians, *yogīs* and medical men versed in *Āyurveda* helped in the impetus given to native wisdom. The invention of steam, the scientific renaissance with many other inventions and discoveries made during the long reign of Queen Victoria, all contributed a share to this flowering in the far south of India, bringing new values into the atmosphere.

The Guru's sensitive spirit responded to the situation surprisingly. Kunjan Pillay Chattambi, who was one of the leaders of the renaissance group, recognised early the potentialities of the Guru Nārāyaṇa and consciously encouraged him to unfold and open out, and by his intelligent elderly guidance, helped the shy, young and retiring Nānu of those days. One of the early compositions of the Guru called *Navamañjarī* (Nine Verses) expressly recognises at the beginning how it came to be written at the instance of the *Śiśu Nāma Guru,* which is the Sanskrit designation for the name of Kunjan Pillay whom the Guru Nārāyaṇa, at the start of his own career avowedly called a 'Guru'. This is as good as calling him his own 'Guru'.

The relation between them has been the subject of some interested controversy, but once on being questioned about the *guru*-hood of the Chattambi Swāmī, the Guru Nārāyaṇa said he saw no objection in taking Chattambi Swāmī as Guru. He readily accepted the senior companion and paid full respect to him, conceding him all priority. Dialectically speaking, the relation must have been something like that existing between John the Baptist and Jesus. The one who comes after is often historically greater, although in terms of baptism with water, one is senior to the other. In these matters as Christ explained to Nicodemus, 'the wind bloweth where it listeth' and nothing more can be said or done about it.[15]

In matters of Yoga, the Guru Nārāyaṇa had another senior guide or *guru*. He was a man employed as 'manager' at the British Residency in Trivandrum. His name was Thykkād Ayyāvu. He was versed in the secret esotericism of Yoga and other obscure allied branches of study which were fast becoming extinct. The Tamil spiritual traditions preserved many secrets of personal psycho-physical discipline which interested the Guru. He explored all the avenues that were open to him, from Chemistry and Astrology to the obscurantisms and cryptical details of Pāṇini's *Grammar,*[16] and went to Thykkād Ayyāvu for instruction in the mysteries of Yoga. Thykkād Ayyāvu was to the Guru Nārāyaṇa somewhat as Ammonius Saccus was to Plotinus.

Both the above *gurus* (Chattambi Swāmī and Thykkād Ayyāvu) may therefore be looked upon as important *upa-gurus* (secondary *gurus*) to the Guru Nārāyaṇa. As Śrī Rāmākṛṣṇā used to say, a crane can teach a man one-pointed attention when it is intent upon catching a fish. At such a time the crane becomes the *guru*. *Guru*-hood and *śiṣya*-hood also, in the final light of dialectics, are interchangeable terms. They can be equated, each one in terms of the other, when wisdom is attained, as when Jesus washes the feet of his disciples. Wisdom that is non-dual relegates all such matters to the background, although they are very important indeed to the novice seeker after wisdom to recognise.

The dates as well as other facts and figures given in the foregoing paragraphs in an effort to present actuality to the person of the Guru, should be treated in a certain contemplative context of their own. In order to explain this, and by way of an apt conclusion to this section, in which we have digressed somewhat from the subject of the Word in order to give some flesh and blood to it, we

---

15. See *St. John's Gospel,* III.8.

16. According to Walter Eugene Clark, writing in *Science in India:* 'His (Panini's) grammar is the earliest scientific grammar in the world, the earliest extant grammar of any language, and one of the greatest ever written.' — *The Legacy of India,* p. 339, Oxford, 1937. Pāṇini's date is uncertain, but is generally given as not later than 400 BC.

shall come to intimate anecdotes. But before concluding in that way, there is one more important subject which we seem to have forgotton. What about the married life of the Guru? This we shall now answer as clearly as the evidence, gathered by the present writer in the village of the one-time wife of the Guru, would permit regarding this long-forgotten story.

The lady was the daughter of a medical man of an ancient school of toxicology (*viṣa vaidyan*) and the cures for poisons. The Guru used frequently to visit this *vaidyan*. The families of the two households, those of the Guru and this medical scholar of Chirayinkil village became intimate. The Guru had two sisters who were interested in seeing that he was married in the usual way by arrangement; and so it was done, without consulting the Guru, as was the custom in those days. A simple wedding took place in which the sisters took the leading initiative in all matters, as custom permitted in the locality. The cloth and gold neck-trinket were exchanged by proxy by the sisters, while the bridegroom sat unconcerned, reading and explaining the *Rāmāyaṇa* — his normal vocation.

All was over. The wife lived in the maternal home, after the matriarchal system which prevailed in Malabār, and still prevails today in the circle of the ruling family of Travancore. The Guru lived under the same roof off and on. About the degree of intimacy of the conjugal relations, the present writer has not been able to draw out any definite evidence, even in spite of his wilful attack on the subject. All that could be extracted from those who knew the couple was a reported remark from the Guru's lips soon after the marriage. He is purported to have said, 'Now the *vaidyan* (Medical man) is happy that all the rooms of his house are occupied.' This was in reference to his taking up residence occasionally in the house of the father of his bride.

A further incident throws some more light on their relations. Once he called another neighbour and asked him to take his wife to a festival in a nearby Bhagavatī or Kālī temple to which she dearly wished to go. With the Guru's better ways, it was too crowded and noisy for him, but the villagers praised its importance very highly. On another occasion the Guru cured his wife who had fainted for some reason, and took some familiar green herb and squeezed the juice into her nostrils. The irritation set aright the circulation in her head and brought her back to normality. These are all the scanty remarks that the present writer is able to make regarding the marital life of the Guru. His wife continued to live in her parent's house in accordance with the matriarchal customs prevailing then in that locality. With the ever-widening path of *guru*-hood that our hero began to tread as more and more years went by, the question of his married life and family relations receded more and more into the background. It was thus naturally and normally transcended. She died, and no children of the marriage are known to have seen the light of day. Subjects such as celibacy, immaculate conception, or virginity, etc., were points which were never raised in connection with either of them. The relation was as neutral and mysterious as the Zero that we have spoken of.

* * * *

The sixtieth birthday of the Guru was celebrated by his disciples and admirers at the Alwaye Ashram where the Guru was resident at the time. The *brahmacārins* (dedicated students) approached the Guru in the morning ceremoniously with flowers in their hands as an offering to him. The Guru recognised them and accepted the honour. Among the flowers were some made of gold, which a rich devotee had put there. He picked up one of them, and simply remarked, 'There are some flowers with no smell.'

Conversation naturally arose on the subject of the Guru's birthday. He saw no meaning in picking out one day as his day of birth. After the manner recorded about Plotinus, he objected to such personal adoration and permitted it only in deference to the wishes of admirers. Also it was only under protest — again like Plotinus — that he would consent to have his likeness taken by the camera.[17]

---

17. Porphyry (233-c. AD 304), the pupil and biolgrapher of Plotinus (AD 205-70), and the 'arranger' of Plotinus' lectures into six sets of nine — the Enneads — begins his account of his Guru as follows: →

On this occasion there seemed to be more insistent objection. 'How do you know' he asked, 'that our birth is on this date?' According to astronomical calculations made by a devotee interested in fixing the date finally, and taking into account the Precession of the Equinoxes which is recognised in some parts but not everywhere in Malabār in determining birthdays, the Guru was born on 28 August 1855, in the month of the Lion (in the Indian calendar) and under the Moon-sign of Satabhiṣā (which lies between the 7th and 21st degree of the zodiacal sign of the Water-bearer, Aquarius). The Moon-sign is called the *nakṣatram.* August 28 corresponds to the Sun-sign in the zodiac (of the West) known as Libra or the Scales.[18]

Versed in astronomy himself, the objection of the Guru was meant to be both an objection in the ordinary and in the

---

→ 'Plotinus, the philosopher our contemporary, seemed ashamed of being in the body. So deeply-rooted was this feeling that he could never be induced to tell of his ancestry, his parentage or his birth-place. He showed, too, an unconquerable reluctance to sit to a painter or a sculptor, and when Amelius persisted in urging him to allow of a portrait being made he asked him, "Is it not enough to carry about this image in which nature has enclosed us ? Do you really think I must also consent to leave, as a desireable spectacle to posterity, an image of the image?" In view of this determined refusal Amelius brought his friend Carterius, the best artist of the day, to the Conferences, which were open to every comer, and saw to it that by long observation of the philosopher he caught his most striking personal traits. From the impressions thus stored in mind the artist drew a first sketch; Amelius made several suggestions towards bringing out the resemblance, and in this way, without the knowledge of Plotinus, the genius of Carterius gave us a life-like portrait.

— Plotinus. *The Ethical Treatises — The First Ennead with Porphyry's Life of Plotinus,* tr. from the Greek by Stephen Mackenna,
Medici Society, London, 1917.

18. The following details of astronomical and astrological interest may not be out of place here. The Precession of the Equinoxes is a shift of the equinoctial points (the points at which the sun crosses the celestial equator) by which the sun reaches the meridian progressively earlier on a given day than a fixed star. It is due to the earth's axis describing a cone figure (like that of the axis of a spinning-top). The completion of the cone-figure takes about 25,800 years.*

In the time of the Gupta astronomer Varāhamihira, the *natural* zodiac beginning with the constellation Aries corresponded with the

→

philosophical sense at once. A *guru* is never 'born' in the usual sense, and if born in the usual sense the event has to be fixed in some reasonable way to the rest of the cosmos, so that it lends itself to no abnormal myth-making.

Protests of this kind made by *guru*s often constitute a cleavage between the Guru and his admirers. They misunderstand him and give him lip veneration while he sits in himself, feeling lonely and apart from the ignoble and gross outwardness of people who come round him. Sometimes, with the best of intentions, they unconsciously slight him, degrade him and made him feel crucified in various ways. His high life is lost on them, and at best they become related to him only though religious emotionalism. A striking example of this is afforded by the following incident.

It was at Śivagiri (Mount of Śiva) and the Guru was standing under a spreading mango-tree. A *brahmacārin* arrived with flowers in a salver early in the morning, at about seven. He had bathed in the spring before daybreak and had picked the flowers, favourite to each of the divinities who presided in the little shrines scattered on the grounds of the Mount of Śiva. The shrines nestled among green trees and shrubs, through which wound neat sand-strewn footpaths immaculately maintained by the Swāmīs in charge of the *āśrama*. Half-open lotus-buds, red ixora, with Jasmine and *tulsī*

→ mathematical or 'precessionised' zodiac. The latter is used in the West, while the former zodiac is in common use in India. The year of correspondence of the two zodiacs was in Varāhamihira's time, in AD 498.

Taken at 50" a year, the increment called *ayanāmśa* in India makes a difference in the year 1950 (1452 years after the time of coincidence) of 20 degrees 10 minutes 0 seconds. Thus the Indian calendar month varies from the world calendar month by a certain amount, while for astrological purposes there is an ever-widening difference between the points of entry into the zodiacal signs. While the entry of the Sun into Aries (*Meṣam*) which marks the Spring Equinox, will be about 21 March in Europe, in India it will be put at a date corresponding to 10 or 11 April.

Another interesting feature in Indian time is the Lunar Zodiac, the belt of the sky covered by the Moon every 28 days. This is divided into portions of 13 degrees 20 minutes 0 seconds called *nakṣatrams*, of which there are 27, each *nakṣatram* (or Asterism as it is popularly called in the West) being again divided into four *pādams*. Hence a person is said to be born in such and such a month (the Solar sign of the natural zodiac) and in such and such a *nakṣatram* (the Lunar sign of the 27-*nakṣatram* zodiac).

(basil) leaves, were ready to be offered with chants to Sarasvatī, the pure white-clad Goddess of Wisdom, corresponding to the original Santa Sophia of Constantinople.

The good-looking youth prostrated himself full-length before the image of the Mother of Wisdom, and from there went on to offer worship at a little shrine where there was established a full-sized painting of the Guru himself. 'The Guru verily is Brahmā, the Guru verily is Viṣṇu, the Guru verily is Maheśvara!' These were the chants he repeated in Sanskrit while he made the offerings. The strong odour from the camphor flame spread out through the morning air, and the incense smoke mounted up, suggestive of strange past associations and habits. A flame was waved round, accompanied by the tinkling of a bell while the worshipper made mystical symbols in the air.

While all this was going on a group of devotees stood around the Guru.

'Look at that', he remarked to the group. 'Here we stand in reality without our breakfast and still waiting for it; but our painting gets all the elaborate ritualist attention. That is due to religion!'

He meant to suggest that religion must as far as possible correspond to reality as such and not get lost without meaning in absurd dualities.

Sometimes, when not controlled or balanced by the actualities of a situation, devotion causes distortions. Misplaced fervour can be like a form of hysteria unconnected and divorced from fact. On another occasion, a devout *brahmacārin* brought the Guru his rice *kanji* (gruel) when he was ill. The Guru asked him if he had salted it properly. The *brahmacārin* replied that he could not do that, because it was wrong to taste any food offered to the Guru. 'Then give it to a dog', the Guru said 'and see if it tastes good to him. The dog doesn't suffer from scruples.'

Religion had to be rid of its distortions and had to be made to reflect reality. This was the secret of the type of spiritual life held up by the Guru as a model. The real and the existent met in neutral truth in all his ways and words, revealing a common human value which was earthly and heavenly at once. All goods or values of life, from the most ordinary, such as a fruit that abated hunger to the highest, to emancipation, in his view thus fell into a certain natural order.

As for himself, he was detached from all. If he took interest in certain goods or values of life it was mainly for the sake of others who still valued them. He was in this world but not of it. He was a detached witness of all without participating in the play himself. Such a silent detachment is of the essence of non-dual mysticism and the Guru himself wrote the following verses with regard to this state of detachment which blends disengagement and personality into one reality of high human value.

What name? caste? trade? how old?
From questions such, when one is free
He gains release.

Come! Go! Go not! Enter! What seekest?
From questions such, when one is free
He gains release.

Departest when ? When arrived? Whence and even who?
From questions such, when one is free
He gains release.

I or thou, this and that, inside or out, or none at all;
From cogitations such, when one is free
He gains release.

To the known and the unknown equalised, differenceless
to one's own or that of others, even to the name of such
indifferent,
From all considerations such, one freed
Himself becomes He, the One Released.[19]

---

19. *Nirvṛti Pañcakam* (Five Verses on Inward Release).

Part-III
Some Poems of the Guru

[Translated from the Sanskrit and Malayalam with comments and word notes.]

21

Translator's Foreword

OUR main object in this volume has been to introduce both the life and teachings of the Guru Nārāyaṇa in a general way. Now that we have covered the personal ways and attitudes of the Guru and elaborated the background and the general mythological, ethnic, religious, social, historical and philosophical setting in which his teachings and the method used have to be viewed, we proceed here to select a few typical samples from his writings, mainly from his early compositions, where much of the imagery is that of the 'stone-language' that we have dealt with in Chapter 15.

We need hardly say why he used such imagery, or why these early writings were clothed in a language of their own, since we have already shown the inevitability of such a language as part of the socio-religious necessary world in which the Guru lived. Such mythology and iconography with all their own 'idioms' as it were, have been alive in the daily life and mentality of the common people of south India from the earliest times, and for everyday use constituted the readiest means available to the Guru for the communication of his own high thoughts.

Essentially, such thoughts were the same as those of his later, more positive and less iconological works and, needless to say, the mystical, philosophical, contemplative or dialectical doctrines contained in all his compositions have remained the same throughout; but there will be many readers outside India, not to speak of those in India, who have lost touch with the old mystical, cultural langauge, who may be puzzled by the two modes of literary expression found in the Guru's writings, the mainly figurative Indian-contextual earlier poetry, and the more openly universally-fronted later productions; and therefore it may be puzzling on the surface to see how both modes of writing are really identical in wisdom-values. This is the background problem which we have tried to clear up.

Shorn of the difference of the linguistic or stylistic mode, both kinds deal with the same subject, breathing the same spirit, always indicating by this or that mode some central human value or good as viewed in the light of pure contemplation. No means of communication or tradition is rejected if it can serve the purpose of indicating such values of help to all. Some of these approaches have academic form and finish, some are in classical Sanskrit, while others view reality from the point of view of the Indian peasant, using popular everyday Tamil and Malayālam. In his earlier verses he spoke as one south Indian peasant to another, using the familiar idiom of a common environment. In his later writings he opened out and became universal, just as he did with his personality. He then took a more positive or definitely universal stand, treating his subject in a correctly academic or contemplative manner which was not only valid for India but global, applicable in any context anywhere.

The compositions we have selected here are just samples of some of these various styles, and, mainly because of space but also because the more serious works are reserved for future treatment, we have kept to the Guru's miscellaneous and shorter writings. The longer works, The *Ātmopadeśa Śatakam* (Centiloquy to Self) and the *Darśana Mālā* (Garland of Visions), each consisting of one hundred verses, since they require extensive comment on account of their profoundly rich philosophical content, require volumes to themselves. In them the Guru's mature and finalised wisdom is contained in a fully developed form. His supreme crowning achievement is the *Darśana Mālā* in which the Guru rises far above what superficially might be esteemed as even his 'own special note,' a statement which lifts philosophy above the philosophical, above the systems, pure and noble, treating of all systematised thought and philosophies in the light of Wisdom itself. But these must wait for future treatment. The last sample selection given in this volume is a foretaste of this kind of wisdom-writing.

We have graded the present selections in a certain order. The first poem, the *Critique of Caste,* has a bearing on an actual problem acutely felt in India, to which the Guru Nārāyaṇa finds a simple solution, without swerving from his own position as a contemplative philosopher. Then in later selections we have the theme centred round essentially real and human values such as *Prenatal Gratitude* and *Kindness to Life.* We pass on to samples in which doctrines of contemplative mysticism covering the psychological or cosmological fields are introduced. Many of the Guru's poems are constructed round the Śiva myth, which has a language all its own, surviving in revalued terms from the earliest times, prehistorically at least as ancient as Mohenjo-Dāro. The distinctive Indian approaches of Sāṅkhya and Yoga philosophy with their specialised features and vocabularies are also covered in our selections. Finally we arrive at the concluding sample, representative of the most sublime form of contemplative writing extant in India or in the world. This conforms to the strict discipline of *brahma-vidyā* or the Science of the Absolute as finalised in the long history of the Guru-Word. Thus through 'politics' in the Aristotelian sense, ascending a ladder of human values contemplatively reviewed and determined, we reach the 'end' of the ladder where there is suspended the glorious crown of the Word-Wisdom.

In conclusion a word might be added to point out that in the following translations I have adhered closely to the original Malayālaṁ or Sanskrit text, perhaps in fact too closely and literally for the comfort of the reader, and thus marring their readability as 'poetry' in the living English language, or even verging into what may seem like doggerel. While conscious of this it must be explained that this is due to a desire to adhere loyally to the original without adding any flourishes of my own, as these might detract from the value of the Guru's own words. However, in some rare instances I have taken what seemed to be an inescapable liberty with the original and employed a slightly different turn of expression. But here too, in order that the reader may not mix up what is mine with what belongs to the Guru's own words in the original, I have taken care to explain all deflections of this kind from the original in the word notes. On the whole, therefore, the reader can rest assured and can verify for himself where necessary the authenticity of the original words of the Guru.

At the end of this volume a complete list of the works of the Guru Nārāyaṇa will be found, with brief particulars about them.

Before taking leave of the reader it is perhaps only fair to explain that this present volume is intended to give only a general idea of the setting and the background and the philosophical purport of the Word of the Guru. We have not been vague on purpose, but of necessity, the subject itself is of such a nature, steeped in antique and unfamiliar details, much of it obscure, in one if not the oldest parts of India. As we have said, this book is only a preliminary volume, a clearing of the ground, and it is our intention in later volumes to present the teachings of the Guru in a modernised, critical, positive, and philosophically 'correct' form as the basis of a new world philosophy on which a fresh integration of humanity can be based.

22

A Critique of Caste
(Jāti Mīmāṁsā)

(*The first verse translated from Sanskrit, the four other verses from Malayālam*)

I

Man's humanity marks out the human kind
Even as bovinity proclaims a cow.
Brāhminhood and such are not thus-wise;
None do see this truth, alas !

II

One of kind, one of faith, and one in God is man;
Of one womb, of one form; difference herein none.

III

Within a species, is it not, that offspring truly breed?
The community of man thus viewed, to a single caste belongs.

IV

Of the human species is even a Brāhmin born, as is the Pariah too,
Where is difference then in caste as between man and man?

V

In bygone days of a Pariah woman the great sage Parāśara was born.
As even he of Vedic-aphorism fame of a virgin of the fisher-folk.

Introductory

This short composition has been selected as an instance where the Guru Nārāyaṇa, who was essentially a contemplative mystical philosopher dedicated to wisdom (*jñāna*), treats critically a subject which at first sight seems to belong merely to the social world, to the domain of obligation or necessity.

Normally, according to the strict methodology of the Vedānta, the Dharma Śāstras or Smṛtis (scriptural commandments or codes) are expected to deal with such questions involving social duties. A closer examination of the contents of these verses, however, will reveal the fact that the Guru here does not treat any aspect of contemplative wisdom other than what reason should confront normally. Although he deals with a question bearing upon or implying social justice or equality, his critique is not conceived or composed as a code.

The final distinction between wisdom and action (*jñāna* and *karma*) should be sought in the obligatory and necessary character of action and the permissive, contingent or commendatory nature of wisdom. When a critique strictly stops short of a programme of necessary action it is still contemplative, and should be considered as belonging to the subject-context of wisdom. A clarified intelligence awake to reality cannot avoid any aspect of reality.

After the Buddhist period the strictly neutral position of wisdom relative to social matters was violated and the necessary aspects of social obligations were stressed by way of a reaction against the 'heterodoxy' implied in Buddhism. We have tried to trace this dialectical action and reaction in a previous chapter. Here, in reviewing the whole matter critically, the Guru Nārāyaṇa brings in characteristics of reality hitherto uncritically treated, within the full scrutiny of contemplative criticism.

Śaṅkara treated the subject of caste as part of the *vyāvahārika* (the world of relative, everyday life), a necessary and given aspect of social obligation taken for granted, as something natural. For various historical reasons the critical revaluation of the subject of caste in the light of the full implications of contemplative, non-dual Self-knowledge was avoided in India. In our own times, as we know, this neglect has led to extreme forms of social inequality and discrimination, known today as caste, exclusive and segregatory, leading to the extremism of untouchability. It is Brāhmin versus Pariah dialectics.

But in the Guru-Way and Word contemplation and common sense come together again without distinction and distortion. Under one discipline existence and reality meet. Everything is brought under the scrutiny of reason in these verses, but at the same time pure reason never degenerates into any kind of injunction or mandate. Here, essentially, the plea is that man should realise his true humanity and unitive solidarity, and realise also that terms like 'Brāhmin' and 'Pariah' are ideas superimposed on the reality that is human nature which is essentially one, and fundamentally of one single sameness.

In the West the idea of equality became accepted publicly and forcefully after the French Revolution. The Age of Reason, with its dialectics between Voltaire and Rousseau, brought this fundamental idea into popularity for the regulation of human relations. Man respected himself and attained a status with a new value never so clearly recognised before. While it is true that, since the time of its pre-Platonic formulation in Greece, democracy had been there, it had hitherto always been qualified by theoretical considerations which complicated the issue, or limited it to a special social group.

This idea of equality is perhaps the greatest single contribution brought by Western culture to the East, where the stress on the individual and the subjective had yielded its full fruition of benefit and had turned toxic to life. As we have seen, during the days of Buddhist decadence the free spiritual life had been smothered by an overpowering weight of grammar-like abstractions; hence the breath of overt reason, a common sense outlook and the revival of a living mystical contemplation were all necessary for the strengthening and emancipation of the life of the common man.

By his status in contemplative Word-wisdom the Guru Nārāyaṇa had the right to revalue and restate the position. He fulfilled this role with that characteristically wistful touch of mysticism which is revealed at the end of the first verse of the poem: 'None do see this truth, alas!' They do not see the truth because the truth can only be known by the contemplative, by the one who knows it and sees it in terms of a Self-realised certitude, from the still centre where such truth resides. That certitude is unlike other kinds of knowledge which can be obtained in the market as usual for the asking, like purchasing a set of volumes of an encyclopaedia. As we have explained elsewhere, such contemplative knowledge requires the *guru-śiṣya* bipolar or mutual relationship, with the necessary corollary of a wholehearted intellectual sympathy by which the intuitive understanding becomes firmly established.

Commentary

I

Man's humanity marks out the human kind,
Even as bovinity proclaims a cow.
Brāhminhood and such are not thus-wise;
None do see this truth, alas!

This verse in aphoristic Sanskrit, while the remaining four verses are in Malayālam, conveys its own meaning, which can only be appreciated in the light of the Word-dialectics and the interplay between the two main Word-formulations as we have described them. Sanskrit is the language in which the idea of caste in the hereditary social sense came about; hence there is a kind of poetic justice in crowning this set of verses with a summary in the classical language. Malayālam itself has a large proportion of Sanskrit in its composition, grafted on to an early Tamil framework, but Malayālam belongs structurally to the non-Vedic Draviḍian context. So here in this poem there is an implied ambivalence in putting the inquiry in the two languages which belong, as it were, to the group representing the Brāhmin and the group representing the Pariah respectively, out of whose interactions the false notion of caste has arisen.

Here the opening line provides the key to the main approach

and method of dealing with the subject. First it is essential to know the truth about caste and then, whatever sociological system there is to be, can have a sure foundation. Caste distinctions have no basis in actuality. Subjected to the most drastic of scientific tests, *homo sapiens* falls *within* the human species. Racial distinctions do not amount to distinctions in the *species* in any strict terms. Like languages and customs, these may give an appearance of variety to the species, but they are only superficial factors of no importance intrinsically to biology.

The writer remembers once having put the following question directly to the Guru:

> If people can develop a healthy rivalry in the name of groups, imaginary or real, within the human species, would it not be good to give recognition to such groups since it would promote human welfare?

To this the Guru had a simple answer. He replied there was actually no difference between man and man. Hence whatever sociological theory or system is erected must rest on sound premisses of truth or fact.

In this *Critique of Caste* all that the Guru denies is that castes such as Brāhmin and Pariah have no reality. While historical, sociological, economic, or even dialectical circumstances may have caused the complex configurations of caste this does not mean that it has a *raison d'être* of its own. Any number of sociological experiments for the improvement of man are possible, but this is another matter like the dream of Utopia or some closed religious doctrine, each experiment requiring examination on its own merits. Whatever the system or theory practised or proposed, the simple fact remains that mankind is one.

Contemplation cannot be erected on a non-factual basis. The higher human values which contemplation incidentally brings to light as its obvious mark cannot ignore truth or fact without being absurd; for truth or fact is indeed the pedestal upon which wisdom of the highest kind rests. Therefore the denial of the non-factual or the non-existent or the superimposed (Sanskrit *adhyasta*) is the correlative and anterior aspect of contemplation, necessary before the reasonings and conclusions of contemplative wisdom can be made. Differences are not seen by the contemplative in any case, and all the more so when actuality or even empirical science denies the difference. Caste, therefore, from both points of view, becomes absurd.

The argument based on bovinity, etc., it will be noticed, never loses its contact with actuality in the usual factual, rational or scientific sense. Contemplation is not divorced from common sense. On the contrary, contemplative wisdom seeks erection on the strictest foundation of a realistic, existential common basis. The discipline of contemplation complements the discipline of science. In the name of the transcendental there is no foisting of any teleological doctrine on the reader, but rather the testing of the ontological here and now put forward as a corrective to all myth-making tendencies that might arise from either the contemplative or the day-to-day practical approach. Thus, exaggeration and distortion in thinking is eliminated. Hysteria is the pathological term for such distortion; and when the factual method is not strictly adhered to, there arise the pseudo-sciences, which, based on non-factual premisses, cause human conduct in society to go astray and awry, resulting in terrible confusion, injustice and suffering in the human world.

The history of the European Middle Ages is sufficient proof of this, while in Indian history the domain of social privileges has been a sacrosanct no-man's-land. Thus in both cases the clever ones got away with many theories whose irrationality was never or rarely or weakly challenged, all of which worked to the advantage of the power-seekers, to the detriment of the trusting and inarticulate masses who were finally segregated to the outermost fringes of social life without even primary human, let alone civic, rights.

If pure contemplation has nothing to do with reformist programmes, at least those who stand for it must refrain from semblance of support of wrong causes, so that at least there should be no possibility of any confusion regarding true human values. When such values are not clearly stated, or unclarified, there is a state of confusion, a kind of smoke-screen wherein injustice and all manner of human wrongs begin to thrive. Contemplation in its 'pure' disciplines must therefore conform to actuality, and if unrighteousness is to disappear it is equally important that the disciplines of the actual world of scientific facts must also be kept pure and in keeping with the universal front presented by contemplation. Only then can the dialectical relation between the two polarities result in a normal recognition of human values, without any extraneous considerations or diversions creeping into the process.

The Brāhmin needs equating with the Pariah so that a central human reality may emerge to view as a simple truth which is both actual and real, both existing and subsisting. Brāhminism is based on a racial distinction which arose from the Vedic penetration into Draviḍian or pre-Vedic India. It implies such 'rules' as the ban on marriage of Brāhmin with non-Brāhmin and a refusal to dine with non-Brāhmins. Two sets of considerations, some actual and some theoretical, have been confused and mixed up, resulting in the strange irrational absurdity which distinguishes caste prejudices in India from similar class-snobberies common elsewhere in the world. These absurdities are held up by the Guru for re-examination and revaluation, in accordance with the standards emerging from a science of contemplation. When inter-marriage or inter-dining between castes in India are prohibited and the false theory therefore made into a dogma of practice, it is on this ground that the Guru steps in to say this is a mistake which must be abolished from the reasoning mind.

'None do see this truth, alas!' In knowing that, even in a contemplative sense, Brāhminhood, Pariahood and all the intermediary classified postulates are neither actual nor rational, there is a need for the Word-wisdom to bring back the true value of life at each level of social complexity. But those who have this Word-wisdom are rare and it becomes, as the *Bhagavad Gītā* points out, of the nature of a secret which the genuine Advaita Vedāntin alone possesses.[1] The *Bhagavad Gītā* also says that contemplatively the notion of Brāhminhood does not exist even theoretically, any more than does the distinctions between an elephant, cow, dog or one who eats dog-flesh.[2]

Thus, bot existentially and subsistentially, the distinctions of caste become meaningless. This question is reminiscent of the relation of genus and species which puzzled theologians throughout the Middle Ages. A paradox is involved here as in the case of the interdependence of the concepts of the One and the Many in Platonic dialectics (e.g., *Parmenides*) and hence this apparently sweeping generalisation becomes justified. Genuine Brāhminhood, to have any meaning at, all must be a subtle personal value revealed to non-dual dialectics, something which has nothing to do with social status, biological heredity or holiness in the ordinary religious sense at all. Where there is the absense of recognition or understanding of this sole possible meaning of Brāhminhood, the consequences are so full of ill-portent for man that the Guru deplores the situation by an apt interjection '*hā!*' which we have rendered 'Alas !'

WORD NOTES

Jāti is rendered here as 'caste'. Although it is the nearest usual equivalent, 'caste' is inadequate. The English word is derived from the Portuguese *casta,* meaning 'unmixed race, breed, race, strain,' and came from the Latin *castus,* 'pure, clean, unpolluted.' *Jāti* has its own complexion on the Indian soil, where ideas of tradition, custom, culture, colour, ethnical groups and ideas of the sacred, all

---

1. *manuṣyānām sahasreṣu kaścid yatati siddhaye*
   yatatam api siddhānām kaścin mām vetti tattvataḥ
   — *Bhagavad Gītā,* VII.3

   Among thousands of men scarcely one strives for perfection; and even among those who strive and are perfect, scarcely one knows Me in truth.

2. *vidyāvinayasampanne brāhmaṇe gavi hastinī*
   śuni cai'va śvapāke ca paṇḍitāḥ samadarśinaḥ
   — *ibid.,* V.18

   In a Brāhmin who is learned and mild, in a cow, in an elephant, even in a dog and in a dog-eater, the wise see the same.

together fuse and blend to form this phenomenon of 'caste,' and throw up the two extreme types called the Brāhmin and the Untouchable. Class enters only feebly into the general concept, and although economic repercussions are inevitable, they are not directly related to the main notion of *jāti*. The dialectical revaluations that have been made throughout history, between the Vedic and non-Vedic concepts, as two sets of values or refinements, may be considered to be at the bottom of the whole question of caste. The sonorous title which is sometimes given to caste, namely *varṇāśrama-dharma* (colour-status-duty), fails to make any definite meaning. It is a confusing compound term consisting of divergent theoretical elements; *varṇa* meaning just colour, *āśrama* normal or stable type of livelihood, and *dharma* incorporating all notions of right living, whether spiritual or social. All these ideas put together produce an opiating black liquid called caste prejudice, without any sense being left of the original meanings of the separate factors making up the compound term. The result is not only irrational but detrimental to well-being from every point of view. Innumerable people, in particular the religious-minded peasantry and illiterate women generally, tend to treat the difference implied in *jāti* almost like a difference in species, for the word etymologically meaning 'kind' means that to speak of this or that *jāti* as of one man or another man, is to separate mankind into different kinds; and hence in this short composition the Guru's aim is to make this position clear.

Manuṣyatvam: 'humanity', means the assemblage of all specific qualities that distinguish man from other beings, including those higher values which are essentially human.

Gotvam: 'bovinity' or 'cow-nature.' In Vedānta this is a favourite example for illustrating the specific qualities of an animal.

Brāḥmaṇādi: meaning here 'the state of Brāhminhood'. This appellation and others of a similar kind, it is pointed out, are not determined or fixed like the specific qualities of a species or kind of living being. They are honorific titles, like the English words 'Lord' and 'commoner', sometimes based on a certain social status, sometimes on a pattern of belief or behaviour which, at a certain period in history, may have been once valid and distinct. The Brāhmin exists because he is not a pariah; thus only doctrinal and not actual difference is involved here.

The word *pariah* is left to stand by itself, but it should not be at all supposed that it has any derogatory significance in the present context. It is merely the existential counterpart of the existence of Brāhmin. The English word pariah is derived from the Tamil *paraiyar,* the plural of *paraiyan,* or 'drummer', the beater of the *parai* or large drum. Thus we are transferred linguistically to the prehistoric age beyond Mohenjo-Dāro times by this simple derivation. Drumming is pre-Vedic, even proto-Draviḍian — the drums that have been thumping 'for ever' as the Guru graphically described it once, as we have noted elsewhere. The Vedic victors had no drummers of their own, and so employed the indigenous drummers, the Pariahs, who specialised in this art which was novel to the invaders, for their festivals, marriages, funerals and other ceremonies, particularly in their penetration into the depths of south India. Thus orginally, as 'drummer', the word only meant those who were clearly outside the Vedic fold. Much later it became synonymous with its present meaning of social ostracisation.

Tatvam: 'truth', implies that Brāhminhood appertains to the subsistential aspect of reality and not to the existential. Brāhminhood belongs to another order of reality altogether. When this distinction is not recognised the entirely false notion of caste arises; a mystical fact with a psychological implication is given an entirely wrong legalistic and social meaning. In view of the fact that even moderns like Gandhi accepted this confused interpretation of caste, the question gains an importance all its own.[3]

II

One of kind, one of faith, and one in God is man;
Of One womb, of one form; difference herein none.

---

3. Cf. articles on caste in *Young India* by Mahatma Gandhi.

III

Within a species, is it not, that offspring truly breed?
The community of man thus viewed, to a single caste belongs.

The solidarity and equality of mankind, both in its existential and subsistential personality aspects, is reviewed here again in the proper scheme of a contemplative science. Self-knowledge is part of this science and the deeper human values have a place in the conception of the human personality when examined in connection with this Self-knowledge. Here we touch the very essence of wisdom. The archetype or the phenotype of genetics to which man or *homo sapiens* belongs by the natural background of necessity is also valid as a general fact which has to be related to all matters involving ideals or wherever problems of a teleological nature arise.

Whether we conceive these ideals or goals by names such as *nirvāṇa*, 'dwelling in the presence of God', or 'attaining eternal life', the position remains the same. In fact, as the Guru Nārāyaṇa admitted in reply to a question, one can substitute some other set of values which omit the theological content or implications. Such for example, would be the case with Buddhist terminology, where the word *dharma* could be substituted for the terms 'One caste', 'One religion', or 'One God'. *Dharma* considered in relation to necessity equates with the idea of one human kind or caste; related or conceived as a means to *nirvāṇa,* it equates with the idea of a single faith or religion; while when it is conceived as a goal, as for example, when the Buddha is referred to as the *dharma-kāya* (the Embodiment of Righteousness), the idea tallies essentially with the idea of a God. In such a context, prospective idealism's teleology gives us God or *dharma,* a purposeful absolute righteousness. The immanent aspects of reality when formulated give us general values such as brotherhood or religion. Conceived in universal terms such values become unitive at each level, retrospective, prospective or immediate, as a series of corresponding ontological excellences.

'Of one womb, of one form', etc. Here we come close to problems such as are dealt with by modern genetics, eugenics and allied subjects. In the West heredity is studied in relation to freaks in nature rather than in relation to the 'eternal' law of heredity. Freaks are exceptions, while the law they prove is the rule. A cat which has had one of its tail bones crushed by something falling on it, may of course have kittens with variously twisted tails reappearing, according to observed laws of heredity, such as those of Mendelism. This, however, does not disprove anything with regard to the main rule or law that father and offspring bear resemblances through generations.

In the search for 'objective' evidence the tendency in the modern laboratory has been to forget the laws that require no experiment. These being *given* to human experience, by common observation and inferred without doubt, they are, for that very reason, taken for granted and forgotton. They are valid outside the laboratory, while the specialist shut up against this sunlight-like evidence, forgets it in his too keen love for his own field of specialist research. This is a tendency needing to be countered by the new science of contemplation. As soon as this kind of 'scientific superstition', as Swāmī Vivekānanda put it, or 'the learned ignorance' that Ramaṇa Maharṣi called it, is abolished, we have once more contemplation and common sense coming together to support the fundamental findings of perennial wisdom or Advaita Vedānta.

Homo sapiens is of the single same phenotype, whatever the dominant or recessive variations may be that enter here and there. The evolution of the species, whether through sudden mutational steps or by slow degrees, never goes beyond the essentially specific characteristics of *homo sapiens* as a prevalent single species or kind. Although some modern thinkers hold that the emergence of a new type or 'race' of human beings is possible, such fancies are far from being strictly scientific.[4] Nothing has so far shown the existence of more than one species whithin mankind, and the possibility must therefore be ruled out for the present.

4. This possibility was alluded to by Bertrand Russell in a speech at Columbia University, New York on 16 November 1950, the *New York Times* reporting him as saying that the armaments race is a genetic competition 'to breed a race stronger, more intelligent, and more resistant to disease than any race of man that has hitherto existed'.

'Within a species, is it not, that offspring truly breed?' The allusion here is to the law of interspecific sterility. A mare can have offspring (the mule) when crossed with a jackass, but the mule is sterile. This is proof of the specific limits existing between the horse and the donkey. Without being a biologist in any modern sense, the Guru is as able as any scientist to state the rule of interspecific sterility, just as he was equally competent to deal with other questions such as evolution, etc. We have here therefore a striking example of the strictly objective and scientific method of reasoning he followed. By the aid of that science of contemplation which we have referred to, the Guru Nārāyaṇa establishes the undoubted fact of human solidarity, whatever may be the approach — of one kind genetically, of one fundamental faith religiously, and of one supreme value considered under the many synonyms of God or the Grand *dharma*.

WORD NOTES

Matam: 'faith', means formulated religion, which is essentially a value regulating human conduct and relations in society. As we have seen, *dharma* or righteousness, social or personal obligations or duties are all the same everywhere when they are shorn of historical or incidental stresses given by each particular expression of religion, and they can then be equated to one or other of the various aspects of wisdom. Thus in the light of contemplative Self-knowledge or neutral Word-wisdom as understood in revalued dialectical terms, all variations become included under one religion, common to humanity as realised in norms of universal, unitive and simple values which remain the same for all men, irrespective of time or clime.

Ākāram: 'form', refers to the typical contours or outline of the body of man, in its species-aspects, the phenotype, deducting those appearances that are incidentally due to variations in climate and food, such as sunburn, skin-colour, thickness or thinness of lips, etc. The Negro's skin is part of his environment as the eyelids of a Mongolian are regulated by hormones coming from other environmental conditions.

Within certain human limits, skin colours can change, when stimulated by secretions produced by long years under special environments, as the study of the ductless glands reveals. The subsoil can also have a similar effect in the absorption or deficiency of certain elements through food and water of particular localities.

A novel written in one language is appreciated when translated into another language because of the essentially human interest it evokes. Similarly, love between different races is common and gives healthier and more virile offspring. Beauty and refinement follow in the footsteps of good economic or educational conditions. A 'pariah' boy taken by the Guru Nārāyaṇa and educated in the Ashram at Varkala was easily mistaken for an orthodox 'Brāhmin,' as the Guru very often demonstrated. In any district in India, in any school, when Scouts in their uniforms are reviewed in line, the fact is again objectively demonstrated how difficult it is to sort out castes based on purely physical features. It is only by the aid of external and easily imitated marks, such as dialects, styles in hairdressing or appropriate 'caste marks,' that any possible caste groupings can be made under such circumstances. Objectively there is no difference, unless the term 'objectively' applies also inclusively to the incidental, superficial or extraneous accretional circumstances, which, from a rational point of view, are strictly irrelevant to the judgement of the subject.

IV

> Of the human species is even a Brāhmin born, as is the
> Pariah too.
> Where is difference then in caste as between man and
> man?

Here the Guru brings together the inevitable dialectical counterparts of the problem. For without the Brāhmin the concept of Pariah as a concept would lose its meaning, and without the Pariah as a background factor, Brāhminhood, at least in the Indian context, would lose its present import: because in the dialectics of history, as we have shown in a previous chapter, the one rises up in response to the other. But both the Brāhmin and the Pariah, in the pure light of reason or contemplation, although they may be historical counterparts, are essentially one in human content. Whatever asymmetry there may be in the 'typical' personality of one or the other is fictitious, they are social vestiges, out of place and incidental to the changed world situation, and quite irrelevant to spirituality. Patterned after the prehistoric Śiva — who is worshipped as a God even by the Brāhmin — the Pariah-drummer (synonymous terms as we have noted) is holy in his own way, while the Brāhmin again embodies as a 'type' certain revalued refinements which are called Āryan virtues, more socialised than the prehistoric ones, and holy in another socialised context. These virtues held up as 'Brāhminhood' consist of certain publicly workable qualities such as a clean diet, monogamy, improved housing conditions, dress and elaborated personal, social charms. A dominant group always has this advantage which justice seeks to abolish in favour of the common masses, the publicans and plebians. The dominated are the 'have-nots' and 'underdogs' because of human injustice, and it is here that contemplation can help in bringing order, balance and equalisation between the two opposites. Fundamentally, as Robert Burns touchingly and poetically summed it up in his grand verses *A Man's a Man for a' That,* it is the good heart and kindliness that unites all classes as 'man' and neither the wealth and extravagance of the strutting 'Lord' or 'Earl' or the grovelling poverty and drunken illiteracy of the 'peasant' or 'worker.' Both Brāhmin and Pariah belong to one and the same essentially human context.

Although this statement is simple enough to understand and even banal when harped upon, yet it is one round which many polemical battles and revolutions have been long and vainly waged. Even Śaṅkara, otherwise so rational and critical a philosopher, and in spite of the strict distinction which he made between the *vyāvahārika* (everyday practical) and *pāramārthika* (ultimate or final idealistic) values in life, left much alone that was irrational in the former, without comment, such as those matters of Vedic ritual and caste obligations, which he treated as if they belonged to the *vyāvahārika* as necessities. But even the necessary need not be irrational; and this is the whole point that the Guru Nārāyaṇa here brings out. Although much of what comes under the necessary has to be taken for granted, as inevitable, like the geographical and climatic variations, *all that comes under the necessary need not be treated irrationally*. If it *is* necessary that we should breathe and communicate, this does *not* mean that it is necessary to tell a lie. Reason can penetrate into the domain of the necessary in order to regulate and rearrange it, after critical scientific scrutiny based on common sense or contemplation.

Contemplation is not intended to condone absurdities, nor to confuse factual issues, but is rather a support and aid to common sense. Common sense and contemplation should be regarded properly as complementary parts of the same discipline, should be conceived as under a strict common methodology and epistemology of wisdom.

In an interesting composition called *Manīṣā Pañcakam* (Five Stanzas on Wisdom), attributed to Śaṅkara, probably correctly, each verse concludes with the statement that whoever represents unitive wisdom, whether he is an outcaste or a Brāhmin, is Śaṅkara's Guru. According to legend the poem was written following an incident in Benāres. Śaṅkara and his followers were returning from their bath in the Ganges when they were confronted by a Pariah who not only refused to get out of the way, but with poignant pertinacy questioned Śaṅkara's caste scruples and orthodoxy. The Pariah did so, not only on ordinary human grounds, as the story goes, but on the basis of Śaṅkara's own Advaitic approach. From the nature of the poem, Śaṅkara is supposed to have learnt the lesson from the Pariah counterpart, of the neutral wisdom of this matter of caste and outcaste. But whether he did or not is doubtful, for a close examination of the various *bhāṣya*s (commentaries) of Śaṅkara on the Upaniṣads, the *Bhagavad Gītā* and the *Brahma-Sūtra* reveals to anyone that he still treated caste distinctions based on Vedic ritualist gradations as something taken for granted. At the most, he is very mildly expostulatory.[5]

Perhaps he was anxious, after the Buddhist decline, to catch up with the pre-Buddhist orthodoxy of the Vedas, which included the social distinctions of caste, and history perhaps justified his lukewarm attitude. The right of the śūdra or lowest caste to have Vedic wisdom is questioned, implicitly and even explicitly. The right of a Pariah to such wisdom does not arise at all, and the inference is that he is to be eliminated rather than made even to serve the Vedic pyramidal superstructure erected on the broad base of the Indian social masses. Further, as Śaṅkara must have known, the Pariah represented a valid Word-wisdom belonging to his own historical context, which Word-wisdom was, as in Tiruvalluvar, even better than the later revalued Vedic-based Word. The anterior Veda typified in the *Kural* was as good at least as the posterior Āryan Veda which latterly became too criticially defective and esoteric. For a fuller examination of this we refer the reader to what we have said already concerning Āryan and proto-Draviḍian dialectics in our discussion of *Blast and Counterblast.*

V

> In bygone days of a Pariah woman the great sage Parāśara was born,
> As even he of Vedic-aphorism fame of a virgin of the fisher-folk.

After treating the matter empirically and dialectically in its various aspects, the Guru finally supports the whole with reference to historical fact. He selects as instances, sages of unquestionable status in the authentic dialectical context of the Vedānta which is the same as that of the Vedas, where this phenomena of caste has to be placed if it is to be understood.

---

5. See *e.g.*, Śaṅkara's introduction to *Bhagavad Gītā Bhāṣya* and his ambiguous comments on such passages as IV.13; and XVIII. 41; and also *Muṇḍaka Upaniṣad Bhāṣya,* II.12; also *Vedānta-Sūtras Bhāṣya,* I.iii.25; I.iii.34-38.

Parāśara was the father of Vyāsa, who was also called the Veda-Vyāsa (Arranger of the Vedas), said to be the author of the *Mahābhārata* and of the *Bhagavad Gītā* contained or 'inserted' in it, which is one of the canonical texts of Vedānta, held in high authority. Parāśara must have been of the prehistoric dialectical context whose characteristics we have already indicated in earlier chapters. Vyāsa and Vedānta are linked up inseparably for ever; so in the very context of the Vedas we find nullifying evidence against caste. Orthodoxy and heterodoxy meet and revaluate themselves in terms of pure wisdom, without heredity or tradition playing any part in the revaluation, which takes place more in spite of than because of heredity. Even if some people hold that Brāhminhood emerges as the culmination of hereditary selection of aptitudes, such a theory or notion is not borne out by historical facts.

The other sage referred to is Vyāsa himself, also mentioned in the *Genesis*-chapters of the Purāṇas as being born of a fisher-maiden. If, as may be, he is also the author of the *Brahma-Sūtras,* the great stringer-together of the wisdom-aphorisms, then here at the heart of what is called roughly 'Hinduism,' we have evidence that blows the false notion of caste to smithereens; for Vyāsa or Bādarəyaṇa — whatever he may be called, sometimes known as Vyāsa the Dark-skinned Sage — is a recognised *brahmarṣi*, taken into the fold as a Brāhmin of the Brāhmins, although not of that line at all.

The Guru's aim here is to reveal to all that these saintly characters, Parāśara and Vyāsa, who are recognised everywhere as ancestors of holy cherished memory and worshipped as such by all castes in every home in the Hindu world, are themselves outstanding reminders that mere prejudice lingers round the notion of caste, since they come from the much-abused and misunderstood Pariah line and not from the Brāhmin stock at all; hence here is the ultimate contradiction to be faced, of the Brāhmin not only accepting and adopting the Pariah Guru but putting him on the topmost pedestal as a sage of supreme value from the Vedic point of view. In the contradictory absurdity thus proved, all caste prejudices based on heredity, dynasty and blind tradition must be dispelled, and the social atmosphere of the present ultimately and finally cleared of this major caste-impediment.

Here it might be permissible to add some concluding remarks on caste, having dealt with it more or less completely in the form of actual textual comments. The Upaniṣads speak of Brahman (Brāhminhood) and kṣātram (kṣatriyahood or the Warrior-pattern) as attitudes of the personality which are superimposed as secondary conditionings on the Self. The *Kaṭha Upaniṣad*[6] treats of these as rice or food, to which the final consummation of specialisation is the dead-end with fixed sauce or pickles added on to the rice base of food as it were, which is called 'death', the cul-de-sac terminus of artificial specialisation. The basic ego is characterless and neutral, but becomes specialised with character as Brāhmin and Kṣatriya which finally attains culmination in the extinction of death. The numinous Self is the neutral basis for all the secondary conditionings, social, psychological or religious, added on to it. Such is the attitude of the highest Upaniṣads with regard to Brāhminhood.

If this attitude is vague, we find in the *Bhagavad Gītā*[7] further indications regarding the four castes:

> The four castes were created by me (i.e., *Kṛṣṇa, the Guru, God, or Ācārya*) in order to divide innate nature and (aptitudes to) action. Know me to be the author thereof as also its undoer, unexpended.

The innate contradiction in this verse where God creates caste and undoes it himself, can be explained only in the light of the dialectical revaluation of caste as it prevailed at the epoch when the verse

6. *yasya brahma ca kṣātram ca ubhe bhavata odanaḥ,*
mṛtyuryasyopaṣecanam ka ittha veda yatra saḥ.
— *Kaṭha Upaniṣad*, II. 25

He for whom Brāhminhood and kṣatriyahood are as food, and death but the sauce, how can one know where that Self is?

7. *cāturvarṇyam mayā sṛṣṭam guṇakarmavibhāgaṣaḥ*
tasya kartāram-api mām viddhy-akartāram-avyayam.
— *Bhagavad Gītā* IV.13

was composed. The four castes based on vocations and corresponding aptitudes being necessary and inevitable in any human society (even as in the Greek society of Plato) had elements of universal validity which were attributable to the Creator of nature. Wisdom, however, transcends nature, and in transcending the practical domain of relative, historical or sociological necessities, seeks pure reason and dissolves what has been built up by prior necessities, by means of new or revalued terms of contingent freedom. In the light of the revival of orthodoxy after the decline of Buddhism, at the time when the above verse was written, such an ambiguous revaluation was all that was possible for the author.

The Guru Nārāyaṇa, however, has no need for this ambiguity and indeed his clarity restates the whole position. He has in these five verses brought about distinct conclusions. Humanity is one and indivisible in kind (*jāti*). There is no room for any multiplicity at any level of human nature, socially, religiously or contemplatively. Neither actuality, empirically examined, let alone contemplative verities, admits of a *raison d'être* for caste; nor does history lend the idea any valid support.

23

Prenatal Gratitude
(Piṇḍa-nandī)

(*Translated from the Malayālam*)

I

Within the womb, O Lord of Good,
Was that lump in hand — this humble self —
With what exceeding love,
Who but Thou, kind One, nurtured it into life !
Ordered by Thee, all comes about.
Thus knowing, this Thy servant
To Thee now surrenders all.

II

Of earth, water, fire, air and ether too,
From each gathered, and firmly shaping in the palm,
Who confines me within a cell with blazing fire alit —
Even from the oppression great of such a feminine
divinity,
Protect and nourish me in Thy nectarine Immortality.

III

Thy Grace it is proclaimed even by
A mere stone-confined creature, impotent.
The very Indra of high heaven
Who within a vase-like lotus dwells —
And all heaven's host besides —
From such a Source do all grow out.

IV

Having no kinsmen, strength or wealth —
How could this ever grow? O marvel picturesque !
My Master's sport is all this !
No darkness is possible in thus knowing.
So to see, do grant Thy Grace, good Master !

V

For months full four and five,
Growing, becoming, by slow degrees,
Even Thou it was who formed eyes one after one,
Ever warding off Death's hand.
All that is now past,
But to my recollective weeping of that prime foetal time,
Listen, O Lord of Good !

VI

Yea, semen it was that mixed with blood;
And thus by sound matured and taking form I lay
mediate.
Then for me there was no mother or father;
So by Thee alone raised, sole parent mine,
All that I am is here today.

VII

If all that now-forgotten suffering should be revived
within,
I would this very day fall and perish in flames, alas!
Alone Thou didst then provide those outlets five of sense,
O Father mine of gold.
Even thus to know, Thou, O Lord, permits.

VIII

That mother of mine who, as a burden bore me within,
With a tender melting heart, vainly breathing many a
sigh,

Fuming hot, in pain she brought me forth,
To lie here, howling on like a jackal.
For once deign to tell me, Lord, what all this can be about.

IX

Full well aware art Thou, good Lord of all,
Hence what need is there for humble me to tell?
Do banish, pray, all agony !
Thy servant has no one here, and if Thou me disown
Then all is lost,
O Saviour coming mounted on a bull !

Introductory

Prayer, piety and questions of the hereafter are matters that are generally given an apocalyptic or liturgical form. But here, in this striking composition, bearing on the subject of spiritual progress, and covering the same contemplative field, the Guru Nārāyaṇa follows a new line, an unusual departure from the normal.

Consistent with the modern spirit of a scientific biologist, he takes the human foetus as his normal starting point and follows up its history very much in the same way as an investigator in experimental science. Continuing this method in terms of Self-knowledge, the Guru is able to traverse a region hitherto overcovered with guesses and rife with age-old speculation. In Europe the hairsplitting of the theologians and scholastic philosophers of the Middle Ages made all thinking minds turn in revolt from their methods of approach, and after the eighteenth century, the age of Voltaire and the full flood of rationalism, the whole subject of piety and devotion was left far behind. Materialism then became the only firm ground upon which human beings could collectively build monuments of common human values such as in the form of what is called civilization. Considering that civilization is a matter for which man is willing to lay down his life, the finding of real values again which suffers from no asymmetry of vision as between the present and the future, the here or the hereafter, and so on, gains ever-renewed importance.

It was Bergson who broke away from the highly theoretical academic idealism of the German philosophers like Hegel and in his own direct and graphic way brought some elements of contemplative metaphysics into the philosophical world. Influenced by Plotinus in his approach, the *êlan vital* (vital spirit or force) of Bergson came nearest to a biological concept of the 'soul' of man which had gone into disrepute with the rise of scientific materialism. Biology, as conceived by Bergson in 'creative' terms of flux and 'pure becoming,' gave a living and breathing reality to the whole problem of spiritual life. He saved metaphysics from being lost in the mere grammar of abstractions and his rhetoric came as a saving factor, making the dry winds of the desert humid and life-giving.

In like manner the Guru Nārāyaṇa here retrieves liturgical, ritualistic or unrealistic piety and gives it an intimately realistic and personal status, so that it yields Self-bliss through the common sentiment of prenatal gratitude.

Commentary

I

Within the womb, O Lord of Good,
Was that lump in hand — this humble self —
With what exceeding love,
Who but Thou, kind One, nurtured it into life !
Ordered by Thee, all comes about.
Thus knowing, this Thy servant
To Thee now surrenders all.

This opening verse sums up the whole position in regard to spiritual progress and the various factors involved. The foetus represents the personality of the seeker or aspirant, as conceived in his most primal simple form without any of those attributes belonging to the world of expansion or action. In the intimate negative recesses of the mother's womb before birth, the self or the ego subsists in direct relation to whatever draws it out into life-manifestation. In this process of life-manifestation there are two poles. There is the self and there is the conception of a Providence, an ultimate or God conceived as a light, perceptual or actual.

Kindness or love is a value that fits into this process as its natural counterpart. Kindness is of the same stuff as bliss or Self-knowledge, while piety or devotion are but words which are soaked in the essential content of kindness, mercy or compassion. When viewed without the asymmetry of a bias towards the subjective or the objective, without the prejudices attached to the *tripuṭi* (the three elements of knowledge) we have a central notion called mercy or kindness which covers an essential human value of a spiritual or contemplative order.

This, regarded as the kind care of Providence, is like the parental concern of a father, and may be called the Father as a spiritual factor, the conscious contemplative conceptualisation of the ultimate or supreme pole of the self, immaterial and invisible, subtle or subsisting, rather than merely existing. This kind One marks the principle which presides over or dominates matter which is merely inert or negative.

It is the touch of this principle or the relation to this pole which enables the whole of life to regulate itself in progressive stages of Self-realised Self-expression or unfoldment. Between these two poles, thus marked out, the whole phenomena of subjective or objective life becomes comprised. Pious surrender is but the recognition of this verity.

'That lump in hand': *Brahmāṇḍa* (the cosmic egg) in Vedāntic writing has for its antinomy, its microcosmic material counterpart, reciprocally in *pinḍāṇḍa.* In this cosmological context, this latter term is not merely the conventional ball of rice that is offered to ancestors in ritualistic Vedic ceremonies, but represents figuratively the substantial material principle of cosmic reality. *Piṇḍa* has here been rendered as a 'lump in hand' which would then correspond to microcosmic aspects of reality as implied when the human personality is considered ontologically in terms of cosmic relations.

'With what exceeding love, who but Thou, kind One, nurtured it into life' ! The treatment here of 'what' and 'who' side by side, as if the difference between them was negligible, suggests that the generosity of the Supreme can be treated personally or impersonally. The pronoun does not make any fundamental difference. There is no limit to the implied generosity, and such an absolute and limitless bounty cannot be attributed to anything but what touches the essence itself of the personality.

'Ordered by Thee, all comes about': This phrase seems to indicate determinism, or a God who directs and designs all according to an inscrutable will. When viewed existentially, there is a law of necessity in nature. This law of determinate necessity of the world of relativity is never abolished as long as the least vestige of duality is supposed to exist between the Supreme and the Self. As this prayer is addressed here to the idea of the Lord of Good (*Bhagavān*), i.e., with Good, as a supreme human value, determinism shifts, in a greatly extended sense, to merge almost into the domain of free-will. The law of determinism itself becomes a principle or criterion of pure reason, an imperative will of goodness, culminating in reflection and Self-knowledge. The object here is to present and explain this mode of operation of the free-will in relation to the actual realistic aspects of life. Such a treatment is meant to make extreme idealism realistic at the same time.

WORD NOTES

Bhagavān has been rendered 'Lord of Good' as the root *Bhag* would indicate.

Piṇḍam, as we have said, is applicable also to the ball of rice offered to ancestors in Vedic ritual. In the Upaniṣads the ball of rice has been further equated to the Self or the Absolute in formulae such as *annam brahmeti,* etc.[1]

II

Of earth, water, fire, air and ether too,
From each gathered, and firmly shaping in the palm,

---

1. *Cf., Bṛhadāraṇyaka Upaniṣad,* V.xii.1; *Taittirīya Upaniṣad,* II. ii.1.

> Who confines me for baking within a cell with blazing fire alit —
> Even from the oppression great of such a feminine divinity,
> Protected and nourished me in Thy nectarine Immortality.

Here the allusion is to the negative principle which is elsewhere referred to as *Māyā*. As long as positive spiritual progress is conceived, we must also postulate for it something as its negative aspect, although in the consciousness of one who is fully established in non-dual wisdom, this *negativitat,* as Hegel would call it, has no place. If the positive principle of spiritual progress is to be *puruṣottama,* the Most High God, then the negative aspect of the same principle, which is finally to be identified with that positive principle, as wisdom gains ground, is justly to be called *Māyā*, the feminine counterpart of the same.

Like the female Pārvatī and the male Parameśvara of Kālidāsa's opening verse in his *Raghuvaṁśa,* they are ever united as Word and its meaning. Every god in Indian mythology and iconography has his *śakti* or counterpart of manifestation or becoming. This *śakti* is the creative urge which is not merely a supposed abstraction of the intellect but something here on the existential side of truth.

The Guru refers to this aspect as something to be transcended, however great its claim may be to be recognised as subservient to the methodology of the Advaita. *Māyā* is not a reality but an inevitable epistemological and methodological necessity, to be used till Self-realisation establishes the full flood of silence in the Absolute beyond words.

Suffering, sin, and evil are all correlated and dependent factors arising out of this concept of the negative side of reality in *Māyā*. They all mean the same when viewed symmetrically, without prejudices arising from our angle of vision as between the cosmological-objective or the psychological-subjective. The good is the nectar that nourishes, while evil is the poison that corrodes the spirit as negative attributes in the gross, inert world of bondage or necessity.

Earth, water and the other elements are considered here as stages in the descending gross manifestation of the negative principle. Although the modern materialist and scientific view of the elements seeks to arrange them round a scheme of 'periodic' laws, the Guru adheres here to a scheme belonging to the contemplative dialectical outlook of Vedānta, the aim of which is mainly to resolve a finally persisting duality in terms of unitive comprehension.

Advaita (non-duality), Viśiṣṭādvaita (non-duality of the specific) and Dvaita (duality) all imply a recognition of this double character in various degrees for purposes of methodological or epistemological emphasis or explanation of one or other of the aspects of reality viewed from the personal level. A detailed discussion of the Vedāntic theory of manifestation of gross inert matter as we see it in nature, which is called *pañcīkaraṇa,* deserves close attention in the light of this implicit dialectics. This we shall undertake later. In the meantime we shall merely keep in mind that the reference in this verse to the elements being gathered into a lump needs examination for its own proper merits quite apart from the modern notions of physics. It requires discussion as a part of the contemplative discipline, as Vedāntins have always done.

'Who confines me for baking within a cell': The cell here can be understood from any of the different ways of regarding reality. Biologically, life begins in a cell bounded by cellular walls. Psychologically the cell represents the limitations of the narrow necessities of conditioned life. Cosmologically the cell is that particular space-time system into which mind and memory are inserted or fitted, in relation to the rest of the universe. An object is subjected to gravity, while gravitation as a principle applies to the universe which can be conceived in terms of electromagnetic or thermodynamic worlds. Whatever the theory there is, it can correspond to the cell mentioned here, in the sense of a limiting context of the 'here and now.'

'With blazing fire alit': This would naturally correspond to the counterpart of the cell. Energy, described for example as electromagnetism, is like a fire; and this, psychologically, would be the fire of consciousness itself, the consciousness of otherness. The pure consciousness, which is itself unlimited, seems to accommodate at its other pole, so to say, its own limited or conditioned aspect. The duality which is the cause of suffering is compared here to baking. The Upaniṣads refer to cooking (*pacyate*) in a similar context.[2] The incubatory process in the foetal state within the womb is actually comparable to subjection to such a slow process of heat as in a baker's oven. The oppression of the feminine divinity is balanced by the protective nourishment which the positive principle represents. We suffer and seek happiness, thus involving the same polarised elements indicated here. One yields place to the other in any spiritual progress at whatever level it may be conceived or formulated.

WORD NOTES

Amr̥tu: 'nectarine Immortality' — like *soma,* the heavenly juice of Indian myth coveted by the *deva*s and *asura*s (the good and evil spirits), symbolises a common human value. This neutral or central value of Good is like food, saving life from death, which latter is negative, representing suffering. When scientists say that the entropy of the universe is tending to a maximal state and that food represents a negative entropy, using thermodynamical language, the same positive and negative sides are involved as here.

III

Thy Grace it is that even now proclaims
This never remained a mere stone-confined creature,
impotent.
The very Indra of high heaven
Who within a vase-like lotus dwells —

---

2. *anupaśya yathā pūrve pratipaśya tathāpare*
śasyamiva martyaḥ pacyate śasyamivājāyate puṇaḥa.
— *Kaṭha Upaniṣad* I.6

Viewing restrospectively, as also prospectively man, like vegetation, is subject to the process of becoming (or cooking) repeatedly (is born again).

And all heaven's host besides —
From such a Source do all grow out.

The life-giving principle is like the little leaven that leaveneth the whole lump. It is both potent and small yet expansive and amplificatory in its effect. On this common ground of life-expression which is of the nature of the Self itself, cosmology and psychology meet. Here that transcendental factor called 'Grace' is the positive aspect of the principle. Grace is not material but is like the 'quality of mercy' which 'droppeth as the gentle rain from heaven' to nourish life beneath. This cycle conceived inclusively both cosmologically and psychologically is implied in the *Bhagavad Gītā* which refers to *evam pravartitam cakram* (such a cyclic motion)[3] where recognition is given to this same process involving positive and negative aspects of reality. Wisdom, within the limits of dialectical method (as well as piety or prayer), implies the postulation, at least for the sake of argument, of a second pole which is sometimes alluded to vaguely as sacrifice.[4]

Whatever the name, Viṣṇu, Puruṣottama or the Most High God, this is the factor constituting the second pole. It is with reference to this alone that it becomes possible for us to discuss the Absolute in any methodical manner. Inevitably, for otherwise the word Absolute itself would fail to have any meaning, and silence on the subject would be the only other alternative. Here Grace is to be understood in contrast with the negative principle of *Māyā* referred to in the previous verse.

'Thy Grace it is . . . .' There is ample evidence of what is meant here by Grace. This Grace is not a mere theological term to be considered in a context of piety or prayer. Grace is a fact inasmuch as whatever its essential nature may be, it is capable of making an embryo develop into a full-fledged personality such as a man. Man appreciates the cosmos and gains philosophical knowledge through

3. *Bhagavad Gītā,* III.16.

4. *sahayajñāḥ prajāḥ sṛṣṭvā. . . .*
— *Bhagavad Gītā,* III.10

Having created the peoples together with sacrifice. . . .

books. He is interested in extra-mundane values and thus gains a status which is unusual in nature taken as a whole.

'The very Indra of high heaven . . . and all heaven's host besides.' As conceived in Indian myth and cosmology Indra is the ideal of such a consummation of human values, and is shown as having originated in the hollow of a lotus bud which symbolises creation, from which even Brahmā the creator first came, with four heads for the directions. What is cosmologically great is psychologically and potently contained within the span of a hollow lotus as in a vase. All the mental constructions which are the further elaborations of this creative urge in consciousness, resulting in hypostatic realities such as gods or angels, belong to the same order as Grace. The names are different, but the reality is the same. Such is the implication of these lines.

'From such a Source do all grow out.' This would seem to point to the fact that the transcendent realities have their source in the immanent. According to the Guru there is no distinction even between the transcendent and the immanent. With intuition it is possible to link these as belonging to one central reality in which there is no duality even though its aspects are named 'transcendent' or 'immanent.' The heavenly beings are grounded in the Self here and now, as the Self is implied in all such notions of heavenly values. These and other matters need more explicit determining in the light of the whole of the philosophy of the Guru, as considered in its various applications both here as elsewhere in his works.

WORD NOTES

Kṛpā: 'Grace' — This could be translated 'kindness', but God's kindness is well known as 'Grace' in the theologies of the West.

Alpa jantu: Rendered 'mere stone-confined creature impotent', should be considered as a worm within a stone which itself is helpless and at the end of its resources in gaining power over its environment.

IV

Having no kinsmen, strength or wealth —
How could this ever grow? O marvel picturesque !
My Master's sport is all this !
No darkness is possible in thus knowing.
So to see, do grant Thy Grace, good Master !

The object of this verse is to draw the distinction between certain secondary factors and the all-important primary factor of Grace which is involved in the growth and progressive adjustment of an organism to its environment. It is true there is the father and mother, and nourishment from the mother's body. But these are only partial explanations of the main cause running through them like a vertical chain of cause and effect in time, rather than in the horizontal world of space or action. The potter is secondary to the basic clay of the pot. Clay is the *prius* in the Aristotelian sense, being the basis of the *entelechia,* the true cause which makes anything what it is in its own perfection, which touches actuality here. The role of the father, mother, wealth or friends who nourish a human being in a social context *after* birth, are seen to be non-operative *before* birth. An invisible numinous cause of an order of the 'thing-in-itself' is then operative as opposed to the incidental factors in which humanity seems to thrive in a socio-economic framework as understood in the usual sense. The contemplative environment of the progress of life or of spirituality is quite another thing. Here the mysterious factors, such as Grace, Presence, the numinous Absolute, the other-worldly, the given, the *a priori* reasoning or intuition, have their prime place. This is but in keeping with the methodology of the Vedānta, as we have seen in earlier chapters.

'O marvel picturesque! My Master's sport is all this!' The numinous aspect of the Absolute or the 'thing-in-itself' as viewed in the light of the non-dual Word-wisdom, is bound to have the character of a marvel or a mystery. It is part of its essential make-up. A central human value, conceived psychologically and cosmologically at once leaves behind only a sense of wonder. In so far as such a wonder fits in with actualities and is normal and harmonised in other ways, without disruption of the personality, it is to be accepted as normally falling within the scheme of contemplative thinking. Sport (*līlā* in Sanskrit) is that field of elusive 'occasionalism' where psychic and cosmic factors enter into inter-play.

'No darkness is possible in thus knowing. So to see, do grant Thy Grace, good Master!' The Guru is aware that these matters lend themselves to various superstitions in the name of religion or spirituality. Followers and teachers of pseudo-sciences and false, interested or asymmetrically constructed doctrines have often in the name of spirituality, erected edifices whose value to human life is often questionable, or suspect in various degrees. One religion may condemn the belief of another. But whatever the variety of belief, the compromise of opposites is inevitably bound to be present in one form or another. This makes the whole matter necessarily speculative when concrete details of doctrine or faith are stated. But this does not make the position fundamentally any different. Knowledge of the Supreme must partake of light, and lack of knowledge must be of darkness. Whatever the form by which we come to know of the higher Grace and its sport or mystery, as knowledge it is illuminative and thus belongs to the side of light rather than to darkness. Grace thus seen unitively is the universal positive principle of the Good, the True and the Beautiful which, whatever its form, cannot be a superstition. Unknowing alone, which is negative, would constitute the essence of superstition. The prayer here is for that Grace which can open the eyes of knowledge towards reality at whatever stage such reality is envisaged.

WORD NOTES

Aho vicitram : 'O marvel picturesque' — The phenomenal world has been attributed to *Māyā* which projects this empty vision, just as a mirage in the desert is also empty of water imagined there. The objective reality affords no final satisfaction to the ever-present thirst for knowledge and such satisfaction comes only when conviction about the real is gained once and for all. In the futile sojourn here one vision after another tantalises the spirit, which is finally lost in the wonder of the Absolute. Such is the goal of non-dual wisdom as known to Vedāntins from classical Sanskrit times. The phenomenal world is a mere presentiment of the will to live, and in this sense is an empty picture which allures without any reality as such. No further settlement of the problem is to be sought. Vedānta ends in the non-dual sense of wonder in the vision of the Absolute.

Andhatvam is 'blindness', or 'superstition', whichever is required by the context, as interpreted philosophically or religiously, as the case may be.

V

For months full four and five,
Growing, becoming, by slow degrees,
Even Thou it was who eyes formed one after one,
Ever warding off Death's hand.
All that is now past,
But to my recollective weeping of that prime foetal time,
Listen, O lord of Good !

The transition of the foetus from a characterless lump of matter to one in which the sense-centres become pronounced stage by stage takes a period of several months from conception, as physiology knows. During this whole period, one steady direction is maintained towards growth and life, with tendencies urging to light and not to darkness. Plants are geotropic and heliotropic while ontogeny repeats the memory of the phylum. The steady direction is a certain development towards a mature phenotype and this is maintained continuously. Metabolism goes on through time without interference from external factors and is protected from their interference. The embryo is thus saved from outside conditionings while innate tendencies are given a chance to assert and strengthen themselves.

In all this process, that principle which was referred to as Grace has its role, which is an important determining factor, as against climatic and other adverse factors, which, if given scope, could at any moment bring an abrupt end to this unfoldment. These are facts well known to biology but even in an extended sense reaching beyond the orthodox limits of biology, the same laws hold good, revealing the organic relation existing and underlying both biology and theology scientifically and correctly conceived in the light of the method and epistemology of the Vedānta which we have already examined.

The conquest of the future is the task of intelligence. This is the path of bliss. Regrets characterise memories which weigh on the Self from an opposite direction, as it were. Retrospection has been recognised as a form of regret by philosophers and psychologists who see in memory the negative weight of inaction and helplessness. Memory is sometimes consoling when attached to pure forms of subjective quietism; but on the whole memory in actual life is linked up with regrets. The feelings roused in the personality when brooding on the past constitute a familiar element in piety which is not perhaps the best form that piety can take. Positive piety rejects the past and lives in possible future freedoms in terms of Self-realisation.

'Eyes formed one after one': Here the 'eyes' are meant to cover all the senses, which are directed to take cognizance of whatever is presented to them in the environment. Biologically the senses, which are situated in close proximity and relation to the higher brain centres anteriorly, constitute together a pole which is opposite to the seat of emotions, often located posteriorly in the viscera or in the tail of certain animals. Evidence of such an ambivalent polarity of the nervous functional centres could be collected, and this would tend to show that all the cognitive centres such as the eyes, form a series, as it were, of concentric rings, the outer and most objective being the eyes, and the most subjective the ears with the sensation of hearing which puts sound and meaning together. Grace may be said to enter into the formation and functioning of the senses and organs, such as sight and the eyes, to the extent that such functioning is independent of memory aspects but rather dependent upon prospective intelligence. The desire to look at light wills the opening of the sense-organs to light. It is in this sense that Grace is to be taken as responsible for the formation of the senses.

'But to my recollective weeping of that time, Listen, O Lord of Good !' Here we have retrospective, regretful piety turning towards the desire for prospective recognition by the higher positive principle of the supreme Good. This sentence gives us the key to the whole technique of contemplative devotion or spiritual practice. The annihilation of the past in terms of the future, and the arrival at an eternal present in the Self, is the basis of contemplation. When thus examined in detail, this prayer of gratitude adheres to the strict epistemological and methodological fundamentals of Advaita Vedānta. Faith is retrospective; hope is prospective; while the resultant charity is the essense of the bliss of Self-realisation. Charity in its widest sense is therefore a contemplative human value.

WORD NOTES

Kālan: translated here as 'Death' is more than a mythological figure, inasmuch as *kāla* means 'Time' in Sanskrit. Time as related to the process of becoming ever new is a great destroyer of the past. The destructive elements of time which are detrimental to life are here personified in the term *kālan,* the God of Death.

Karuvinkal has been rendered 'in prime foetal,' *Karu* is the soft kernel or essential part of a fruit or nut. It is the substratum of life at its inception.

VI

Yea, semen it was that mixed with blood;
And thus by sound matured and taking form I lay mediate.
Then for me there was no mother or father;
So by Thee alone raised, sole parent mine,
All that I am is here today.

The intermediate stages of the incubation and formation of the foetal personality are now under reference. The biological picture of fertilisation given here corresponds exactly to that of science. The ovaries and principles connected with them are referred to generally as 'blood' while the spermatozoa is referred to as 'semen'. Without going into microscopic details, this corresponds to the biological picture in general terms, inasmuch as blood would represent the basic aspect and semen the factor which gives character and individuality to the mass fertilised. The two principles that were antinomies are again here referred to, side by side.

Beyond and besides the material basis for the proliferation of the cells to form the organs, there is introduced the idea of sound as the factor which makes the whole organism mature in the contemplative sense. Sound, as we have noted, is the meeting point of Word and meaning; the outer and inner principles meeting through the common 'sound' conceived as a principle. This theory of the relation of sound to the maturing of matter into organisms finds support vaguely in various Vedāntic writings, in connection with the theory of *pañcīkaraṇa,* and has been the subject of recent investigation by some Western scholars. This has relationship with the mystery of number itself which was one of the subjects of Eleatic philosophy, dealing with order and music in regular patterns and scales, expounded by Pythagoras and beginning to be reaffirmed by scientists like Jeans and Eddington.

Whatever the final theoretical implications may be, for our present purposes it will be sufficient to know that sound is the medium where the subjective and the objective meet, and where the mind may be said to be inserted in general consciousness. The foetus is no more a mere inert lump, but gains a certain degree of self-consciousness, however low or feebly initiated, at this stage. This self thus integrated, connects positive and negative aspects, and holds them together in unitive knowledge. In this inceptual stage of consciousness, such a self knows nothing of a father or mother. It is innocent of all relations, innocent of the outer world's superimpositions which come only later. Thus by origin, the personality is essentially independent of external human relations. These belong to a social context of a later stage.

'I lay mediate' can refer to the position of the foetus whithin the maternal body in an actual sense, or it might be understood in a psychic or symbolic sense. This self, at its inception, was neither postitive nor negative in its adjustment to the environment. It was a neutral entity, balanced between the two extremes, and thus represented the principle of being in its purest form. The essential nature of the personality pertains to this neutral self, and it is in this sense that the later remark in the verse applies, namely, that the self is to be looked upon as raised solely by the Grace of God, as the child of immortality.

WORD NOTES

En tātan: 'Father mine', is here rendered 'sole parent mine.' *Tātan* is a word of endearment applied to any parent, including the grandfather, and sometimes even to a child. It has no relevance for the particular generation. Ancestor and heir become interchangeable in its intimately pure connotation. It is representative of the protective principle in the abstract, whether conceived prospectively or retrospectively.

VII

> If all that now-forgotten suffering should be revived within,
> I would this very day fall and perish in flames, alas !
> Alone Thou didst then provide those outlets five of sense,
> O Father mine of gold.
> Even thus to know, Thou, O Lord, permits.

Retrospection when overladen with regretful memories of suffering must be detrimental to progress in the usual sense. It is of the nature of a self-consuming fire as the Sanskrit word *tāpam* (regret) sufficiently well recognises (i.e., *tāp* — to burn). In this negative state of self-immolating memory, the senses have a corrective or balancing role. They hold the interests on newer and ever-newer objects. Life is thus diverted into progressive channels of normal activity. This helps to balance and maintain the metabolisms and the life of the tender being in normal consciousness. Integrated and unified consciousness can reflect on its own nature, and thus, through the balancing of the senses, the personality is able to attain to full human knowledge. Such Self-knowledge can imply more theoretically. As the Guru Nārāyaṇa himself points out, lucid retrospection need not be an impediment to wisdom.[5] The implications here deserve detailed and separate examination which we shall defer for later consideration.

'Alone Thou didst then provide those outlets five of sense. . . .' The ambivalent aspects of life have to be maintained at a certain equilibrium so that life and Self-realisation may be possible. The higher values depend on the more basic ones as when the *Bhagavad Gītā* says that the gods are to be propitiated by sacrifice, and they in turn would then shower graces on man.[6] A reciprocity is suggested here between what memory implies and what the senses represent. One cannot exist without the other. Like sin and grace in theological discussions, the relation here is to be understood in both its implications at once. As the Tamil *Tiru-Kural* puts it, in connection with rain, 'Should the sky run dry, there would be neither festivals nor worship for the gods here.'[7] The circulation of ambivalent factors and values of good and bad goes hand in hand and has to be understood intuitively in its global entirety.

'O Father mine of gold' — The reference to a father of gold is to indicate that matter itself is not to be thought of as divorced from any idea of the supreme principle. The thinking substance of Spinoza comes near to this way of looking at the reality which is at once immanent and transcendent.

WORD NOTES

Uṇarnāl, rendered 'should be revived within', means more literally, 'waking to the past.' Sleep and dream are like memories in the subconscious. At the conscious level we are awake where another set of tendencies come into operation, more in relation to the objective, empirical or actual.

Poṟvātil, rendered 'outlets five of sense,' would be more literally

---

5. *Ātmopadeśa Śatakam,* Verse 64.
6. *Bhagavad Gītā,* III.11.
7. *Kural,* II. 8.

'doors.' The senses have been compared to windows, and, together with the other bodily orifices, they have been referred to in the *Bhagavad Gītā* as the gates of a city.[8] Reflexive thought is also a higher function involving the positive aspects of the personality.

VIII

> That mother of mine who, as a burden bore me within,
> With a tender melting heart, vainly breathing many a sigh,
> Fuming hot, in pain she brought me forth,
> To lie here, howling on like a jackal.
> For once deign to tell me, Lord, what all this can be about.

The picture painted here is so realistic that it calls for little comment. There is even a touch of humour in this very realistic form of adoration, especially at its tail-end, like the sting of an epigram.

'With a tender melting heart . . . in pain . . . howling on like a jackal.' The painful heat and the tenderness of feelings alternate in the mother, making life a pendulum swinging between two extreme poles. The mother has pain in giving birth, as the child shows pain in being born, by crying. The final question is therefore pertinent and cannot be answered with logic one way or the other. The cyclic rotation of *saṁsāra* or the wheel of life is here summed up. It revolves between the ambivalent factors and tendencies at the root of life itself — a continuous cyclic movement. No philosophy or science offers an answer to these questions which involve an understanding of the numinous Absolute. Only the silence of the Guru can represent an answer.

WORD NOTES

Ventullazhiññu, literally 'cooked and melted loose within,' has been rendered 'fuming hot . . . with a tender melting heart' and shifted round to give the meaning in English.

---

8. *Bhagavad Gītā,* V.13.

IX

Full well aware art Thou, good Lord of all,
Hence what need is there for humble me to tell?
Do banish, pray, all agony !
Thy servant has no one here, and if Thou me disown,
Then all is lost,
O Saviour coming mounted on a bull !

In the last lines the Guru links up the whole composition with the prehistoric Śiva tradition and affiliates the entire theme to the doctrines of the perennial philosophy or mysticism. The duality as between the Supreme Providence and the adoring Self here is the cause of all the agony or suffering referred to above. Mutual recognition of the bipolar interdependence between the Supreme and the ontological Self is strikingly restated here by way of conclusion; the two aspects being brought together into close reciprocity for purposes of contemplative understanding of the one in terms of the other.

The allusion in the last line is to Śiva who rides a bull and saves lives, as against Yama or Kāla, the God of Death who is represented symbolically as riding on a black buffalo. This final reference to the Śiva-bull who is the white Nandi, adds that characteristic depth to the composition, reaching back to prehistory and to that virile principle of positive life in the symbology and mythology of Śiva which we have outlined in earlier chapters.

The *Mārkaṇḍeya Purāṇa* describes the way in which Śiva mounted on a white bull (the Nandi) appears on the scene at the very last moment of the death of a young man who was destined to die at the age of sixteen. Death (or Kāla) claims the life at the appointed hour, but the saviour on the white bull comes at last as the youth's final refuge, in his hour of extreme despair. Such is one of the images which this verse reverses in the time-honoured context of contemplative Word-wisdom.

24

Kindness to Life
(Jīva-kruṇya-pañcakam)

(Translated from the Malayālam)

I

All are of one Self-fraternity.
Such being the dictum to avow,
In such a light, how can we take life,
And devoid of least pity go on to eat ?

II

The non-killing vow is great indeed,
And, greater still, not-eating to observe;
All in all, should we not say, O men of righteousness,
Even to this amounts the essence of all religions ?

III

If killing were applied to oneself,
Who, as a favour, would treat such a dire destiny ?
As touching all in equality, O ye wise ones,
Should that not be our declaration for a regulated life?

IV

No killer would there be if no other to eat there was —
Perforce, himself must eat !
In eating thus abides the cruder ill
In that it killing makes.

V

Not-killing makes a human good —
Else an animal's equal he becomes,

No refuge has the taker of life,
Although to him all other goods accrue.

Introductory

This short composition of five verses shows that ethics arises directly out of the contemplative way of life. In fact, we see here how contemplation and matters which primarily concern the commandments of a religion can be brought together under one general principle of wisdom and rational living. The ethic here is dictated by the inner voice of contemplative reasoning when a man wants to be fully human. Leaving aside on the one hand epicurean, hedonistic or utilitarian views of life, which are based upon satisfactions too ordinary for the dignity of man, and on the other hand preventing such commandments from becoming mere dead letters, which might happen if divorced from all human considerations, the Guru here follows a line of contemplative reasoning which is full of true humanity and dignity. The pious man of prayer seeks refuge in God while denying what might give a similar refuge to animals. The contradiction in such a unilateral attitude of prayer, with the subsequent conflict which it brings about, is forthrightly abolished here, with a tenderness that is touching and which even has some humour.

Commentary

I

All are of one Self-fraternity.
Such being the dictum to avow,
In such a light, how can we take life,
And devoid of least pity go on to eat?

When piety and kindness are hinged one on the other, they together constitute an important article of faith, a law or axiom of contemplation. In the very first verse, Nārāyaṇa Guru relates it to the axiom of the Advaitic or non-dual reality of the Self. The Self is universal and unitive and therefore cannot countenance conflict between life and life. This is the first corollary arising out of the pure contemplation of *a priori* truth. When it is accepted that killing is wrong, the same holds good *a fortiori* with the question of eating. Kindness emerges naturally as the argument of the second degree which partakes of the logic of the emotions to at least an equal measure as it is itself based on pure reason. To the Advaitin one is as valid as the other since the principle involved is the same.

The need to be kind to one's fellow creatures does not require the support of argument. One does not have to look for this justification in any book. It is self-evident and, consciously or unconsciously, humanity treats it as such. All civilised governments provide laws for the protection of wild life, even though instituted for aesthetic rather than ethical reasons. The promiscuous destruction of nature is beginning to be recognised as at least undignified behaviour for those calling themselves civilised.

However, much vagueness clings to this subject. Some consider kindness as being sentimental, and others as an impractical ideal. Killing in some form being incidental to life, such as that involved, for example, in agriculture, there is a condoning of killing or a conniving of it in various degrees without any real criticism. There is even a popular saying in Malabār that the sin of killing is abolished by eating. Killing a man is murder (except in the case of war), while slaying a beautiful deer in the woods is not. Cannibalism, again, cannot be treated at the same level as the consumption of microscopic beings in milk or other food. Confusion between the inevitable and the contingent aspects of the question gives rise to the prevalence of an uncritical vagueness, creating a no-man's-land of absurdities.

But here the Guru marks out the field of rational contemplative norms of conduct in terms of the dignity of man. Man is the measure of all things as Self-realisation in universal terms is his goal, when intellectually conceived. After understanding critically the position in regard to this question of killing and eating, it is for each man to make up his mind where he will draw the line of demarcation between what is necessary according to him and what he should avoid in the name of kindness. But the palate here should not be the preponderant consideration.

Duty, piety, righteousness and religion are matters involved here more than a merely rational outlook. Here reason is affiliated to a humanitarian outlook. This attitude is of the essence of religion, whatever the verbal form it may assume. Man is seeking spiritual consolation as a refuge from suffering and sin, or even seeking emancipation in wisdom in ultimate terms of pure reason. The generosity of the absolute principle is always there as an inevitable factor to be dealt with, whatever path of wisdom or piety a particular aspirant may place before himself as his ideal. In times of stress all men pray for mercy of some kind, and that same prayer must bind us all to acts of mercy as Shakespeare says. A man who was sure that he would never need mercy might perhaps be the only one who could logically escape from being merciful. Only in the context of neutral wisdom is such an indifference to mercy imaginable, and when such a neutrality is really gained, it becomes tantamount to being one with the Absolute. Then the question of mercy does not arise. In all other cases mercy becomes a necessary and inevitable form of obligation, even in the most contemplative of disciplines. Mercy, however, should not be mixed up with sentimental regret or retrospective self-pity. The kindness meant in this poem is that tender feeling of universal sympathy which is based on an open and rational outlook.

In this first verse the doctrine of non-duality, as conceived in universal terms is invoked to support the idea of kindness as an obligation to be rightfully recognised by man. Reason makes kindness binding. Otherwise ethics would depend upon necessity and would be left for its support on instinct or animal nature. Non-dual contemplation requires reason to be taken as a corrective to instinct. Instincts must always be subjected to the sublimating purification of reason.

'Self-fraternity' — *Ātma sahodarar* in the original means the same as that universal brotherhood or equality in the eyes of God spoken of by religious people. Such terms as 'created in the image of God' are sufficiently recognised in the study of comparative theologies of all religions to be clear to the general reader.

II

The non-killing vow is great indeed,
And, greater still, not-eating to observe;
All in all, should we not say, O men of righteousness,
Even to this amounts the essence of all religions?

There is no religion which does not stress one form or another of universal brotherhood, and which does not advocate kindness to all living things. The commandment 'Thou shalt not kill' which Christianity and Islam inherited from Hebraic and perhaps from proto-Hebraic sources confirms this view and, taken side by side with facts in practice such as the prohibitions and injunctions regarding killing on certain days and of certain animals (such as a red or a stray cow or bull), we can gather, even in the religions of the non-vegetarian peoples an acceptance, in principle at least, of the non-killing commandment. And there is the general acceptance by the Semitic religions that a form of grace accompanies fasting and abstention from meat-eating on certain days. Buddhism in principle (though not in practice in Burma for instance) is solidly based on non-hurting (*ahiṁsā*), and Jainism marks the high level of this principle. The universal principle of brotherhood of all life and general equality becomes confined to 'humans only' in those climes where animal food becomes more excusable than, say, in the southern latitudes of Asia. Making allowances for local differences due to necessity, non-killing, in principle, is enjoined by all religions.

'O men of righteousness' — This verse is addressed particularly to those who think in terms of organised and active religions which try to keep the faithful on the path of righteousness and virtue by edict and law. The more contemplative religions accept it in the axiomatic form which does not require legalisation.

III

If killing were applied to oneself,
Who, as a favour, would treat such a dire destiny?
As touching all in equality, O ye wise ones,
Should that not be our declaration for a regulated life?

The appeal in this verse is to those endowed with wisdom or education. Equity leads inevitably to the notion of equality. The argument here is against unilateral attitudes of equity. Reciprocated equity applied to both sides concerned without difference, and based on a uniformly general principle, becomes equality, which the wise are here asked to recognise so that they may lead humanity along such lines.

WORD NOTES

Dharmyam has been rendered 'for a regulated life,' i.e., conducive to a life lived according to the first principles which have been stated already. When *karma* or conduct is controlled by considerations of first principles, it becomes *dharma* or right action, and anything which promotes the prevalence of such activities in group life is *dharmyam* — what conduces to a regulated life.

IV

No killer would there be if no other to eat there was —
Perforce, himself must eat !
In eating thus abides the cruder ill
In that it killing makes.

We often hear the argument that someone else has done the killing and therefore one can eat without any qualms of conscience. The hollowness of such an argument is exposed here with a certain touch of humour. The picture arises of a lone huntsman having brought down a deer and being faced with the problem of consuming it all himself. This readily brings home the absurd relation between killer and eater, and in the argument, is not without its humorous side.

WORD NOTES

Agham: 'evil', has been translated 'ill'.

V

Not-killing makes a human good —
Else an animal's equal he becomes.

No refuge has the taker of life,
Although to him all other goods accrue.

This last verse appeals to human dignity and, in its name, puts in its final plea against killing. Even if all the other arguments should be logically unconvincing, here is an appeal to a higher value in man which is reasonable. Man becomes the equal of an animal by wanting to kill it for the pleasure of his palate or for the pleasure of hunting, which are motives of a very ordinary order, common to more uninformed levels of life.

'Although to him all other goods accrue.' — There are values and values. Those in the form of goods which we enjoy here are many and varied and may be had in a unilateral fashion even when one is undeserving. But the essential good as a value, such as grace or refuge or sanctuary in God, comes from the unitive, presiding principle of Good with which a bilateral and unitive relationship is necessary. One cannot think of bribing God for a partial favour based on no principles. To be loved of God one has to love one's fellow creatures, all in all.

25

Song of The Kuṇḍalinı Snake
(Kuṇḍalinī-Paṭṭu)

(*Translated from the Malayālam*)

REFRAIN

Dance, cobra, dance !
Thy burrow seek and witness
The bliss of grace in wild display.
Dance, cobra, dance !

I

Keep close the foot so lotus-red
Sacred of the Lord who dons
The crescent moon and cassia bloom, and
(*repeat refrain*) Dance, cobra, dance . . . . !

II

Besmeared with ash and bright His holy form shines.
Thy tears for Him in streams do shed,
And thus steadily
(*repeat refrain*) Dance, cobra, dance . . . !

III

Upon this burning ground
Where ghost and also corpse are born
United well with what subsists, its counterpart supreme
(*repeat refrain*) Dance, cobra, dance . . . !

Śiva Dancing with the right leg raised, early Pāṇḍya, 10th century AD.

IV

The tresses of hair so fragrant
Excelling flowers of sweet aroma
In shade they lie in shame.
Beside this beauteous form, which view, and
(*repeat refrain*) Dance, cobra, dance . . . . !

V

A spotted leopard-skin surrounds
His form of tender bloom.
'Within the Self he dances' say, and
(*repeat refrain*) Dance, cobra, dance . . . . !

VI

Upon the silver-hill what gleams
As Vedic wisdom's quintessence.
Say 'That in me is dancing too,' and
(*repeat refrain*) Dance, cobra, dance . . . . !

VII

He for whom a sportive snake
An ornament becomes
His home it is in us; so
(*repeat refrain*) Dance, cobra, dance . . . . !

VIII

No one has seen, not he of blossom's bloom
Nor even that holy garlanded one,
This flower-form of thine, so
(*repeat refrain*) Dance, cobra, dance . . . . !

IX

Auṁ and all the rest that form
The essence of ten million charms —
We now do know and so keep on, and
(*repeat refrain*) Dance, cobra, dance . . . . !

X

To the One who conjures down
Who all things here bring out,
To His leaf-tender foot adhere, and
(*repeat refrain*) Dance, cobra, dance . . . . !

XI

From lettered charm of Śiva-praise
To every formula of truth —
Even from sound do they come out, so
(*repeat refrain*) Dance, cobra, dance . . . . !

XII

Ten thousand millions
Of that Ananta snake art Thou;
Thy million hoods then open out, and
(*repeat refrain*) Dance, cobra, dance . . . . !

XIII

This body here, no truth it has;
Owner another in it resides.
Such wisdom do thou gain, and thus
(*repeat refrain*) Dance, cobra, dance . . . . !

XIV

Uniting body and owner too,
Radiant, who abides as one,
Such there is to know, as well, so
(*repeat refrain*) Dance, cobra, dance . . . . !

XV

What swallows all, with rival none,
Such is the omnipresent Word
Which swallow thou, and steadily
(*repeat refrain*) Dance, cobra, dance . . . . !

XVI

Consuming all the words there are
As the supporting wall for all
Even on such do take thy stand, and
(*repeat refrain*) Dance, cobra, dance . . . . !

XVII

From very name this great expanse
And even earth as well did come
As a presentiment in thought, so
(*repeat refrain*) Dance, cobra, dance . . . . !

Introductory

Kuṇḍalī is the seat of the *kuṇḍalinī* which is often spoken of in Yoga as a snake lying coiled at the base of the vertebral column. It is supposed to represent a ganglium, plexus or storehouse of nervous energy which irradiates upwards to the higher centres of the nervous system. Although anatomists have tried to locate this *kuṇḍalinī śakti* (basic nervous energy) in histologic, organic or functional terms more precisely in modern scientific language, all such attempts remain unconvincing and resemble the efforts of a pseudo-science, for the very simple reason that this psychic energy is not reflected directly in objective organs or functions.

The subjective and the objective come together here, hand in hand, as the methodology and epistemology of Vedānta would necessarily require. Where inner and outer values are spoken of together, a certain vagueness is bound to be present, at least according to the objective standards of science with its great stress on what is visible. Under suitable attitudes and spiritual disciplines known to Yoga, the coiled-up snake at the base of the vertebral column is capable of uncoiling itself. The roused up serpent power then reaches higher and higher levels, touching or attaining successive plexes often referred to as lotuses or central points from which nervous energy of a spiritual order radiate.

Of these, the highest ranking is somewhere at the base of the brain, beyond the soft palate, which the tongue's tip, when trained, can touch and stimulate. This is the centre of the thousand petalled lotus (*sahasrāra padma*), of the full radiance of positive wisdom in which all relative knowing becomes absorbed. This is like the burrow of a snake situated on high. And when the snake reaches this home on high it is lost inside it and all 'becoming' is absorbed finally in 'being.' Such is the imagery underlying this composition.

The cobra charmed by music lifts its hood and swings and sways in response to it like a dance or play. This is a familiar sight in the Indian scene and affords the author an apt literary device around which to build his mystical doctrines and philosophy of the Self. The whole process is attended with a certain sense of exaltation, joy or bliss which the *yogī* feels, like a poet or artist who reaches out from one sublime vision of the psycho-physical universe to another one higher or still more superb.

In order to appreciate the suggestive meanings of mystical import in this naive-looking form of poetry, one has to be sufficiently familiar with the dancing Śiva legends. The bronze of Naṭarāja, now so well known in the West, represents this dance which is both cosmological as well as psychological in symbology, fused into one creative image based on the myth or prehistoric personality of Śiva, such as we have traced in our earlier chapters.

Snake symbology has been in the tradition of many lands, Crete, and Egypt as well as India (where the tradition still lives on). The snake cosmologically is the principle of time, continuity, or eternity. Ādiśeṣa and Ananta (the cosmic serpent of time) are two well-known snakes of mythology, inseparable attendants upon Viṣṇu, and whose long coils form the couch upon which this form of the divine principle reposes.

With Śiva the snake comes in as an ornament worn round the neck of this cosmo-psychic God. It represents again the principle of becoming, memory or time, with a personality of its own which may be said to represent some mystical attitudes on the lines of the *kuṇḍalinī* snake we have already referred to particularly in the Yoga context.

In the present composition of the Guru Nārāyaṇa the snake

symbolises the soul or self in its progress. It represents aspects of the numinous and the Absolute made living and real for purposes of helping to explain mystical doctrines, over which otherwise we should be obliged to pass in silence. The whole composition should thus be treated figuratively, as explanatory by an apt literary device, of some aspects of Word-wisdom.

The verses are meant to be suggestive mystically, and belong to the world of intuitive imagination, and therefore we shall refrain from explanations in cut-and-dried doctrinal terms. The elusive and ineffable character of the style is meant to be left untouched by mere logical anyalsis. We shall confine our remarks to show on the one hand how the lines can be dovetailed into a context of Self-knowledge, and on the other hand, to indicate the symbology which has grown traditionally around the personality of Śiva in India. Śiva symbology pervades prehistory and comes to us even in the West through the Dionysian mysteries and frenzies into the heart of Christianity itself, especially in its mystical aspects. Perennial philosophy and mysticism with contemplative visions contain elements of this wisdom which we see represented in this example of the Guru's writings.

Commentary

REFRAIN

Dance, cobra, dance !
Thy burrow seek and witness
The bliss of grace in wild display.
Dance, cobra, dance !

While the psyche seeks realisation in terms of perfect Self-knowledge, the phenomenal world is seen as a presentiment to the self or the will. In the process of transcending this visible phenomenal aspect, the psyche takes a dispassionate view of the whole and witnesses it without particularised emotions, but with a global sense of bliss. As electricity implies magnetism secondarily, the phenomenal is secondary to the main search for truth in terms of Self-knowledge. The display is here referred to as wild or meaningless because the values involved in the field of the relative are all evanescent, tantalising and elusive. They have no substratum of reality except in terms of knowledge which is the main object of the search by the aspirant.

WORD NOTES

Āḍu: here rendered 'Dance', could be equally 'play' or 'sway'. This swaying movement reflects the movements in the phenomenal aspects of life which also alternate.

Kūthu is any exhibition of dance, implying movements without much meaning, here translated 'wild display.'

I

Keep close the foot so lotus-red
Sacred of the Lord who dons
The crescent moon and cassia bloom, and
(*repeat refrain*) Dance, cobra, dance . . . . !

The clear tender light of the crescent moon has always been associated with the cosmic picture of Śiva who wears the crescent on his dark knotted hair. The cassia flower is also held traditionally to belong to the Śiva context. It might have some prehistoric associations with the personality of Śiva. Sarasvatī is often addressed as one who lives in the forest of Kadamba trees. The red lotus-foot suggests that subtle aspect of creation, tender and ruddy, like oxidised mango leaves in the Indian spring. In all references to the foot in this symbolic language the ontological aspects are implied, whereas references to the head signify teleological or transcendental meanings. The light of the crescent moon thus refers to the latter. Both foot and head aspects meet in the personality of the Dancing Śiva.

II

Besmeared with ash and bright His holy form shines.
Thy tears for Him in streams do shed,
And thus steadily
(*repeat refrain*) Dance, cobra, dance . . . . !

Holy ashes are associated with the Śiva symbolism. The burning *ghāṭ* is the favourite haunt of Śiva. This indicates that death and its terrors have first to be transcended for spiritual attainment. Vitalistic levels fall short of the implied vision, while the light grey ashes are the pure residue remaining after all the vitalistic elements which cling to the instinctive personality are burned. Passions and emotions have all to be sublimated and surpassed. This burning of the instincts does not destroy the essential principle of the Self as pure consciousness, which is immortal, and which lives on in a life that is eternal as accepted by many theologies. This uncompromising renunciation of Śiva has its counterpart in the tenderly emotional attitude of the seeker, which is here depicted by the tears which the snake is asked to shed.

III

Upon this burning ground
Where ghost and also corpse are born
United well with what subsists, its counterpart supreme,
(*repeat refrain*) Dance, cobra, dance . . . !

The two grounds of spiritual life are here distinguished. The corpse is the objective body, considered as matter. The ghost is the immaterial counterpart. Some aspects of the human personality are just matter while certain other aspects of the personality persist in the form of subtle tendencies. These affect the minds of others and to that extent belong to a certain order of reality which, contemplatively, there is no special interest in abolishing. The Guru thus speaks of 'ghost' incidentally, as he might speak of higher hypostatic principles, always in a figurative sense. He is not directly concerned here with concrete scientific proof for the existence of disembodied spirits called ghosts. They are as much mental fixations to the Advaita Vedāntin as the phenomenal world itself, and are treated alike as will-presentiments or dream-stuff. The concept of a concrete ghost does not arise here, in the sense which might be assumed by an objective scientist.

Here all that is legitimately implied is that there are certain subtle tendencies besides the material body, which go towards the total structure of what we call the personality as known here and now. This ontological immanent aspect has its second pole in the Supreme which is 'beyond' in the Platonic sense. Although this 'beyond' has finally to be identified with the ground 'here' when the arguments and suppositions are completed, the Supreme has to be understood before a full sense of the mystery of the Śiva presence, as representing the numinous Absolute, can be grasped even intuitively. The existing aspects have their subsisting counterparts which are supreme and trancendental.

WORD NOTES

Peyum piṇavum: 'Ghost and Corpse' — these are ambivalent aspects of the human personality. The first is given to the mind and the second is given to the senses. In so far as suppositions affect human conduct, they are realities of everyday life. The question of the existence of ghosts on a status of their own does not arise here. Viewed empirically, this world consists of dead bodies after life has been lived, and some other factor known as life which meets matter and makes the personality whole. This life principle has to be supposed in one form or another, and the term *pey* or 'ghost' just applies to the ontological aspect of such a factor as an entity, even though it may be treated as a mere mental hallucination.

Êlum param porul has been paraphrased in the third line to keep as close to the original as possible. *Porul* would suggest a substance, while *param* implies the Supreme or the transcendent, while *êlum* implies 'having as a counterpart.'

IV

The tresses of hair so fragrant,
Excelling flowers of sweet aroma
In shade they lie in shame.
Beside this beauteous form, which view, and
(*repeat refrain*) Dance, cobra, dance . . . . !

The reference here is possibly to the tresses of Pārvatī which is said to have a natural perfume.

This would then be an indirect reference to that type of mysticism of a poetical kind similar to Solomon's *Song of Songs* of the Bible. But the intensity of this mystical sense of beauty is weak when compared with the virile and direct expression of life which the Śiva symbology in its pure form is meant to revive here. The Śiva approach trancends lyrical effects and bucolic comedy, reaching tragic heights in Śiva's radical dance of frenzy in the name of the Absolute. Erotic mysticism is lukewarm when compared with the full-flooded cosmic vision of the Dancing Śiva.

WORD NOTES

Pū maṇakkum-kuzhal — literally 'tress of natural perfume.' The suggestion here is that the perfume is indirectly suggested in the hair while in Śiva the bloom of beauty itself is seen directly. Immediacy of vision is here implied. A certain amount of whole-hearted, confident attachment or loyalty to the mystical principle is also implicit in this emphasis, as when a child says 'I have the best of all fathers,' etc. The aim is merely to compare levels of mysticism as within lyrical emotional limits or in attaining 'tragic' heights of sublimity.

V

A spotted leopard-skin surrounds
His form of tender bloom.
'Within the Self he dances' say, and
(*repeat refrain*) Dance, cobra, dance . . . . !

The unconventional and anti-social ways of Śiva are well known. Although his inner personality belongs, like that of all such figures, to a perennial context of Word-wisdom, Śiva outwardly belongs to a prehistoric stratum, and he has never caught up with the refinements of a later age. Śiva's enemies, to test him, set a tiger or leopard, to kill him, but Śiva killed the leopard and thereafter wore its skin. Then — according to the same legend — an elephant was sent, and he also killed it and its skin was also donned. Viewed in the light of mystical symbology, these skins represent external material aspects of the personality of the cosmic principle. The tough elephant skin is dark, the negative side of objective life, full of inertia and lethargy. The spotted leopard represents the harsh or louder aspects of creation, the positive wilfulness of uncontrolled instinctive life. Both are but outer coverings to the spirit which dances in bliss within.

VI

Upon the silver-hill what gleams
As Vedic wisdom's quintessence,
Say 'That in me is dancing too,' and
(*repeat refrain*) Dance, cobra, dance . . . . !

Śiva's abode is often referred to as the great Hill of Silver. He is said to live in the snowy white peaks of the Himālaya, in Kailās, with Gaurī, otherwise known as Pārvatī, Kālī or Sarasvatī — who are all different consorts varying according to the mythological contexts of the many branched Śiva legends. When south Indian wisdom attains the heights of Mount Kailās and becomes allied to Vedic wisdom this rouses the ire of Rāvaṇa, who may have been a prehistoric ruler of Ceylon (Sri Lanka). Rāvaṇa is said to have disturbed the happiness of Śiva and Pārvatī when they took up their north Indian abode. In the light of the historical blast and counterblast in the formulation of the Word-wisdom in India, this legend gains pointed significance. Here we note that the Guru Nārāyaṇa alludes to the Vedas as teaching essentially the same wisdom as that of the ancient indigenous Śiva-wisdom. The two currents of Word-wisdom meet in the Śiva-symbology which dominates India even to the present day, inasmuch as the chief diety of Benāres is Śiva in the form of Kāśī Viśvanāth. Śaṅkara dedicated Vedāntic verses to this deity of Maṇikarṇikā, considered the holiest of holy places for the Hindus, on the banks of Mother Ganges. In thus bringing Vedic wisdom in accord with the Śiva tradition, the Guru is here conforming to the principal trend of spiritual life in India.

VII

He for whom a sportive snake
An ornament becomes,
His home it is in us; so
(*repeat refrain*) Dance, cobra, dance . . . . !

This states the converse of what was said in verse three. The earthy snake is an ornament to the supreme Absolute, just as the 'here and now' aspect of the Absolute is common to all devotees or to humanity in general. These two poles are evident also in the Christian 'Lord's Prayer' when it reads 'They will be done in earth as it is in heaven.'[1]

VIII

No one has seen, not he of blossom's bloom
Nor even that holy garlanded one,
This flower-form of thine, so
(*repeat refrain*) Dance, cobra, dance . . . . !

The Lord of all creation and the first created is Brahmā the four-faced God born out of a lotus flower. (Brahmā the God is not to be confused with *Brahman* the Absolute.) Brahmā himself being produced out of a flower, as the flower itself emerges from its stem, is poetically described as 'blossom's bloom.' Viṣṇu is the consort of Lakṣmī the Goddess of prosperity, in her name as Śrī or Holy, summing up all that is good or auspicious in the Viṣṇu context. Here again is a comparison of the relative depth of mystical feeling implied in the two sets of symbols — one extolling widening values of ease and prosperity and the other the soaring, virile, radical principle of cosmic mysticism reaching to the heights of tragedy.

IX

Auṁ and all the rest that form
The essence of ten million charms —
We now do know and so keep on, and
(*repeat refrain*) Dance, cobra, dance . . . . !

1. *St. Mathew,* VI.10.

Auṁ is the key or root charm which symbolically implies all its further elaborations, variants or branches in whatever other religious or spiritual context they may occur on the tree of wisdom. *Auṁ* represents *Brahman* the Absolute and contains all the mystical secrets in its single syllable. This is explained in the Upaniṣads, especially in the short *Māṇḍūkya Upaniṣad*, which is wholly dedicated to a discussion of complete spirituality as related to this one syllable in its articulate and inarticulate forms. The aspects of the personality and all the psychic states possible to man are masterfully correlated round this little word. Thus the ten million other symbol-words or charms (*mantra*s) are unnecessary to anyone who understands the wisdom implied in the one holiest of holy charms represented by the three letters *A*, *U* and Ṁ.

X

To the One who conjures down
Who all things here brings out,
To His leaf-tender foot adhere, and
(*repeat refrain*) Dance, cobra, dance . . . . !

The hypostatic (heaven) world above is related to the hierophantic (priest or ritual) world below in the idolatrous or existing sense by something like magic. The natural chains of cause and effect have to be somewhat reversed in the descending dialectics implied here. At the lower levels of realism the higher abstractions emerge with various names and forms in the multiplicity of creation; but in every creation there is a revertive unitive principle of the invisible and the Supreme which participates and neutralises the multiple and many-named into the uniate. This theory, which we have developed throughout our earlier chapters, is illustrated here by an apt instance wherein the Guru expounds some of the aspects of the mystical doctrine.

The familiar image which is evoked is that of an Indian juggler who is also a snake charmer. Sometimes the juggler materialises a mango tree as if drawing it into being on earth with sweeps of his arms from above downwards. The serpent that belongs to the same mysterious or magical setting of the Absolute is representative of the Self seeking emancipation. An understanding of the whole situation can be gained by closely adhering to existing realities, here symbolised by the magician's feet, the holy feet of God or Śiva; this being the lowliest or ultimate earthy aspect of the human form which is accessible or amenable in terms of human behaviour — touching the feet of the Lord the source of the world-emanation and re-absorption.

XI

From lettered charm of Śiva-praise
To every formula of truth —
Even from sound do they come out, so
(*repeat refrain*) Dance, cobra, dance . . . . !

Na-Maḥ-Śi-Vā-Yā is the five-lettered (syllabled) sacred charm which is given to a disciple as the pass-word and motto which the disciple has to treasure as his lifetime secret. This is the holy *mantram* which is obtained after many years of disciplinary trials. There are other *mantrams*, but all gain their potency in their common affiliation to a basic truth. Sound is such a basic principle. Sound that is heard meets, mingles and coalesces with the sound that is of the inner ear, and both together form what is here referred to as the principle of sound, a principle in which all names and forms, letters and their audible sounds or even their meanings have their being. Nominalism and phenomenalism can be fitted into this basic meeting-point when the principle of sound is conceived neutrally, that is to say, conceived as between its perceptual and its actual aspects, as intended in this verse. All secret teachings such as that suggested here are meant to reveal the numinous Absolute through sound.

XII

Ten thousand millions
Of that Ananta snake art Thou;
Thy million hoods then open out, and
(*repeat refrain*) Dance,cobra, dance . . . . !

Ananta is the snake of the Viṣṇu symbology representing eternity (*an:* 'not' or 'without', *anta:* 'end'). By the multiplication of such an idea of endless time, eternity as a new quality of time emerges. It becomes qualitative instead of quantitative. Ādiśeṣa is another snake which means 'First-Remaining' or ever remaining in the eternal present, which is an emergent mystical quality independent of duration. Present, past or future lose their meanings in the bliss of the 'eternal now' as Plotinus would call such a 'moment.' This moment — now being full of joy — the Guru calls upon this timeless principle of pure duration so that Self-bliss may be enjoyed. The million hoods mean the many-sided appraisal of the eternal now in the universe and not mere subjectivism which is lost in the past or the future in a closed or individual sense.

XIII

This body here, no truth it has;
Owner another in it resides.
Such wisdom do thou gain, and thus
(*repeat refrain*) Dance, cobra, dance . . . . !

'This mortal coil' as the body has been called by Shakespeare,[2] is divided into more and more centralised zones of subjectivity, like the successive layers of peel of an onion. These zones, concentrically arranged, are graded from the gross to the subtle, from the physiological to the psychological. The deeper seats of consciousness have their cosmic counterparts such as moonlight or starlight, whose beauty and presence is appraised by subtle senses or a globally artistic sensibility to beauty. It is here in these inner zones that the personality attains its full spiritual stature as an abstract principle, just as when we say 'the kingdom of God is whithin you.'[3] The introspective approach to metaphysics is an inevitable part of the method of Advaita Vedānta which speaks of five *koṣa*s or sheaths, beginning from *annamaya* and up to *ānandamaya* (i.e., from 'food-formed outermost sheath' to the 'subtlest innermost ground of value').

---

2. *Hamlet,* III.i.
3. *Luke,* XVII.21.

XIV

Uniting body and owner too,
Radiant, who abides as one,
Such there is to know, as well, so
(repeat refrain) Dance, cobra, dance . . . . !

Understanding the double nature of the body on one side and its subtler counterparts on the other side, is one step in knowledge. There follows the further step of treating this dialectical pair unitively. To know the terms of an equation in mathematics is one step and to actually perform the equation, arriving at a result, is another process. But these two phases are neither mutually exclusive nor are they contradictory. Duality as a supposition is abolished in non-dual awareness, thus indicating two steps in a contemplative method whose result is the final triumph of Self-realisation as a central experience.

WORD NOTES

Deham is 'the body'. *Dehi* is 'one who occupies the body' the agent or subject thereof.

XV

What swallows all, with rival none,
Is the omnipresent Word.
Which swallow thou, and steadily
(repeat refrain) Dance, cobra, dance . . . . !

Having traced the Absolute to the principle of sound and noted how reciprocal aspects meet conversely and reversely in the manner of the terms of an equation, it is not hard to see that the Word conceived in terms of nominalism or conceptualism can imply and contain the pure principle of the Absolute of the Vedānta. The Word can include all reality in one conceptual synthesis of the Self-contemplative act. This act is compared in this verse to swallowing, as if intuitively making one's own the essence of a syllable such as *auṁ* with all its philosophical implications correctly understood in its Advaitic or non-dual context, as part of the science of *brahma-vidyā* which we have tried to outline in previous chapters.

XVI

Consuming all the words there are
As the supporting wall for all
Even on such do take thy stand, and
(*repeat refrain*) Dance, cobra, dance . . . . !

The universally existing, which is the prime substance, is both transcendent and immanent as the basic support of all that can be conceived. No picture can be seen without a wall. A canvas is needed for a painting. The screen is needed for the cinema-film. Similarly the experience of the mystical state becomes possible only when there is a mainstay. This is the supporting 'wall'. The phrase here is common place in the ordinary language of south India, but elsewhere such popular wisdom lives on the fringes of life or has to be sought out with trouble. This maintaining, supporting 'wall' is the *sat* or the *satyam* as explained in the *Bhagavad Gītā* in its extended meanings and implications, comprising values, realities and existence.[4]

XVII

From very name this great expanse
And even earth as well did come
As a presentiment in thought, so
(*repeat refrain*) Dance, cobra, dance . . . . !

The Guru abolishes this final idea of universal substances by relating such directly to their concrete-seeming counterparts such as the earth and other empirical realities, and by reducing all to the terms of nominalism. Such a nominalism sums up rather than

---

4. *sadbhāve sādhubhāve ca sad-ity-etat-prayujyate*
praśaste karmāṇi tathā sacchabdaḥ pārtha yujyate
yajñe tapasi dāne ca sthithiḥ sad-iti co-'cyate
karma cai-'va tadarthīyam sad-ity-evā-'bhidhīyate
— *Bhagavad Gītā,* XVII.26-27

The word *sat* is used in the sense of *existence* and of *goodness*, and so also, O Pārtha, the word *sat* is used in the sense of a *praise-worthy act.*

Steadfastness in sacrifice, austerity, and gift-bestowing is also called *sat;* and even action for the sake of That is called *sat.*

contradicts the notion of the Absolute. Name is the last dividing factor keeping subject and object apart. When the nominative factor is removed and the last trace of division dispelled, then Self-realisation reigns fully. Beyond this there is pure consciousness alone.

26

Thought and Inertia
(Cit-jaḍaṅgal)

(*Translated from the Malayālam*)

I

Should ten million suns rising all at once
Eclipse the earth, fire and water and all else,
That ascendent presence of Thine
Radiant ever abide.

II

Be it askance, pray, give but one glance
From the corner of Thy keen eyes, O Umā's spouse.
Inertia shall vanish, no place has it in aught that is,
Such is Thy servant's cherished desire.

III

On earth as in fire and in evenly flowing water,
In air and in the sky, that state of Thine
Which in all these five steadily endures,
Do give again and again, this even is our sole refuge.

IV

Mind first, then smell, and wakefully all five
Up to Grace is the will's domain of mind-stuff made;
From earth we touch to darkness' boundary — Alas ! —
Inertia gross extends. These twain do all comprise.

V

All of yore such doctrine held Śuka Sage and others.
Easily attained they thought it and in varied forms,
They did transmit it down from age to age.
Such the Māyā mystery of the Blessed One. Ah, how great !

VI

Great, small and middling too, steady and waveless it rises,
O Mental-Firmament ! From sinking into Māyā's dross,
From mind confused and foothold lost, O save
And grant Thy grace of erect immobility.

VII

O Grace that round Thy sacred Presence wraps
O darkness-light, O nook and public space,
O core and what within the core as treasure dwells,
O Burner famed of the cities three !

VIII

Holding aloft the flambeau how Thy presence divine
Descending, while reigning still in thought's blue dome,
As that city of fame — Chidambaram — is called,
Could yet the cities three burn down, a marvel that is !

IX

Fresh mango bloom, O flower's nectar, confection sweet,
O honey, luscious fruit, O rich juice, O Master mine !
Ever sought by gods, both of Providence and Grace,
Thy lotus foot alone my final refuge is !

X

Refuge art Thou alone for this supplicant, O Thou
Who elephant's skin did strip and wear, O Presence of mind-
stuff made !
O chase somewhat at least this treacherous dark,
And grant this servant Thine Thy grace !

Introductory

The duality of mind and body and an occasionalism which made them interact, was the doctrine of Descartes, for whom the body was like a machine. This picture of the relation between the two aspects of the Self or the Personality has held the field in spite of the non-dual doctrines that have been put forward later. Synergism, antinomialism, bipolarity, ambivalence and other theories implying duality have been in vogue in various branches of knowledge. Some have been stated psychologically and others elaborated cosmologically.

In earlier chapters we have had occasion to refer to these methods of approach under different settings, so that it will be hardly necessary for us to enter into any fresh discussion here of what they imply. If truth itself is not to be dually conceived, at least the method of arriving at truth and making truth prevail in life requires the recognition of some sort of duality. Contemplation stated in terms of a goal or end needs taking account of the positive and negative division of what we call right reason or understanding as a means for the guidance of all aspirants to higher unitive wisdom. The contemplative mind, confronted by multiplicity, has to categorise and deal methodically and critically with the subject according to an implied science on somewhat the same rational footing as in mathematics. Understanding or certainty needs the form of an equation, and before any worthwhile conviction can result, the terms at least of the equation have to be intelligently related. It therefore follows that it is necessary for us to have correct notions about what we mean by 'mental' and 'material', or as the *Bhagavad Gītā* puts it, about the distinction between 'the field' and 'the knower of the field'.[1] This distinction and the understanding of one in terms of the other is of the essence of wisdom.

---

1. *idam śarīram kauteya kṣetram-ity-abhidhīyate*
etad-yo vetti tam prāhuḥ kṣetrajña iti tadvidaḥ
kṣetrajñam ca-'pi mām viddhi sarvakṣetreṣu bhārata
kṣetrakṣetrajñayor-jñānam yat-taj-jñānam matam mama.
— *Bhagavad Gītā*, XIII.1-2

'This body, O son of Kuntī, is called the field, that which knows it, they who know call the Knower of the Field'.

In this present composition from the pen of the Guru Nārāyaṇa this very problem is confronted in his own unique way, in a blending of devotion, contemplative mysticism and critical elements, the whole affording a basis of life for the *brahmacārin*, for one who would walk in the path of *Brahman*, for one dedicated to the wisdom of the Absolute, or to that 'divine Ground' which is neither thought nor inertia, but in which these are 'inserted' or basically established.

Commentary

I

Should ten million suns rising all at once
Eclipse the earth, fire and water and all else,
That ascendent presence of Thine,
Radiant ever abide.

The imagery here aims to sublimate, as it were, the material aspects of the five elements (earth, water, fire, air and space-ether) conceived phenomenally into a numinous presence. In such a process of contemplative transmutation of values from the grossest tangible or earthy to the spiritual, the reference to the rising of ten million suns is both apt and necessary. The quantitative aspects of the vision have to be converted into the qualitative before the real import of what constitutes the divine presence can be understood with any degree of rationality or positiveness. Inert conditions of the gross, earthy material world have to be conceived in terms of the omnipresent, all filling principle of light. The ontological aspects of reality are thus transformed in real and living terms into transcendent or teleological aspects, disclosing the mechanism of their relation and possible interaction. The two aspects are not so distinct after all as they are represented to be in systematised doctrines or articles of faith. By an intuitive grasp of the whole in non-dual vision one can think of one in terms of the other as counterparts or ambivalent equivalents. When the contemplative

→ And understand Me (Kṛṣṇa) as the Knower of the Field in all fields, O Bhārata. Knowledge as to the field and the Knower of the Field is deemed by Me as the knowledge.

vision dominates the personality, then the lethargic heavy inertia yields place to the resplendence which fills all; while the outside phenomenal world is inserted without conflict into the psychological or inner world of the Self. Transient cross-sections of reality give way to the eternal flux of pure becoming. Eternity itself gains a new and purer meaning, removed from the relative aspects of time. Such are some of the suggestions contained in this opening verse.

WORD NOTES

Koṭi means 'crore' the Indian numerical term for ten million.

Kedumāru: 'So as to extinguish' has been rendered 'should . . . eclipse.'

II

Be it askance, pray, give but one glance
From the corner of Thy keen eyes, O Umā's spouse.
Inertia shall vanish, no place has it in aught that is;
Such is Thy servant's cherished desire.

'Umā's spouse' is a reference to Śiva as the husband of Pārvatī (also called Umā). The mystical union of the two blends ambivalent counterparts. The God who can make Umā happy by his understanding of feminine nature, and able to deal with it as befits the unitive vision of contemplation, has also a certain compassionate attitude and kind look for all. This look makes us think of one keen eye rather than of one who sees actuality with the two eyes open. Śiva is sometimes represented also as being androgynous and as having a central eye in the middle of the forehead. The Guru here does not refer to this middle eye as a distinct organ, but prefers the psycho-physical imagery of a keen meeting point of the glance of kindness in poetic terms, familiar in the context of love.

The word 'askance' suggests that the full glance of the God of grace may not be fully deserved by the devotee with his sense of humility and surrender to the higher principle. Being related to this higher principle of kindness or grace helps in the sublimation of the lower order of living. The inert view we take of the physical world loses its importance when the contemplative way begins to prevail and becomes more and more firmly established, as it advances in terms of grace or higher value.

The indirect reference here to Śiva as the consort of Umā, the daughter of the Himālaya, white-clad and pure, the principle of Beauty as mentioned in the *Kena Upaniṣad*[2] has its own relevance. Like the Beatrice of Dante, this principle of Beauty is the intermediate stepping stone to the appreciation of the divine grace in the abstract, in relation to the Absolute principle. It takes a great God like Śiva to be happy and confer happiness on Umā. The supreme Principle can transcend all and prevail as the final Value of bounty or grace. When affiliated to such a higher principle, the mind is lifted out of the setting of inert matter which has no reality, no existence by itself, apart from its relation to the higher principle of all truth.

III

On earth as in fire and in evenly flowing water,
In air and in the sky, that state of Thine,
Which in all these five steadily endures,
Do give again and again, this even is our sole refuge.

Just as gravitation is a principle regulating the movements of bodies in the universe, so it is possible through contemplation to arrive at a sustaining and preserving principle which gives continuity, and therefore a permanence by contrast, to phenomenal expressions. The sectional view which the mind persists in taking of the physical world, results from inability to appraise this principle of continuity.

When this new or vertical view is taken we find that *terra firma* has a new status in reality as something of human value which endures more than space. But thin air or space, on the other hand,

---

2. *sa tasminnevākāśe striyamājagāma bahuśobhamānām* ।
umām haimava tīm tām hovāca kimetad yakṣam iti.
—*Kena Upaniṣd*, III.12

He (Indra) beheld in that very spot a woman, Umā, very beautiful daughter of the Himālaya. He said to her, 'What is this great Spirit?'

suggests the ineffable spiritual aspects. Between these extremes of solidity and space there are the states of fluidity as in water, the fire that burns upwards, and the still thinner condition of air. Throughout these graded levels there is a constant axis of interrelationships which shows the same reciprocal diphasic interdependence or bipolarity which is the dual manifestation of the unitive reality of Advaita (non-duality). Gravitation is common to all objects and yet objects in relation to the earth in particular instances are said to come under the earth's 'gravity' as if it was a quality of the earth only.

Whatever the variation in the name, the universal principle when conceived as it ought to be in its entirety, satisfies the requirements of an all-comprehensive law of ponderable matter, both in electro-magnetic and gravitational terms. Similarly, this universal ordering unitive principle is the enduring state of grace or goodness alluded to here, in this verse. This can be seen to correspond to either a law of reality in the terminology of a positive science, or as a principle of divine grace in a more or less theological sense.

The expositionary style, whether academic, monastic, lay or expert, should not make any difference to the subject-matter. Without violating the methodology or terms of knowing of any one of these, the Guru is able here to state the case for a contemplative and comprehensive view of reality with as little sophistry as possible, in a setting of reverence and devotion, which need not itself be treated as unscientific.

IV

Mind first, then smell, and wakefully all five
Up to the Grace is the will's domain of mind- stuff made;
From earth we touch to darkness' boundary — Alas ! —
Inertia gross extends. These twain do all comprise.

The central doctrine is expounded in this verse with unmistakable clarity. The contemplative way, to have a proper method of its own in order to arrive at any convincing results, must needs divide all reality broadly into two primary categories such as envisaged in the expression in the *Bhagavad Gītā* already referred to, about the Field and the Knower of the Field.

In this verse the question of the perceptual and the actual, which is one of the recognised problems of modern philosophers, is confronted. The categories and laws of thought have to be determined *a priori*. No experimental methods can be employed here to reduce such factors into the terminology of the applied sciences. Such a treatment is precluded by the pure principles involved. The only way open is to subject our own inner experience to a closely focused scrutiny without confusion.

We know we have a physical world surrounding us. We touch the ground and stand on it while talking of abstract realities. On one side extends this gross aspect of reality, and when we focus our attention on it, it becomes more and more inscrutable. It is like a cloud of unknowing, of negation, fear, inertia and ignorance into which we sink as if into a deep morass of darkness. Past memories and associations make this region doubly dark with all sorts of vaguely suggestive memory factors in which all is lost.

On the other side, mental factors begin to assert themselves. Through the mediation of the senses such as smell which, like taste, is nearest to the tactile sensations, consciousness opens out fanwise or funnel-like, giving contact with the vast world of light. The sensible light has its own limits and at its fringes it again merges into the mystery of the unknown Grace. This Grace is a mystery looked at from either end with, in each case, its own specific implications. There are negative and positive ends of unknowing, and both meet in the numinous mystery in which all is comprised as stated in the last line of this verse.

WORD NOTES

Cin-mayam, rendered 'of mind-stuff made'; *cit* being 'mind-stuff' and *mayam* 'wholly made of.'

Jaḍam has been translated 'inertia gross'.

V

All of yore such doctrine held Śuka Sage and others.
Easily attained they thought it and in varied forms;
They did transmit it down from age to age.
Such the Māyā mystery of the Blessed One. Ah, how great !

The perennial character and mysterious content of the wisdom which is the heritage of humanity is affirmed in this verse. The contemplative law of non-duality of the never ending becoming and the eternal being enunciated in the previous verse is no new invention or ingenious discovery. Even in the setting of India from the time the Purāṇas were written by Vyāsa and others and especially in the *Bhāgavata Purāṇa,* ways of spiritual life in relation to higher values are seen expounded. The outer form of the mystical garb of holiness can vary, but the message which can be gleaned out of these varied doctrines or disciplines is common to all — an attitude and way of life — always implying a correct appraisal of the two categories already mentioned. These two categories belong to the basic formula of all contemplative disciplines, whether in the East or in the West. Sage Śuka of the *Bhāgavata* is cited here as a typical example.

Although this doctrine has been known for ages it is not of the nature of open public knowledge, determined only by the visible and objective, to the detriment of the mental or perceptual. Actualities are more readily accepted by the public than truths which pertain to subtler facts of personal life. These subtler facts form the subject-matter of doctrines understood and expounded by a few contemplative philosophers of each generation who take the trouble of passing on the doctrine to their disciples. These hierarchical inheritors keep the doctrine alive in modified form until, kindled into flame by another intuitive soul who responds to the age-old message as if spontaneously, the torch of wisdom once again flares up brightly.

WORD NOTES

Akhilarkum: 'All of yore' means all those original contemplative thinkers who exist in every country and every age. This is evidence of the perennial and universal nature of the *matam* or 'doctrine' enunicated above.

Paramparā is the 'vertical line of successive generations.' In Tamil people refer to the immortality of the banana tree, one tree being replaced by another young one growing out from the same underground stem; making for an everlasting continuity of succession, just like the immortality of the amoeba. What is meant here is a vertical continuity in time.

VI

Great, small and middling too, steady and waveless it rises,
O Mental-Firmament ! From sinking into *Māyā*'s dross,
From mind confused and foothold lost, O save
And grant Thy grace of erect immobility.

In the understanding of the doctrine of contemplative wisdom, this verse recommends the need for gaining a certain steady balance. Only then can the peaceful life of contemplation and happiness be established. The upward sweep of wisdom-dialectics takes account of all things, rising into the regions of higher and higher hypotheses, and in the process constructing hierophantic or hypostatic mental entities which may be big either spatially or in psychic potency and content. When conceived unitively, all these make for a hierarchy of 'monads', with God as the greatest of them all, hidden away and unknowable in the idea of the holiest, most supreme 'Absolute' or 'intelligible' entity. This entity is the steadying factor countering all unholy haste and motion in this world of variety and appearances of the actualities seen through the senses.

Māyā is that factor allied to memory, whose tendency is to drag down the spirit in its flight to the higher values attained by contemplative insight. *Māyā* is the negative drag which, when we yield to it, displaces unitive insight by a confusing and bewildering multiplicity of phenomenal aspects.

Nature and instinct range themselves on the side of this *Māyā*, always tending to destroy the steady calm outlook which contemplation or grace instils into the spirit of man. As the Chinese

Tao philosophy recognises, water symbolises this natural negative tendency. It spreads all around and is opposed to being gathered up unitively under one steadily enduring law of solidity or rigidity. It takes any shape while just finding its level passively without any will or effort. The ocean of *saṁvit* (knowledge) is referred to in Vedānta in a similar way as being essentially spatial, yielding and passive, while the erect principle of immobility running through this passivity links such a principle to the principle of supreme values. The neutrality of the psychological principle of immobility gives support to the dedicatory aspiration of the aspirant, producing a steadying influence on the Self or Personality. Through this steadying influence the mind is oriented to the positive factors which transcend the dull level of nature.

WORD NOTES

Cin-ambaram 'Mental-Firmament' has also been rendered in verse 8 below as 'thought's blue dome' with a little more freedom.

VII

O Grace that round Thy sacred Presence wraps
O darkness-light, O nook and public space,
O core and what within the core as treasure dwells,
O Burner famed of the cities three !

The sacred Presence is a hierophantic entity, while Grace is hypostatic as coming from the supreme invisible God on high. In the next line the 'darkness' is brought into close relationship with the idea of the open 'light'. The recess or 'nook' is also placed *vis-a-vis* 'public' or open 'space'. In both cases there is the same kind of affinity — reciprocity as existing between two aspects of the same reality. The ambivalent is not only expressed by opposite extremes or poles, components of the same 'magnet' as it were, but it is also to be imagined as belonging to different zones of the personality. The more interior the zone, the closer the resulting value becomes as a counterpart of the cosmic. Thought and substance meet in such a central concept — the 'core' mentioned in the third line; thought and substance becoming interchangeable terms; while hidden within is the priceless glory, the 'treasure' referred to. The virtue of the shell consists in its precious kernel, while the kernel needs the protection of the shell. Only by unitive vision is the duality of shell and kernel abolished.

The symbolic myth of Śiva as Burner of the three cities of metal is continued in the next verse, where it is both explained and left intact. With the touch of divine neutralising Grace, the gross inert material heaviness vanishes. Thought and matter meet in a central expression of life 'as such' in the Absolute as revealed by contemplative introspection.

WORD NOTES

Tiru meni: rendered 'sacred Presence'. *Irule:* 'O darkness' is in the vocative case, although it remains the object of the 'wraps' of the previous line.

Karale which has been translated as 'core' or heart, actually refers to any inner organ such as the liver.

Arum porul: 'treasure' — *arum:* rare; *porul;* thing, reality.

VIII

Holding aloft the flambeau how Thy Presence divine
Descending, while reigning still in thought's blue dome,
As that city of fame — Cidambaram — is called,
Could yet the cities three burn down, a marvel that is!

All phenomena is based on duality. Any recognition of actuality leads us to the implied duality between aspects of reality such as we have tried to distinguish. A neutral position has to be taken before the equation of mind in terms of matter and vice versa can be correctly treated contemplatively, to yield the non-dual reality underlying both. This non-dual Absolute is a mystery and its functions and operations are bound to remain enigmatic. The hand of the Lord is not given to any one here to go any further in unravelling the mystery of the Absolute. Philosophers are in the habit of treating the idea of the Absolute without any enthusiasm or appreciation of any value implied in the concept. Only in the light of the science of Self-knowledge does this value emerge and the mystery become acceptable as a reality in itself. To say that the reality is Absolute, or that it is a mystery, or even that it is a numinous Presence, are only different ways of stating the same truth.

Cidambaram is both the actual name of a city in south India where the famous Dancing Śiva is adored by thousands still today, as well as the name of the 'most high God' symbolic of a highly philosophical idea of reality, derived from the two words *cit* or 'mind' and *ambaram,* 'sky.' This 'most high God' is one of the factors, which, taken together with its counterpart in the sense of the 'actual here' as representing the 'field' of manifestation or phenomena, yields the key to the mystery of creation, or conversely, its destruction — the city on high is the reflected necessary counterpart of the city on earth.

WORD NOTES

Puram is a city, but in psychological references in Vedānta it signifies psychic classes or units as when the term *puryāṣṭakam* meaning the 'eight cities of the subtle body' (*sūkṣma śarīra*) is used. In Vedāntic literature such as the Vāsiṣṭha there are also cosmological references to various cities in the sky. One of the names of Śiva is Tripurāntaka, i.e., 'The One who finished the three cities', which refers to the same myth or prehistoric legend.

IX

Fresh mango bloom, O flower's nectar, confection sweet,
O honey, luscious fruit, O rich juice, O Master mine !
Ever sought by gods, both of Providence and Grace,
Thy lotus foot alone my final refuge is !

Academic, philosophical or contemplative aloofness to reality is abandoned here in favour of an intimacy such as that felt between a lover and beloved. Lavish lyrical extravagance is unreservedly expressed to show the intimate value and personal meaning which truth, both existential and subsistential has for the seeker or aspirant. Here is a crescendo of rhapsody. It breaks through all convention into the intimate cultivation of the Presence of the Supreme in the language of ecstasy, exaltation or bliss. This marks the ultimate appraisal of reality as a value and not merely as an intellectual abstraction.

By scanning the adjectives or attributes piled up here one finds that now one leans on 'origin' or 'cause' and in the next moment on the 'result' or 'effect', 'fruition' or 'flowering.' Freshness and antiquity are both suggested side by side making this verse a sweet delicacy, a rare joy, suggesting teleological and ontological values together and immediate.

The juice mentioned here is reminiscent of the *soma* juice which is mentioned in ancient Indian literature, which is sometimes a herbal extract, a honey, or an ambrosial essence or drink of the immortal gods of Indra's heaven. Soma is also sometimes the principle of the moon, while the King Soma of the Vedas suggests life and vitality. Soma is always a symbol of the *r̥tam* or the existential, as opposed to the *satyam* or subsistential aspect of reality or truth. Here in this verse both aspects are referred to together non-dualistically as the underlying principle of life, both prospective or retrospective, immanent or transcendent. The reference to the gods of Providence as well as Grace in the same line is suggestive of the non-dual position taken.

WORD NOTES

Vidhi and *mādhavar:* 'Providence' in the sense of necessary fate, and 'conferring principle of Grace' are justifiable by the implicit derivation of the divinities suggested by the verse. These are to be thought of as presiding principles, the one of 'necessary law' or *vidhi,* the other of 'contingent Grace.' More simply, in the symbolic language of Indian religious thought, they can stand for Brahmā as Lord of Creation and Viṣṇu as the Principle of Preservation.

X

Refuge art Thou alone for this supplicant, O Thou
Who elephant's skin did strip and wear, O Presence of mind-
stuff made!

O chase somewhat at least this treacherous dark,
And grant this servant Thine Thy grace !

In this sequence of ten verses the implied scheme of the various aspects of reality as examined under the two primary categories has been covered. In this last verse we have a pointed reference to the gross-inert aspect of the harsh actuality of life where the problems of evil reside. The dark unknown beyond is on the other side of visible light, and there is also that darkness which is that other kind, thick and crude as the stripped hide of a large elephant. This typifies the monstrous, sinister, macabre side of the dark unknown aspect of the Absolute as conceived realistically.

This treacherous dark aspect can be banished only by the light of Grace which is the intuitive understanding; and by relation with the opposite pole for which the lower is only an attribute. The higher Grace absorbs the lower terminal and abolishes it, making of it part and parcel of its own higher personality. The higher category includes the lower, in the same relation as a simple item, instance, appendage or attribute or raiment is to the supreme person. The raiment can be rejected or donned at will by the wearer. When understood, the pure principle can thus make the evil aspects of life and suffering as of no importance. These are then considered incidental, being taken for granted instead of being considered as factors of worrying import. It is in this sense that contemplation of the supreme principle as personified in the Śiva or any other personality treated similarly, can be taken to be the last refuge for a suffering supplicant who is really the aspirant for Self-realisation. In this a doctrine of the double negation of evil is implicitly intended.

WORD NOTES

Cin-mayam has been rendered, as in Verse IV, 'mind-stuff made' which is vocatively employed here for one made of mind-stuff.

The legend of Śiva stripping the elephant to make apparel from its skin, refers expressly to a gruesome aspect of reality in the name of realism. The allusion has been explained already.

27

Scriptures of Mercy
(Anukampā-daśakam)

(Translated from the Malayālam)

I

Such Mercy that even to an ant
Would brook not the least harm to befall,
O Mercy-Maker do vouchsafe with contemplation
Which from Thy pure Presence never strays.

II

Grace yields blessedness; a heart Love-empty
Disaster spells of every kind.
Darkness as Love's effacer and as suffering's core,
Is seed to everything.

III

Grace, Love, Mercy — all the three —
Stand for one same reality — Life's Star.
'He who loves is he who really lives.' Do learn
These syllables nine by heart in place of lettered charm.

IV

Without the gift of Grace, a mere body
Of bone and skin and tissue foul is man
Like water lost in desert sand,
Like flower bereft of smell or fruit.

V

Those phases six that life do overtake

Invade not wisdom's pure domain;
Likewise the Mercy-quality, when human form has gone,
As good reputation's form endures.

VI

That Dispenser of Mercy, could He not be that reality
Who proclaiming words of supreme import, the chariot drives,
Or Compassion's ocean, ever impatient for all creation,
Or who in terms clear non-dual wisdom expounds, the Guru?

VII

In human semblance here is He a divinity,
Or perhaps the law of right in sacred human form?
Is He the pure begotten Son of the Lord Most High?
Or kindly Prophet Nabi, pearl and gem in one?

VIII

Is He that soul personified who with holy ashes once
Fever drove away and many wonders worked?
Or yet that other of psychic power who wandering in agony,
Allayed His ventral distress even with song?

IX

Else is He that Sage of crowning fame who uttered once again
That holy script already known and writ in Hara's name ?
Or He devoted to the Value of the Lord Supreme
Who here departed bodily ere life for him was stilled?

X

Dealing bounty here on earth and taking human form
Is He that Kāma-Dhenu cow of all-providing good?
Or perhaps that wonder-tree of heaven supreme,
The Deva-Taru which to each its gifts bestows?

ENVOI

High scripture's meaning, antique, rare,
Or meaning as by Guru taught,
And what mildly a sage conveys,
And wisdom's branches of every stage,
Together they all belong,
As one in essence, in substance same.

Introductory

Here we have another sequence of ten verses around the central concept of kindliness, compassion, grace or mercy. The slighest inclination one way or the other of the meaning of this central concept gives us various representations, some based on hypostatic, and others on hierophantic principles. The substance of reality can be conceived ontologically as the immanent, the transcendent or the teleological. Generally speaking when we take most other concepts the divergence between these aspects seems to widen. But given a central concept or factor of human value touching life in a direct way, it is possible to focus discussion of all possible variants of what is commonly understood to constitute the good, virtuous or holy life.

The concept of Mercy affords such a pivotal factor. Shakespeare's oft-quoted passage on Mercy treats the subject in this globally comprehensive impartial manner as a central common human value. It is the 'twice blest' state of the personality, irrespective of donor or receiver, subject or object. In fact, it is identical with blessedness, which objectively would be grace, and subjectively would be bounty, generosity or compassion. One acts compassionately and receives grace. Blessedness is a central and neutral state which neither refers to objective or subjective factors. The difference between a state of being in love and that of blessedness, when conceived in their widest and most universal connotations, is negligible. The negation of such love is the negation of life and thus of all wisdom.

Such are some of the arguments inferred here, whether explicitly stated or not. Contemplation itself depends on the middle way implied in a loving and positive attitude. Exclusiveness, hatred, a unilateral position, stressing duality, all suggest the negation of life and love. Love and consideration for other living creatures is the basis of the good life and upheld as the central doctrine and commandment of all the world's religions. We have touched upon this theme already in the Guru's poems, but here spiritual expressions are correlated over a wide and varied range.

Commentary

I

Such Mercy that even to an ant
Would brook not the least harm to befall,
O Mercy-Maker do vouchsafe with contemplation
Which from Thy pure Presence never strays.

This opening verse reciprocally links the one who prays and the object of prayer through the intermediacy of the one and same concept of Mercy. The kindness shown to an ant is of the same measureless quality as the Mercy we expect from God in the form of grace. Both refer to one common central value belonging to the human personality. To love a brother is natural and instinctive, but to love a lowly creature like the ant demands an intelligent sympathy which thinks in universal terms.

When this universal idea of kindness applies to one and all, including the Self, without any asymmetry or difference, the essential attitude belonging to contemplation is attained. Such contemplation knows neither distinction of subject or object but equates all factors impartially according to fundamental laws of knowing, which means reducing one factor in accord with its natural and normal dialectical counterpart.

Here the 'pure Presence' is the Absolute conceived as a human value; while 'contemplation' is the intellectual or spiritual approach implied in appraising such a personalised value. The quality of mercy which 'blesseth him that gives and him that takes,' is the common real living and actual factor which induces contemplation to yield a consciousness of the presence of the pure or the sacred in the sense of the Absolute. Neutral or global awareness as Self-realisation amounts to the same thing. Philosophically conceived as 'knowledge', psychologically conceived as 'self', cosmologically conceived as 'the supreme divinity' or ethically and religiously conceived in the universal language of 'brotherhood' or 'mercy', all these, representing existence, truth and value, meet in this central concept which the Guru has chosen as the normative principle or correlation for all the various forms of spiritual expression.

WORD NOTES

Anukampā: 'Mercy'. More literally it is nearer to the word 'sympathy' (*anu:* 'after'; *kampā:* 'to move').

Karuṇākara has been rendered 'Mercy-Maker' closely in keeping with the original.

Cintā has been rendered 'contemplation.'

II

Grace yields blessedness; a heart Love-empty
Disaster spells of every kind.
Darkness as Love's effacer and as suffering's core,
Is seed to everything.

The interrelation of factors is here stated concisely, both the joy-yielding positive and the suffering-productive negative forces. Grace is first equated to love on the positive side. Darkness and suffering are also to be understood as referring to the negative side of the personality. Just as knowledge tends to make a man generous and universal in his sympathy and outlook, opening out the restraining limiting power of the ego, so ignorance is the cause of hatred. All factors which produce the idea of value in connection with the Self or personality of man are joined together in a certain way with the ambivalent principle underlying the whole. This principle regulates personal relations according to a subtle dialectics of wisdom. This consists in viewing all neutrally in the light of the Absolute. This is a marvel too great for words. In common language we refer to such a reality as God. If we do not do so strictly all the time, at least we ought to do so. For then concepts like love and grace begin to have a consistently rational, convincing, non-dogmatic and even some kind of scientific meaning. Grace is only the positive side of one's own love of life. We can place it in a heaven or in the heart of each man. Sin and grace must be taken together and fitted into a common context of Self-knowledge so that all values have their place in the general scheme. When this is accomplished it would help to minimise ideological conflicts.

WORD NOTES

Arul: translated 'grace' is not so strictly connative of 'divine' grace as in Tamil and the south Indian prehistoric languages. It can mean just compassion or the welling-up of sympathy in oneself, in a poet or in a mystic. In English it is perhaps more exclusively used in a theological sense.

Inpam: 'Blessedness' — *per inpam* is 'great blessedness' and *cit-inpam* is 'little or worldly well-being or happiness'. Both meanings are comprised here.

Allal: 'disaster' is just 'evil' or 'ill'.

Karu, rendered 'core' is the tender nuclear part of a living organism where life-factors are concentrated and from whence all action is initiated as in the central nervous system.

III

Grace, Love, Mercy — all the three —
Stand for one same reality — Life's Star.
'He who loves is he who really lives.' Do learn
These syllables nine by heart in place of lettered charm.

Here the positive factors are brought closer to one another to indicate the one dominant human value intimately related to life itself. Doctrinal religion tends to reduce faith into dry liturgical formulae and creeds to be repeated mechanically for a promised salvation. The aspirant who seeks instruction in *Brahman*-wisdom or knowledge of the Absolute often becomes a slave to its deadening, mechanically repetitive word-features, which is the word that kills and not the bread of life, though such word-features can be potent in their own way in a purely perceptual context.

It is not enough to understand love as a doctrine and say that one believes in it as an article of faith. This and other values have to enter into intimate union with the Self as part of a life that is lived. But even such a life, where theory and practice meet, involves an intuitive apprehension of reality in the most intimate understanding of Self-realisation. On the one hand, one has to enter into the spirit of the words, and then on the other hand, the manna of the Word has to be made effectively true again in the everyday living meaning of daily bread.

In the first formula the value which ought to dominate life is indicated as a star to guide the mariner on the sea of existence, and then it is related backwards as it were to real living in the here and now. Thus in both ways the unity of life and love is affirmed. The whole object here is to bring ethics, piety and knowledge unitively under one dominant conception of a human value, in accord with the fundamental method and theory of the Advaita Vedānta which affirms 'That Thou Art' (*tat-tvam-asi*).

WORD NOTES

Arul, anpu and *anukampā:* 'Grace, Love, Mercy' have somewhat the same connotations in both English and Malayālam. Sympathy, compassion, misericorde and pity contain also the same value, some implying more distinction between subject and object than others. The attempt here is to strike those meanings of value which are common to subject and object and, if possible, to abolish all asymmetry and thus reveal the central single value of Good implied in Self-realisation.

IV

Without the gift of Grace, a mere body
Of bone and skin and tissue foul is man

Like water lost in desert sand,
Like flower bereft of fruit or smell.

The frustrated Self buried in its own desert sands does not emerge into positive levels of goodness either to humanity or to its own true nature. When grace has gone and love has weakened, the body loses its beauty. A flower through its fragrance confers some benefit, and fruit too has its positive smell-taste virtue. These are the opposites of the inert bodily aspects. Flower and smell complement each other producing the total value of a good flower. Similarly the bird and bird-song can be equated, together resulting as joy for the poet. Water lost in sand cannot allay the traveller's thirst or be of use to plants; and with the non-satisfaction of simple needs, more refined cravings for luxury are out of the question. At the personally hedonistic, the collectively utilitarian and the universal Platonic levels there are corresponding emergent factors which tend to complete the personality, bringing into existence an integrated central value compounded proportionately of both 'positive' and 'negative' factors. Contemplation stabilises, harmonises and equalises these opposing factors, producing the good life at all levels in different forms, as indicated in the various ways discussed in this composition.

WORD NOTES

Sira has been rendered 'tissue.' What is meant is the small lymphatic or other vessels taken collectively. The idea of cell units as seen microscopically, which constitutes tissue as understood today, was not meant by the term *sira*.

V

Those phases six that life do overtake
Invade not wisdom's pure domain;
Likewise the Mercy-quality, when human form has gone,
As good reputation's form endures.

The perfume of a flower can leave its traces in its surroundings till breezes carry the scent across the fields. In a similar way when we come to human values which are subtler than the perfume of a flower, it is possible to imagine how the behaviour of a good man in a certain locality can create around him associations and memory-factors which we generally call, vaguely, the 'atmosphere' of a place. Sometimes this results from the contribution of many personalities who have lived a life of goodness.

In the case of a highly spiritual man of the status of a harmonised contemplative or sage, this ineffable influence affects the surroundings almost permanently. The reputation of a Christ or of a Buddha belongs to this category. It does not depend upon the passing away of the body. The body is the phenomenal aspect of reality which suffers change. Metabolic changes, and changes through the larger cycles of life and its extinction (such as the six phases usually mentioned in the terminology of Vedānta, viz., existence, birth, growth, transformation, decline and death) affect only one aspect of the personality. The subtler, purer or inner life tends to become independent of states and the last lingering traces of duality vanish in Self-realisation, which is the innermost awareness of all, the *vijnānamaya kośa* (zone of pure consciousness), where Plotinus' 'flight of the alone to the Alone' takes place.

Even when this final consummation is unattained, at whatever intermediate level it may be that we consider the matter, the antinomial principle makes for a fundamental distinction between the bodily and other subtler, positive aspects, successively sublimating and approaching pure reason as contemplation gains ground. When human values enter into the conduct of a wise man, as it ought to in a normal way at every stage of his spiritual progress from the real to the ideal, the higher aspects of the personality leave various traces on his environment. Actually, all this good influence remains as a favourable appreciation on the part of humanity, which is often grateful for the good implied in a certain way of life. This reputation is the life after death recognised here. There is no confusion of false esoterics in a public or scientific sense.

VI

That Dispenser of Mercy, could He, not be that reality
Who proclaiming words of supreme import, the chariot
drives,

Or Compassion's ocean, ever impatient for all creation,
Or who in terms clear non-dual wisdom expounds, the
Guru?

The allusions here are to three ways of appreciation of the central human value called kindliness in three different contexts. God Himself is first referred to as the Dispenser of Mercy as He was Mercy-Maker in the first verse of the poem. Functionally, God is Mercy's Author. Generosity, goodness and bounty are integral parts of His absolute nature in the usual sense of the positive, transcendental immaterial Principle.

As representative of this Principle, conceived as a human value, which makes human beings more human, in the same sense that they are distinguished from less intelligent animals, we have Vyāsa who, in the *Bhagavad Gītā* represents Kṛṣṇa as a Guru or Teacher of contemplative wisdom. Kṛṣṇa drives the chariot of Arjuna into the midst of the battle. In this capacity Kṛṣṇa was Arjuna's friend and equal, but as a Teacher of wisdom he was at the same time an *ācārya* or *guru*. The historical Kṛṣṇa is the friend, but when the *Bhagavad Gītā* refers to Word-wisdom, the Teacher-quality gives Kṛṣṇa another status. He then represents in his person the Word or the Wisdom such as the Logos meant to the Greeks. This is an objective aspect of reality but should be conceived in pure terms. Such a reality is the 'stuff' or 'substance' here (*porul* in the original).

In the third line of the verse the reference is to that type of wisdom which expresses itself realistically at the level of daily life. Buddha's ethics had this character. The boundless human sympathy which welled up within the Buddha overflowed and reached out to all life in the quest of a universal synthesis, taking in life as a whole realistically and rationally. The universal elements present in Buddha's sympathy gave it a mystical character which is described here as a restless ocean ever seeking to make good prevail in human affairs.

Śaṅkara can easily be taken to be a typical example of the Guru referred to in the last line, although many others could also be taken as examples.

WORD NOTES

Bhūta dayā: 'Kindness to creation'; here translated 'ever impatient for all creation.'

Sarala: 'clear', 'unequivocal.'

Advaita-bhāṣya-kāra: 'Commentator on non-dual wisdom' suggests Śaṅkara as directly as necessary.

VII

In human semblance here is He a divinity,
Or perhaps the law of right in sacred human form ?
Is He the pure begotten Son of the Lord Most High?
Or kindly Prophet Nabi, pearl and gem in one?

When we say 'Son of God,' this means the same as when in another place we read 'Son of Man.' The second Person of the Trinity is the meeting point of two aspects of reality. In Vedānta we have the famous example of the sentence 'This is that Devadatta.' The syntactical and grammatical relations of the different-seeming but identically semantically 'this' and 'that' helps to fix the identity of Devadatta, as if from two opposite poles of reality. Much Vedāntic scholasticism has been continued round these attributes which meet in the Absolute neutral, central, actual or numinous reality. This central Value is to be recognised intuitively by the contemplative mind. By the reversal of a proposition, e.g., analytical judgement in synthetical terms, and so on, we arrive at central notions.

In the present verse the same contemplative method of examination is carried out. The 'man-god' is the same as the 'god-man.' In some cases it is easy to see the antinomial features. In other cases where the pure and the practical coalesce more closely in the person of a prophet or spiritual teacher, the two aspects adhere almost without distinction, like the two sides of the same gold coin.

According to the Guru Nārāyaṇa, the Nabi or the Prophet Mohammed has this last described quality. He is called 'kindly Prophet Nabi, pearl and gem in one.' The pearl found in the ocean's depth represents perfection. It symbolises an integrated normal value in human affairs. The gem is a similar beauty-value with many facets. There is a certain pure severity combined with a lavish sense of richness and kindness combined in the character and personality of Mohammed the Prophet. The *Koran* is full of practical injunctions based on a sense of justice in the name of the Most High and Generous God. Mohammedan art provides an example of this double character. The gems inset in the Taj Mahal and the pure pearly perfection of Islamic architecture reflect this austerely severe love of purity, combined with beauty and justice. Islam's success as a religion further testifies to these qualities.

WORD NOTES

Parameśa: 'Lord Most High';

Pavitra: 'Pure';

Puthran: 'Son'. These three words refer to Christ.

Dharma: 'Law of right' in the second line, refers again to the founder of an ethical religion, and could mean Mahāvīra of Jainism or Buddha.

VIII

Is He that soul personified who with holy ashes once
Fever drove away and many wonders worked?
Or yet that other of psychic power who wandering in agony,
Allayed His ventral distress even with song?

Reference is made here to the early seventh-century Tamil saints, last representatives of the Śiva tradition, who after the decadence of Śaivism in the south, by a strange appeal to the emotional aspects of the ancient traditional religion, were able to give it new life once more in the Tamil country at a time when foreign ideologies from the north were beginning to confuse the life of the people. They were able again to revive in the masses a simple pious response to Śiva. The ashes and the snake were inseparable counterparts of this old prehistoric cult which we have elsewhere traced from the times of the Mohenjo-Dāro seals.

When Jaina influences came to the south and when the ruling families were being converted one after another to the Jaina ways, these saints demonstrated how healing and psychic wonders of faith occurred when older, atavistic or memory reactions in reference to wisdom were revived. Ventral troubles are often due to emotional maladjustments which get healed when deeper memory factors are revived by atavistic group behaviour or the like. Even fever can come from excitement and overwork due to lack of balancing interests in life.

The devotional character of these saints is revealed in the profuse songs they poured out in praise of the ancient god Śiva. All the accumulated imagery, rich in mystical import — the heritage of ages of the Tamil genius, reaching back into prehistory — came back to the surface and gave a specific character to these songs. With all these connected associations, and with the 'miracles' which, as in the case of Jesus, were possible and actually in the air, along with rumours of all kinds, these Tamil saints lived and moved among the kings and the common people of the period.

Appār, Sundarar, Manikkavācakar and Tirujñāna Sambandar were four of the great names in this early era. The first two lines here refer to Appar who is said to have healed the Pallava king Mahendravarman I, of his chronic fever. It was evidently faith-healing to the credit of the Śiva cult, by which Appar became famous. The last two lines refer to Sundarar. The object here is to show that bodily health depends on a balance of emotional and intellectual factors. Most 'miracles' examined in the light of the ambivalent factors in the psyche lose their mystery. This domain of psycho-pathology must not lure us into any lengthy discussion here.

IX

Else is He that Sage of crowning fame who uttered once again
That holy script already known and writ in Hara's name ?
Or He devoted to the Value of the Lord Supreme
Who here departed bodily ere life for him was stilled?

The author of the *Kural,* that monumental Tamil masterpiece dating from the beginning of the Christian era, or earlier, and based on the background of prehistoric Śiva, who is also known as Hara, is referred to here.

The Hara-cult was widely prevalent in ancient times, and it is even likely that its influence was wafted across the seas and deserts to far-off shores and lands outside India, as we have tried to depict in previous chapters. It had its own scriptures, some of which are extant to the present day, but much of it has been overcovered by the debris of time. The allusion to favourite trees, stones and animals in the seals and ideograms through its long history reveal sufficient of its character to identify it with what still persists in popular myth, legend and fable even to this day.

Tiruvalluvar, the author of the *Kural,* is held in high esteem in the Tamil country and the *Kural* itself with its ethical and philosophical implications of deep significance is understood by Tamil scholars who can still read meanings into its 1330 verses correctly and with great richness of insight. The work, being conceived correctly as Word-wisdom, is a monument of remarkable importance in the Tamil world, and no child is unfamiliar with at least a few of its proverbial apothegmatic sayings. The Guru Nārāyaṇa revives here this classic and its author who is so often forgotten and overlaid by later expressions of spirituality on the Indian soil. The perennial nature of the Word-wisdom as formulated in the systematically and critically constructed chapters of the *Kural,* draws out the just homage from a *guru* of a later age, who gives it an honoured place in these verses extolling representations of the Word-wisdom throughout the world.

The idea of the dialectical revaluation of the Word-wisdom is suggested in the second line and at the end of the first: 'once again.' Wisdom lives on, ever and again revalued and restated by great sages and the person of such a sage capable of revaluating Word-wisdom critically and methodically attains a supreme status as the counterpart of such wisdom when objectively and correctly considered.

In the last two lines the reference is to the common belief held in the Tamil-speaking south India that certain great saints like Nandanār and other more recent devotees were able to pass from this state here of life to one beyond the threshold of life by a new adjustment of their life tendencies in relation to ultimate and transcendental values. The Guru here seems to give some verisimilitude at least to the theory implied in such a belief, though not in realistic terms of actuality.

The death of certain saints can be of the type of an enigma as viewed in the usual sense, inasmuch as they did not die in the normal sense of death where life energies get spent in a certain way. On the contrary, the Guru here implies that it is possible for a person who dedicates himself to the life of the hereafter, and to those transcendental values which lie on the side of the Ultimate and the Supreme, as personified in a divine being, by earnest dedication to such ideals, to die a special kind of death. The physiological aspects do not come to their end by fatigue but by a special exaltation which occurs in which nervous stress or pressure increases due to intense other-worldly interests.

Cases have been known of bursting of certain blood-vessels due to psychic intensity rather than to physiological causes. The passing away of Swāmī Vivekānanda, as gathered from the intimate personal reports given by those present at the time, as the present writer heard directly, bore some resemblance to these ultra-biological traits. Some *yogīs* go into long-lasting trances and lie without any consciousness (like hibernating animals) in the normal sense. Food looks strange in their eyes, and they do not seem to need it, and ultimately, by a long process of wasting away, life comes to a radiant and beautiful end.

The Guru Nārāyaṇa himself was one who passed away in this gradual and willed fashion, as those who have been at his bedside during his last days had ample evidence to know. After recording some details in the earlier chapters, the present writer has had additional confirmation on this matter on his return to India from his first visit overseas. The body of the Guru was absorbed by gradual stages of unconsciousness into peaceful *samādhi* or Passing into the Peace Beyond. Such a happening can be seen to be normal and possible if the two-sided nature of the psyche is imaginatively understood and applied to the case of understanding of the phenomenon known as death. The lyre becomes its music and this is seen to be its death here. But contemplatively it is a fuller life.

WORD NOTES

Maṟa is the name applied to any scripture of the status and canonical authority of the Vedas in India. The *Kural* is often spoken of as the Tamil Veda.

Mā munīndran: 'the great Indra among Munis (sages)' has been rendered simply 'sage of crowning fame.'

Pararthya: 'devoted to the Value of the Lord Supreme' — from *Para*: 'beyond', and *arthya* 'something desired.' It is in relation to *bhakta:* 'devotee.'

X

Dealing bounty here on earth and taking human form
Is He that Kāma-Dhenu cow of all-providing good?
Or perhaps that wonder-tree of heaven supreme,
The Deva-Taru which to each its gifts bestows?

After alluding to various forms in which the counterparts made the Absolute Presence real to us in its various manifestations in different contexts, we come here to more matter-of-fact expressions of the emergent value of Good in human affairs. The pragmatic 'good' consists of distributing benefits in a concrete sense. The Kāma-Dhenu is the fabulous cow of plenty. It is a mythical symbol of certain values of general good or prosperity. It stands for the common-weal as when social reformers speak of the greatest good of the greatest number in collective or individual terms. The man who wants to do good becomes elevated to a status of holiness by his very intention. He aims at an ideal which, equated with himself, yields that numinous factor which is a supreme value.

The heavenly cow is like a generous man on earth. Aspects meet to reveal the same value, though in apparently different forms. This central value is kindness or Mercy. A tree or an animal can

The Juma Masjid at Delhi, showing "The pearly perfection of Islamic architecture" and the solidarity of the Prophet's faith.

have, hierophantically, the same status in the Absolute as hypostatically conceived angels or spirits. Good is always the centrally emergent factor, and Mercy is that same Good stated in realistic language. A good man can be equated to a tree, and, vice versa, a cow of plenty can be equated to a generous man. Whatever the terms used in the understanding of value, it has the same worth as a 'Guiding Star' in contemplative life.

WORD NOTES

Anukampā āṇḍavan: 'the one who mercy has' has been translated according to the grammatical needs in each verse. In this verse it is the 'Is he . . .', etc., *āṇḍavan* by itself stands for God, thus *anukampā āṇḍavan* would denote divinity or humanity indifferently, according to its usage and derivation.

ENVOI

High scripture's meaning, antique, rare,
Or meaning as by Guru taught,
And what mildly a sage conveys,
And wisdom's branches of every stage,
Together they all belong,
As one in essence, in substance same.

This concluding verse sums up the position in conformity with convention, as the first verse also did in a certain way, in explaining the general subject-matter without entering into it too deeply.

The mystical doctrines contained in the body of the composition apply directly to a spiritual life without any special religious or academic colouration. In fact it is above such distinctions and considerations. Vedānta, particularly Advaita Vedānta, is no substitute religion or scripture, but is a synthetic approach to all scripture. The verses above should not be taken to be a new religion or any religion based on Mercy as a creed or doctrine. Mercy is a transcending human value running through all expressions of spirituality, whether pre-Vedic, Vedic, post-Vedic or non-Vedic. The Āgamas are all the various later ramifications and elaborations of the primary attitude of Mercy implied in the highest scriptures.

The Guru is generally one who teaches in critically systematic and philosophical terms instead of through myth or fable. The *muni* is the silent recluse who does not talk much, but by practising self-control in seclusion coveys his messsage of Mercy and who, examined closely in the light of the discussion above, is not different from the Guru.

In this verse the Guru wants to ensure that there is no mistake made in this matter. The Vedas, the Upaniṣads and the later wisdom literature based on them, whether they take the form of philosophy or asceticism, express the same human value which has been chosen as the central subject-matter of this composition.

WORD NOTES

Arumāmaṟa: 'High scripture . . . antique, rare'.

Artham can be 'meaning', or 'value' such as wealth.

Muni is generally a silent ascetic of self-control. The *guru* type and the *muni* type represent the same wisdom expressed in two personal styles which are only to be treated as incidental.

Porul is the substantial content which is the same as the *artham* or value. Both indicate value which is here the central idea of Mercy.

28

The Science of the Absolute
(Brahma-vidyā-pañcakam)

(*Translated from Sanskrit*)

I

Even through the discrimination of the lasting from the transient,
Attaining well unto detachment, the well-instructed one,
Duly well adorned with the six initial conditions known,
Such as calmness, control, and so on,
And thus keenly desirous of liberation here on earth;
He then greets with prostrations
A *Brahman*-knower superior,
Pleased and favourable by anterior attentions and service;
Thereafter should he ask of such a Guru:
'O Master, this 'I' here, what is it?
Whence this world phenomenal?
O teach me this, great One.'

II

Thou verily art *Brahman*, not senses, not mind,
Neither intellect, consciousness, nor body;
Even life and ego have no reality, being but conditioned.
By nescience, superimposed on the prime Self.
Everything phenomenal here, as object of perception, is gross.
Outside of thine own Self, this world manifested is nought,
And Self-hood alone does shine thus
Mirage-like in variegated display.

III

What all things here, both moveable and immoveable, pervades,
As the clay substance does the pot and jug,
Whose inward awareness even Self-hood here constitutes, wherein everything exists.
And whereunto resolved what still remains, instilled with reality unborn,
And That which all else do follow —
Know That to be the Real, through clear insight,
As That same which one adores for immortal bliss !

IV

Nature having emanated, what thereafter, therein entry makes,
What sustains and gives life, both as the enjoyer
Of the divided objectivity outside,
As the 'I' of the deep subconsciousness of dreamless sleep.
Whose Self-hood even shines as the 'I',
Within the consciousnesses each of the peoples too —
That same in which well-being stands founded firm at every step;
Such a plenitude of Perfection; hear ! 'That verily Thou Art !'

V

'Intelligence Supreme, even That I am ! That verily Thou art !'
That *Brahman* is the Self here !' Singing thus full well,
And so established in peace of mind;
And reborn to pure ways in life by the dawn of *Brahman*-wisdom,
Where could there be for thee the bondage of action
Whether of the past, present, or future?
For everything is but superimposed conditioning on thy prime Self.
Thou verily art That existing-subsisting One of pure intelligence, the Lord.

Introductory

In this our last selection of this volume, we have a Sanskrit composition of five symmetrically conceived verses dealing with the Absolute-value in the terminology of Self-knowledge. Such wisdom has a long tradition as a branch of exact knowledge or science. It is the flowering and culmination of the Vedāntic trend of thought on the Indian soil. This composition has for its subject-matter an ultimate personal Value which is appraised through contemplative dialectics. Immanent and transcendent realities are considered in such a way as to reduce them all unitively in relation to Self-realisation, to *Brahman* or the Absolute. The composition is a complete and positively conceived whole.

Brahmā[1] is the cosmological god of creation of Hindu mythology. He is the first person of the Hindu Trinity, consisting of Brahmā, Viṣṇu, and Maheśvara (or Śiva). Although called a 'Trinity' because of the three divinities brought together, this is meant to be understood historically, or at the most cosmologically, rather than theologically as in the case of the Christian Trinity. Brahmā as the first member of a trio of divinities who have dominated the Indian mind through its long history, is considered the first of all creation — although Maheśvara or Śiva, can claim historical priority and precedence. The rival claims of these divinities finds place in many a legend bringing these three together. When they are taken together, different values of the spiritual world are fused, but the discussion of their relative primacy is a favourite subject of the Indian *paṇḍita*.

Brahman, the Absolute of the Upaniṣads, should not be confused with any divinity, whether theological, cosmological or historical. Although arising terminologically from the male Brahmā of the Vedic background, in the effort to explain reality in as 'real' terms as possible, in the post-Vedic literature the philosophical nature of the *Brahman* stands out unmistakably. Here it is the unknowable Absolute, the numinous presence which can be

1. The word Brahmā which is masculine, should not be confused with *Brahman* which is neuter (see explanation in next paragraph).

conceived cosmologically or psychologically at the same time, and in which transcendence or immanence have no importance. Its truth is meant to be both ontological and teleological, and all philosophical approaches and religious attitudes only lead up to it.

In some of our earlier chapters we have attempted to lay the foundations for the proper understanding of the concept of the Absolute as implied in the meaning of *Brahman* as it belongs to a science of *brahma-vidyā* (*Brahman*-Wisdom). Here in these stanzas the Guru Nārāyaṇa outlines the scope, method and epistemology of this *brahma-vidyā* as understood dialectically as a revision or a revaluation of human knowledge of high import.

The *guru* and the *śiṣya*, the Teacher and inquiring Disciple, are inevitable counterparts of such a dialectical revaluation, or progressive culmination of Vedāntic wisdom. A bipolar relation is established between them when the preliminary conditions have been fulfilled. When such a relationship gains firmness and directness, the Guru begins to represent in his person those aspects of the unknown which are outside or complementary to himself. The silent teaching of the Guru implies special lines of reasoning which are outlined here as an indication of its nature, content or scope. One inquirer approaches the great subject ontologically and cosmologically, while another has a psychological bias. Each has his own way of stating problems.

The problems themselves are first clearly stated in the form of questions of the typical kinds put at the end of the first verse by the *śiṣya* to the *guru*. After covering the questions in a certain order in which all philosophies and theologies and ethics are incidentally brought to a focus on the subject of the Absolute in terms of Self-knowledge, the stanzas go on to cover the whole field of wisdom. They leave no major gaps in free and easy reasoning for either the pragmatist's or idealist's 'buts' and 'ifs'. Both theological and philosophical questions are answered by implication. Ethics and eschatology are also brought into the scheme. The four walls within which contemplative wisdom has to live, move and have its being are definitely indicated.

Action is not wisdom's domain. According to these verses knowledge is freedom and all-sufficing power. Self-knowledge is the foundation or opening for all other knowledge which is secondary to it. The duality of man and God is finally and boldly abolished, not in favour of self-conceit, egotism or self-deification, but as a dedication to the high cause of Self-realisation. In this sense as the Upaniṣads declare, the *Brahman* knower attains the status of *Brahman* Itself. Knowledge and *Brahman* thus mean the same, the Value underlying all values.

Commentary

I

Even through the discrimination of the lasting from the
transient,
Attaining well unto detachment, the well-instructed one,
Duly well adorned with the six initial conditions known,
Such as calmness, control, and so on,
And thus keenly desirous of liberation here on earth;
He then greets with prostrations
A *Brahman*-knower superior,
Pleased and favourable by anterior attentions and service;
Thereafter should he ask of such a Guru:
'O Master, this 'I' here, what is it?
Whence this world phenomenal?
O teach me this, great One.'

The unmistakable imprint of the Śaṅkara tradition is to be recognised here in this first verse. The metrical form and the style of all the five verses are also strongly reminiscent of some similar compositions of Śaṅkara, such as the *Dakṣiṇā-Mūrti-Stava,* where Vedānta is discussed with the name of the ancient *guru* of the south as the object of adoration. This accepted *guru* tradition is carried over by the Guru Nārāyaṇa entirely in the present composition.

In this verse all that Śaṅkara discussed through the first part of his famous work, the *Viveka-Cūḍāmaṇi* (Crest Jewel of Wisdom) which altogether consists of nearly 600 verses, is summarised and quickly reviewed by way of preparation of the ground for the four later verses. Here the basis is laid for the construction of the superstructure of doctrines to be stated later, as the findings and conclusions of the Vedānta. The basis indicated covers such topics as the requirements and qualifications on the part of the seeker for wisdom, the main problems of the contemplative philosophy stated in brief, and the necessity of having that bipolar relationship which inevitably belongs to the dialectics of wisdom.

Within the span of these five stanzas there is a symmetry and methodical presentation of the whole inquiry and its result, dealing with preparation, complication and resolution in the progress to wisdom. The facets of each step are well defined. The six initial conditions or qualifications required of the *śiṣya* are found in verses 22 to 26 of the *Viveka-Cūḍāmaṇi* already mentioned in Chapter 13. These are *sāma* (calmness), *dāma* (control), *uparati* (breaking of other interests), *titikṣā* (endurance), *śraddhā* (earnest trust) and *samādhāna* (steadfastness). These mark the six stages of withdrawal from actual action while gaining self-control; as training and practice before actual wisdom is imparted. It represents the preparing of the soil before the implanting of the seed.

II

Thou verily art *Brahman*, not senses, not mind,
Neither intellect, consciousness, nor body;
Even life and ego have no reality, being but conditioned
By nescience, superimposed on the prime Self.
Everything phenomenal here, as object of perception, is
gross.
Outside of thine own Self, this world manifested is nought,
And Self-hood alone does shine thus
Mirage-like in variegated display.

The Absolute *Brahman* is the real, and 'That Thou Art'. This is the finalised doctrine of the Vedānta as taught by the Guru here in response to the question of the disciple in the previous verse.

By a process of systematic elimination of the outer or extraneous factors related to the Self, beginning from the mind to its various bodily and other appendages and attributes, one succeeds by the *neti ! neti !* (Not this ! Not this!) of the Upaniṣads, identical with the *via negativa* of the teaching of Dionysius the Areopagite in Western mystical theology, to arrive at what constitutes the 'thinking substance.' which is the essence of the Self, which itself is neutral to subjective and objective aspects, as the Absolute *Brahman* as represented by the purest state of the prime Self of man.

The phenomenal vision which we see ever changeful and tantalising, with its many value-contents, is a mirage-like play of psychic constituents, which has no reality but is only appearance. Its reality, if any, is that of the Absolute. The inside reflects the outside or vice versa, and put together they meet in the mirror of wisdom, which reflects reflections as well as originals indifferently. The Self on one side and the phenomenal on the other make for the variegated display, by alternation of conditioned mental states. The whole doctrine of the Vedānta is thus summarily reviewed in this second stanza, in answer to the problems stated in the first.

WORD NOTES

Buddhi has been translated as 'Intelligence.'

Manas means 'mind.' When this mind expresses itself in a more integrated and unitive manner through the ego, it attains different levels of willed thinking, the totality of such functional expression being named *buddhi.* It is thus just will above just passive thinking which is the normal function of the mind.

Cittam, here translated 'consciousness,' is also on the side of intelligence, implying purer reasoning.

Avidyā, rendered 'nescience'.

Svātmani: 'on the prime Self'.

Kalpitam means conditioned or superimposed secondary reality outside the Self.

Jaḍam: 'Gross'.

III

What all things here, both moveable and immoveable,
pervades,
As the clay substance does the pot and jug,
Whose inward awareness even Self-hood here constitutes,
wherein everything exists.
And whereunto resolved what still remains, instilled with
reality unborn,
And That which all else do follow —
Know That to be the Real, through clear insight,
As That same which one adores for immortal bliss !

The conscious substratum of all life, responsible for all the actual and subtle manifestations of reality here, is like the clay to the pot, the common universal and primal basis. Ontologically approached in this manner, we reach our own Self as the factor involved in our appraisal and awareness of the world around us. Consciousness turns round the Self, and is of the same stuff as the matter which it represents round itself in its outer zones. We know ourselves and our own ego.

It is here that the 'mind' and 'self' come into our being, with the visible world as one of its aspects. This outer aspect is manifested and absorbed again into consciousness, according to its life-phases or states. Even when absorbed or dissolved into the prime nature of the Self it remains a reality as a 'prius.' Conversely, it can be thought of as something which leads and is followed by all. By whatever method it is treated, according to an ascending or a descending dialectics, it remains the same reality. Intuitive insight has to result in such a contemplative wisdom, and the attitude of mind implied in the insight is the same as reverence, adoration or worship as known in other and different spiritual contexts. The result is bliss in Self-realisation.

WORD NOTES

Mṛt sattā has been rendered 'clay substance.'

Dhī, buddhi and *manas* are degrees of integration of

consciousness; *manas* being the mind in its most general non-integrated sense, *dhi* representing 'will' or well-integrated consciousness.

Nirmala dhī is 'pure or clear insight.'

IV

Nature having emanated, what thereafter, therein entry makes,
What sustains and gives life, both as the enjoyer
Of the divided objectivity outside,
As the 'I' of the deep subconsciousness of dreamless sleep,
Whose Self-hood even shines as the 'I',
Within the consciousness each of the peoples too —
That same in which well-being stands founded firm at every step;
Such a plenitude of Perfection; hear ! 'That verily Thou Art !'

Reality is viewed here from the side of nature. The actual manifestations of variegated nature and multiplicity is one extreme pole of reality. The existing aspects of reality are pervaded by the subsisting principle which comes to it, as it were, from the other pole. In the Upaniṣads also there is this same idea of two aspects of the Absolute, one being manifested and absorbed into the other.

The creation of nature first, without form, like water, and its later characterisation as the Absolute principle is a figurative illustration bringing out the bipolarity inherent in reality. The *Taittirīya* Upaniṣad discusses this later figurative entry of *Brahman* into its own creation in a very striking passage which reads: 'Having performed austerity he created this whole world, whatever there is here. Having created it, into it, indeed entered.'[2] The figurative nature of this entry has been explained by Śaṅkara in his commentary on this passage. In the light of the bipolarity and ambivalence which we have discussed in our earlier chapters the 'figurative' nature of the two-fold character becomes further clarified. No duality is to be finally countenanced in Advaita

2. *Taittirīya Upaniṣad*, II Vallī, 6th Anuvāka.

Vedānta. From the point of view of the actual, however, it becomes necessary to recognise duality, at least for purposes of argument.

WORD NOTES

Pravibhakta bhuk: 'Enjoyer of the divided objectivity outside.'

Suṣuptau is 'dreamless sleep' being a technical name for the third state of life where the *kāraṇa* or causal body or Self is marked out for discussion. This is *prajñā.*

Jāgrat, svapna, suṣupti and *turīya* are the four states of 'waking', 'dream', 'deep sleep' and 'absolute consciousness' respectively.

Pratyantaraṅgam: rendered 'subconsciousness,' could also be translated 'unconsciousness.' Inasmuch as the word refers to the collective and individual ego it implies one and many (*vyūha*).

V

'Intelligence Supreme, even That I am ! That verily Thou art!'
'That *Brahman* is the Self here!' Singing thus full well,
And so established in peace of mind;
And reborn to pure ways in life by the dawn of *Brahman*-wisdom,
Where could there be for thee the bondage of action
Whether of the past, present, or future?
For everything is but superimposed conditioning on thy prime Self.
Thou verily art That existing-subsisting One of pure intelligence, the Lord.

The *Aitareya Upaniṣad* reduces all into unitive terms of intelligence. It reads: 'All this is guided by intelligence, is based on intelligence. The world is guided by intelligence. The basis is intelligence. *Brahman* is intelligence.'[3] Here we arrive at a finalised doctrine of the Vedānta which takes the extremely pantheistic and idealistic position of reducing all into the unitive terms of intelligence which

3. *Aitareya Upaniṣad*, III.v.3.

is supreme and all inclusive. The *mahā-vākyas* (Great Utterances) like *tat-tvam asi* (That Thou Art), etc., are variously stated in different texts in the first, second or the third person, according to the psychological, metaphysical or cosmological setting. They are all meant to mark the supreme synthesis of all dual factors into one unitive idea. Consciousness and its aspects are all equated, one to the other, till all differences vanish in a final contemplative vision.

The present verse brings out such a culminating doctrine of the Advaita Vedānta. The Guru here recognises the divine and absolute nature of the disciple, whom wisdom has made one of pure re-born ways, as when one is called a Brāhmin or when he is said to be baptised in the Holy Ghost. Whether the baptism is with water or with the fire of wisdom, it is accomplished by supreme and final knowledge, of all reality in unitive absolute terms. Peace comes to the man who has this understanding, and all those considerations of relative good and bad, virtue or vice, that are associated with the Self as conceived in relative consciousness, have no reason or need any more to be. From the position thus taken these questions do not arise. *Karma* is transcended. Duality, even in a theological sense as between the worshipper and the worshipped, is finally effaced, as implied when we say one 'lives in God.'

WORD NOTES

Vipra caraḥ: Vipra is the twice-born Brāhmin, here 'one of pure life;' *caraḥ* means 'one who moves or lives' (as when we say *brahmacārin,* i.e., 'One who walks in the path of *Brahman*'). The combined meaning of *vipra caraḥ* has been rendered 'reborn to pure ways in life.'

Appendix-I

Essential biographical data of Nārāyaṇa Guru

1854 Birth 20 August at Vayal Vāram house in Chempazhanty, a village ten miles north of Trivandrum, capital of Kerala, south India.

Parents : Māḍan Āśān (father) and Kuṭṭy Amma (mother).

1872 First part of education concluded. Death of mother before he is 18.

*c.*1877 Higher studies in Sanskrit at Karunāgappalli.

1884 Death of father. Goes to Aruvippuram. Period of wandering. Settles down on bank of river. Śiva temple established. Composition of earlier poems, incorporating Śiva mythology into Advaita Vedānta.

1894 Finds Kumāran Āśān and takes him to Bangalore for education. (Kumāran Āśān later becomes poet of Malayālam renaissance.)

1897 Composition of *Ātmopadeśa-Śatakam,* original Vedānta textbook, at Aruvippuram.

1901 Role of Guru recognised by public. State census records him as erudite Sanskrit scholar.

1903 Association known as Śrī Nārāyaṇa Dharma Paripālana Yogam (S.N.D.P.Y.) founded. (This body has now a very large membership all over the Malayalam-speaking region.)

Tours Cochin State. Wider public response. State exempts him from attending courts. Travancore Law Report notices his influence in helping to decrease litigation.

c.1904 Settles at Śivagiri, Varkala, on the coast, 25 miles north of Trivandrum.

Founding of temples at Anjengo and Perungoṭṭukara.

1906 Founding of temple at Trichur.

1907 Founding of temple at Cannanore.

November, Severe attack of cholera.

1908 Founding of temple at Tellicherry.

1910 Founding of temples at Calicut and Mangalore.

1912 Founding of Śāradā temple at Śivagiri, Varkala.

1913 Establishment of Advaita Ashram at Alwaye, near Cochin.

1916 Widespread celebrtion of his 60th birthday throughout the West Coast and elsewhere, marking further recognition as a spiritual leader and Guru. (*Note*: there is uncertainty of his year of birth, which the Guru left unrecorded).

Composition of *Darśana Mālā* about this time, representing a high level of mystical literature.

1918 First tour of Ceylon (Sri Lanka).

Śrī Nārāyaṇa Smṛti (*Dharma Śāstra*) written as a guide to his lay followers.

1921 Conference on Brotherhood at Alwaye.

1923 Second visit to Ceylon (Sri Lanka).

1924 Conference of All Religions at Alwaye, inaugurating study of comparative religions and suggesting the foundation of a University for the Science of the Absolute (Brahma-Vidyā Mandiram).

1926 Visits Coimbatore and Nilgiris. (7,000 ft plateau).

1928 Serious illness. Passes away at Varkala, 20 September.

Appendix-II

Works of Nārāyaṇa Guru

(In chronological order of composition)

1881 *Cijjaḍa-Cintanam* (Reflections on Mind and Inertia)

Daiva Cintanam (Reflections on the Divine)

Both these works are in Malayālam prose. The remainder of the Guru's works are in verse.

1884 *Vināyaka Aṣṭakam* (Hymn in Praise of Vināyaka, the Elephant God). Eight verses in Sanskrit.

" *Guha-Aṣṭakam* (Eight Verses to Guha or Subrahmaṇya), in Sanskrit.

" *Śrī Vāsudeva Aṣṭakam* (Eight Verses to Śrī Vāsudeva), in Sanskrit.

" *Bhadra-Kālī-Aṣṭakam* (Eight Verses to Bhadra-Kālī), in Sanskrit.

" *Navamañjarī* (A Cluster of Nine Verses), in two series, one in Sanskrit, the other in Malayālam.

" *Vairāgya Daśakam* (Ten Verses on Detachment), in Malayālam.

1887 *Śiva-Aṣṭakam* (Eight Verses to Śiva), in Malayālam.

" *Thevarappathikangal* (Five hymn-sequences about God), in classical Tamil.

" *Subrahmaṇya-Aṣṭakam* (Eight Verses to Subrahmaṇya), in Malayālam.

" *Saravana-Bhava-Stotram* (Hymn to the Lake-born God, Subrahmaṇya), in Malayālam.

1887-97 *Cit-Jaḍaṅṅal* (Thought and Inertia). Ten verses in Malayālam. Translated with commentary in Part III of this volume.

" *Kuṇḍalinī-Pāṭṭu* (Song of the Kuṇḍalinī Snake). Seventeen verses, with a refrain, in Malayālam. Translated with commentary in Part III of this volume.

" *Piṇḍa-Nandī* (Prenatal Gratitude). Nine verses in Malayālam. Translated with commentary in Part III of this volume.

" *Sadāśiva-Darśanam* (Vision of the Eternal Śiva). Eight verses in Malayālam.

" *Devi-Stavam* (Hymn to the Goddess). Ten verses, in two parts, one in Sanskrit, the other in Malayālam.

" *Subrahmaṇya-Stotram* (Hymn in Praise of Subrahmaṇyam). Fifteen verses in Malayālam.

" *Indriya-Vairāgyam* (Sense Detachment). Ten verses in Malayālam.

" *Ṣaṇmukha-Stavam* (In Praise of the six-faced God, Subrahmaṇyam). Nineteen verses in Malayālam.

" *Kālī Nāṭakam* (The Dance of Kālī, i.e., Time). A long euphonic poem of over a hundred lines in Malayālam.

" *Bāhuleya-Aṣṭakam* (Eight Verses to Bāhuleya, i.e., Kārttikeya or Subrahmaṇya), in Malayālam.

" *Cit-Ambara-Aṣṭakam* (Eight Verses to the Mental Sky, i.e., Naṭarāja or Śiva), in Malayālam.

" *Śiva-Prasāda-Pañcakam* (Five Verses to the Grace of Śiva), in Malayālam.

" *15 Oṟṟapadyaṅṅal* (A Sequence of Fifteen Verses), in Malayālam.

1887-97 *Arivu* (Knowledge), fifteen verses in Malayālam.

" *Brahma-Vidyā-Pañcakam* (Five Verses on the Science of the Absolute) in Sanskrit. Translated with commentary in Part III of this volume.

" *Īśāvāsya-Upaniṣad,* Translated from the Sanskrit into Malayālam verse.

Advaita-Dīpikā (The Lamp of non-dual Wisdom). Nineteen verses in Malayālam.

1894 *Svānubhava-Gīti* (Song of Self-Realisation). Originally about 100 verses, but only 60 extant, in Malayālam.

" *Ardhanārīśvara-Stavam* (Hymn to the Androgynous Śiva), five verses in Malayālam.

" *Tiru-Kural,* Thirty verses translated from the Tamil original of Tiruvalluvar, into Malayālam.

" *Oẓhivil-Oṭukkam* Translated from the Tamil into Malayālam.

1897 *Atmopadeśa-Śatakam* (One Hundred Verses of Self-Instruction). One hundred verses in Malayālam.

1909 *Jananī-Nava-Ratna-Mañjarī* (A Cluster of Nine Verse-Gems to Mother), in Malayālam.

1914 *Daiva-Daśakam* (Ten Verses to God), in Malayālam. Translated at end of Chapter 6, Part I of this volume.

" *Jāti-Mīmāṁsā* (A Critique of Caste). Five verses, the first in Sanskrit, the remaining four in Malayālam. Translated with commentary in Part III of this volume.

" *Anukampā-Daśakam* (Ten Verses on Mercy, Scriptures of Mercy), in Malayālam. Translated with commentary in Part III of this volume.

" *Jīva-Kāruṇya-Pañcakam* (Five Verses on Kindness to Life), in Malayālam. Translated with commentary in Part III of this volume.

1915 *Nirvṛti-Pañcakam* (Five Verses on Inward Release, or Detachment), in Sanskrit. Translated at the end of Part II, Chapter 20, of this volume.

1916 *Darśana-Mālā* (Garland of Visions). One Hundred verses, in ten sections, in Sanskrit.

" *Municaryā-Pañcakam* (Five Verses on the Way of the renounced Recluse), in Sanskrit.

1918 *Śrī Nārāyaṇa Smṛti.* A *Dharma Śāstra* or work on religious or spiritual conduct as conceived in the light of the Guru's teachings, consisting of 302 Sanskrit stanzas dealing with problems of the common man from birth to death.

1924 *Homa Mantram,* beginning '*Agne tava yat-tejah . . . .*' prescribed as the essence of Vedic ritual, and adapted for use in *āśrama*s dedicated to wisdom.

" *Vedānta Sūtram* (Summarisation of the Essence of Vedānta in 24 Aphorisms), in Sanskrit.

Glossary

Popular interpretations of meanings are not always correct, and so some of the explanations of terms or phrases given here, though not opposed to etymology, indeed in some cases closer to derivation, may seem novel. The words already translated and explained in the Word Notes of Part III have not been included.

Ācārya: Teacher, especially one with religious authority.

Advaita: Non-duality. The final establishment of unitive vision, when the vestiges of every shade of duality, whether psychological or cosmological, have been transcended by the man of philosophical vision.

Agastya: One of the first of the Vedic *ṛṣis* supposed to have crossed the Vindhya mountains and come to the south. His relation to Tamil literature and his status in the spiritual life of south India (which was up to then shut off apart from the north) from historic times have brought Agastya and Subrahmaṇya (*q.v.*) into relation of *guru* and *śiṣya*. Agastya is the *cirañjīvī* or everliving, and Subrahmaṇya is the lightning-born son of Śiva. In the dialectical process of the revaluation of Indian, and particularly south Indian spirituality, there is a mutual recognition of the importance of these two figures in whom myth and history are blended. Agastya is also famed as the sage who drank up the seven seas.

Agni-hotra: The burnt offering or fire sacrifice of the Vedas.

Aham Brahma Asmi: (see *Mahā-vākya*).

Ahiṁsā: The vow of non-hurting or compassion as understood in the Buddhist or Jaina religious systems. With Gandhi it meant non-violence in political struggles.

Akula: Literally, one without *kula* or clan. A term applied to Śiva, who was a disturber of sacrifices and an outcaste or non-caste.

Alaṅkāra: Rhetoric, especially treating of figures of speech. This with *kāvya* (*q.v.*) and *nāṭaka* (*q.v.*) are covered by students of Sanskrit.

Amitābha: Literally 'boundless light', which became hypostatised in northern Buddhism along the lines of the Gods and Goddesses of the Indian pantheon.

Ānanda: Bliss. Should be understood in the context of the Good in Western philosophy as a supreme Value. Bounty, goodness and kindness are all conceptions depending upon a notion of value. *Sat,* existence; *Cit,* substantial being in a rational sense; and *ānanda* as a supreme value, are terms conjointly used to describe the Absolute in Vedānta, representing three stages in the appraisal of the true from the point of view of human intelligence. *Ānanda*, is thus supreme bliss or goodness and describes the Absolute in terms of human feeling.

Ananta: Literally 'endless'. Name of the snake upon which Viṣṇu is supposed to sleep, resting on the primordial milk-ocean of universal goodness. The name stands for eternity. The counterpart name is Ādi-Śeṣa meaning 'what originally remains', i.e., the eternal present from the most ancient antiquity. This snake is many-headed, signifying the multi-sided nature of creation at any given moment.

Ante-vāsī: One who dwells near. Term applied to a disciple in the ancient *gurukula*s of India, where the disciples spent years in the household of the *guru*, serving the master and maintaining the fires of the household.

Anubhava: (*Anu,* according; *bhava,* to become) When the mind by intellectual sympathy enters into the reality of a subject with full sense of identity with it, as when a man of wisdom enters *Brahman*-knowledge and thus *becomes Brahman* in effect, his is a state of *anubhava.*

Apara: see *Para.*

Āraṇyaka: The four Vedas were later supplemented and appended with extra portions dealing with many injunctions and laws connected with various rituals. The simplicity of Vedic worship gave place to elaborate discussions on the merits of certain rituals and their validity, etc. Before attaining to the status of proper critical discussion, this body of literature came to be known as *Āraṇyaka,* both because of the complicated nature of the teaching (a forest — *araṇya*), as also perhaps because of the stage of forest-life (*vānaprastha*) to which the injunctions often referred. They mark the pre-Upaniṣadic stage in the development of Vedic lore as it developed through the centuries.

Artha-vāda: The exegesis of Vedānta. Discussion of meaning, as opposed to *vidhi* (*q.v.*) which implies ritualist injunctions.

Āryan: Name applied vaguely by historians to tribes who crossed over the Himālaya and penetrated into the matrix of the Indian life of prehistoric time which consisted of various amorphous formations including the so-called proto-Draviḍians.

Āśrama: A place of retreat for peaceful cessation of duties or ritualistic activities, where those who have become *saṁnyāsīs* or those who are initiates in such a path or way of life live in small self-sufficient communities, independent of the surrounding society, and with an universal outlook on life as members of an open world community. It may have been derived from *ā,* prefix meaning up to the point, of, and *śrama,* effort, as *āśramas* are places where all the preparatory stages to spiritual effort may be carried out in peace and seclusion.

Asuras: The opposite of *suras* or *devas* (the fair or bright entities inhabiting the Vedic heaven). Demons. These might have come into being with reference to anyone who opposed the Āryan penetration ideologically or in historical actuality. *Bhū-Sura*, the earthly god is a term which would seem to lend support to this view, as it connotes a Brāhmin complete with sacrifices and his twice-born quality on wearing the sacred thread, which is a kind of baptism in Brāhminhood. The conflict between the *devas* and *asuras* permeates the whole of the spiritual literature of the Vedic Indians and has to be understood historically or in pure dialectics according to the requirements of the context. Max-Müller thinks there is an affinity between Ahura (Ahura Mazda) of the Zoroastrians and *asura*.

Aśvamedha: Form of Horse-Sacrifice of Vedic times, in which a ruler re-established his right to *de facto* rulership of his kingdom by letting loose a white horse. Any rival could stop the horse, which was equivalent to taking up the gauntlet against him. The king's prowess was proved by vanquishing such rivals and by the emptying of his treasury and bestowal of gifts. The *aśvamedha* was said to have taken place every ten years. The later Rāma story *Uttara-rāma-carita* (*q.v.*) centres round this theme.

Ātman: The Real viewed psychologically as the Supreme or universal Self. The *ātman* is further distinguishable as the *paramātman,* the Supreme Self, and the *jīvātman* or Individual Self respectively.

Auṁ: As the Word of Words, this represents the Absolute, combining *Logos* and *Nous* as understood in the Greek context. The three letters *A*, *U* and *Ṁ* are said to correspond to the open, the half-closed or subtle and the closed or the purely psychic, worlds; thus inclusively covering the cosmological, psychological and spiritual grounds of being or reality as conceived in terms of the Absolute.

Āvaraṇa: Anything which veils the vision or reality, as in the case of a thin cloth or smokescreen. A subtle and general state of ignorance is suggested, also a lazy or negative state of mind, as in the case of a cow frightened by a red cloth. Degrees of *āvaraṇa* can be imagined, and the philosopher has to have a vision cleared of this smoke.

Avatāra: Manifestation of divinity in human form, implying descent from above, and associated primarily with Vaiṣṇavite religion. The ten *avatāras* of Viṣṇu are (1) *Matsya,* the Fish; (2) *Varāha,* the Boar; (3) *Kūrma,* the Tortoise; (4) *Narasiṁha,* the Man-Lion; (5) *Vāmana,* the Dwarf-Brāhmin (*q.v.*); (6) *Paraśurāma,* Rāma-of-the-Axe; (7) *Rāma* (*q.v.*); (8) *Balarāma;* (9) *Buddha,* and (10) *Kalki,* the *avatāra* yet to come.

Avidyā: Nescience; equivalent of *Māyā* (*q.v.*) or darkness, and the opposite of *vidyā* (*q.v.*).

Āyurveda: Medical lore descending from Vedic times though having nothing to do directly with religion, is often called *Āyurveda*, or the wisdom pertaining to *āyus* or life.

Bāhuleya: Another name for the six-headed god, Subrahmaṇya (*q.v.*).

Bhadra-Kālī: That aspect of Kālī, the feminine creative urge of becoming which is personifed in the symbology of the Śiva system. *Bhadra* suggests safety or protection to the devotee.

Bhagavad Gītā: A part of the *Mahābhārata* (*q.v.*) consisting of eighteen chapters, in which Kṛṣṇa as God instructs Arjuna, who is one of the Pāṇḍavas fighting the Kauravas, in the secrets of the mystical science of contemplation called *brahma-vidyā* or *yoga-śāstra.* It is supposed to contain the quintessence of all the Upaniṣads, and to continue Vedic tradition without breaking with orthodoxy, but in revalued terms. It is fundamentally a dialogue or *saṁvāda* between a Teacher and Disciple (*guru* and *śiṣya*), which for reasons of an epic setting in this case are Kṛṣṇa and Arjuna. They serve the philosophical subject-matter as apt literary devised figures in the strikingly realistic situation of a battlefield, where problems face them most squarely.

Bhakti: The devotional type of religious life in which emotions have a large place. In his writings the Guru Nārāyaṇa, however, makes no distinction between meditation or self-reflection and devotion in the sense of *bhakti.*

Bhāṣya: Commentary, particularly on philosophic texts.

Bhikṣu: Originally referred to the mendicant religious priests of the Buddhist religion. The *saṁnyāsī* of later Indian society conformed to this pattern of *bhikṣu* in the revalued terms of the *Bhagavad- Gītā. Bhikṣu* means alms, so that the *bhikṣu* is one who lives on alms and has given up all other social roles applicable to the four castes, or in recognised positions in the normal workaday life of society. (See *Madhukara bhikṣā.*)

Bhīma: The second of the five Pāṇḍava brothers of the *Mahābhārata* war, who faced the Kauravas, the numerous tribe of Kuru. He was a man of gigantic proportions, thus conforming to pre-historic stalwart standards. Quantitative brute force as opposed to the refined spiritual quality of a later epoch were personified in this character.

Bīja-akṣara: Seed Word; *auṁ*.This *Auṁ* contains, synoptically, all Vedāntic Word-wisdom, and this is expounded in the *Māṇḍūkya Upaniṣad,* where cosmology and psychology meet in one central notion of the Logos. (See *Auṁ.*)

Brahmā: One of the members of the Indian pantheon as the first creator and source. He is four-faced, representing the four directions (with an up and down, zenith-nadir fifth sometimes added). As creator he is distinguished from the neutral *Brahman*, the Absolute, which is no god, but a philosophical Reality.

Brahmacarya: (from *Brahman* the Absolute, and *cara* to move). Moving in the path of *Brahman*. As a corollary, secondarily, this would include such disciplines as continence as helpful to realisation; but sex is only one of the implied considerations in the discipline of a *brahmacārī,* who can continue to walk the path of *Brahman* as a married man later in his life when he has sufficiently controlled his instincts. In recent years undue stress has been laid on sex in relation to *brahmacarya*, so that some even treat it as synonymous with continence in sex. But, as evidenced many times in the Upaniṣads, *ṛṣis* have been married and still been able to walk the path of *Brahman*.

Brahma-sūtra: Original aphorisms of canonical rank, which, together with *Bhagavad Gītā* and the Upaniṣads are known as the *prasthāna trayas* or the three bases of belief. The *sūtras* sometimes called *Vedānta Sūtras,* are attributed to Bādarāyaṇa, sometimes identified with Vyāsa (*q.v.*) or Veda-Vyāsa. Their importance is enhanced as Śaṅkara commented upon them, as also Madhva and Rāmānuja. Their study thus gives a thorough grounding for a *brahmacārī* in Vedānta in its anterior and posterior forms, as re-stated by Śaṅkara.

Brahma-vidyā: The Science of the Absolute as understood in the Vedāntic context of non-dual wisdom.

Brāhmin: One who conforms to the religion of the Vedas and initiated or confirmed by the bestowal of the sacred thread which causes him to be known as a 'twice-born' (*dvija*) and fit thereby to assist at ceremonies of burnt offerings to the Gods of the Vedas. Socially he is the highest of the types of castes statically viewed in the Indian world of caste hierarchies, the others being kṣatriya (warrior), vaiśya (merchant) and śūdra (servant). Vedic learning and ritual accompanied the Brāhmin as priest in the formation of society as it stratified with the penetration of the Āryans into the Indian matrix, about 1500 BC (See *Pariah, Caste, Untouchable, Cheri.*)

Caste: This word originated with the Portuguese who came to India and founded mutually exclusive groups here who would not interdine or intermarry. (Port, *casta,* from *casto,* pure; from Latin *castus,* pure, related to *castigare,* to cleanse or punish, *castrare,* to cut, and *carere,* to be without, lack). The idea of preserving a certain purity of racial, religious or traditional strain based on a certain notion of chastity or purity was what the Portuguese observed. It has been used synonymously with the Sanskrit word *jāti,* meaning species, or kind. In the period of Indian decadence the original concept became stratified in social life, giving rise to the well-known phenomenon of rigid caste distinctions, with untouchability as its extreme manifestation. Sonorous titles such as *varṇāśrama dharma* have been vaguely used in connection with this phenomenon of caste in India, and philosophical rationalisation is sometimes sought by certain authorities for attachment to this purely instinctive and natural tendency to form closed static groups within society — a tendency sufficiently familiar, though in simpler forms, all over the world, to be in no need of further elaboration. (See also *Brāhmin* and *Pariah, Untouchable, Cheri.*)

Cārvāka: Literally 'sweet-tongued'. Materialists of the Indian philosophical context comparable to the Epicureans. If Epicureans are said to have preferred the red side of an apple, the Cārvākas were supposed to have taken butter (ghee) even at the risk of being in debt for it. Though despised as materialists in Greece and India, much rational philosophy gets its initiative from the matter-of-fact attitude of the Cārvāka-Epicurean materialists. The sceptic is here seen in his best light as opposed to a mere dogmatist.

Cheri: Tamil name applied to clusters of huts where 'low-castes', generally live. Para-cheri is the place where Pariahs (*q.v.*) live. These places might be compared to Indian reserves in USA. although in India there is no legal reserved area.

Cingam or Siṁha: The constellation Leo which marks out the first of the zodiacal months in Malabar (quite apart from *Meṣam* or Aries, which is used for calculations, astrology, etc.).

Dakṣa: Evidently a person of some status in Vedic society, and for that reason refused to give his daughter in marriage to Śiva because he was an *akula* (*q.v.*) However, the marriage does take place mysteriously in spite of Dakṣa's objections. Dākṣāyaṇī the daughter later proves her loyalty to Śiva, whom Dakṣa continues to slight, by her death at Dakṣa's famous sacrifice which is held without inviting Śiva.

Dakṣiṇā-Mūrti: Literary 'the deity of the south'. Name applied to a form of Śiva in which this god-hero is the *guru* to the Vedic *ṛṣis*. He is represented as seated on a stone facing the south under a spreading tree with meditative light on his features and the *jñāna-mudrā* (*q.v.*) or wisdom-gesture formed by his right hand. Here in this image, Śiva gains ascendancy over Vedic wisdom and also triumphs in Kailās (the seat of the Vedic gods.) In the context of *guru*-wisdom Dakṣiṇā-Mūrti affords the archetype for *guru*-hood; as this same pattern of a wise man seated under a tree runs right through historic tradition in perennial philosophy down to the most ancient of periods known on the Indian soil.

Dama: Checking and turning away of the mind from its distractions.

Darśana: Vision of certain aspect, especially as seen from the particular point of view of a given system of philosophy. Facets of truth can be strung together systematically, so as to bring out the particularity of each while revealing the truth of truth underlying the whole. In Vedānta, *darśana*s are thus studied in an interrelated fashion, as in the *Sarva-Darśana-Saṁgraha* and the *Sarva-Darśana-Siddhānta-Saṁgraha* which method finds its culminating example in modern times in the *Darśana-Mālā* (Garland of Visions) of a hundred verses in ten sections or *darśana*s of ten verses each, of the Guru Nārāyaṇa. The German word *Anschauung* corresponds to what is meant by *darśana*.

Devas: Vedic heavenly entities, as opposed to *asuras* (*q.v.*).

Dharma-kṣetra: *Dharma* stands for generalised religious or spiritual duty, while *kṣetra* is 'field'; so that the term would suggest a field, real or imaginary, in which the question of spiritual duty rests as a basis. More simply it is explained as the actual battlefield on which the *Mahābhārata* (*q.v.*) war was waged.

Draviḍian: Referred to by historians as being unlike the Āryans (*q.v.*) in colour and physiognomy and supposed to represent the most important proto-Āryan ethnic group, especially persisting to the present day in the south of India, and also represented by various hill-tribes in pockets and in isolated areas all over India.

Droṇa or Droṇa ācārya: As teacher was the family priest on the side of the Kauravas in the *Māhābhārata* war. He conformed to the Vedic priestly type. (See *Mahā-bhārata.*)

Dvaita: or Śuddhādvaita is that school of Indian philosophy, such as that of Madhvācārya which stops short at the recognition of the dual nature of God and devotee, as belonging to two final or irreducible categories in life. Monistic belief is implicit in the idea of Godhead, and the duality is only the colouration of the particular method adopted by this school.

Ekalavya: Prince of a hunter-tribe who was refused instruction in archery by Droṇa, who had caste prejudice. Ekalavya, however, managed to master the art indirectly by devotion to a dummy of Droṇa on which he concentrated to obtain the required skill. Discovering this violation of his rights, Droṇa penalised Ekalavya in a damaging way, by demanding his thumb to be cut off by way of Guru's remuneration, thus spitefully disabling Ekalavya as an archer.

Gaṇeśa: The elephant-headed god, the eldest born to Śiva and Pārvatī. He is also called Gaṇapati, which would suggest that he is the first of the *gaṇa*s or beings (from *gaṇa* to count; and *pati,* chief). Gaṇapati has always to be propitiated first in prayers or ceremonies so that no hindrances may befall an undertaking, such as the writing of a book, etc. Gaṇapati is pot-bellied and has the rat or field-mouse as his *vāhana,* or vehicle. One of his tusks is also broken, and with the broken piece he is supposed to have written the *Mahābhārata* to the dictated recitation on the epic by its author, Vyāsa.

Gaṅgā: The river Ganges. Often spoken of as representing the creative urge originating in the head of Śiva. This sky or mind-river (Ākāsa-Gaṅgā) was brought down to earth by the penance of Bhagīratha, and when it did descend for the benefit of humanity it came in such torrents that Śiva had to make it flow through his locks of hair lest it should be catastrophic to mankind. Creation has its benefits for humanity and the good value represented by water is the overflowing bounty of God in the symbolic form of the Ganges, or Gaṅgā.

Gokarṇa-Nāth: Name given by the Guru Nārāyaṇa to a temple which he established in Mangalore.

Gaurī: One of the *Śakti*s of Śiva. (See *Pārvatī*) The white rather than the dark or terrible aspect (See *Kālī.*)

Gṛhastha: The householder, as a stage in life, in the scale of spiritual progress outlined in Indian religious books. (See also *Vānaprastha.*) This stage corresponds to that of a married man who has his social obligations and duties in-keeping with the scriptures, in particular as laid down in the Vedas, which must be adhered to by necessity.

Guṇa: Quality or functional peculiarity in nature. *Sattva, rajas* and *tamas* (*q.v.*) are the three specialising *guṇa*s found in nature, besides other numerous manifested qualities or functions.

Guru: (from *gu* darkness, and *ru* to counteract). The banisher of darkness or ignorance. A spiritual teacher or preceptor.

Haimavatī or Haimatīśvarī: Haimavatī, daughter of the Snows or Himālaya; Īśvarī, goddess. The same as Umā (see *Umā* and *Pārvatī*). One of the *śakti*s of Śiva.

Hara: Original name signifying Śiva, counterpart of Hari who is Viṣṇu incarnate. In later times Hara and Hari became fused as Harihara, thus bringing into coalescence the Viṣṇu and Śiva currents of religious symbology.

Hīnayāna: The Lesser Path. Used to mark out the southern Buddhist teachings in a somewhat derogatory way.

Hitopadeśa: Stories with moral precepts, found in Sanskrit literature. *Hita,* beneficent; *upadeśa,* precept. Widely used by students.

Indra: The first of the gods of the Vedic heaven with Mitra, Varuṇa and other presiding deities of phenomenal aspects. Indra's heaven is one where all desires are fulfilled, and where plenty prevails.

Īśvara: Master of the World; One Supreme.

Jagat: The derived meaning suggests something that moves or revolves according to the movement, sometimes cyclic, like *saṁsāra.* The phenomenal world of cycles of seasons or of births and deaths is implied.

Jagat-guru: A *guru* or preceptor as distinguished from the patriarch of a tribe or the leader of a parochial religion. What is stressed is the universal nature of the authority and the teaching here. All mystical teachers or contemplatives who identify themselves with no closed or static group may be said to be world or universal Teachers in this sense.

Jātakas: Birth-stories. Used to describe the various incarnations of the Buddha and the *bodhisattva*s.

Jīvan-mukta: One who attains release in life.

Jīvātmā: Individual soul veiwed as a living being. This individual soul or *jīva* which has spiritual elements implicit in its nature, is the subject of transmigration from body to body as described in chapter XV of the *Bhagavad Gītā.*

Jñāna-mudrā: The *mudrā* is a finger-gesture. These are found in icons in India and have their conventional meanings, forming indeed an important part of the dance-dramas of India, where speech can be conveyed by *mudrā*s. The *mudrā* referred to here is that which is interposed between a *guru* and his disciple, as in the case of Dakṣiṇā-Mūrti (*q.v.*). It is evidence that the teaching concerns wisdom (*jñāna*), and is formed by the junction of the index and thumb tip to tip to form a circle, the other three fingers being together rigid in line with the palm. (See *Dakṣiṇā-Mūrti.*)

Jñānin: One who has attained enlightenment. *Jñāna* means wisdom, as contrasted with *karma* (works). The *Jñāna-mārga* or the way of wisdom gives primacy to reason and intuition.

Kālī: (from *kāla,* time) Dark and terrible aspects of time personified as the process of creative becoming. In its tragic aspect it is Kālī. The smoky flame of a sacrificial fire is also called Kālī or dark, in the *Muṇḍaka Upaniṣad* (I.ii.4.).

Kāma or Kāmadeva: The Eros of India. Rati is his consort. The central eye of Śiva which erupts fire is said to have burnt Kāma to ashes when Kāma aimed his flowery-arrow at Śiva in order to make him erotic, as commissioned by the gods who needed a martial deity. The war-god was born, however, without erotic love in circumstances portrayed by Kālīdāsa in his poem called *Kumāra-sambhava* (The Birth of the War-God) (*q.v.*).

Kāmadhenu: The wish-fulfilling cow of Indian mythology.

Kāṇḍa: As in *karma-kāṇḍa* refers to section or part. *Jñāna-kāṇḍa* designates the philosophical section, while the *karma-kāṇḍa* refers to the ritualistic or religious section.

Kāñjī: Rice gruel. This has become almost an English word. *Kāñjī* is the basic food of the poeple of south India, including Malabar. It is perhaps the most primary form of cooked food existing in any part of the world.

Kanyā-Kumārī: (Cape) Comorin, the extreme southern tip of the Indian peninsula. On the grey-black rocks there is an ancient temple dedicated to the memory of the Mother-Principle which has a very ancient history. It is mentioned by the ancient Greek author of the *Periplus of the Erythraean Sea* (first century AD). Rāma (in the *Rāmāyaṇa* epic, *q.v.*) worships at Kanyā-Kumārī, thus sanctifying the place in the later Viṣṇu context of Indian spirituality. *Kanyā* is a virgin, *Kumāri,* a maid; and so Kanyā-Kumāri equates with the Christian concept of the Virgin Mary.

Karma: All action is included under this term, more especially ritualistic action. In individual psychology it stands for the accumulation of tendencies referring to past habits recorded in the personality, as it lives and is determined by the conditionings of the past. The accumulated effect of habits from the past culminates as a fatal Nemesis. When the tendency to be active is regulated or sublimated by higher considerations and disciplines, it is referred to as *karma-yoga.* Ethically revised action or *karma* becomes *dharma* or right action in the sense of religious duty.

Kātyāyanī: One of the *śakti*s of Śiva. (See *Parvati.*)

Kārttikeya: Another name for Subrahmaṇya (*q.v.*).

Kāvya: Minor heroic poetical work in Sanskrit, such as Kālidāsa's *Kumārasambhava* (*q.v.*).

Khaddar (*or Khādī*): A Hindī word meaning homespun and hand-woven stuff, whether of cotton, silk or wool, but more usually cotton.

Kṛṣṇa: Chief of the Yādava tribes: and an incarnation of Viṣṇu. (see *Yādava, Mahābhārata, Bhagavad Gītā, etc.*).

Kṣetra-Kṣetrajña: Field and Knower of the Field. Field or ground can be psychological or spiritual as well as actual. These terms correspond to the actual and perceptual aspects of reality. The entire XIII chapter of the *Bhagavad Gītā* is devoted to this discussion and the distinction between these two aspects of field and knower, in itself constitutes one of the central problems of philosophy.

Kumārasambhava: A minor Sanskrit epic of Kālīdasa, literally. 'The Birth of the War-god Kumāra'. In their struggle against the demons (*asura*s) the gods (*deva*s) badly needed a warrior god and approached Brahmā to this end, who counselled that they should somehow make Śiva, who was then steeped in meditation, fall in love with a woman. Kāmadeva (Eros) (*q.v.*) was selected to tempt him for this purpose, and Kāmadeva came with his wife Rati, choosing the moment when Umā (*q.v.*) came with offerings, to let fly at him the flowered dart of erotic temptation. Śiva caught Kāmadeva before the arrow left his bow, and in his anger, Śiva opened his third eye whose glance reduced Kāmadeva to ashes.

Kural: See *Tiru Kural.*

Kurukṣetra: The same as *dharmakṣetra* (*q.v.*) whereon the battle between the Pāṇḍavas and the Kauravas was waged as mentioned at the beginning of the *Bhagavad Gītā*. Literally it means the Field of Kuru, and is a geographically identifiable locality as opposed to *dharma-kṣetra* which is ideological only.

Lakṣaṇārtha: Figurative sense of statement as opposed to its actual or literal meaning. If not understood figuratively, many of the sayings in the Upaniṣads become puerile or enigmatic. Śaṅkara justifies many passages which at first sight seem to be contradictory by making this distinction between *vācyārtha* (literal) (*q.v.*) and *lakṣaṇārtha* (metaphorical or figurative) meaning.

Lakṣmī: The consort of Viṣṇu; the personification of the principle of plenty and prosperity. She is lotus-born and with four arms; one of the first results of the churning of the ocean of good and evil, symbolising a central human value when looked at from the utilitarian point of view. After the highly negative and lifeless values of decadent Buddhist periods Lakṣmī or Śrī as a principle of good or godhead gained popularity in India which she holds to the present day. Often suggesting even a sloppy love of comfort in certain pleasure-loving minds.

Laṅkā: Ancient name for Ceylon (Sri Lanka). In the time of the *Rāmāyaṇa* (*q.v.*) the ruler of Laṅkā was Rāvaṇa.

Liṅgam: Literally anything that constitutes a sign or symbol. The male and female sex-organs as symbols are referred to as *liṅgams*, *pulliṅgam* meaning male sex symbol, and *striliṅgam* marking the feminine. The *śiva-liṅgam* which is the phallic symbol of Śiva is a spherical stone which is an object of worship in India from prehistoric times. It is dressed up, anointed or washed with ablutive waters by way of respect or adoration in memory of the antique god Śiva.

Madhukara bhikṣā: The *saṁnyāsin* is not supposed to enter a house where the kitchen fire is still smoking. As Manu prescribes he is not to impose himself at meal times without invitation. The best method for receiving alms is collection as the bee gathers nectar from many flowers, becoming rich without depriving anyone of a large portion. *Madhukara* is the honey-making bee; *bhikṣā* is receiving alms without making a nuisance of oneself. (See *Bhikṣu*)

Mahābali: One of the last of the Buddhist emperors whose rule extended to south India. Popular folk-song in Malabar preserves his name as Maveli which is interpreted to be the same as Mahābali Cakravartī. Vāmana (*q.v.*) is said to have cheated him of his kingdom by a trick. This mythical and historical episode is perhaps meant to convey the dominating ascendancy of Viṣṇu as Trivikrama or Vāmana after the decadent last days of Buddhism in India which became displaced by more living human values as embodied in the Viṣṇu religion which was restated and revalued at the time of Rāmānuja and others.

Mahābhārata: The greatest of the Indian epics, named after Bharata, an emperor of ancient India. Like Homer's *Odyssey* it contains the account of the exploits of two rival groups, in this case the Pāṇḍavas and the Kauravas, and is recorded in verse, presumably by the sage Vyāsa, who also wrote or edited the Vedas. (See also *Bhagavad Gītā*)

Mahātmā: (*Mahā,* great; *ātmā,* soul) One of great soul. A spiritual man of God.

Mahāvākya: Literally, 'great word'. Applied to the conclusive formulae of Vedāntic wisdom, such as *aham brahma-asmi* (I am Brahman); *tat-tvam-asi* (That thou art); *auṁ tat sat* (*auṁ*, That is what is Real); *ayamātmā-brahma* (This Self is *Brahman*); *prajñānam brahma* (*Brahman* is consciousness).

Mahāyāna: The Great Path. Used to mark out the northern Buddhist teachings, in a somewhat superior way.

Maheśvara: The Great God. Applied to Śiva as last of the members of the so-called Hindu trinity with his function of destroyer as against creator (Brahmā) and preserver (Viṣṇu). These three Brahmā-Viṣṇu-Śiva form the Trimūrti symbol which emerged as a result of synthetic assimilation and revaluation of spirituality.

Mālā: Garland; rosary (of pearls or beads).

Malaya: Region referred to by Kālidāsa and others in Sanskrit; the pepper and coconut coastal region of the West Coast of south India. (See end of Apte's *Sanskrit Dictionary.*)

Malayālma: A script almost extinct, belonging to the early days of the Malayālam language.

Mantra: An aphoristic formula to be repeated for psychic or cosmic effects to follow as a consequence. Any short, effective, or potent saying.

Mārga: Path, applied to various approaches to wisdom or salvation.

Māyā: Connotes a factor of epistemological and methodological importance in Śaṅkara's Vedānta especially, and in the Upaniṣadic lore generally. Whatever is postulated as the cause of the unreal spoken of in the most generic of categorical terms in philosophy, as against theology, is to be laid at the door of Māyā. It is the basis of duality or synergic antinomies. The nearest Western equivalent is the *Negativitat* of Hegel's system.

Mīmāṁsā: Literature of the Vedic or Vedāntic tradition treated critically. Critique or Inquiry.

Mokṣa: 'release', signifying final emancipation.

Mukti: Normally refers to release that is gained after death.

Mumukṣutva: The state of being an aspirant for wisdom or having a resistless desire for liberation.

Naciketas: Youth mentioned in the *Kaṭha Upaniṣad* who has a discussion with Death who instructs him in higher wisdom, as distinct from mere ritual. He represents the youthful, bright, spirit of man desirous of emancipation, while his father typifies the failure and bankruptcy of life dominated by ritual and longing for heaven.

Naimittika: When applied to *karma* or actions refers to such acts as are not daily or routine (see *Nitya*) but which arise incidentally from a given situation not anticipated in the usual course of daily routine life. Both *naimittika* and *nitya* actions belong to the domain of necessary life activity.

Nārada: A dubious sort of holy figure or *ṛṣi* who moves between the *devas* (*q.v.*) and men and used perhaps in Indian literature whenever the Āryan and pre-Āryan sets of spiritual values had to be related through the aid of literary devices. He is a tale-bearer, reporting the vicious and virtuous, and recommending appropriate reward and punishment. Nārada is the reputed author of the *Bhakti Sūtras* or Aphorisms of Devotion, and he carries a stringed instrument as he moves from one plane of existence to another. He is more Vedic than pre-Vedic.

Nārāyaṇa: One who sleeps on the primordial waters (*nara,* water; *ayana,* to lie in repose). Creation, before Brahmā gave it the four directions, symbolised by his four heads, has the indefinite nature of all-pervading water ('God moved upon the face of the waters' as *Genesis,* I, 2 puts it) on which the numinous principle of life or creation was supposed to recline. This image of creation formed the background of the later Viṣṇu tradition which itself suffered many changes through history and became the Vāsudeva (*q.v.*) tradition of the *Bhagavad Gītā* (*q.v.*) epoch. In the original Nārāyaṇa scheme, Śiva, Viṣṇu and Brahmā met without distinction as the Ādi-Nārāyaṇa, the first divinity of creation, or the primordial Man or Nara, when called Nara-Nārāyaṇa.

Nāṭaka: Drama.

Naṭarāja: The dancing Śiva. The virile cosmic principle which Śiva stands for is seen dancing on a demon in the familiar bronze statues. The Śiva dance is referred to in various mythic contexts, where the glory of Śiva is emphasised as against later intrusions into this prehistoric tradition.

Neti-neti: This refers to the method of negative reasoning which is at the basis of the Vedāntic approach to wisdom. Literally it means 'Not this, not this'. By the elimination of the irrelevant and extraneous factors which prevent the coming of wisdom, illumination results automatically, without effort or action. This corresponds to the *via negativa* of the European mystics, such as Eckhart, Tauler, Boehme, Dionysius the Areopagite, etc. The *nivṛtti mārga* (*q.v.*) or path of withdrawal, which is often opposed to the *pravṛtti mārga* (*q.v.*) or path of action, means also the same attitude of disciplined negation.

Nīlakaṇṭha: Blue-throated. Reference to Śiva, whose neck was turned blue and remained so for ever as a distinguishing mark, after he drank the *hālāhala* poison which was first thrown up when the milk-ocean was churned under his auspices by the gods (*deva*s) and the demons (*asura*s) of later Vaiṣṇavite mythology. Beneficent values succeed harmful ones, representing extreme positions. If the poison had not been quaffed by the kindness of Śiva who was immune to poisons, humanity would have been destroyed. The worst that it could do was to leave the permanent spectral blue band on his throat.

Nimitta kāraṇa: Indian schools of logic or reasoning admit of different classes of causes. To take a favourite example, the pot has its material cause in the mud. The potter makes the pot by mixing mud and shaping it on his wheel. This is incidental and not essential to the situation. In this sense this instrumental cause is the *nimitta kāraṇa.*

Nirvāṇa: Extinction of all desires in a kind of pure void of the Absolute consciousness.

Nirvikalpa: Without *vikalpa* (mental acts) involved. It is a term applied to the state of enlightenment which in its highest sense is said to be devoid of mental activities in any form. The lower stage is distinguished as *savikalpa* with mentation as its condition.

Nirviśeṣa: Non-specialised; term used by different schools of Vedāntic philosophy. Not giving primacy to effect but to the basic ontological aspect of reality. (See *Satkāraṇa-vāda, Satkārya-vāda* and *Viśiṣṭadvaita.*)

Niṣkāma (*karma*): (*Niṣ,* without; *kāma,* passion) That kind of necessary activity which the *yogī* or aspirant adopts, cleared of all desire motivation; as if dedicated to the good of humanity or to a universal principle of Good or God, which thus tends to diminish rather than increase the urge or pressure of the instincts.

Nitya: When applied to *karma* or actions means all the routine of necessary actions which follow one another in the course of daily life, like eating and bathing, etc. (See *Naimittika.*)

Nivṛtti-mārga: The path of withdrawal. The word *nirvāṇa* comes from the same root. This is related to '*neti, neti*' (*q.v.*), or the *via negativa.* It means sinking into one's own true nature by withdrawing the mind from outward-going attachments, the final culmination of this process being *nirvāṇa*.

Pañcatantra: A Sanskrit book of stories and fables sometimes thought to be the prototype for such works as *Aesop's Fables* and other similar collections in the West.

Para: Beyond; pertaining to the Ultimate or Supreme; as opposed to the immanent here and now aspect of reality which is *apara.* It could mean transcendent (cognisant with English word 'far').

Parama-Haṁsa: Literally 'Supreme Swan'. Spoken of as signifying the ultimate stage of detachment, illumination and peace reached by the mystic or *yogī.* May be cognisant with the analogy in Plato where he describes the soul as a bird whose feathers grow as it looks upwards beyond the world of dualities, and ultimately surpasses even the middle-region of the gods in its winged flight to supreme freedom or happiness.

Pāramārthika: This is contrasted with *vyāvahārika* (*q.v.*). The pure, rational or idealist aspect of life which has little or nothing to do with social or other obligations or necessities. (*Parama,* ultimate; and *ārtika,* as the aim.)

Paramātmā: The Supreme or the Absolutely conceived Self. Can be equated cosmologically with the concept of *Brahman*, or ethically with *ānanda* or Bliss as a supreme value.

Parāsara: The father of Vyāsa, otherwise called the Veda-Vyāsa (see *Vyāsa*). Parāsara was born of a Pariah woman, which must mean that he was non-Āryan in origin and Vyāsa was born from a fisherwoman.

Pariah: The proto-Āryan remnants of the civilization which was overrun by Vedic civilization were mostly to be recognised as drummers on ceremonial occasions in the vanguard of processions. They were the vanquished and were outside the pale of the new Āryanised formation. Comprising many of the tribes or groups who live away from the village, they were considered untouchables, although in the purely spiritual context of India they have always occupied a very important, though little-recognised place. The word 'pariah' is derived from 'para' the drum, thus revealing affinities with the pre-historic drummer of the Indian scene. (See also *Brāhmin* and *Caste, Untouchable, Cheri.*)

Pārvatī: The consort or *śakti* aspect of Śiva. She is the daughter of the Himālaya and is also a huntress, and known under various aspects in mythology and iconography.

Paśu-pati: Both this term and *pāśam* are basic concepts in the ancient Śiva religion. *Paśu* is creation, in the sense of beasts or animals of all kinds, while *pati* is the master or creator. *Pāśam* is the bondage in which all life is trapped. Paśupati is Śiva visualised as surrounded by animals, thus bringing together dialectical counterparts belonging to a situation which is typical of the spiritual attitude cultivated by the Śaivites.

Pāṭhaśālā: (*Pāṭha,* lesson; *Śālā,* house) 'The old school-house'.

Prachanna Bauddha: Nickname sometimes applied by orthodox ritualists in India of the type of Kumārila Bhaṭṭa and Maṇḍana Miśra to Śaṅkara, who in their eyes seemed to be hiding his heterodox Buddhist views under a false garb. The term means Buddhist in disguise.

Prajāpati: Name applied to the creator as the progenitor or originator of all people, who are his subjects, and representing an ontological version of Brahmā the creator conceived in a human relationship.

Pratyakṣa: Given to the senses in a strictly empirical sense: as when we see and touch a pot. This is a form of knowledge of which *parokṣa* or conceptual knowledge is the opposite counterpart in the parlance of Vedānta.

Pravr̥tti-mārga: The Path of Action, as opposed to the Path of Negation. (See *Nivr̥tti-mārga.*) Here the mind goes forward to the outer world and wins domination over the forces of nature through ritual or science. Here primacy is given to the objective approach.

Preṣṭa: Friend; one who is dear. A term sometimes applied by a *guru* to an intelligent disciple who is often a questioner, like Theaetetus to Socrates. The term of endearment between a *guru* and a *śiṣya* is a natural attitude in the teacher-disciple relationship of contemplation.

Priya: Anything of value capable of giving pleasure whether applied to things, persons or ideas. *Asti, bhāti* and *priya* are the three philosophical categories pertaining to the Real which can exist, enter consciousness and be desirable, respectively.

Purāṇa: Literally, ancient. The accumulation of legends of antiquity.

Puruṣottama: The Absolute principle of Godhead as distinct from demi-urges and divinites of various religious expressions. *Puruṣa* in Sānkhya philosophy is the spiritual principle, as contrasted with *prakr̥ti,* or nature. When Advaita revalues this concept of *puruṣa* in an effort to raise it above all taint of dual implications, the idea of Puruṣottama arises, as in the chapter XVof the *Bhagavad Gītā,* where there is a transcendence of both the eternal and the transient aspects of reality. Probably akin to *The Most High* of the *Bible.*

Pūrva Mīmāṁsā: For purposes of classification, Vedic lore has been divided into *pūrva* or former, earlier, and *uttara* later division. This division has to be understood both in the historical and literary sense. The *Pūrva Mīmāṁsā* (Earlier Critique) is where ritualist injunctions and obligatory rules are discussed critically by Jaimini. (See *Uttara Mīmāṁsā.*)

Pūrva-Pakṣin: (from *pūrva-pakṣa,* prior side). The anterior position of doubt represented by the disciple in his dialogue-relations with the *guru*. The *guru*'s finalised standpoint in the argument is the *siddhānta,* meaning the attained end, or conclusion.

Pūṣan: One of the Vedic divinities pertaining to the Sun.

Rajas: The stage in nature in which the equilibrium is disturbed so as to produce every action in the form of fighting or sport. In the human type represented by the warrior. (See *Sattva, Tamas* and *Guṇa.*)

Rāma: Hero of the *Rāmāyaṇa* (*q.v.*). He was the personification of political, royal and Āryan virtues, as understood by Vālmīki (*q.v.*), the author of the original *Rāmāyaṇa.*

Rāma-rājya: (*Rājya,* kingdom or regime). Refers to the relationship, much praised as the ideal state by Gandhi, as between the ruler and the ruled, at the time of Rāma. (See *Rāmāyaṇa, Sītā, Uttara-Rāma-carita.*)

Rāmāyaṇa: An epic (like the *Mahābhārata*) composed by Vālmīki (*q.v.*) centred round the history of Rāma (*q.v.*), King of Ayodhyā, who travelled to the extreme south of India and to Ceylon. The *Rāmāyaṇa* brings into juxtaposition the Āryan and the proto-Āryan civilizations of India. (See *Uttara-Rāma-carita, Sītā.*)

Rati: Passions; forms of affectivity or attachment and considered impediments to spiritual progress. In mythology Rati is personified as the wife of Kāmadeva (*q.v.*).

Ṛṣi: Name applied to wise sages of ancient India who lived generally in the seclusion of forests and wrote holy scriptures of canonical importance and classical value. They were not necessarily monks, and many of them had their wives living with them. *Maharṣi* means a great *ṛṣi*.

Ṛtam: In the Vedas and Upaniṣads a subtle distinction is often implied between what is real in its 'here and now' aspect and the real as conceived conceptually. The latter is often referred to as *satyam* or the true, while the former would refer to existent aspects of reality.

Sahodaryam: Brotherhood.

Sama: Calm resting of the mind on the goal to be attained.

Samādhāna: A settled and peaceful state of mind non-agitated by fancy, curiosity or imagination, but firmly established in the Real or *Brahman*.

Samādhi: Ultimate peace or illumination, that goal which the *yogī* is said to attain.

Sambhūti: The process of becoming, as in creation. Contrasted with *vināśa* (in the *Īśa Upaniṣad*) or dissolution. A pair of dialectical counterparts.

Samuccaya: Taken together. Used in speaking of mixing of *jñāna-karma* (wisdom and works). This mixing has been questioned by Śaṅkara. According to him such joining of contrary aims leads to absurdities philosophically and practically. *Jñāna* (wisdom) alone, to him, can lead to release or *mokṣa*.

Sanat-Kumāra: A typical sage of the Vedic context. Sanaka, Sananda, and Sanat-Kumāra were the Himālayan *ṛṣis* who were taught by Dakṣiṇā-Mūrti (*q.v.*) or Śiva, when he attained to Kailās as the *guru* of all *gurus*. These ancient teachers are sometimes portrayed as youthful Brāhmins who learnt wisdom of the negative type from the southern *guru* or god Dakṣiṇā-Mūrti.

Saṁgraha: Synopsis; summarised account. Description applied to works such as *Sarva-Darśana-Saṁgraha* which reviews the philosophical position of former philosophers so as to bring them into line historically to a developed culmination in thought such as the Vedānta of Śaṅkara. The authorship of the *Sarva-Darśana-Saṁgraha* has been questioned on internal evidence, and it is often attributed to a disciple of, rather than to Śaṅkara himself. The *Darśana-Mālā* of the Guru Nārāyaṇa also reviews philosophy in this style but presents it in a more symmetrically conceived framework of epistemology and methodology.

Saṁnyāsa: The act of renunciation, especially ritualistic Vedic religious life in favour of monastic life of austerity, where philosophy gains the foreground and has primacy in the life of the individual.

Saṁnyāsin: One who has taken to *saṁnyāsa*. Generally in India the *saṁnyāsin* or renouncer wears a yellow ochre dress, has a shaven head, and carries a *daṇḍa* or staff and a *kamaṇḍalu* or water-pot. He wanders homeless and depends upon *bhikṣā* or freely given alms. In the post-Buddhist period, under the leadership of Śaṅkara, this order became more and more prevalent and recognised in India.

Śāradā: Synonym for the feminine counterpart of the Śiva principle, called *śakti,* which is a creative urge as viewed in cosmic manifestation or existence. *Śakti* is 'becoming' as against 'being'. This same principle has been variously described in mild or terrible forms in relation with black Kālī, who is time with its consuming terrors personified. Umā, Haimavatī and other goddesses also represent *śakti* in varying grades, but Sarasvatī or Śāradā is praised by Kālidāsa and Śaṅkara as the most refined and cultured personification as visualised in classical Sanskrit and in Vedānta. At the other end of this scale, as the crudest and harshest aspect would come Bhadra-Kālī.

Sarasvatī: Otherwise known as Śāradā or Bhāratī: The goddess of learning. Though born of a low-caste, occupies by the side of Śiva, as one of his consorts, a high place in the Indian pantheon. She is clad in pure white and carries a book and a musical instrument (the *vīṇā*) as marks of culture and the fine arts; as opposed to her anterior counterpart Kālī or Bhadra-Kālī, who represents darker and more tragic aspects of cosmic reality personified in female form.

Sarvajña: The all-knower; one who his attained to wisdom regarding everything in a philosophic sense.

Sarvatra: Everywhere.

Sarva-vit: (Śee *Sarvajña*) All-knower.

Sat-cit-ānanda: (See *Ānanda*).

Satkāraṇa-vāda: That mode of argument or doctrine which gives primacy to *cause* as against *effect*. Advaita Vedānta as understood by Śaṅkara is essentially of the *Satkāraṇa-vāda* tendency in its methodology.

Satkārya-vāda: That mode of argument or that doctrine in which primacy is given to *effect* as against *cause*. All Vaiśeṣika schools in the Indian philosophical scene conform to this mode.

Sattva: To be understood in conjunction with *rajas* and *tamas* (*q.v.*). *Prakṛti* or nature in its normal form, when subjected to the process of creative specialisation, manifests in three different levels. *Tamas* is the lowest of these in which there is inertia and lack of brilliance. In the human type this would be typified by Caliban. *Sattva* is the opposite of *tamas*. *Rajas* is intermediate and implies some sort of activity. (See *Guṇa*.)

Satya-āgraha: (*Satya*, truth; *āgraha*, desire) A word coined and used by Mahatma Gandhi to describe his method of non-violent resistance to certain forms of injustice. The term can mean a variety of politico-social duties or *dharma* as understood in the teachings of Gandhi.

Satya-dharman: Term found in *Īśa Upaniṣad* used to describe the worshipper who, himself aspiring to truth (*satya*) and righteousness (*dharma*), becomes the subjective counterpart of these ideas.

Satyam: (See *Ṛtam*).

Sevā-āśrama: *Āśrama* (*q.v.*) which combines some sort of social service in the sense of 'good works' as understood in the West. This type of *āśrama* became known in modern India under the leadership of Swāmā Vivekānanda and others who stood for Śiva and Sevā, religion and service, as conceived unitively.

Śakuntalā: Daughter of Menakā, a beautiful goddess who gives birth to her on earth after a love affair with a mortal. Unable herself to look after the girl she leaves her at the *āśrama* of Kaṇva in a forest. The episode of Śakuntalā's love of King Duṣyanta who comes to the *āśrama* while hunting, is the theme of the immortal Sanskrit drama of Kālīdāsa called *Śākuntalam,* which has become world-famous today.

Śāstra: Scientific treatise with definitions and following a certain method and conforming to recognised theories of knowledge. Thus the *Bhagavad Gītā* is referred to as a *Yoga-Śāstra* at the end of each of its chapters. All knowledge handed down in this way, whether religious or secular could be called a *śāstra*. (See *Smṛti.*)

Ṣaṭ-sampatti: Literally, the six treasures — the qualities which a person who wishes to tread the path of wisdom should possess. These include: *sāma, dāma, uparati, titikṣā, śraddhā,* and *samādhāna* (*q.v.*).

Śraddhā: Intelligent confidence in the words of the *guru*s of the past as preserved in their writings as well as full trust in the teachings of the present Guru. This is often mistaken to be 'faith' in the sense of blind belief. It is faith in an intelligent sense.

Śruti: Learning directly heard and learnt from a teacher fit to impart wisdom. All scriptures dealing with pure Vedāntic wisdom.

Siddhānta: Finalised position of knowledge taken as a conclusion of a set of arguments in philosophy, as opposed to the anterior position or *pūrva-pakṣa* which represents the sceptics' or the disciples' point of view, which is the starting-point in the discussion.

Śikhā: The tuft of hair allowed to grow posteriorly on the cranium; associated with ritualistic life. The rest of the hair is often shaved. When the whole head is shaven the significance is that all ritual has been given up for ever as with the *saṁnyāsin* or *bhikṣu*.

Śiṣya: One who submits himself for learning from a *guru*. *Guru* and *śiṣya* are inseparable counterparts, the one having no meaning independent of the other.

Sītā: Wife and queen of Rāma, hero of the *Rāmāyaṇa* (*q.v.*). Rāvaṇa the demon-king of Laṅkā, infuriated by the insult of Rāma to his sister Śūrpanakhā, carried Sītā from north India to Ceylon (Laṅkā), and the *Rāmāyaṇa* tells the story of her recapture and return to Rāma's capital, Ayodhyā. For the later story, see *Uttara-Rāma- carita,* which deals with Sītā's exile and ultimate disappearance into the womb of the Earth-Mother.

Śiva: The ancient hero-God from the times of prehistory associated with radical virility and renunciation. He is an unconventional god like Dionysius, wearing skins and dancing in ecstasy, drunk with cosmic consciousness. He is the most ancient and the most important figure of the Indian pantheon, and occupies his seat in Benāres and Kailās.

Śiva-Rātri: A festival in honour of Śiva, the anceint god of dance, or the prehistoric hunter-hero (see *Śiva*). Crowds keep awake on this occasion throughout the whole night, with lights and drums.

Śivo-'Ham: Literally, 'I am Śiva.' Corresponds to the *Mahā-vākya* (*q.v.*) in the Śiva context of Vedānta. One of Śaṅkara's compositions ends with the refrain *śivo'ham.*

Smārtta: Pertaining to the *Smṛtis* (*q.v.*) or to those applied aspects of Upaniṣadic learning which influence the life of the disciple when he enters the life of a householder. The memory of what he has learnt directly from the *guru* which is the Upaniṣadic way of life as understood by him is translated into the terms of everyday activity. This primary meaning has come to mean, in south India at least, a sect of 'Brāhmins', treated as a hereditary caste who are Śiva worshippers as opposed to Viṣṇu worshippers. But the Smārttas can also worship Viṣṇu and Śaṅkara is accepted as their *guru* in Madras and south India generally.

Smṛti: Learning or scriptural lore remembered by a student when he applies pure wisdom-teachings to his practical life. Obligatory conduct and works of religious duty (*Dharmaśāstra*s) belong to this category.

Subrahmaṇya: Synonymous with Kārttikeya and Bāhuleya who was supposed to be born in a lake by the light or glance of Śiva which fell there. Subrahmaṇya rides the peacock and is six-headed, being born to six mothers. This myth is supposed to be astronomical also in its import, as there is a group of six stars with the same name (possibly the Pleiades). Subrahmaṇya is younger brother to Gaṇeśa, thc elephant-headed son of Śiva. Subrahmaṇya is much adored in south India, and is mentioned also in the Vedas. (See *Gaṇesa* and *Śiva*.)

Tamas: Inert aspect of nature. The opposite of *sattva.* Heavy and dull. (See *Sattva, Rajas* and *Guṇa.*)

Tapas: (from root, *tap* to burn) Intense self-discipline in a secluded place or forest, aimed at spiritual illumination. It involves effort in Self-realisation in which all instinctive impurities are burnt up.

Then-Galais: (*Then,* south; *Galai* or *Kala,* aspect) Term applied to Viṣṇu worshipping sect of south India claiming to have originated from the south, as opposed to the *Vada-Galais,* or north-origin sect (*q.v.*). Wear white Y mark with central red streak on forehead. Followers of Rāmānuja.

Tiru-Kural: A Tamil work by Tiruvalluvar who belongs to the first century AD. Ethics, philosophy and mysticism blend in a wholesome perennial form of wisdom in this work which may be said to be a continuation of wisdom of the 'pre-historic' India, more or less independent of the Vedic tradition. Tiruvalluvar was not a Brāhmin, but a non-caste Indian, who in spite of this circumstance still holds a high place among the authoritative sages of India.

Titikṣā: Endurance of the troubles incidental to the life of discipline without petulance or self-pity.

Tripuṭi: Having three bases. Technical term in Vedānta referring to three aspects of cognition, namely the subjective, the objective and the process itself. The knower of the pot and and the object called the pot and the knowledge of the pot would illustrate the three ways by which the same cognition could be viewed. Absolute knowledge is without this triple-based difference.

Tṛtīyam sthānam: The third place or factor which is denied in the epistemology and methodology of the Vedānta, at least according to Śaṅkara's system. Like purgatory between heaven and hell, it is the ground of absurdities which belong neither to the here and now nor to the ultimate.

Tulsī: (*Ocimum sanctum*) A kind of basil plant of the labiate family, considered holy and said to have a purifying, antiseptic or antitoxic effect. It is planted in front of orthodox Indian houses where women and children decorate it and adore it for its holiness. The Bel or Bilva (*Aegle marmelos*) and Tumbai (*Leucas aspera*) the latter also a labiate are sacred to Śiva or even Viṣṇu. In most temples it is common to find these leaves dipped in holy water and sprinkled on idols as a preliminary to worship.

Uhā-poha: That intuitive faculty which is akin to imagination or insight, or even critical acumen, which like statemanship, chivalry or even craftsmanship is a gift with which certain persons are more endowed than others. It is more than what mere scholarship can give.

Umā: One of the *śaktis* of Śiva, as the beautiful and radiant daughter of the Himālaya, portrayed in Kālidāsa's *Kumārasambhava* and in the *Kaṭha Upaniṣad* (Khaṇḍa III, 12.) (See *Pārvatī.*)

Untouchable: One whose touch is supposed to pollute a high caste Indian. For economic and cultural reasons certain dominated sections of Indian society were considered so inferior to others that even approaching within a certain range of distance was itself objectionable, in certain areas where extreme caste segregation prevailed. (See under *Caste, Brāhmin,* and *Pariah.*)

Upādāna-kāraṇa: Material cause.

Upaniṣad: When the chapter of *karma* or ritualistic action has been transcended by a religious student or *brahmacārin*, he is ready to receive the posterior philosophical teachings which constitute the Vedānta (i.e. 'the end of the Vedas'). The Vedānta is non-theological, concerned with the Absolute or *Brahman*. The word is said to be derived from *Upa,* beside and *Niṣad,* sitting; so that it is a teaching received by a disciple when he is allowed to sit and listen to philosophical teaching near, or by the side of the Guru. (See also *Vedānta.*)

Uparati: Cessation of desire-motivation, especially when it applies to merit in the ritualistic sense of the Vedas. The seeking of heavenly pleasures would thus come under *rati,* in the sense implied here as Prof. Max-Müller has pointed out. (fn. ch. I, *The Vedānta Philosophy.*)

Uttara Kāṇḍa: Later chapter or section. Refers to the philosophical developments arising out of the Vedic tradition.

Uttara-Mīmāṁsā: One of the two divisions of Vedic lore (*Uttara,* later; as contrasted with *Pūrva-Mīmāṁsā,* (*q.v.*) or earlier inquiry or critique). *Uttara-Mīmāṁsā,* Later Critique, comprises all the critical literature where reason and *artha-vāda* or discussion of meaning find a large place. All Vedāntic works of a critical, rational character fall under this group.

Uttara-Rāma-carita: The posterior happenings in the life of Rāma of the *Rāmāyaṇa* (*q.v.*) of Vālmīki (*q.v.*), as represented in the drama written by Bhavabhūti. It relates how Sītā (*q.v.*) was banished to please popular opinion regarding chastity. Rumour held that Sītā's chastity was sullied when she dwelt in the custody of Rāvaṇa, the demon-ruler of Laṅkā (*q.v.*). This act of political integrity has been the subject of much criticism inasmuch as private and public morality clash in this event. Lava and Kuśa, twin sons of Rāma, are born to Sītā while she is in exile in the *āśrama* of Vālmīki; and as youths they engage in battle against Rāma himself under the circumstances of the *Aśvamedha* (*q.v.*), Horse Sacrifice. The resolution of the situation occurs when their mother Sītā comes to the scene of the battle and helps the children to recognise their own father whose name has hitherto been kept secret from them. After reconciliation Sītā is taken by Mother Earth into her domain and engulfed in a mysteriously tragic manner.

Vācyārtha: Literal sense of statement as opposed to its figurative meaning. (See *Lakṣaṇārtha.*)

Vada-Galais: (*Vada,* north; *Galai* or *Kāla,* aspect) Term applied to Viṣṇu worshipping sect of south India, claiming origin from north. (See *Then-Galais.*) Wear U-mark on forehead; followers of Rāmānuja, and therefore Viśiṣṭādvaitins.

Vairāgya: The state of being without *rāga* or passion, refers generally to detachment in the system of Vedāntic self-discipline.

Vaiṣṇava: Pertaining to the worship of Viṣṇu; secondarily means certain virtues and holy traits belonging to the Viṣṇu way of life. Gandhi's favourite song describes these qualities; it begins 'Vaiṣṇava janato. . . .'

Vallī: Name of a Kurava (or hunter) girl whom Subrahmaṇya, (*q.v.*) is supposed to have espoused at the instance of his father Śiva. The god Subrahmaṇya is familiarly called the husband of Vallī who is a low-caste girl.

Vālmīki: The *ṛṣi* or sage who composed the *Rāmāyaṇa* (*q.v.*) in Sanskrit. He is said to have been the contemporary of Rāma the hero of the epic, and in later parts of the epic, the *Uttara-Rāma-carita* (Later History of Rāma) (*q.v.*) Vālmīki himself figures with Rāma's queen, Sītā, (*q.v.*) whom he protects in his hermitage. Vālmīki may be said to belong to the context of Vedic orthodoxy.

Vāmana: One of the *avatāra*s of Viṣṇu. In the legend he was a dwarf Brāhmin who cheated Mahābali (possibly one of the last of the Buddhist emperors of Kerala, the West Coast kingdom) of his kingdom by a ruse. As elaborated the legend says Vāmana asked the generous Mahābali for a piece of land of just three paces in extent. But the 'three paces' of this *avatāra* covered earth, heaven and underworld, including Mahābali who placed his head for the third 'step'. (See *Mahābali, Avatāra.*)

Vānaprastha: One who has entered the forest-life which is the third or penultimate stage of life. The other stages are the religious student (*brahmacārī*), householder (*gṛhastha*), both former, and the renunciate (*saṁnyāsī*) (see under each).

Vardhamāna-Mahāvīra: Leader of the Jain religion which flourished about the same time as Buddhism, and having the same ethical tendencies, with special stress on *ahiṁsā* or non-hurting *Mahāvīra*, or the Great Hero, as the founder was called, had colossal nude statues erected in his honour all over India at that period.

Varṇāśrama: (*varṇa*, colour) (see *āśrama*): A term loosely applied to caste duties, formed of two component parts which belong to two contradictory contexts. *Āśrama*, besides signifying a place of retreat for *saṁnyāsins*, is used to mark stages of life such as that of *brahmacārin*-student, householder and forest-dweller. In the domain of necessity where colour and class come in, *varṇāśrama* would signify a certain pattern of conduct based on caste-distinctions in its primitive form or as rationalised by Manu and others.

Vāsudeva: Became the popular name for Viṣṇu during the period of the *Bhagavad Gītā*. *Ekāntika bhakti* or one-pointed and solitary devotion to the God Vāsudeva, as understood in the revalued terms of the post-Buddhist orthodoxy, has this form of Viṣṇu as its top, displacing all other less perfected concepts of the Godhead as understood at that epoch. Kṛṣṇa, the Yādava tribe hero, was the son of Vasudeva and Devakī and it is from the former that the name is derived.

Vedānta: When the Vedic teachings had been revalued in philosophical terms by later *ṛṣi*s and sages, a body of literature called Vedānta arose in the history of Indian thought. These often go contrary to the Vedic tendencies of ritual and obligations, announcing freedom and stressing Self-realisation. Later, we find Śaṅkara, Rāmānuja and Madhva referred to as three typical Vedāntic philosophers, although the *guru*s of the Vedāntic line (or *paramparā*) are many. (See also *Upaniṣad.*)

Vedas: The early Sanskrit writings in praise of Indra, Varuṇa and other phenomenal gods of nature; later displaced by the philosophical concept of the Absolute *Brahman* in the

Upaniṣads. The four chief Vedas are the *Ṛg, Sāma, Yajur* and *Atharvan.*

Vidhi: Obligatory injunction, such as the ritualist rules found in the Vedas, which have to be obeyed without choice by Vedic followers, as they are conceived as relating to actual laws of nature or existence. In the later philosophical scriptures of the Upaniṣads, this strictness is relaxed; and instead of *vidhi* we have the method of *artha-vāda* or discussion, in which there is freedom of opinion.

Vidvān: One endowed with *vidyā* or learning.

Vidyā: Science in its empirical or rational connotations. It is posited contra *avidyā* or nescience, but gains a meaning of its own independently when pure notions of reality gain ascendancy. Then the word transcends duality and is known through its own light without the negative contrast of darkness.

Viṣa vaidyan: Medical practitioner of the Indian Āyurvedic school who specialises in toxins and poisoning such as from snakebite, etc., and their cure.

Viṣṇu: The second of the so-called Hindu Trinity, of which Brahmā the creator is first and Maheśvara or Śiva is the last. Śiva is also the destroyer. Viṣṇu is referred to as the preserver, although taken by themselves each of them is in turn preserver and destroyer. These result from the fusing of three cosmological and psychological currents of religious thought in India.

Viśiṣṭādvaita: *Viśeṣa* is the specialised aspect of nature or creation. The supreme divinity is the culminating stage of such specialisation as the highest of its effects or the flower of perfection. That school of Vedānta as revalued by Rāmānuja which holds that this perfected being, while retaining his status as a specialised aspect of reality, could still represent non-duality in its philosophical implications, is called the Viśiṣṭādvaita school of Vedānta.

Viśvāmitra: A priest and religious leader of the Vedic religion. He is often represented as a rival or counterpart of Vasiṣṭha.

Viveka: Wakeful and discriminating state of mind which is conducive to wisdom. One who is not carried away by momentary prejudices is a *vivekī* or man of discrimination in the usual sense, and, beginning with scientific knowledge which avoids false or vague notions, up to wisdom in its highest sense, all come under this term.

Vyāsa: The son of Parāśara (*q.v.*), born of a fisher-maid. Otherwise known as Veda-Vyāsa. He was also the author of the *Brahma-Sūtra.* He was also called Bādarāyaṇa and a dark-coloured *brahmaṛṣi*. He is the most important of the personalities of Brāhmin orthodoxy.

Vyāvahārika: Pertaining to the workaday world of relations and affairs in the usually understood sense. It covers the world of practical living and social behaviour as opposed to *pāramārthika,* which refers to the real and ideal without compromises to the actual empirical or pragmatic exigencies of life.

Yādava: Cowherd caste. Also the name of a kingdom near modern Gujarat which had for its leader the historic Kṛṣṇa, later identified as an incarnation of Viṣṇu. The Yādavas were kinsmen to the Pāṇḍavas through marriage with Kṛṣṇa, their leader or king. (See *Kṛṣṇa.*)

Yakṣa: A genie or mysterious apparition belonging to the series of angelic or awesome denizens of the spirit world mentioned in Sanskrit literature, including besides Yakṣa, the Rakṣa, Gandharva and Kinnara, as differing grades of beings.

Yāta-tatya: State of being as it should be itself (*yāta,* how; *tata,* thus; and *-tya,* nominal suffix). In the domain of the objective world, right scientific knowledge could be called *yāta-tatya.*

Yavanas: Presumably derived from Ionians or Greeks, who were the Europeans known in India 2,000 years ago and earlier.

Yoga: (from root *yuj,* to join) Psychic union of the self with the Self. In the history of Indian spirituality Yoga has often been associated with psycho-physical self-discipline, and has many branches such as *haṭha-yoga* where the physical postures gain primacy, and *rāja-yoga* (meaning royal, public or rational *yoga*) which is very little if at all distinguishable from philosophical or global attitudes, or contemplative stages of the personality in a philosophic context. Thus there is *jñāna* (wisdom) *yoga*, *karma* (action) *yoga*, and *bhakti* (devotion) yoga, besides *rāja-yoga*. The last is associated with the system of Patañjali, while the *Nārada Sūtras* may be said to be the basis of *bhakti-yoga*. *Jñāna* and *karma* are the two broad divisions of *yoga*. The former is philosophical while the latter is connected with activity and discipline, religious or psycho-physical. In its broadest connotation *yoga* can only mean contemplative vision, as we find the word employed, for instance, at the end of each of the eighteen chapters of the *Bhagavad Gītā,* where even the distress of Arjuna is called *Arjuna-viṣāda-yoga*. *Yoga* thus means just a unitive contemplative way.

Yogī: One who accepts the way of *yoga* in his life and meditation. (See *Yoga.*)

Bibliography

Aristotle, *Works, in* Jowett's translation.

Aṣṭāvakra Gītā, tr. by Swami Nityaswarūpānanda, Advaita Ashrama, Almora, 1940.

Attar, Faridu'd-din, *Conference of the Birds,* tr. by R.P. Masani, Oxford University Press, 1924.

Augustine, St., *City of God; Confessions* (numerous editions).

Bacon, Francis, *Works* (numerous editions).

Bergson, Henri, *Creative Evolution* (1907); *An Introduction to Metaphysics* (Macmillan, London, 1913); *The Two Sources of Morality and Religion* (1935).

Bhagavad Gītā, tr. by Annie Besant and Bhagvān Dās, Theosophical Pub. House, Madras, 1940; also tr. with Commentary of Śaṅkara, by A. Mahādeva Shastri, Madras, 1897. Both reliable.

Brahma-Sūtra (Vedānta Sutras), with the Commentary of Śaṅkarācārya, tr. by George Thibaut, vols. XXXIV, 1890, and XXXVIII, 1896 of Sacred Books of the East; Clarendon Press, Oxford, Inelegant but fair translation.

Canat, Rene, *La Litterature Francaise par les Textes*, Librarie Classique Paul Delaplane, Paris, 1906.

Chuang Tzu, *Writings,* tr. by James Legge, Vols. XXXIX and XL of Sacred Books of the East — *Texts of Taoism;* Clarendon Press, Oxford, 1891. Faithful, but style archaic.

Comte, Auguste, *Works* (numerous editions).

Descartes, Rene, *Works* (numerous editions).

Deussen, Paul, *Outline of the Vedānta System of Philosophy According to Śaṅkara,* tr. by Woods and Runkle, Grafton Press, New York, 1906; *The Philosophy of the Upanishads,* tr. by A.S. Geden, Clark, Edinburgh, 1906.

Dionysius the Areopagite, *On the Divine Names and the Mystical Theology,* tr. by C.E. Rolt, London, 1920.

Essington, Sir A.S., *The Nature of the Physical World* (1928); *The Expanding Universe* (1933).

Elliade, Mircea, *Traite d'Histoire des Religions,* Payot, Paris, 1949. Full of original thought.

Encyclopaedia Britannica 15th edn, Chicago.

Encylopedia, Columbia, New York, 1950.

Estruscans, Phaidon Press.

Euripides, *Bacchae, etc,* tr. by Gilbert Murray, Allen and Unwin, London, 1917.

Evans, Sir Arthur, *The Palace of Minos,* 3 vols. 1921-30.

Evans-Wentz, W.Y. in Collaboration with late Lama Kazi Dawa-Samdup, *Tibet's Great Yogi, Milarepa* New York, 1928; *Tibetan Yoga and Secret Doctrines,* New York, 1935.

Garratt, G.T., (ed.), *The Legacy of India,* Clarendon Press, Oxford, 1937. Contains valuable material presented by foreign experts, such as H.G. Rawlinson, W.E. Clark, etc.

Goddard, Dwight (ed.), *A Buddhist Bible,* pub. by editor, Thetford, Maine, USA, 1938.

Harrison, Jane, *Myths of Greece and Rome,* Benn, London, 1928.

Hegel, W.F., *Works* (numerous editions).

Hume, David, *Works* (numerous editions).

Imitation of Christ of Thomas à Kempis, tr. by Whitford, New York, 1931.

Inge, W.R., *Christian Mysticism,* London, 1899.

Kālidāsa, *Kumāra Sambhava.*

Kant, Immanuel, *Works* (numerous editions).

Kural of Tiruvalluvar, (1) tr. by Prof. M.R. Rājagopal Aiyar (pub. S. Viswanāthan, 56, Broadway, Madras, 1950), a faily reliable translation; (2) tr. by Dr. G.U. Pope (London, 1886), good for its vast glossary and references, but spoiled by verse rendering; (3) *Selections,* by H.A. Popley (Oxford University Press, 1931), good for general picture of life and times of Tiruvalluvar, but too brief to be of any reference value.

Lacombe, Olivier, *L'Absolu Selon le Vedānta*, Librairie Orientaliste Paul Geuthner, Paris, 1937. One of the best works extant and a monument to French scholarship.

Laṅkāvatāra Sūtra, tr. by D.T. Suzuki, Routledge, London, 1932.

Lawrence, D.H., *Etruscan Places,*Penguin Books, 1950.

Lin Yutang, *Wisdom of China* Michael Joseph, London, 1948. Conveys Confucian spirit of China. Tao philosophy is brought out much clearer by James Legge, even though Lin Yutang has an admirable poetic style.

Mahābhārata (numerous editions).

Maharshi, Sri Ramana, *Maharshi's Gospel,* Sri Rāmanāśrama, Tiruvannamalai, S. India, 1946. A precious little memento of Word-Dialectics.

Marshall, Sir John, *Mohenjo-Dāro and the Indus Civilization,* 3 vols. Arthur Probsthain, London, 1931. Contains outstanding proof of proto-Dravidian, pre-Aryan culture, making a revolution in historical religious thought.

Milinda Questions, tr. by T.W. Rhys-Davids, Vols. XXXV and XXXVI of Sacred Books of the East, Clarendon Press, Oxford, 1925. Contains *guru-śiṣya* dialectics of Buddhism.

Muller, Max, *Chips from a German Workshop,* 4 Vols.,1895.

Narasinhacharya, R., *History of the Kannada Language,* University of Mysore, 1934.

Nielsen, D. *Mythology of All Races*, Archaeological Institute of America, Boston, 1931.

Panchatantra, tr. by Arthur W. Ryder, Jaico Pub. House, Bombay, 1940.

Periplus of the Erythraean Sea, tr. and annotated by Wilfred H. Schoff Longmans Green and Co., New York, 1912. First century commercial navigator's guide to the West Coast of India.

Perry, W.J., *The Growth of Civilization,* Penguin Books, London, 1937.

Piggott, Stuart, *Prehistoric India,* Penguin Books, 1950.

Plato, *Works,* Jowett's translation.

Plotinus, *Enneads,* tr. by Stephen Mackenna, Philip Lee Warner for the Medici Society, Ltd., London, 1907-30. A model translation in impeccable English, sumptuously produced. A slightly altered otherwise handy selection is the compilation, *The Essence of*

Plotinus, by Grace H. Turnbull Oxford University Press, New York, 1948.

Pycraft, W.P. (ed.), *The Standard Natural History,* Warne and Co., London, 1931.

Koran (numerous editions).

Rāmāyaṇa (numerous editions).

Rolland, Romain, *La Vie de Rāmakrishna,* Librairie Stock, Paris, 1930. Also tr. by E.F. Malcolm-Smith, *The Life of Rāmakrishna*, Advaita Ashrama, Almora.

Rousseau, Jean-Jacques, *Works* (numerous editions).

Russell, Bertrand, *History of Western Philosophy,* Allen and Unwin, London, 1946.

Śaṅkara, *The Bhagavad Gītā with the Commentary of Shri Śaṅkarācārya* tr. by A. Mahādeva Shāstri (Madras, 1897); *Select Works of Sri Shankarācharya,* tr. by. S. Venkatarāmanan (Natesan and Co., Madras); *Self-Knowledge,* tr. by Swāmī Nikhilānanda (Sri Ramakrishna Math, Madras, 1947); *Vedānta Sūtras* (or *Brahma-Sūtra*) *with Śaṅkara's Commentary,* tr. by George Thibaut (Sacred Books of the East, vols. XXXIV 1890 and XXXVIII 1896, Clarendon Press, Oxford): *Viveka-Cūḍāmaṇi* tr. by Swāmī Madhavananda (Advaita Ashrama, Almora, 1944); *Upadeśa-Sahasrī, (A Thousand Teachings)*, tr. by Swami Jagadānanda (Sri Rāmakrishna Math, Madras, 1949); *Upanishads and Sri Śaṅkara's Commentary,* tr. by S. Sītīrāma Sastri (Natesan and Co., Madras, 1898).

Sarva-Darśana-Saṁgraha (Synopsis of All the Systems or Philosophic Visions), of Mādhava Ācārya, tr. by E.B. Cowell and A.E. Gough, Kegan Paul, Trench, Trubner, and Co., Ltd., London, 1894.

Schmidt, W., *Culture-Historical Method of Ethnology* (1939), and *Primitive Revelation* (1939).

Schopenhauer, Arthur, *Works* (numerous editions).

Sen, Gertrude Emerson, *The Pageant of Indian History,* vol. I, Longmans Green and Co., New York, 1948.

Sengupta, Padmini, *Everday Life in Ancient India,* Oxford University Press, 1950.

Spinoza, Baruch, *Works* (numerous editions)

Srinivas Iyengar, P.T., *History of the Tamils*, Madras, 1929.

Stein, Aurel, *Serindia,* 6 vols. (1921); *Ruins of Desert Cathay,* 2 vols. (1912).

Tao Te Ching, tr. by James Legge, Sacred Books of the East, *Texts of Taoism,* vol. XXXIX; Clarendon Press, Oxford, 1891. Basic text indispensable to understanding the Word-Wisdom as expressed in China; profound, humorous, practical; one of the greatest books in the world. Dialectically revalued and commented upon most originally with wit by Chuang Tzu (see above).

Tawakley, Iswar Dayal, *Thesis on Sarva Darsana Sangraha,* Jouve et Cie, Paris, 1927.

Toynbee, Arnold J., *A Study of History,* 6 vols. (1934-39); Abridgment by D.C. Somervell, Oxford University Press, 1946.

Tyndall, John, *Fragments of Science for Unscientific People* (1871).

Upanishads, the Thirteen Principal, tr. by Robert Ernest Hume, Oxford University Press, 1934. A competent, thorough work, with useful appendices.

Underhill, Evelyn, *Mysticism,* London, 1930.

Voltaire, F.M.A. De., *Works* (numerous editions).

Wyld, Henry Cecil (ed.), *Universal Dictionary of the English Language,* Routledge, London, 1940.

Young India, Madras.

Yule, Sir Henry (ed.), *The Book of Ser Marco Polo,* 2 vols., Hackluyt Society, 1903.

Zimmern, Alfred E., *Greek Commonwealth*, Clarendon Press, Oxford, 1922. .

Index

Note: Certain words, alone or in combination, (e.g., Absolute, Advaita, Contemplation, Dialectics, Guru, India, Value, Vedānta, Wisdom, The Word, etc.) belonging to the subject-matter of the book, occur so frequently that they have been omitted, as their inclusion would inordinately lengthen the index.